AID
STATE

AID
STATE

ELITE PANIC,
DISASTER CAPITALISM, AND
THE BATTLE TO CONTROL
HAITI

JAKE JOHNSTON

ST. MARTIN'S PRESS
NEW YORK

First published in the United States by St. Martin's Press, an imprint of St. Martin's Publishing Group

AID STATE. Copyright © 2024 by Jake Johnston. All rights reserved. Printed in the United States of America. For information, address St. Martin's Publishing Group, 120 Broadway, New York, NY 10271.

www.stmartins.com

Library of Congress Cataloging-in-Publication Data

Names: Johnston, Jake, author.
Title: Aid state : elite panic, disaster capitalism, and the battle to control Haiti / Jake Johnston.
Other titles: Elite panic, disaster capitalism, and the battle to control Haiti
Description: First edition. | New York : St. Martin's Press, 2024. | Includes bibliographical references and index.
Identifiers: LCCN 2023036033 | ISBN 9781250284679 (hardcover) | ISBN 9781250284686 (ebook)
Subjects: LCSH: United States—Foreign relations—Haiti. | Haiti—Foregin relations—United States. | Economic assistance, American—Haiti. | Haiti—Economic conditions. | Haiti—Politics and government—1804–
Classification: LCC E183.8.H2 J66 2024 | DDC 327.7307294—dc23/eng/20230926
LC record available at https://lccn.loc.gov/2023036033

Our books may be purchased in bulk for promotional, educational, or business use. Please contact your local bookseller or the Macmillan Corporate and Premium Sales Department at 1-800-221-7945, extension 5442, or by email at MacmillanSpecialMarkets@macmillan.com.

First Edition: 2024

10 9 8 7 6 5 4 3 2 1

To all the friends I've made along the way

CONTENTS

AID
STATE

PROLOGUE

———

On August 14, 2021, about one hundred miles to the west of Port-au-Prince, the capital of Haiti, the tectonic plates lurking beneath the earth's surface slipped, producing a 7.2 magnitude earthquake—twice as powerful as the one that had hit in 2010, an event that had forever altered the history of the nation (and where this book begins in chapter 1). Once again, hospitals and schools collapsed, homes were destroyed, entire communities were cut off from the outside world. Thousands died. This time, however, the capital was spared the worst. And yet, coming just over a month after the assassination of Haiti's president Jovenel Moïse (where this book ends), the government was in no better a position to respond than it had been eleven years earlier. If the measure of success after a natural disaster is how much better prepared the country is for the next one, the 2021 quake served as a punctuation mark on the failures of the decade-long reconstruction period.

The next day, thousands of miles away, a different kind of earthquake shook the foundations of another nation. On August 15, Afghanistan's president fled into exile and Kabul fell to the Taliban. It occurred just as the US neared completion of its troop withdrawal after two decades, a deployment that had only recently surpassed the early twentieth century occupation of Haiti as the longest in US history.[1] Though on their surface the events appear distinct and unrelated, the earthquake in Haiti and the Taliban takeover in Afghanistan revealed a deeper commonality.[2]

After the fall of Kabul, Washington's foreign policy establishment lit up with experts asking and answering the question of why "nation-building" in Afghanistan had failed so miserably. But few seemed to be wondering the same about Haiti. In the latter's case, the president's assassination and the earthquake simply proved that Haiti was a failed state all on its own. But America's foray into "nation-building" had not been confined to Afghanistan.[3] US troops landed in Port-au-Prince a few years after deploying to Kabul; they were, however, quickly replaced by some ten thousand United Nations soldiers. Though the occupation occurred largely outside the public's view, a parallel effort to that in Afghanistan had been taking place in Haiti for nearly as many years.

The histories and futures of the two countries are not defined by the actions of foreign powers alone, of course. But, in both nations, the governments' eventual collapses were driven by remarkably similar internationally led policy choices. In Afghanistan, the US spent billions in an effort to prop up unpopular presidents, from Hamid Karzai to Ashraf Ghani. As in Haiti, the only thing keeping these leaders in power had been foreign support. Ghani, for example, won reelection in 2019 in a voting process supported by the US, United Nations, and other outside actors. Turnout had only been about 20 percent.[4] As you will read in this book, that mirrors precisely what had transpired in Haiti. Regardless of the location, it was a tried-and-true recipe for disaster. The reality is that a state cannot be imposed from outside; its legitimacy must be homegrown.

Over twenty years of foreign-led state building, Haiti and Afghanistan became two of the most aid-dependent countries on the planet, the public sectors de facto replaced by an alphabet soup of multilateral organizations, NGOs, and development companies. In Afghanistan, donors financed roughly three-quarters of public spending. It was a "house of cards built on aid," as a foreign official with more than a decade of experience there described it to me. When the fantastically corrupt and Western-backed president fled for exile and the Taliban took power, those donor flows stopped virtually overnight. The "house of cards" collapsed instantly.[5]

In Haiti, the collapse has been taking place in slow motion over multiple years. The UN withdrew the last of its troops in 2017, but there was no organized and armed Haitian force on the scale of the Taliban to immediately seize power. Unlike in Afghanistan, the foreign-backed regime remains in power, and donor funds continue to flow. The collapse is ongoing. Still, the result—hollowed-out public institutions, handpicked leaders with little popular legitimacy, and a population left behind by the state—has been much the same.

By 2021, about half the population in both Afghanistan and Haiti were facing food insecurity. Remarkably, those levels were practically unchanged after twenty years. And so, it should have come as little surprise that tens of thousands from both nations would want to seek a better life outside their own borders. Nearly every American was well aware of their country's efforts in Afghanistan, and polls showed a strong majority favored allowing Afghans entrance into the US. The root causes that drove thousands to leave their home country were impossible to overlook. The Taliban was a common enemy. There was even bipartisan support. The Biden administration responded by evacuating an initial 37,000 Afghans to the US for resettlement.[6]

When it came Haiti, however, the reaction was different. The first nation to permanently abolish slavery, Haiti's inequities, and the role of the United States in perpetuating them, had been systematically obscured from public view for centuries. Few Americans had ever learned about the 1804 revolution, or that the nation was forced to pay a financially crippling "freedom ransom" for nearly 150 years. The US had occupied the country for nearly twenty years in the early 1900s, but how many knew that, a century later, foreign troops had been in Haiti for nearly that long again?[7] Haiti was, as the obligatory journalistic descriptor went, "the poorest country in the Western Hemisphere," no explanation needed. The country was "politically unstable," but few cared to ponder why.

When it came to Haitians, fleeing the failures of the forgotten twenty-first-century occupation in the world's first independent Black republic, there would be no dignity nor compassion.

* * *

MIRARD JOSEPH AND his wife, Madeleine Prospere, left Haiti in 2017—two of some 100,000 Haitians who migrated to Chile that year. In 2020, the couple welcomed their first child, a baby girl. But the COVID pandemic changed everything. The economy cooled; businesses shuttered amid lockdowns. Worse, the conservative president in Chile took the pandemic as an opportunity to crack down on the recent increase in immigration, especially of Haitians.

Joseph, Prospere, and their one-year-old daughter were forced to flee yet again. They joined thousands of others on the well-trodden path from South America to Mexico, crossing the Darien Gap and traversing Central America before reaching the Texas border. They arrived in Del Rio in early September and were told to wait their turn for processing in a makeshift camp under a bridge.[8]

The right to asylum is enshrined in international law, but under Donald Trump, the US had eviscerated the process. With the COVID pandemic as an excuse, the Trump administration used the authority of an arcane law called Title 42, a public health order, to turn away all those arriving at the US border without so much as their legally required asylum hearing.[9]

Joe Biden campaigned explicitly in opposition to Trump's hard-line immigration policies, which Democrats chastised as racist and illegal. But like so many of his predecessors, Biden walked back much of that promise once in office. In June 2021, border apprehensions reached a two-decade high. The influx, though largely a product of the draconian policies of his predecessor, was a political headache for the new president. "He knows the damage this can do and what a gift this is to Republicans," one official explained.[10] In August, the administration extended Trump's Title 42 policy.[11]

It did little to stop the flow of Haitians, however. By September, with the temperatures along the arid Texas border still reaching into triple digits, more and more families—like Mirard Joseph's—arrived under the Del Rio bridge. By the middle of the month, there were some fourteen thousand sheltering there—nearly all of them Haitian. Officials were monitoring the route from South America. Tens of thousands more were on their way.[12]

The dust under the bridge, on the banks of the Rio Grande, was all consuming, covering the skin and penetrating the lungs. Joseph and his family slept on a piece of cardboard. They were given one diaper per day. After a few days, their daughter developed a respiratory illness. Border Patrol agents, who "managed" the Del Rio encampment, distributed some bread and the occasional bottle of water, but it was never enough. That was probably the point, an extension of America's long-standing policy of deterrence.

Many would travel back to Mexico, to find basic supplies and food, making the dangerous cross through the Rio Grande on a near daily basis. On September 19, Joseph was on his way back to the Del Rio camp with two plastic bags full of food when he saw them. The administration had dispatched hundreds of additional Border Patrol agents to Del Rio; now some were on horseback watching as he and dozens of others waded through the water.

As Joseph emerged onto US soil, an agent charged at him, lashing with his reins. The agent grabbed his collar and began to drag him back to the Rio Grande. A photojournalist happened to be standing nearby and captured the entire episode in heart-wrenching detail. The images went viral and shocked the nation's conscience. Black men, women, and children, simply wanting a chance at a better life, chased, beaten, and rounded up; it was impossible not to make a connection to the era of chattel slavery, with the Black population terrorized and whipped by men on horseback.[13]

Even top officials in the Biden administration, including Vice President Kamala Harris, denounced the behavior of the Border Patrol. But it didn't stop the administration from its efforts to close the Del Rio camp. Two days later, Joseph was cuffed, shackled, and placed on an airplane to be expelled to Haiti.

Being attacked by the agent on horseback "was the most humiliating experience of my life," Joseph later said. "The second most humiliating moment was when they handcuffed and chained me to go back to Haiti."

It was the beginning of the largest air-based mass expulsion of migrants in US history. In less than two weeks, the US had sent more than fifty planes carrying nearly seven thousand people back to Haiti.[14] In

Biden's first year in office, more than twenty thousand individuals, including pregnant women and young children, were flown to Haiti. It was nearly as many as under the prior three presidents combined.[15]

THE DAY AFTER Joseph and his family landed in Haiti, the United States special envoy to Haiti submitted his letter of resignation. "I will not be associated with the United States' inhumane, counterproductive decision to deport thousands of Haitian refugees," wrote Daniel Foote, who had been appointed just two months earlier in the aftermath of the assassination.[16]

Foote, like many diplomats who passed through Port-au-Prince, had worked in Haiti before—and Iraq and Afghanistan. The State Department saw the similarities, even if much of the public didn't. Writing that his recommendations had been ignored or misrepresented to superiors, he called the general US policy approach to Haiti "deeply flawed." In his resignation letter, Foote connected the broader migration "crisis" to that flawed policy. Haiti needs security and humanitarian assistance, he wrote. "But what our Haitian friends really want, and need, is the opportunity to chart their own course, without international puppeteering and favored candidates but with genuine support for that course," Foote observed. "I do not believe that Haiti can enjoy stability until her citizens have the dignity of truly choosing their own leaders fairly and acceptably."

And, he pointed out, the US and its allies in the international community were doing it again—backing an unelected prime minister, Ariel Henry, who had taken office after the assassination of President Moïse, rather than a broad-based initiative led by Haitian civil society organizations. "The hubris that makes us believe we should pick the winner—again—is impressive."

What Foote said didn't come as a surprise to most Haitians. Over the decade-plus I had been traveling to Haiti, I had heard a similar analysis countless times. What was surprising was that a US diplomat had said it.

I sat down with Foote nearly a year later at a restaurant just a few blocks from his former employer, the State Department. Shockingly little had changed in Haiti. The de facto prime minister was still in office, wielding unprecedented power—to little or no positive effect. After a brief respite in the immediate aftermath of the assassination, violence and insecurity had only worsened. Homicides and kidnappings were approaching record levels, and the victims included US citizens.[17]

"The only way out of this is a Haitian-led political solution," Foote explained. You can enforce stability, at least temporarily, he said. "Come in, roll hard, kill a bunch of people." It's what we had done with each military intervention in the past. It had happened in 1994, 2004, and, to an extent, after the earthquake in 2010. But that wasn't going to "resolve the social issues that you need to fix before you have real stability."

"The people are going to rise up, it is inevitable," he cautioned.

"In the name of stability, they are making instability inevitable," I responded. So, I asked, did he think Haiti was a failed state?

"They never had a chance to fail!" he countered with a chuckle. "I know we will fail, I am certain of it. I've never been more certain of anything in my life, but there is a chance Haitians could fix it. So why not let them try?"

For the diplomat, there was one thing standing in the way: the US continuing to prop up the unelected prime minister whom they had helped place in power after the assassination. Worse, Foote believed the prime minister had been "in the middle" of the plot to kill the president.[18]

IN EARLY OCTOBER 2022, Ariel Henry, the US-backed prime minister, requested a foreign military intervention to help "restore order" and address the ongoing humanitarian emergency in Haiti. The plea came less than twenty-four hours after a meeting with the US secretary of state and the head of the Organization of American States (OAS). Protests calling for his resignation had been building for months, and negotiations over a political accord that could shore up the embattled leader's legitimacy had fallen apart. Most observers recognized Henry's appeal for foreign reinforcements as a desperate attempt to cling to power amid unprecedented dissent. Still, the request received the support of the US and the United Nations.[19] As I write this in early 2023, the debate over yet another deployment of foreign troops to Haiti remains unsettled.

In the past eighteen months, starting with the assassination of President Jovenel Moïse, the nation of Haiti has received more international media attention than it has in a decade—since the 2010 earthquake. "Haiti in Crisis" has been plastered on front pages and strewn across cable news banners, seemingly on repeat. There is no functioning government, no president, no legislature, not even a working supreme court. It would be hard to identify one state institution that is operating as it should. Armed groups, closely linked with politicians and the economic elite, control more than half the capital. Political scientists and academics include Haiti alongside nations like Yemen, Syria, Afghanistan, and the Central African Republic atop lists of "failed" or "fragile" states. In Washington, DC, where I live and work, a baseline assumption seems to have taken hold: we have to do something. History, as they say, is bound to repeat itself.

At the time of the assassination, I was already working on this book. I had first started focusing on Haiti in the aftermath of the 2010 earthquake, when the world pledged more than $10 billion to "build back better." Where was the money going? What was being planned? The answers could be found in official reports and contracting databases—generally available only in English—of NGOs, multilateral banks, and government agencies. It quickly became clear that, from my office in DC, I had more access to information about the foreign-led reconstruction efforts than those communities supposedly on the receiving end of all that support.

For more than ten years, I followed the money, encountering waste and fraud, good intentions, and outright corrupt schemes. But in searching for an answer to where the money had gone, I was confronted by a far bigger story. It wasn't just where it had gone, but why it had gone there in the first place. It wasn't just about an earthquake, but about a revolution that had begun more than two hundred years earlier and remained unfinished.

A land of magic and mystery, of devastation and dictatorship—Western perceptions of Haiti have been shaped by centuries of colonialism and racism. Though many scholars have referred to Haiti as a "failed state," this book puts forth a new designation: "Aid State," the latest in a long series of foreign-led attempts to manage Haiti. The basic principle underlying the analysis, that the Haitian state has become divorced from the interests and needs of the Haitian people themselves, is something Haitian scholars have filled libraries examining for well over a century. It is their work that informs this contemporary application.[20]

I'm often asked what motivates US government policy in Haiti. Migration? Economic development? Political stability? These are often the publicly stated reasons, but they don't capture the reality. Most simply, I answer, during the past decade, US officials have wanted to keep Haiti out of the news. If it's in the US media, it means there could be a domestic political cost to whatever is generating the headlines. But I think there's something more: officials just don't really want the public to see. For two centuries Haiti has been a mirror of morality held up to the world. And we continue to fail the test. Analyzing US policy in Haiti means confronting the hypocrisy at the core of our own origin story.

Another question is, why Haiti? I'm not Haitian; there are plenty of other countries in the world worth focusing on. So, why Haiti? For me, focusing on Haiti began as a lens to better understand US foreign policy—though I quickly realized it was more like a magnifying glass. Usually, the sausage-making remains in the shadows. In Haiti, it was in your face. Impossible to ignore. Eventually, I fell for the country itself: the people, the beauty, the history. Over the past decade, I've learned more about my own country and the effects of its policies abroad—not to mention about love, family, solidarity, and community—by talking to Haitians than from any university classroom or DC think-tank event. The Haitian people are the ones who live with the results of decisions made in Washington, DC.

I am not just an observer. Since the 2010 quake, I've worked with members of Congress, advocates, grassroots and civil society organizations in Haiti, to push US policy toward a more rational, respectful, and progressive path. And I've worked with journalists at just about every major news outlet to keep Haiti in the news, even as attention faded with each passing year after the 2010 earthquake. Many have interpreted the lack of sustained attention from Washington, DC, and US policy makers as not caring about Haiti. But, if I've learned one thing over the last decade, it is that the US and other world powers care deeply about what happens in Haiti—even if they'd rather nobody else look too closely.

What has happened in Haiti over the past year and a half is not random. It is not an accident. It is not due to "progress-resistant cultural influences," as David Brooks opined in *The New York Times* after the 2010 quake, nor to a "pact with the devil," as the televangelist Pat Robertson spewed. As I argue in this book, what has occurred is the result of specific policies pursued by the world's great powers; the natural result of the Aid State's imposition and inevitable collapse.

Today, in Washington, New York, Ottawa, Paris, and Brussels, the question pertaining to Haiti is framed as a decision between intervening or not; the reality is that foreign intervention never stopped. The question therefore is whether to continue intervening or, at long last, to stand in solidarity with the Haitian people as they chart their own future free from foreign meddling and elite state capture.

1

THE "COMPASSIONATE INVASION"

On January 12, 2010, Haitian president René Préval left his office in the white-domed National Palace, in the capital city of Port-au-Prince, a little earlier than usual. He and his wife, Elisabeth, wanted to stop home before attending a gala that Tuesday evening hosted by the US ambassador. The president pulled into the driveway of their private compound, got out of the car, and noticed his eight-month-old granddaughter Alessa in the courtyard with her nanny. He picked her up and pulled her close. It was 4:53 P.M.[1]

Eight miles underground, two tectonic plates shifted. The friction produced an explosion equivalent to some 475,000 pounds of dynamite.[2] A deep rumble rose from the earth. The land beneath the Prévals' feet began to shake. He fell to his knees; his wife was knocked back onto the ground. Their house swayed, and then they watched it collapse, unsure if their two daughters had been trapped inside. Within thirty seconds, the sky was dark—the low evening sun obscured by hazy clouds of dust and debris. Elisabeth turned to her husband.

"Let's get out of here before the ground opens up," she said, frightened.

But they stayed instead, and soon opened the gates of their compound and invited those in the street, confused, injured, in shock, to join them. Nobody could fully grasp what had happened, what was still happening. The earth shook again. The phone lines were down. The power was out. The president was unable to reach his aides or ministers.

Soon, the minister of the interior arrived on the lawn, covered in dust. The prime minister, Jean-Max Bellerive, arrived a short time later on a motorcycle. His car had been crushed. The chief of police, the justice minister, and a number of top advisors followed. The National Palace had collapsed, Préval learned. So had the Parliament, the police headquarters, the justice ministry. When the dust-clouded sun fell beneath the horizon line at 5:30 P.M., Port-au-Prince was darker than anybody remembered seeing it before.

Unable to communicate with anyone not already in his front yard, the president hired a handful of motorcycle taxis, *motos* as they're known in Haiti. He sent an emissary on one to the US ambassador's residence. The president got on the back of another and set off to tour the city, the magnitude of the death and destruction becoming more apparent with each turn. He passed the palace, seeing for himself the sunken white dome, the broken symmetry of the French renaissance–style façade. Throngs of people crowded outside the country's largest public hospital, part of which lay in ruins. He continued to the Parliament, where nearby residents were scrambling to pull bodies, including the head of the Senate, from the rubble.[3]

Préval stayed on the streets until the sun rose the following morning. Since the initial fissure, the earth had barely stood still. By the time the president returned home after his all-night tour of the crumbled Haitian capital, there had been more than thirty aftershocks. All but one of the government's twenty-nine ministry buildings had collapsed.[4] Many of those who hadn't left work early remained trapped in the rubble, buried under tons of mangled iron rebar and substandard concrete. "I went to a poor neighborhood called Bel Air, and everywhere there, there were dead," Préval later remembered. "This is when I discovered the horror of the catastrophe."[5]

For twenty years, Préval had stood at the forefront of Haiti's democratic trajectory. Since the fall of the dictatorship in 1986, Haiti had seen more than ten heads of state[6]; only Préval had managed to get elected, serve a complete term, and then hand power over to another elected leader. He was scheduled to do so again in 2010. He had served as prime minister under Haiti's first freely elected president, the liberation theologian priest Jean-Bertrand Aristide, and as president himself twice. Préval was Haiti's "indispensable man" and "likely the only politician capable of imposing his will on Haiti—if so inclined," the US ambassador had written to Washington the year before the quake.[7] Despite their nearly two decades of familiarity, the US was still wary of Préval and his left-leaning background.

In contrast to his political stature, his friends called him Ti-René or Little René. With a neatly cropped salt-and-pepper beard framing his mostly bald head, Préval was always more comfortable behind the scenes. He once told a journalist that, when he retired, he just wanted to run a cigarette stall in a local street market.[8] He preferred Marlboros. His lack of formality extended to how he dressed—most commonly in a white button-down shirt, slacks, and sandals, regardless of the circumstance. That's what the president was wearing as he sat in his yard the morning after the quake, contemplating what he had just seen and what he would do next.[9]

The country and the government, which Préval had tried for two decades to build up, was now in pieces, parts of it scattered in his front yard. The images from his firsthand look at the devastation were planted deep in his psyche. In a matter of seconds, the country had changed, and so had he. He was criticized for not making any public statement that first night. The reality was that he had no idea what he could say to families who had just lost everything, who were still frantically trying to pull loved ones from the rubble. "As a person, I was paralyzed," he remembered months later. "I couldn't find the words."[10]

But he had asked for help, starting with the US ambassador. He may not have had the words, but after his all-night tour of the city, one thing was clear. "The catastrophe was beyond the means of Haiti to respond," he said.

ON A MAP, Haiti looks like a crab's claw, open and reaching west into the Caribbean Sea from the Dominican Republic, the country with which Haiti shares the island of Hispaniola. Port-au-Prince, the capital and the center of the country's economic and political life, is the claw's hinge and sits just thirty miles from the border. Deeply impoverished communities occupying the land nearest to the bay surround the palace and most government buildings. Unlike most of its Caribbean neighbors, the capital's shoreline is devoid of hotel chains or beach resorts. Instead, the land has long been used for industrial manufacturing and squatter camps for workers. The real estate is coveted by developers, producing an inherent tension over Port-au-Prince's land use. Préval's presidential compound, a white, boxlike, two-story home with a smaller guest house where his aides work, sits on a curving hillside to the southeast, higher up into the mountain range that protects the city and the country's elite. The US ambassador's residence stands about halfway between the top of the mountains and the bay.

On the afternoon of that same tragic Tuesday, US Ambassador Kenneth Merten had hosted Lieutenant General P. K. "Ken" Keen, the second-in-command of US Southern Command, or SOUTHCOM, the Pentagon wing that oversees operations in Latin America and the Caribbean. A former Army Ranger and Special Forces commander, he was on a routine visit from his Florida headquarters. After a long day, the two sat on the veranda of the ambassador's residence, enjoying the setting sun and drinking a couple of Diet Cokes.[11] Upstairs, Merten's wife, Susan, and their two daughters were reviewing the guest list for a reception to be held in Keen's honor, the reception that President Préval had left the office early to attend.[12]

At 4:53 PM, as the ground began to shake, Mrs. Merten noticed the palatial staircase inside the front entrance rippling "like waves in the ocean" while actual waves spilled over the edges of the pool outside.[13] But the residence, constructed in 1938, stood. From the hillside perch, the city below appeared gone, hidden by a rapidly expanding cloud of dust. They could hear screams coming from the city's densely packed neighborhoods in the distance and the collapsed Hotel Montana nearby, where the team accompanying Keen had been staying. On a typical day, one could see the historic hotel from the front of the home. The ambassador rushed around the corners of his property. There was nothing but a dark fog of debris in the foreground. The hotel was nowhere to be seen.[14]

Merten, at forty-eight, was a career foreign service officer and a portrait of US diplomacy—white, balding, slightly overweight, and friendly with everyone he was supposed to be friendly with. He had joined the State Department in 1987 and only a year later was sent to Port-au-Prince during the chaotic years following the end of the dictatorship and Jean-Claude "Baby Doc" Duvalier's exile to France. After another two-year posting in the late 1990s, President Barack Obama nominated him for the ambassadorial position in June 2009. Twenty years after his first posting, Merten spoke fluent Kreyòl and had developed close personal relationships among Haiti's political and economic elite.

Earlier in the day, he and General Keen had been discussing disaster preparedness for the upcoming hurricane season. Nothing, however, could have prepared him for what was happening now. In a panic, Merten attempted to reach the State Department in Washington, DC. There was no cell phone service. They were two miles from the US Embassy compound, but eventually, with a spotty landline, a two-way radio, and the general's BlackBerry, they set in motion what would end up being the most expensive response to a natural disaster the world had ever seen.[15]

Fifty-nine minutes after the magnitude 7 quake, President Obama was briefed on the situation in Haiti, while an aftershock, the fourth in less than an hour, rattled Port-au-Prince once more.[16] As the shockwaves continued to reverberate from the quake's epicenter just sixteen miles southwest from the capital, reports of widespread ruin echoed throughout the mostly empty early-evening concrete halls of the federal government buildings in DC. At six o'clock, before Préval had even been able to speak with most of his ministers, a joint planning group met in Washington, bringing the US Agency for International Development (USAID) together with officials from the State Department and the Department of Defense.[17]

At nine o'clock, before Préval had even gotten on the back of a *moto* to survey the crisis, SOUTHCOM held an emergency meeting with the State Department. They still had no hard information about the situation on the ground but feared general lawlessness and widespread violence could take hold. According to a directive from the US Embassy, the immediate priority was the evacuation of American citizens. There were nearly fifty thousand of them in Haiti. By the time Préval's aide had arrived at Merten's residence, the US response was already in motion.[18]

Planning meetings continued throughout the evening. Just after one in the morning, SOUTHCOM reported to the State Department that two Coast Guard cutters were en route to Haiti.[19] An hour later, the military Joint Chiefs convened via video conference. US troops had been sent to Haiti twice in the preceding fifteen years, once to help restore the ousted Jean-Bertrand Aristide to the presidency and then again to help stabilize the government after Aristide was overthrown a second time. The Pentagon continued to keep a close eye on the country, with confidential intelligence briefs prepared by SOUTHCOM in the months before the quake, providing leadership with regular updates on the number of Haitians attempting to migrate to America and any possible risks to stability.[20] The earthquake, they determined, was a threat to US national security. The Joint Chiefs' most immediate fear was that if the situation was not quickly stabilized, there would be a "mass exodus toward Cuba and the US," according to an after-action report prepared by the US military.[21]

Unlike the palace and the president's residence, the US Embassy in Port-au-Prince, one of the largest structures in American diplomacy, remained standing. But the day after the earthquake, most of its employees were told to pack their belongings and leave. By daybreak on the following morning, as Préval was finally returning home from his tour, the first US ships had arrived off the coast, and a helicopter began evacuations of three or four people at a time, starting with a few injured embassy employees. Later, a steady stream of black SUVs ferried staff, their families, and their pets in heavily guarded convoys to the airport.[22] With the control tower damaged, however, most planes could not take off or land.

MONA AUGUSTIN, HEAVYSET with thick dreadlocks wrapped up and over his head, had spent the early part of January 12 at his modest home in Delmas 30, a middle-class neighborhood between the seaside shantytowns of downtown and the relatively wealthy suburbs that filled out the hills above.[23] Delmas is the main road between the two areas, and traveling up the hill is like climbing Haiti's socioeconomic ladder. The street numbers increase as you go, and the higher the number, the wealthier the neighborhood.

Most days, in the afternoon, Augustin walked to St. Vincent's School for Handicapped Children, where he volunteered teaching music. He played guitar and was the lead singer in a Haitian folk band. On January 12, however, Mona was ill. He'd tossed and turned in bed most of the day, fighting violent stomach pains and an aching fever. He never went to St. Vincent's, where the school collapsed, killing almost all the children and teachers. When the earth shook, Augustin, too, had been buried in the debris of his home.

It was impossibly dark when Augustin initially came to. He was trapped, but it was as if the earthquake had shaken the illness from him. He was *alive*. And his wasn't the only house on the block to collapse. He could hear neighbors calling to him, pulling up shards of concrete, zinc metal roofing, and splintered wood to release him. He listened to the screams of other neighbors just a few feet away. Somehow, he did not suffer any major injuries. A few blocks away, the Delimart, one of the biggest supermarkets in the capital, had folded into itself, trapping dozens of shoppers and employees inside. Other screams of pain and cries for help sounded far away and seemed to echo forever. After the first devastating blow, the fear and panic had not subsided as the ground had continued to convulse for hours. No structure in the neighborhood seemed safe. Augustin and about two hundred others sought some sort of refuge in a drainage canal. He blindly probed the fetid knee-deep swirl of dark water and debris, searching for a pair of sandals or something he could use to cover his feet, still bare since he had emerged from the rubble.

He'd lost a sense of time, he'd later say, but it was, at least, a few hours before the fear of a tsunami convinced Augustin and most of the others in the canal that it was time to look for safer ground. He started walking. Eventually, amid the wreckage, he arrived at a familiar empty lot. He wasn't even sure how he got there, but he knew the space well.

Neighborhood vendors set up their food stalls here, and neighborhood kids played soccer on the vacant and often trash-clogged field set back off the street.

Many others kept walking in search of higher ground, but Augustin stayed. By the next morning he knew this field was where he had to be and where his old neighbors needed to come. Through his band, Augustin had international connections and friends with places for him to sleep. Still, something greater seemed to be pulling him toward this nondescript, grassy lot. "People were injured," Mona later remembered. "One person was missing a leg, but there was nothing for them. I said, 'Wow, I need to do something. I need to help.'"

PRESIDENT OBAMA ISSUED a statement at 10:20 A.M. the following morning of January 13, 2010. He had just spoken briefly with Préval by satellite phone. "We are just now beginning to learn the extent of the devastation," Obama told the press. "The reports and images that we've seen of collapsed hospitals, crumbled homes, and men and women carrying their injured neighbors through the streets are truly heart-wrenching," he said, before pledging the "unwavering support" of the United States. The military was already at work repairing the airport's control tower at Préval's request. Thankfully, the runways hadn't been damaged too severely. Aid flights could start landing soon, Obama said.[24]

A few hours after Obama spoke, General Douglas Fraser, the commander of SOUTHCOM, addressed reporters at the Pentagon's briefing room in Arlington, Virginia. "We have a very robust effort headed in that direction," he said. Préval had requested assistance, but SOUTHCOM didn't have a plan in place for a humanitarian response of this nature. "The bottom line," Fraser told reporters, "is we don't have a clear assessment, right now, of what the situation on the ground is, what the needs within Port-au-Prince are, how extensive the situation is." The military had coordinated relief efforts before, both at home and abroad. But General Fraser was, first and foremost, mobilizing the Pentagon's assets to protect US interests.[25]

Fearing a seaborne exodus and with fifty thousand US citizens on the ground, the Pentagon simply pushed as many resources as possible toward Haiti. The USS *Carl Vinson,* an aircraft carrier, was dispatched along with the USS *Bataan,* an assault ship. A battalion from the Army's 82nd Airborne Division was put on standby, as were two thousand members of the 22nd Marine Expeditionary Unit.

By late morning the day after the quake, after traveling by land from the Dominican Republic, a CNN news crew had finally made it to the airport in Port-au-Prince. Medical correspondent Sanjay Gupta held a microphone to Préval, who was wearing the same white button-down shirt from the day before, though somehow his wife had found a few moments to wash and press it earlier that morning. Gupta asked where the president was going to sleep that night.

"I don't know," Préval responded.

"It is striking," Gupta said, addressing the camera directly. "The president of this country doesn't know where he's going to sleep tonight."

"No," Préval said, correcting the CNN reporter. "I have plenty of time to look for a bed, but now I am working [on] how to rescue the people."

The streets had to be cleaned, he said, the rubble cleared. There were people crowding outside hospitals, and there was an urgent need for medical assistance. The president seemed to be staring off into the distance as he spoke.

Gupta asked if he was worried about violence breaking out as people became desperate for food and water in the coming days.

"No," Préval again responded flatly, suggesting the question missed the concerns of the Haitian president and the needs of his country, still in the throes of this horrific, life-and-death crisis.[26]

That evening, the first US military plane touched down at the airport.[27]

It wasn't until early afternoon on January 14—forty-eight hours after the first great shock—that President Préval formally sat down with international officials, including Merten. He reiterated his appeal for assistance and laid out his government's priorities: "Re-establish telephone communications; clear the streets of debris and bodies; provide food and water to the population; bury cadavers; treat the injured; coordination." Security remained absent from the list.[28] The president's stated needs stood in stark contrast to the fears of violence expressed by Gupta, the concerns about mass emigration away from Haiti, and what was becoming an increasingly militarized relief effort.

The same day, the Pentagon formally initiated Joint Task Force Haiti, with General Keen taking command and control in Port-au-Prince. C-130 planes stuffed with relief supplies and infantry body armor rolled into the airport, now under the general's authority. The battalion from the 82nd Airborne stepped out from their helicopters onto the grass outside the collapsed National Palace. It was the beginning, as *TIME* magazine put it, of the "compassionate invasion."[29]

2

THE FEAR

———

At the peak of the military response, on January 31, 2010, there were more than twenty-two thousand American soldiers in or off the shores of Haiti, a country about the size of Massachusetts.[1] Canada, coordinating closely with Washington, sent two thousand additional troops and two naval ships. Israel, the Dominican Republic, and more than two dozen other countries also provided significant military assets, including elite search and rescue teams centered in Port-au-Prince. They joined more than twelve thousand United Nations peacekeepers, whose presence on Haitian soil predated the quake. It was as if forty thousand foreign troops had descended on Boston. At the time, there were about seventy thousand troops in all of Afghanistan, where the US was actively engaged in a war.

Thirty-three US Naval and Coast Guard vessels served as offshore hospitals and helicopter landing pads, largely for relief and evacuation purposes, but also functioning as floating barriers to contain the potential waves of immigrants pushing offshore. More than three hundred military aircraft were conducting aid distributions and evacuations. It had taken the military less than twenty-four hours to reopen the airport. The US evacuated more than sixteen thousand of its citizens, the largest such operation since World War II. The Pentagon reported delivering 2.5 million liters of water, 17 million pounds of bulk food, and 5.7 million individual meals. Military doctors performed more than a thousand surgeries and treated more than nine thousand patients.[2]

The numbers are impressive, and the response saved thousands of lives. But the military security took precedence over the list of other basic needs that Préval had communicated to the international community and that were readily apparent to anyone on the ground in Port-au-Prince. The US military response alone cost more than $500 million—nearly 8 percent of Haiti's GDP.[3] Tens of millions were spent on fuel as helicopters and SUVs sat idling. Twenty million dollars went to Agility, a logistics contractor once blacklisted by the US for fraud in Iraq.[4] At one point, a US Air Force plane made daily flights over Haiti broadcasting a message in Kreyòl. "If you think you will reach the US and all the doors will be wide open to you, that's not at all the case. And they will intercept you right on the water and send you back home where you came from," the message bellowed.[5] In the end, most soldiers never even set foot on Haitian soil; instead, they waited on ships offshore or dropped meal kits from low-flying helicopters.

For weeks, however, the military's every move was broadcast internationally on CNN, ABC, NBC, and Fox News. CNN alone had more than forty journalists and staff members in-country at one point.[6] Images of soldiers handing out humanitarian kits to seemingly needy and desperate survivors provided a welcome reprieve for the Pentagon during a national debate over its post-invasion actions in Iraq. Each potential survivor found in the rubble became headline news. At one point, six different international rescue teams were stationed at the ruined Hotel Montana, searching for survivors among the two hundred or so who had been staying there, almost all of whom were foreigners.[7] Correspondents beamed the live stream to eager audiences across the world. It was the most covered international event since the 2004 Indian Ocean earthquake and tsunami. Americans followed the situation in Haiti more closely than any natural disaster since Hurricane Katrina.

The round-the-clock coverage was pumped into the homes of hundreds of millions of Americans on a nightly basis, often with a prompt at the bottom of the screen to donate ten dollars to relief efforts. Nearly half of all American families did, many via a simple text, a suddenly new, real-time fundraising tool.[8] The American Red Cross raised more than $21 million in the first week through text and eventually raised $500 million.[9] Everyone, it seemed, wanted to help Haiti.

Haiti had long captured the West's attention, though rarely for the right reasons or good purpose. It was, to many, a dark place of dictators and military coups, of political violence and unimaginable savagery, of child slaves and HIV-infected "boat people." In much of the popular imagination, if Haiti existed at all, it remained a mystical island under the control of Vodou, where even the outlandish seemed possible. Royal Caribbean cruise ships made regular stops to a remote beach in Haiti that it leased, but for years didn't even disclose to passengers that they were, in fact, in Haiti.[10] After the earthquake, in the opinion pages of *The New York Times,* award-winning columnist David Brooks lamented the "progress-resistant cultural influences" present in Haitian society that had contributed to the ruin.[11] Christian televangelist Pat Robertson suggested it was retribution for Haiti's "pact with the devil," a reference to the belief among many Evangelicals that followers of Vodou worship the devil.[12] The post-quake focus on security was a product of and fed into the West's worst perceptions of Haiti. Americans watched the drama from their living rooms, waiting for a zombie apocalypse.

"Elites tend to believe in a venal, selfish, and essentially monstrous version of human nature," explained Rebecca Solnit, the author of *A Paradise Built in Hell,* which chronicles how humanity responds to disaster, for example, in San Francisco after its 1906 quake or in New Orleans after Katrina. Solnit wasn't describing post-quake Haiti, but she may as well have done so. "They believe that only their power keeps the rest of us in line and that when it somehow shrinks away, our seething violence will rise to the surface."[13]

Solnit's work brought the concept of "elite panic," a term coined by disaster researchers more than fifty years earlier, into the mainstream. That "panic" helps to explain why few foreigners questioned the vast deployment of military assets or why there were already thousands of foreign troops in Haiti when the quake hit. And it's not simply that the elite fear random violence after a disaster. "There's also an elite fear," Solnit said, "that there will be urban insurrection."[14] And those fears aren't entirely unfounded. Researchers have established a historical correlation between the occurrence of natural disasters and social or political uprisings.

Haitian president Paul Magloire's corrupt response to a devastating hurricane in 1954 eventually led to his exile, while the 1985 earthquake in Mexico precipitated the collapse of more than seventy years of one-party rule as the population rose up against a political system unable to address the disaster. In the absence of authority, impacted communities do not descend into anarchy, Solnit found. Instead, they come together, often with revolutionary effect. And in Haiti, a revolution that started more than two hundred years earlier had remained unfinished; the out-sized military response suggested that America and other powerful nations feared it would be percolating once again.

AT THE TIME of the earthquake, perhaps the most well-known fact about Haiti, the product of its incessant repetition in foreign media, was its distinction as "the poorest country in the Western Hemisphere." In the late eighteenth century, however, the world had never seen a colony so prosperous as French-held Saint-Domingue. "The Pearl of the Antil-les," as the island was gaudily referred to, exported more sugar than the colonies in Jamaica, Cuba, and Brazil combined and was more valuable to the French than all the original North American colonies were to the British. Saint-Domingue was the object of every imperialist nation's de-sires, and indeed, Britain, France, Germany, and others had spent much of the preceding decades fighting for control of the territory.[15]

But even then, as Haitian sociologist and historian Jean Casimir has noted, Haitians themselves were still the poorest people in the Ameri-cas.[16] Ninety percent of the population were captives forced into slavery, most of whom had been born and raised in Africa. The colony may have produced riches for slave-owners and merchants, but not for those who lived and toiled there. They had resisted their enslavement continually and formally planted the seeds of revolution at a clandestine meeting in a forest outside the northern port city of Cap-Haïtien in 1791. Within days, the lush agricultural plains in the north were in flames, and a rev-olution that would last thirteen years had begun.

Twice, the French sent troops to put down the revolution. Despite Napoleon Bonaparte's reputation as one of the greatest military commanders in history, in the end, it wasn't the most-well-funded military force in the world that emerged victorious. On January 1, 1804, Jean-Jacques Dessalines, a former slave himself, declared Haiti an independent nation, promising to "forever ensure the empire of liberty in the country that gave us birth." Haiti was the first nation in the world to permanently ban the institution of slavery, becoming a beacon of hope for all those resisting and fighting for their independence and freedom.[17]

The successful revolution on Hispaniola changed the course of history,[18] including for the hemisphere's only other independent nation at the time, the United States. Haitians had dealt such a blow to Napoleon's troops that he was forced to abandon his plans to continue sailing to the US. Instead, the US acquired French holdings, at a considerable discount, via the Louisiana Purchase. The revolution's impact spread south as well. In 1815, following a military defeat at the hands of the Spanish, Simón Bolívar, the South American continent's eventual independence hero, was granted refuge in Haiti. Bolívar was given arms, manpower, and money by Haiti's newly independent leaders—on the condition he would abolish slavery upon his eventual victory over the Spanish. In 1819, Bolívar founded Gran Colombia, covering most of northern South America and even some of Panama.

Haiti, however, was forced to pay dearly for both its freedom and the hope it provided the enslaved elsewhere. It is no surprise that some, like David Brooks, see in Haiti a "progress-resistant" culture. Since 1791, when the revolution began, local and foreign actors have worked tirelessly to ensure that Haiti could not succeed—at least, not on the terms of the vast majority of its citizens. It took twenty-one years for France to recognize Haitian independence, and only then, on condition that it pay 150 million francs as reimbursement for the imperial nation's loss of property, i.e., those it had enslaved. With a flotilla of warships off the coast, the Haitian administration acquiesced, and subsequent governments continued to pay the independence debt until 1947. Haiti's economic loss from this "ransom" is estimated to be between $21 billion and $121 billion in today's dollars.[19]

Haiti served as a hope but also as a warning. Fearful of the message the newly free nation was sending to its own enslaved population, Southern members of the US Congress banned the use of the word "Haiti" in the Capitol Building. It took America even longer than France, failing to recognize the nation of Haiti until 1862 after the secession of Southern states. Even Bolívar did not send diplomatic representation to Haiti. Though an abolitionist, Bolívar had little desire to see real power handed over to the masses.[20] Few revolutionary leaders in Haiti did, either. Though the nation had achieved independence, its leaders failed to create a state that represented the people, the vast majority of whom had been born and raised in Africa. The economic model of extraction continued. And thus, the revolution was never completed. As Jean Casimir writes in *The Haitians: A Decolonial History,* "The very oligarchs who had sustained the colonial world were, to a large extent, those who took charge of the future of the new state during the nineteenth century."[21]

However, the new elite and public administration were unable to impose their will on a population that refused to obey and continued to resist. At the point of independence, it was the interplay of three distinct social blocks that determined the state of Haitian society. They were the local elite, foreign powers, and *pep la*—the masses. For two hundred years, the former two groups have sought to manage the latter to ensure the continuation of the extractive policies of the colonial era. This economic system consolidated further under the brutal Duvalier family's dictatorship. The state did not provide for the population but rather served as a means of enrichment for those politically connected and as a repressive force able to maintain control over the silenced majority. But the constant resistance from the masses has meant that Haiti's position at the forefront of the struggle for independence has not been confined to the nation's colonial history. It has also ensured that foreign powers and the local elite have never stopped trying to control the population.

3

THE BLUE HELMETS

———

There was too much going on at eye level for most to look up, but the airspace above the capital must have looked unnaturally crowded on the afternoon of January 14, 2010. At one point, eleven planes circulated overhead,[1] pilots waiting for clearance to land, hoping they had enough fuel to make it to the Dominican Republic or back to Miami if that clearance never came. Fuel supplies at the airport were running low. Meanwhile, friends and family members were still digging through piles of crumbled concrete looking for survivors, taking stock of what was left of their belongings, and worrying about where their next meal might come from.

Edmond Mulet still didn't know the fate the earth's movement had delivered to his colleagues at the Hotel Christophe. Short and slender, with a rapidly receding hairline, rimless glasses, and a neatly trimmed white mustache, Mulet more closely resembled a tenured history professor than a career politician and bullheaded diplomat. He certainly did not look like someone who should have been hanging on to the wall inside a C-130 circling a disaster zone. From inside the massive body of the cargo plane amid the plastic-wrapped pallets of relief supplies, he couldn't even see the traffic jam in the sky.

Mulet, a former president of the Guatemalan Congress, a veteran of the Central American peace process, and then an ambassador to the US, had managed the UN's peacekeeping mission in Haiti, which had deployed in 2004. He had since moved to New York to oversee the entire peacekeeping department, but the operation in Haiti continued. The troops, who came from more than two dozen countries and were led by a Brazilian general, comprised the UN Stabilization Mission in Haiti, or MINUSTAH by its French acronym. Many Haitians called them tourists—or occupiers. The world knew them as the "Blue Helmets." To US policymakers, they were a "bargain."

Circling above Port-au-Prince, Mulet's thoughts were on his former colleagues.[2] He had arrived in Haiti in 2006, just a few months after Préval's second election. Mulet's mandate had been to deliver stability, which, in US terms, meant open and safe for foreign investment and resistant to a further leftward political shift. On that front, he felt he had succeeded, or at least made progress. The US had agreed. In 2008, its ambassador wrote in a confidential cable that a "premature departure" of the UN mission would result in "an exodus of seaborne migrants, a sharp drop in foreign and domestic investment, and resurgent populist and anti-market economy political forces—reversing gains of the last two years."[3]

But now, as Mulet waited for the final descent into Port-au-Prince, jostling in the cargo hold, things were anything but stable. The gains attributed to Mulet's ironfisted leadership of the UN mission had been reduced to rubble. Information was incomplete, but a few local staff members had managed to reach the UN's headquarters in Haiti. They told Mulet that it had been "pulverized," though nobody knew how many had been inside or if there were any survivors. At least he knew the force's commanding officer, a Brazilian who had attended the National War College with General Keen, was in Miami at the time of the quake. The Brazilian had arrived in Haiti on another Coast Guard flight a day earlier and informed Mulet that hundreds of prisoners had escaped from the largest prison in the capital in the chaos after the quake. Many of them had likely been put there during the UN diplomat's last time in-country. Mulet wasn't just going back to Haiti to save his friends; he was going back to save his legacy, a legacy he shared with the international community.

*　*　*

THE CONCEPT OF stability is rooted in military action. The initial stability operations carried out by the US military occurred in North America, as the newly independent nation expanded westward. Troops helped lay down roads, and, of course, removed potential sources of instability, in this case the indigenous population. Since that time, the US has engaged in eleven conventional wars, but many hundreds more military engagements that are considered stability operations.[4] In 1915, the US dispatched Marines to Haiti under the banner of stability. They stayed for nineteen years and drastically reoriented the nation's political and economic life. Stability operations came to define US military engagement across the Caribbean in the early twentieth century and expanded greatly during the Cold War era. The Global War on Terror put stability operations into overdrive.

In two centuries, there has not been a single decade where the US has declined to newly engage its military in one of these lesser-known missions. US boots have literally been on the ground continuously since the Spanish-American War began in 1898, constituting a true forever war for global stability as defined by the US and its local political allies of choice. And, by the early twenty-first century, the policy had come full circle back to Haiti.

The night of January 14, 2010, CNN's Wolf Blitzer interviewed former secretary of state Colin Powell. "Here's what I'm worried about in the immediate next few days," Blitzer began. "I'm afraid of the tensions [that] could get going. There could be rioting, there could be looting. There could be some serious violence." The opening followed a disconcerting pattern of fearmongering from the US media. Blitzer then asked Powell if the US military was going to be involved if that was the case. Fear of thousands of Haitians arriving by boat on the shores of Miami, and fear of anarchy as those who remained fought for their survival, was already taking hold in the media and foreign capitals.

"Well, you have the Haitian police force," Powell told Blitzer. "But you also have UN peacekeepers who are in Haiti . . . and with the addition of US troops . . . that should be enough to stabilize things," he continued. "A very small military force in the course of Haitian history has been able to control that population."[5]

That wasn't a conclusion Powell had reached casually. As a retired four-star general, he was assuredly familiar with the US military's long history of stability operations, including the original "compassionate invasion" of Haiti. Further, in the two decades preceding the 2010 earthquake, Powell himself had been intimately involved in planning two large-scale military operations in Haiti: once under a Democrat, Bill Clinton, and once under a Republican, George W. Bush.

By 2010, US policy in Haiti had become a rare point of bipartisan agreement. The two former presidents even launched a joint fund for Haitian relief efforts just days after the quake. It was more than bipartisan: it was global. The Blue Helmets on the ground were the sixth UN-led mission since the midnineties. And that's why the UN mission was such a bargain for US policymakers. "Without a UN-sanctioned peacekeeping and stabilization force, we would be getting far less help from our hemispheric and European partners in managing Haiti," the ambassador explained in a 2008 diplomatic cable.[6]

Just as foreign powers had attempted to manage Haiti's affairs for centuries, after the 1986 popular uprising that pushed Baby Doc Duvalier into exile, they sought to ensure the nation's transition to democracy didn't mean a shift out of the American-led global economic order. The US had given the final push to get their former Cold War ally out the door and on to a US military jet bound for France, but a democracy proved far more difficult to manage than a dictatorship.[7] In 1990, when Haiti held her first free and fair election, the US and major donors were convinced the winner would be a World Bank economist who had served under Duvalier. Instead, it was a priest who had waged a war of words against Baby Doc and the nation's elite from his pulpit in Cité Soleil. It was Jean-Bertrand Aristide who won with 67.5 percent of the vote.

The newly elected government lasted only seven months before a military coup backed by the country's kleptocratic oligarchy chased Aristide and Préval, his then prime minister, into exile. The George H. W. Bush administration denounced the coup, but had also provided covert support for the Haitian military.[8] In 1993, after President Bill Clinton took office, the Pentagon started actively planning an operation in Haiti to help restore democracy and rebuild the country.

"US forces would have no combat role but rather would focus on the Pentagon's 'nation-building' capabilities aimed at speeding recovery after the devastation of war or natural disasters," the Associated Press reported at the time. "Such military forces, now primarily in the reserves, were developed to put a conquered nation back on its feet."[9] The next day, a Pentagon official told the AP: "It's classic nation-building. It was stuff that they were never able to use in Iraq, the kind of thing an occupation force would have to do."[10] Sixteen months later, Clinton authorized the deployment of up to twenty thousand soldiers to pave the way for the return of Aristide. Foreign troops stayed as part of a UN-led mission for nearly two years through the 1996 inauguration of Préval. It took only eight years for US troops to arrive again.

REPUBLICANS HAD BEEN highly critical of the Clinton administration's intervention in Haiti. Then presidential candidate George W. Bush was asked about it during a debate in 2000 with Al Gore, Clinton's vice president. "I don't think our troops ought to be used for what's called nation-building. I think our troops ought to be used to fight and win war," Bush said.[11] By 2004, of course, Bush and his neocon cabinet were already deep into their nation-building exercises in Afghanistan and Iraq. The former cold warriors saw an opportunity in Haiti, which, by then, had seen the feared Aristide return to the presidency.

In early 2004, Fulton Armstrong, a CIA analyst covering Haiti, began to notice arms caches coming from the Dominican Republic and getting into the hands of former Haitian military officers who were rumored to be preparing a bloody rebellion aimed at toppling Aristide. "They really had good logistics, good comms," he remembered. "It had all the markings of a US operation." But, he continued, it wasn't the agency behind it. When he looked more into it, he discovered it was the State Department. "All indications were, incredibly, that the State Department's Bureau of Western Hemisphere Affairs—charged with managing relations with Aristide but managed by people who'd opposed him for years— was behind it." The final push came when the administration blocked a US security company that had been protecting Aristide from providing reinforcements and renewing its license to provide his security. "That was a dirty trick," he recalled.[12]

On February 29, 2004, with the paramilitaries approaching the capital, Aristide boarded a US-registered airplane previously used for illegal rendition flights and was flown into exile. When he eventually landed in the Central African Republic, he told the press that US diplomatic and military personnel had been present at his residence and that he had been "kidnapped."[13] Powell, then secretary of state, categorically denied Aristide's characterization.

The same day that Aristide was forced from office, the United Nations Security Council authorized the deployment of an international military force to Haiti, to be led by two thousand US Marines. The authorization occurred under the UN's Chapter VII, invoked only when a situation threatens international peace and security. It gave the international body the right to send soldiers and use deadly force without Haiti's formal authorization. UN Secretary-General Kofi Annan pledged a long-term global commitment to the country. "The international community is not going to put a band-aid on [Haiti], and that we are not only going to help stabilize the current situation, but assist the Haitians over the long haul and really help them pick up the pieces and build a stable country," Annan told the press.[14] The international community was again jumping headfirst into nation-building in Haiti.

The military-led nation-building in the Western Hemisphere, in the world's first independent Black nation, took place without significant pushback whatsoever. By 2004, opposition to the Iraq War was growing exponentially. The initial justification that the government there possessed weapons of mass destruction had been exposed as belligerent propaganda. The UN Security Council had never even authorized the invasion. Though the US had cobbled together its "coalition of the willing," support was fading. But the possibility of a long-term military engagement in Haiti enjoyed bipartisan support in the US.

In April 2004, the Center for American Progress, an influential liberal think tank, released an article titled "Nation Building in Haiti: Can We Do Better This Time?" The brief report recommended that it would be better for the US to share in the responsibilities of managing

Haiti. "One possible solution to the challenge of nation-building," the report concluded, "is a permanent UN force with units for policing, infrastructure-building, tax collection, education and other essential state functions."[15] Few among the political establishment in the US or international community questioned why foreign troops were necessary on the ground in Haiti in the first place.

Later that month, the Security Council authorized the deployment of 6,700 soldiers and 1,622 police officers to Haiti. The mission's primary goal was to ensure the stability of the unelected transitional government that took power after Aristide's ouster. The new prime minister had been in retirement in Florida when the coup took place.[16] The mandate, however, was far broader than just keeping the peace. Among its many provisions, it included support for elections, justice sector reform, police training, and humanitarian operations.

However, the major success for the US was handing off control of the mission to Brazil. It was the first time in the history of UN peacekeeping that a country from the Global South would take on such a role in the region.

The peacekeeping mission in Haiti was significantly different than other UN missions. The first-ever official UN peacekeeping mission had been in 1948, to enforce a cease-fire in the Middle East between Israel and its neighbors. Over time, the missions' scopes expanded. UN Blue Helmets took more active roles in complex nation-building operations across the globe and especially in Africa. Most think of peacekeepers in relation to their activities in both Bosnia and Rwanda, their presence on the ground ineffective in the face of genocide. In many regards, however, the UN peacekeeping missions simply served as a replacement for stability missions previously undertaken by the US military. In Haiti, for example, there was no war, no widespread civil conflict at all. The UN troops' 2004 deployment was a response to political instability, not a sectarian armed conflict. That came once they were on the ground.

In Haiti, the Blue Helmets launched a brutal crackdown on the capital's poorest neighborhoods, many of which remained Aristide strongholds. After the fall of the dictatorship, the popular neighborhoods[17] of Port-au-Prince had organized themselves around community groups known as *baz,* the Kreyòl term for "base." Long excluded from the state, these communities formed the backbone of the movement that had delivered Aristide to the presidency—twice. They had formed in the absence of the state and as explicitly political actors, working to bridge the divide between the forgotten masses and the political and NGO class to ensure their communities could benefit from otherwise inaccessible state and foreign resources.[18]

After the deployment of the Blue Helmets, the *baz*—referred to internationally as gangs—engaged in an armed conflict with what they viewed as an occupying force sent to consolidate a coup d'état. These communities were the sources of instability that the foreign troops were there to neutralize. In one such raid that ended up killing and injuring dozens of civilians, Brazilian troops fired more than twenty thousand rounds of ammunition into the crowded neighborhood of Cité Soleil.[19] The UN imposed stability with lethal force.

The intervention, however, was as political as it was militaristic. After the deployment of the troops came the installation of the "Core Group" of international donors, consisting of the UN mission, the Organization of American States, as well as the ambassadors of Brazil, Canada, the European Union, France, Germany, Spain, and, of course, the United States of America. This Core Group of diplomats became a de facto fourth branch of government.

Initially given a six-month mandate, each year the Security Council had voted to reauthorize. But the mission, and its heavy reliance on South American soldiers, was becoming increasingly untenable by the time of the 2010 earthquake. Haiti was not the crime-ridden island many believed it was. Outside of a few neighborhoods in the capital, the country was far more peaceful than most of its neighbors, including the Dominican Republic. United Nations security officers began internally referring to their mission not as a PKO, or "peacekeeping operation," but as a BKO, or "beach-keeping operation," since they spent most weekends on the pristine Caribbean shores outside the capital, drinking Prestige—Haiti's national beer—or rum sours.

Public opposition was also growing. The mission had been involved in a series of ever-more-public sexual abuse scandals during its time in

Haiti. In 2007, more than one hundred Sri Lankan soldiers were sent back to their home country after being caught exploiting children as part of a sex ring. There had been no arrests.[20] And the hemisphere's political landscape had continued to shift. Throughout South America, left-wing political leaders had taken power through the ballot box and were becoming more responsive to their citizens' calls to stop participating in the long-running occupation of Haiti. The US had pushed back. "The UN Stabilization Mission in Haiti is an indispensable tool in realizing core USG policy interests in Haiti," the US ambassador wrote to Washington in 2008. "The fundamental USG policy goal in Haiti is to make it a viable state that does not post [sic] a threat to the region through domestic political turmoil or an exodus of illegal migrants."[21]

The "compassionate invasion" wasn't an isolated event, in other words. Instead, it must be seen as part of a two-decade effort to manage Haiti's long transition from dictatorship to democracy. It had played out in fits and starts since Clinton had sent troops in 1994. Still, by the time of the earthquake, Haiti was well into its second decade of an internationally led nation-building effort, though one that had taken place largely outside the view of the US public. And the quake had given new life to the faltering UN mission. Speaking before the US Congress a few weeks after the earthquake, James Dobbins, a former diplomat working with the RAND Corporation, explained that "as the result of the earthquake, we basically have to set the clock back to zero and assume that a UN peacekeeping force is going to be required there, probably for another decade at least."[22]

ON JANUARY 17, five days after the earthquake, Al Jazeera reported that the US military had built a ten-foot fence around its base of operations at the Port-au-Prince airport, named after Toussaint Louverture, a beloved hero of Haiti's revolution. US forces had erected a "mini-Green Zone," Al Jazeera's correspondent said, in reference to the military's much larger compound in Baghdad at the time.[23] There was no doubt the Pentagon had tremendous logistical capabilities, as demonstrated by its rapid reopening of the airport. However, the security buildup served to confirm the media's fears of impending chaos and hampered relief efforts.

The World Food Programme, desperate to get supplies into the country, could not land at the airport until January 16, and complained of landing spots being reserved for US military supplies. "Their priorities are to secure the country. Ours are to feed."[24]

On the first day that the Air Force had control of the airport, seventy-three planes landed. One-third of them were US military assets. In the weeks after, a plane carrying Church of Scientology members landed, as did a plane carrying diapers from Canada. CNN's Anderson Cooper managed to land at the Port-au-Prince airport. One-half of a field hospital arrived, but the other half was diverted to the Dominican Republic. Doctors Without Borders complained they had had multiple flights, each with tons of medical supplies, that were refused landing spots.[25]

Brazil and France both lodged formal complaints with the US. The airport, said France's ambassador in Haiti, was "an annex of Washington" and not for the international community's use. France's aid coordinator scuffled with an American inside the airport's control tower on the eighteenth. "This is about helping Haiti, not about occupying Haiti," the Frenchman said afterward.[26]

Even when aid did get into Haiti, the fear of violence often prevented it from actually reaching those in need. As many organizations were unwilling to travel without robust security details, planned aid distributions were canceled or delayed. Relief supplies piled up behind the ten-foot fence that the US military had built at the airport. Pallets of bottled water and MREs (meals ready to eat) baked in the Caribbean sun. The fear of an impromptu riot led the UN to evacuate doctors from a medical tent. Seeing the doctors leaving, CNN's Sanjay Gupta turned his film crew into a crack medical team and stayed through the night.[27]

The elite rescue teams that arrived to pull survivors from the rubble of collapsed buildings generally avoided the capital's most impoverished neighborhoods as well. In contrast to the "green zone" at the airport, these neighborhoods were labeled "red zones" by the UN mission, meaning foreigners should not dare enter. Instead, rescue teams did most of their work at hotels where the foreign and local elite had been at the time of the earthquake, like the Hotel Montana. Other teams were at the Hotel Christophe, where more than a hundred UN officials had been. The various international rescue teams cost hundreds of millions of dollars. At most, their efforts saved about 140 lives, many of whom were foreigners.[28]

The militarized response saved some lives, but the fear that drove it had cost untold more. And as time passed, the predicted widespread violence or mass migration never happened. "No one knew what the response of the Haitian people would be to this terrible event," an Air Force general explained to the press in mid-February. "So yes, we did send in men and women with guns, and we have not needed to use them." It was a stunning admission, and one that passed with little regard for its deeper meaning.[29]

Instead of the US military, it was the Blue Helmets that provided security. The UN Security Council upped the number of troops by four thousand after the earthquake. Natural first responders after such a disaster, the soldiers instead largely stayed in their fortified barracks. When they did patrol, it wasn't to provide urgent medical care to the hundreds of thousands of wounded. Viewing the desperation from behind bulletproof glass, they stayed in their armored vehicles. "The only time I've seen one of these UN troops jump out of the back of a truck was to beat up on somebody or take a shot at them," a member of the US 82nd Airborne Division told Reuters in late February.

"I still have to patrol," Edmond Mulet said, justifying the mission's prioritization of security. "I still have to go after all these criminals and bandits that escaped from the national penitentiary, the gang leaders, the criminals, the killers, the kidnappers. I cannot really distract myself from doing that."[30]

IN RETROSPECT, THE focus on security in those first weeks and months looks like a tragic mistake and one borne more of racism and misplaced fear than anything else.[31] It was taken as a given that Haiti needed external supervision, that, amid the unfolding crisis, the savagery of the Haitian people would rise to the surface. Haitians have been branded as inherently violent people since 1791, and that narrative has been fraudulently perpetuated for centuries. The victims of imperial aggression and their humanity are rarely recognized by citizens of aggressor nations. After January 12, rather than fighting one another or foreign aid workers, Haitians did indeed come together. They came together to provide for one another, to care for one another as they had been doing for more than two hundred years. Rural residents took in hundreds of thousands fleeing the capital, providing far more humanitarian relief than any aircraft carrier or body-armored soldier. "Looters"—primarily people looking to survive—had assuredly saved more Haitian lives as they sifted through the rubble than all the elite teams from abroad combined. And the Haitian diaspora, sending whatever they could to friends and family, provided more direct assistance than any donor or NGO.

In the end, the US military's "compassionate invasion" lasted less than six months. Powell was right, the UN troops were more than enough to "control the population."

The Pentagon was on standby, the Blue Helmets kept the order, but it was a different occupation, one that had been ongoing in parallel for years, that now appeared more entrenched than ever. The aid industry was taking over. The massive military deployment and round-the-clock coverage had drawn millions of eyes to Haiti and helped raise billions of dollars for what was shaping up to be an unprecedented humanitarian effort. Foreign assistance, however, is about more than just disaster relief; it is an integral part of the international community's nation-building tool kit.

Following the collapse of the Soviet Union, the US poured billions of dollars of aid into Eastern European states, hoping to bring them more into line with the West's vision of democracy and development. In the twenty-three years since the end of the dictatorship in Haiti, the international community had spent $8 billion pursuing the same. Two decades into this nation-building experiment, all that the international community had to show for their effort was the evisceration of the Haitian state, as the government's absence after the quake had demonstrated. What the response to the earthquake revealed, however, was that this was no accident. Donors hadn't helped build a modern Haitian state; what they had created was its replacement, the Aid State. In the decades before the earthquake, most of the state had been outsourced to foreign actors. After 2004, the Core Group of international diplomats acted as the local management team. With a world-historic reconstruction effort coming, the Aid State was about to get even stronger.

4

THE OPPORTUNITY

———

Two major fault lines run right through the island of Hispaniola. One is in the north, and the other is in the south, near Haiti's capital. They are strike-slip faults, the same type as the San Andreas Fault. Before 2010, the last major earthquake along the southern fault occurred in 1770.

The pressure had, quite literally, been building for centuries.

Goudougoudou is what Haitians called the January 12, 2010, tremblor. It is an onomatopoeia, named after the sound emanating from the ground as it began to shake. The center of the quake, where the pressure along the fault initially broke, was located about eight miles under the town of Léogâne, which itself sits to the southwest of Port-au-Prince. After that initial crack, the force extended along the fault, explaining the powerful aftershocks that echoed for days. Amazingly, more than ten years later, scientists are still investigating the exact cause of the *Goudougoudou*. Some now suspect that a more minor, previously unknown fault was the cause, meaning the super-quake may be yet to come.

The force of the 2010 Haiti quake, 7.0, was significant but not abnormal. Each year, globally, about six quakes of similar size occur. There hasn't been a year without a 7.0 since 1960.[1] The scale used to measure the energy released by the shifting faults is logarithmic. With each point, the force increases ten times. The San Francisco quake of 1906, a 7.9, was equivalent to nearly fifteen million tons of TNT exploding. The Haiti quake was closer to 475,000 tons, or the equivalent of about thirty of the atomic bombs the US dropped in Hiroshima.[2] That was the natural disaster. There was nothing that any government could do to stop it. But the magnitude of the devastation tells another story.

The numbers are shocking. The earthquake is estimated to have killed between 60,000 and 220,000 people;[3] either way, it was one of the worst natural disasters in terms of lives lost in modern history. More than 300,000 were injured. More than 500,000 fled the capital, seeking refuge with families, friends, or complete strangers in rural areas. The damage to infrastructure was immense. At least 105,000 homes were destroyed, and 208,000 damaged. Over fifty hospitals collapsed or were too unstable to be used. The same was true for more than 1,300 schools.[4] All but one of the government's ministry buildings fell. The Inter-American Development Bank estimated the total damages to be at least eight billion dollars, an amount larger than the Haitian economy.[5] There was nothing natural about a loss of this magnitude.

Throughout the first decade of the twenty-first century, natural disasters claimed more than 84,000 lives annually. As our earth warms, scientists warn that the frequency and severity of those events—though not necessarily earthquakes—will continue to increase. In the 1970s, there was an average of ninety-one major natural disasters recorded each year. During 2000–2009, that figure had reached 447.[6] To be sure, record-keeping has improved, as has the instrumentation used to measure such events. Still, the trend is clear. On the other hand, the loss of human lives due to these so-called natural disasters has consistently fallen. With each passing storm, the world becomes better prepared to face the next. What determines the extent of the damage from a natural disaster is not simply the magnitude of the event but rather how well prepared the affected country is. The event itself is natural; the devastation is often human-made.

In December 2009, one month before the earthquake, the head of the government's Bureau of Mines and Energy, Dr. Claude Prepetit, gave an interview to Le Nouvelliste, Haiti's oldest newspaper. He warned, as he had been doing for years at international conferences, in university

classrooms, and in meetings with government officials and foreign donors, that pressure was continuing to build along the fault lines hidden
under the denuded ground. "The day when it cracks the consequences
will be catastrophic for the region," he had told the paper. For Prepetit,
it was simple mathematics. It had been 240 years since the last major
eruption; with the plates moving an average of seven millimeters a year,
a 1.4-meter gap had developed. A rupture of that size, Prepetit concluded, would equate to a magnitude 7.3 earthquake.

While Prepetit was sure it would happen, he couldn't predict when
with any accuracy. He had asked the government to invest in new equipment that could detect the imperceptible-to-humans movements of the
earth that often precede massive quakes. "The government listened to
me, but they had other priorities," Prepetit recalled.[7] The future is un-
certain; immediate needs, on the other hand, are guaranteed. Do you
invest in preparing for an earthquake that could be decades off, or do
you distribute food to those who need it now? In 2009, the Haitian
government's budget was about half the size of the city of Boston's but
for a population sixteen times greater. The choice, if there was one at all,
was simple.

Few, however, seemed willing to ask why the Haitian government
was forced to make that trade-off in the first place. Haiti is one of the
most aid-dependent nations on earth. From the fall of the dictatorship
in 1986 through 2009, official development assistance to Haiti had to-
taled nearly $8 billion—equivalent to the estimated cost of the dam-
age the quake had caused in less than a minute.[8] However, that money
hadn't been managed by the Haitian government. And just as politicians in aid-recipient countries are prone to choose immediate needs
over long-term disaster preparation, so, too, are donors. In the humanitarian world, the metric most used to show progress is the number of
people who received some benefit from the project. Investing in the future does not fit neatly into this evaluation system. Rather, almost all of
those billions went to stopgap measures for perpetually pressing needs
such as food insecurity and medical care, needs that were compounded
by each successive hurricane, drought, or flood. Precious little went to
preparing for the next disaster, even less for the looming super-quake.

After a natural disaster, the ultimate measure of success goes beyond how many individuals receive some sort of assistance. Success comes from the community, the city, the state, the country, or the entire region being better prepared to face the next disaster. After the earthquake, the plans for how to ensure that happened diverged significantly.

THE *GOUDOUGOUDOU* KNOCKED out cell towers and the transmission of most radio stations, but a few, including Signal FM, did manage to stay on the air throughout.[9] The day after, Préval sent a taped message in which he provided a staid rundown of the destruction before calmly asking citizens to *kenbe*—or "hold on." But in the weeks after, he had barely been heard from in public. Radio hosts ended up stepping into the role of disaster coordinator, fielding calls and airing pleas for assistance. In a country with high levels of illiteracy and little print media outside the capital, community radio is king; there are thousands of stations, and virtually every household owns a radio. Though the official language of the government is French, about 90 percent of the population only speaks Kreyòl. Surveys indicate roughly the same percent of the population relies on radio broadcasts, generally in Kreyòl, for information.[10] Across the country, Haitians listened intently, and they heard firsthand reports from loved ones and others fleeing the capital. Little outside assistance was getting to those in need on the ground in Port-au-Prince.

Meanwhile, aid supplies piled up at the airport, logistical challenges and security concerns preventing their rapid distribution. Even in the best of times, Haiti relies on imports to feed the country. But that didn't mean there was nothing to be had locally after the earthquake. Though much of the capital had been destroyed, including many of the storage units that had served as food depots for the thousands who bring fresh produce from the countryside to be sold in the markets of Port-au-Prince, those informal vendors, known as *Madan Sara,* continued to operate almost without interruption. Though not reported as such in the US and international media, these were the true first responders who provided food to those in need. Foreign officials were worried about chaos in the absence of public authority, but Haitians had been managing, for better or worse, without such an authority for centuries.

In rural Haiti, stories of the absence of the centralized state came as little surprise; there was a reason people referred to the capital as the Republic of Port-au-Prince. Following independence and the end of the plantation economy, outlying Haitian society had rebuilt itself around these rural families and rural communities. This explicitly anti-plantation and autonomous social organization was based around the *lakou,* a system of customary land management and community-led development. By the early twentieth century, Haiti had one of the most equal distributions of land in the world, and its constitution prevented foreigners from owning any of it. That changed with the 1915 US occupation. At the urging of the occupying force, the constitution was rewritten, and foreigners were invited to take over large tracts. Political and economic power, which had been largely decentralized, was consolidated in Port-au-Prince.

In the years after the Marines left, that trend had only accelerated. Hurricane Hazel, in 1954, forced thousands of peasants to leave their land and seek opportunities in the capital. The urban-to-rural migration was compounded by globalization, specifically the promotion of Haiti as a low-cost manufacturing hub in the 1970s and '80s—an aggressive effort supported financially by foreign assistance from Washington and international lenders. The creation of the densely packed neighborhoods along the bay of Port-au-Prince that had seen so much devastation in the quake had begun decades earlier with haphazard construction to provide shelter for workers in the American-owned sweatshops of the capital.[11]

By the time of the quake, Port-au-Prince and its surrounding areas were home to some three million people, more than a third of the country's population. In the quake's aftermath, radio shows in Haiti became the center of hours-long debates about the future of the state, the damning legacies of past foreign interventions, and the long-term neglect of rural communities. With the capital in ruins after the earthquake, perhaps there was an opportunity to reverse this damaging legacy.

That a natural disaster, like any crisis, can present an opportunity may sound callous. But amid collective trauma and human suffering, there will always be those looking to the future and using the current landscape to alter it. The question then becomes, to the benefit of whom? In the United States, the Bush administration used the rising tide of nationalism following the September 11 attacks to advance its long-desired plans of occupying Iraq, plans that had been partially tested out earlier in Haiti. Politicians may seize on the opportunity that a disaster presents to push through legislation that never previously stood a chance—for example, the Patriot Act in the US, a 342-page law that was introduced in its entirety just days after September 11.

That said, internal solidarity—in traditionally marginalized communities—built in the face of a crisis over the longer term can also become a potent force for structural change of a different kind.

In rubble-strewn neighborhoods, in rural townships, in the rice fields of the Artibonite, on the factory floors in the industrial parks, and under already-fraying blue and gray tarps throughout the capital, there was a moment when it seemed possible that a door was opening to the systemic change the Haitian people had struggled to achieve for centuries. The state, which throughout most of the nation's history had not protected the people but rather elite local and foreign interests, was gone. The disaster was an opportunity to build the nation promised with Haiti's 1804 independence.

Several grassroots organizations started meeting to discuss organizing a broad coalition around a common agenda. On January 27, more than a dozen groups, representing peasant collectives, human rights defenders, and even community radio stations, released a statement under the banner of the Coordinating Committee of Progressive Organizations. They had all lost friends, family, and colleagues. But, the organizations continued, it was vital that Haitians paused and drew lessons from the disaster so as to continue their struggle for a different country, "capable of overcoming the cycle of dependency and destruction and rising to the level of the dreams of universal emancipation of its founders and of all the people of Haiti."[12]

In a mid-February interview with a local journalist, Patrick Elie, a prominent pro-democracy activist and former Haitian government official, appealed to all Haitians to continue in this spirit of solidarity. Solidarity, he said, is what had saved so many lives in the crucial first days when nobody else was there. Solidarity, he continued, would be necessary for Haiti to rebuild. "It is this solidarity, a far cry from the political instability and social polarization we have known," Elie said, "that must ensure that a few local and international interests do not end up coopting the majority of the funds targeted for Haiti's reconstruction."[13]

Of course, those local and international interests were also eyeing the quake as an opportunity, albeit a very different one than imagined by Elie and the Coordinating Committee of Progressive Organizations. Only days after the earthquake, an aide to the Haitian president had been pitched on the idea of a new industrial park for foreign investors. The idea had been on the table for years, but now, it seemed, there would be the necessary resources to lure a big multinational company to Haiti. "This is what the earthquake is today—an opportunity, a huge opportunity," Reginald Boulos, the patriarch of one of Haiti's most notoriously wealthy families, told the *Washington Post* a month later.[14]

Incredibly, in Washington, DC, the conversation had quickly shifted to whether or not Haiti could even continue to exist as an independent state. Twenty years of nation-building and billions in aid hadn't been enough to save Haiti from itself. Should it become a UN or US protectorate, wondered many in the Haitian diaspora—approaching a million in the US alone by 2010—and the Washington foreign policy community. Reporters were curious about who the new Paul Bremer would be, referring to the man the Bush administration placed in charge of the Coalition Provisional Authority that managed Iraq after the invasion.[15]

"Is it too wild a suggestion to be talking about, at least temporarily, some sort of receivership?" asked Senator Chris Dodd, a Democrat from Connecticut, during a Senate hearing in late January. His Republican colleague from Tennessee, Bob Corker, who had first traveled to the country in 1982 with a local church group, believed it would take even more. "We just need to be in charge, and that's what's happening," Corker said. "The international community is in charge."[16]

After the earthquake, the two-hundred-year history of the independent Haitian nation appeared to hang in the balance. Corker was right about the state of affairs in the first few weeks after the earthquake. The international community was in charge. But whose vision of the future was going to win out in Haiti? Those controlling the billions in antici- pated aid were likely going to determine the answer.

5

THE PLAN

The earthquake in Haiti occurred at a critical time for the global aid industry. In the early twenty-first century, major donor nations had begun to reconsider how they provided foreign assistance. Under the auspices of the Organisation for Economic Co-operation and Development, or OECD, the world's wealthiest nations came together in 2003 to begin discussing how best to reshape their assistance programs. In 2005, more than one hundred countries and the leading development banks endorsed the Paris Declaration on Aid Effectiveness.[1] For too long, the signatories agreed, aid had been inefficient and dictated from abroad. Instead, it suggested that "recipient countries" come up with a development plan that donors could support. It sounded good in theory, though even at the time, many pointed out that this new aid paradigm, designed to get donors to work more with local governments, was still written by a club of rich countries.

Implementation, especially by the US, proved more difficult. In the end, few wealthy nations wanted to give up control over how they spent their foreign assistance funds. In 2009, however, the Obama administration made an early pledge to bring its practices in line with these emerging global standards. Secretary of State Clinton made Haiti the first place the administration would translate the lessons into action. She gave the job to her chief of staff, Cheryl Mills, who had been deputy White House counsel during President Bill Clinton's impeachment trial.

The trusted confidante led a comprehensive review of US aid for Haiti. She turned in her final report on the afternoon of January 12, just hours before the quake upended the nation.[2]

The US, the review found, had spent more than $4 billion since 1990 but had precious little to show for it. Aid programs had been haphazard, poorly coordinated, and spread over too many different sectors; most of the money had gone to private contractors or NGOs. Worse, there had never been real plans to transition aid programs to the control of the Haitian government. The earthquake was an opportunity to make right. And there were two of the most influential people in the world standing onstage pledging to make that a reality. They were former president Bill Clinton, named UN special envoy to Haiti in 2009, and his wife, Secretary of State Hillary Clinton.

The Clintons first traveled to Haiti as a young couple in 1975 and have often referenced the profound impact that trip had on them. They took to calling it a "delayed honeymoon," as Bill Clinton told CNN's Wolf Blitzer just a day after the earthquake.[3] It wasn't actually what they had planned for their honeymoon, which they took with family in Acapulco; it was a wedding gift from David Edwards, a Citibank executive and close friend who had business in Haiti.[4] Fast-forward thirty-five years, and the Clintons were at the forefront of a concerted international effort to redevelop Haiti into the type of place where Americans might once again honeymoon—and where banking executives might once again do business.

A series of three devastating hurricanes swept across the island during a span of just thirty days during the late summer and early fall of 2008. The resulting flooding buried whole cities and left hundreds of people dead. Soon afterward, the Clinton Foundation, the family's post-presidency global NGO, started its first project in Haiti. Later that year, the Clinton Global Initiative (CGI), with its longtime partner Citibank, initiated the Haiti Action Network to channel corporate cash to Haitian development. By 2009, it was also donor cash they were marshaling. In April of that year, Secretary of State Clinton headlined a donor conference to help raise funds for the hurricane response at the

Inter-American Development Bank (IDB) in Washington. The future of Haiti, she told the room of diplomats and development experts, "will be shaped to a large extent by the decisions that we make."[5]

Her words would prove prophetic, though the donor conference raised only $353 million in pledges, a paltry amount given the extent of the damage. Haiti's woes were low on the priority list for the world's rich countries already mired in a global recession. And donors had attended similar conferences in the past. They had pledged vast sums, and yet every few years, they'd be called back to be told that Haiti remained, as the mantra went, "the poorest country in the Western Hemisphere," and then be asked to donate once more to its cause. There had been too many disasters and too many wasted millions. "Donor fatigue," in industry parlance, had set in. About a month later, Bill Clinton was named UN special envoy.[6] He was the high-profile name needed to mobilize international funding for Haiti's development.

The appointment wasn't met so warmly by many among Haiti's political class. The president of the Senate asked why Haiti needed a special envoy at all, given that they are reserved for "places where there are crises and conflicts." He wondered about the actual mandate of the former United States president. "Where do his powers end?" the senator asked during an interview with a member of the Haitian press. *Le Nouvelliste* called Clinton the new "Governor General," in reference to the colonial-era title France gave to its local representative.[7]

Despite the pushback, the Clintons had a close ally within the Haitian government at the time. Two years before his UN appointment, Bill Clinton had met with Haitian president René Préval at Ronald Reagan National Airport outside Washington. Clinton was arriving and Préval was on his way to Miami. With their paths crossing, they met inside a conference room the Haitian ambassador in DC had reserved.

When Bill Clinton entered, he greeted Préval with a hug. "Mr. President, I cannot tell you how happy I am to see you as president again," the Haitian ambassador recalled Clinton saying. "Because I know when you were president the first time, Aristide didn't let you do anything that you wanted to do. Now that you are president in your own right, how can I help?"

On the way out, Préval turned to his ambassador.

"Ambassador, now Clinton is mine."[8]

With Clinton firmly in his camp, Préval believed he would finally be able to consolidate the support of the donor class. When the former US president took the special envoy position in 2009, Préval's prime minister referred to Clinton as "a great friend of Haiti" and praised the appointment in the press. "We will work with him to better make the case of Haiti to the international community and to build a new, solid and efficient partnership to improve the Haitian people's living conditions," she said.[9] Nobody could have expected that, less than a year later, the earthquake would serve as the perfect opportunity to turn that into a reality.

IN FEBRUARY 2010, a month after the earthquake, major donors announced they would hold another aid conference at the United Nations. There, the Haitian government would present its plan for reconstruction, and donors would be asked to pledge financial support to its implementation. The conference cohosts were Préval, Hillary Clinton, and Bill Clinton. They called the conference Towards a New Future in Haiti.

Haitians themselves, however, remained skeptical. A survey commissioned by the global NGO Oxfam found that only 17.5 percent of Haitians believed the plan would be responsive to their needs. The majority, the poll showed, felt "that Haitian governments have never fulfilled their promises and have always favored the economic elites of the country." Fewer than 7 percent believed their government should lead the reconstruction effort. Remarkably, nearly 40 percent said they would support a foreign government taking over.[10]

Many others, however, believed that a foreign takeover had already happened. Ten days before donors were set to meet in New York, a group of more than two dozen Haitian organizations and social movements, including those that had organized under the Coordinating Committee of Progressive Organizations, issued a press release decrying the local population's near total exclusion from the formulation of the development plan. The organizations wanted a break from the past, but instead what they saw were donors, with the acquiescence of the Haitian government, perpetuating the same old development model. They had a point.

In late 2008, UN Secretary-General Ban Ki-moon had dispatched Paul Collier, an Oxford economist and author of *The Bottom Billion: Why the Poorest Countries Are Failing and What Can Be Done About It,* to Haiti. Collier's work was championed by Ban, and the book's thesis, that a drastic rethink in foreign assistance was necessary, dovetailed nicely with the aid rethink happening at the State Department. After a short research trip to the country, the economist produced an official report titled *Haiti: From Natural Catastrophe to Economic Security.* It became known as the Collier Report.[11]

Haiti was considered a "fragile state"—on its way to failed state status—Collier wrote. But it shouldn't be. It was in a relatively peaceful part of the world and was not beset by ethnic conflict. The UN's peacekeeping troops were there to provide security, and it was geographically close to the world's largest market, the US. Since the introduction of US legislation in 2007, Haiti had been the beneficiary of duty-free access for manufactured goods. And "due to its poverty and relatively unregulated labor market, Haiti has labor costs that are fully competitive with China," Collier argued. At its core, his report called for low-cost garment manufacturing and export-oriented agricultural production—hardly a historic revelation. These were precisely the policies that had helped drive the rural-to-urban migration that precipitated the massive devastation in the quake. In Collier's estimation, the problem was not the model of development but rather the inability of the government to provide a stable environment for foreign investors to prosper. What was supposed to be different this time, Collier argued, was aid.

Foreign assistance was becoming increasingly irrelevant. In sub-Saharan Africa, for example, the flow of *private* capital had already surpassed official development aid. The same logic underpinned the Clinton Foundation, especially its Global Initiative. Donor governments were tired of giving, but if the little money left could be focused on catalyzing foreign investment, Haiti's future might look a lot brighter. If disparate donor aid flows were pooled together, aid money could be channeled to big-ticket items that foreign companies wanted to see before investing, like critical infrastructure and reliable energy. Foreign assistance, the theory went, could reduce the perceived risk associated with private-sector investment in Haiti. What Haiti needed in order to operational-ize the Collier plan was an entity that could manage the donors' funds and ensure they were well coordinated. An entity that could deliver the stability that the Haitian government couldn't, Collier stressed.

Collier and his colleagues inside the UN and the State Department had partially drawn on lessons learned from the response to the Aceh tsunami in 2004. There, a reconstruction commission run by the Indo-nesian government had earned international plaudits for its response coordination. Bill Clinton had been involved in the effort. The slogan had been "build back better," and it seemed like they actually had. The region ended up better prepared for the next disaster.[12]

Unlike in Indonesia, however, the assessment of the US and other major donors was that such a commission couldn't function with the Haitian government in charge. That analysis had been remarkably con-sistent for at least one hundred years. In 1914, the United States had proposed embedding a formal US financial advisor within the Haitian state to help improve its creditworthiness and provide necessary "checks against graft," as the State Department put it.[13] At the time, servicing for-eign debt took up some 80 percent of Haiti's budget. When the Haitian government balked, the US loaded the country's central bank reserves onto a ship and took them to New York for safekeeping at National City Bank, the precursor to Citibank. The following year the US Marines invaded. Even after they left, a financial advisor remained embedded in the government until the mid-1940s. In public after the quake, donors talked about the need to support the Haitian government. However, be-hind closed doors, those same officials had determined the government was still too weak and too corrupt to manage the billions in expected assistance.

The US and the UN had first put together a draft for such an author-ity in mid-2009. The donor conference that year, however, had raised only a few hundred million dollars. Not enough to put the plan into action. The earthquake changed everything.

On January 20, Collier emailed a top State Department staffer. "To avoid a coordination nightmare, try to get a structure in which there is a single authority with some temporary power," he wrote. He suggested Bill Clinton as a cochair alongside a "senior Haitian official." The authority, Collier wrote, could be supported by a council "where you can put the key parties on so they dont [sic] feel excluded (e.g. EU which will otherwise sulk)."[14]

In late March, the Haitian government presented its development plan to representatives of more than one hundred nations at the UN's New York headquarters. At its core, it was the Collier Plan on steroids, though it had been neatly repackaged using the post-quake rhetoric of supporting the Haitian government and strengthening public institutions. At the conference, Reginald Boulos, a well-connected Haitian businessman, spoke on behalf of the Haitian private sector. By the end of the weekend, fifty-eight donors, from the US, Canada, and France, to Estonia and Algeria, pledged $10 billion. The US alone committed $1 billion. It was the largest-ever mobilization of international resources to respond to a natural disaster. To oversee this massive effort, donors and the Haitian government announced the formation of a development authority similar to that which had been used in Indonesia. They called it the Interim Haiti Reconstruction Commission.

Just as Collier had suggested in the weeks after the earthquake, Bill Clinton accepted the position as codirector to serve alongside Prime Minister Jean-Max Bellerive. Donors who pledged at least $30 million at the conference received a seat at the table. So, too, did an equal number of Haitians drawn from civil society, the government, and the private sector, including Mr. Boulos. After eighteen months, this supranational entity planned to hand full control to the Haitian government. This new framework, the former president said, name-checking the slogan of a different reconstruction effort, was Haiti's opportunity to "build back better."[15]

It was Boulos, however, who had most succinctly described the concept a week before the donor conference in a closed-door meeting between Haitian businesspeople and former president Clinton in Port-au-Prince.

"A responsible elite," Boulos said, "laying out and implementing a vision of development that benefits all Haitians."[16]

THE LATE-MARCH PLEDGE of $10 billion, an amount larger than the Haitian economy, raised hopes for the future, even if there remained legitimate questions over how that money would be spent. In the present, however, the needs were more immediate, and the rainy season was fast approaching. In Delmas 30, Mona Augustin had helped organize the 126 families that eventually settled on the former soccer field. Their new community even had a name, Mozayik.[17] Any bit of open land in the capital seemed to be occupied by makeshift shelters. In humanitarian speak, those living in camps such as Mozayik were referred to as internally displaced people, IDPs, since everything needed an acronym. The camps were at the center of the aid effort. NGOs, unable or unwilling to go into poor communities, provided services—water, food, hygiene kits, hundreds of thousands of tarps, and even temporary jobs—only to those living in officially registered camps. The population grew as more and more families were drawn to the resources.[18] Somewhere near a million people were facing the prospect of a significant storm with little more than a tarp for shelter. Hundreds of thousands hadn't even received one of those.

To ensure access to aid and that it would get to those among them who needed it most, Mona and the residents of Mozayik formed an internal system of governance. They maintained an up-to-date census and developed community decision-making processes. Mona stopped focusing on his music in order to help manage the camp full-time. He shuttled between friends' houses in the hills and the Delmas 30 camp, using whatever connections he had to help pull together resources. For residents, the camps were no longer just a necessity to survive; they were the best bet for starting anew.[19]

The situation was being driven not by the state but by the NGOs in the camps, their coffers full of text message donations, church group offerings, and multimillion-dollar government contracts or grants. In theory, that was why the Clinton-led reconstruction commission was in place, to coordinate those disparate actors and ensure they were working in support of the Haitian government, not instead of the Haitian government. To make sure that when the next disaster struck, the state *could* be the one to respond. Somebody might even take the advice of Dr. Prepetit, the government official who had warned of a super-quake for years. In the meantime, it came as no surprise that NGOs were in the lead given how donors had historically administered their foreign aid budgets.

Haiti was not, however, the failed state that so many believed it was. By the time of the earthquake, the Haitian state had been shaped by decades of foreign assistance and centuries of foreign intervention; it was a nation shackled, politically and economically, by the very actors ostensibly there to help. The reconstruction commission served as the culmination of this long process. If the "Core Group" of donors had formed a de facto fourth branch of government, the Clinton-led body went further, taking on powers of both the legislative and executive branches. With the judiciary under the auspices of the Blue Helmets, virtually the entirety of the Haitian government was being overseen or even directly managed by foreign actors.

By 2010, public services had already been outsourced to the Aid State. Some 80 percent of social services across Haiti were provided by the private sector, primarily contractors, NGOs, and religious organizations. The vast majority were foreign-financed and foreign-owned. These actors accounted for some 70 percent of coverage in the health sector and 85 percent in education.[20] Collier's plan, however, did not view this as a problem. With the commission, funding would be centralized, but the actual provision of public goods would remain primarily in private hands. These non-state actors had proliferated for decades, but after the quake, some estimates put the number as high as ten thousand. Together, they constituted a parallel state, the Republic of NGOs.

6

THE AID-INDUSTRIAL COMPLEX

―――――――

On May 13, 2010—four months after the devastating earthquake—the global agribusiness conglomerate Monsanto issued a press release. "Haitian farmers, who otherwise may not have had sufficient seeds to plant this season in their earthquake-ravaged country, are receiving help from a unique public and private partnership," the company wrote.[1] Monsanto, one of the companies that manufactured Agent Orange for the US military during the Vietnam War, had since become the world's largest purveyor of hybrid and genetically modified seeds, and they were offering Haiti 130 tons of them free of charge.[2] The first batch would be distributed through a costly USAID-financed project called WINNER, aiming to help revitalize Haitian agriculture. It was being run by a for-profit company based in Washington, DC, Chemonics International. On the ground, the project was overseen by Jean-Robert Estimé, a onetime prominent member of the Duvalier dictatorship.

The earthquake struck just weeks before the beginning of the spring planting season. Many farmers had just harvested and were sitting on relatively large stocks, but if they couldn't sell quickly, they wouldn't have the money to buy seeds for the next planting. It was no secret that agricultural degradation had precipitated much of the haphazard urbanization in the capital. But with five hundred thousand leaving the city for the relative comfort and safety of rural Haiti, there was an opportunity to reverse this corrosive trend.

In the camps of the capital, NGOs and UN agencies were leading massive food distributions. In just the first two months after the quake, humanitarian organizations distributed more than forty million pounds of food. Almost all of it was imported. For many local farmers, that was a death sentence. There was simply no way they could compete with free. The Monsanto donation was a response to a genuine need. Farmers did need to replant their crops. The Food and Agriculture Organization (FAO) and other international organizations were also pursuing wide-scale seed distributions.

But Haitian farmers didn't need seed, and they especially didn't need foreign seeds that they'd never worked with before. They needed cash. There were plenty of local seeds on the market they could buy if they had the resources. For only about $80 million a year, a small fraction of what had been pledged in March, foreign donors could have purchased the entire amount of rice needed for food aid from local producers.[3] It would have provided a necessary stimulus to the rural economy and food for those in need. It didn't happen.

Why didn't more people ask if seeds were really what farmers needed after the earthquake? First, aid officials and the media kept describing Haiti as the "poorest country in the Western Hemisphere" and saying the government had abdicated its responsibility. The perception was that Haiti could use whatever help it could get and that Haitians would be eager to receive it. Of course, those interests aligned with those of Monsanto. Once farmers get used to hybrid seeds, which need to be purchased anew each year, the company would have a new market. Nonprofits, however, function in similar ways. Even if motivated by good intentions and responding to actual needs, NGOs and their employees face their own unique interests.

In the summer of 2010, Louise Sperling, an expert in the field, authored a 115-page report analyzing the need for seeds. The determination was that Haitian farmers were not facing a seed emergency at all. Many foreign NGOs "seem to see delivering seed aid as easy," Sperling explained. "They welcome the overhead (money)—even if their actions may hurt poor farmers."[4] When most of us think about NGOs, we think of nonprofits. But the term "nonprofit" is a bit of a misnomer. While the organization does not exist to make money for its shareholders or owners, that overhead goes to pay salaries, issue bonuses, invest in new buildings, run public relations campaigns, and compete for the next government contract or grant. The CEO of the American Red Cross, for example, earned $500,000 in base pay in 2010.[5]

The term "nongovernmental organization" formally entered the world's vernacular in 1945 with the charter of the United Nations. NGOs proliferated through the second half of the twentieth century. By the 2010 earthquake in Haiti, the number worldwide had reached beyond one million. The term encompasses more than just the humanitarian world. However, even there, it covers a vast array of different entities, from a small-town church group's charity to global players like the Red Cross, Catholic Relief Services, Oxfam, and Doctors Without Borders. Thousands of these humanitarian actors arrived on the ground after the quake, though only a few dozen were formally registered with the Haitian government. These disparate players received at least $800 million in donations in the first couple of months after the earthquake, and that is almost certainly a gross underestimate.

The humanitarian world doesn't run strictly on private donations, however. The eight billion dollars that donors offered in foreign assistance from 1986 to 2010 mainly had gone to NGOs. By that point, the definition of the term had expanded to include explicitly for-profit companies as well. Aid had become big business, not just in Haiti but across the world. It had spawned into a multibillion-dollar global industry, one that had become too big to fail and too big to reform. This history is, in many ways, the story of Chemonics International, the company that distributed Monsanto seeds after the earthquake. It helps explain how the promotion of US economic interests through foreign assistance undermined local markets and why, after the earthquake, the same players who had long dominated the aid game were the first on the ground. In fact, one could draw a relatively straight line from the aid-industrial complex of the twenty-first century to a series of conscious policy decisions made by diplomats in Haiti half a century earlier.

* * *

IN THE FALL of 1954, Hurricane Hazel made landfall in the southern peninsula of Haiti. The storm's heavy rains and record wind speeds tore through the country and devastated agricultural production. At the time, Haiti was led by Paul Magloire. A former high-ranking military official and police chief of Port-au-Prince, Magloire secured power by helping overthrow the progressive Dumarsais Estimé, whose son, Jean-Robert, went on to manage Chemonics' post-quake aid program.

During the Magloire years, the country experienced a brief period of political stability. His rabid anti-communism won allies in Washington, and Haiti became a favorite tourist destination for American and European travelers. "Impressed by the boom in Caribbean travel and the phenomenal 500 per cent jump in the number of visitors since 1950, Haiti has mobilized to offer more facilities for vacationists—more night-club fun, more first-class hotel rooms, new beaches, sports areas and shopping centers," The New York Times reported in November 1956.[6]

But the destruction wrought by Hazel, and the government's inability to respond to its citizens' needs as opposed to those of tourists, ultimately led to the general's downfall. Engulfed in corruption allegations and facing increasing internal unrest, Magloire fled into exile in 1956, less than a month after that article. Subsequent "elections," held under tight military control in 1957, brought the first Duvalier to power: François "Papa Doc" Duvalier, a physician by training. Since the revolution, Haiti's population had remained extremely stratified between the lighter-skinned mulattos and the darker-skinned majority. Papa Doc, like Estimé, was a noiriste. It was the term for those who believed that, since the US occupation, the elite mulattos had oppressed the Black majority.

Once safely inside the National Palace, however, Duvalier consolidated his power with ruthless repression and abandoned the pro-poor rhetoric. And though he continued the anti-communist stance of his predecessor, he also rejected outright American control of his affairs.

In 1961, the United States government provided $6 million in direct budget support (the equivalent of more than $45 million today).[7] But the following year, Duvalier demanded control over USAID's programs.

Haitians in exile had been pushing the US to suspend aid to the despotic regime for years, but it was Duvalier's decision that convinced the US to act.

Duvalier ruled ruthlessly, and the embassy was aware that any direct financial support would likely be siphoned off due to corruption—not to mention potentially cause a public relations problem as news reports of the regime's horrors proliferated. While the US had suspended direct financial assistance, it covertly increased support through "voluntary service organizations," known as VSOs, including Catholic Relief Services and CARE, another religiously affiliated relief organization.

In December 1965, Melville E. Osborne, a US foreign service officer, wrote a memo to the ambassador in Haiti that suggested dividing the country into regions and assigning these American VSOs to each one. They would provide support for health, education, security, and other basic services. Osborne argued that taking over these traditionally public roles would have "long term political effects." In the late fifties and early sixties, more aid had gone directly to the government, allowing Duvalier to brand the programs as his own. "[François Duvalier] wants money to spend, jobs to give, and political credit to take," Osborne wrote. "These are precisely the items we would want to withhold from him." The policy, he believed, would eventually undermine the dictatorship and precipitate its collapse.[8]

The new aid policy failed to fatally undermine Papa Doc Duvalier, who consolidated a dictatorship and ruled the country for twenty-nine years with his son, Baby Doc. The Duvaliers didn't need foreign assistance to maintain power; for that they had the feared Tonton Macoutes, the extra-official state security forces that brutally imposed their leader's will. But the aid policy did have long-term political effects, as Osborne had predicted. The decision to bypass the government disassociated the provision of public services from the state. In its place, a parallel state formed, one consisting of hundreds, if not thousands, of nongovernmental actors, each with their own unique set of interests. Within this new creation existed missionary groups spreading Christianity to the "devil-worshipping" Haitians, humanitarian organizations providing direct assistance, and for-profit players like Chemonics, who helped open new markets for US economic interests. It was little wonder that, over time, these explicitly non-state actors had eroded or even replaced the Haitian state—that, after all, had been the intention of foreign officials from the beginning.

After the earthquake, while the rhetoric had shifted, the money flow hadn't. Forty-five years after Osborne's memo, Paul Collier had made a similar argument in the report that became the template for Haiti's post-quake rebuilding plan. While resources had to be consolidated under one authority, the actual provision of basic services should remain in private hands, he said. The Haitian government was supposed to be in charge, but in the initial relief phase, 99 percent of donor money bypassed the local government entirely, an analysis performed by the United Nations later found.[9] The vast majority ended up in the hands of foreign NGOs and for-profit development companies like Chemonics International.

In 1964, Thurston "Tony" Teele left government after more than a decade in the US Foreign Service, including several years in the newly created USAID. When he left, the agency employed some seventeen thousand who oversaw and directly implemented aid programs worldwide. Teele wasn't leaving the development world, however. Instead, he began to work as a private consultant on USAID projects. Teele and his partner, a retired Air Force pilot with a background in agricultural science, sensed an opportunity years before the full ramifications of the changing USAID landscape could be known to the outside world. In 1975, they founded a consulting firm, Chemonics International.[10] They discovered an eager investor in Gerald Murphy, a Harvard Business School graduate and the CEO of Erly Industries, a global agriculture and chemical conglomerate. Chemonics became part of the Erly family in 1976 because, as Murphy would later recall, he had always wanted to do two things: "one, have my own CIA, and two, be helpful to people."[11]

However, the Los Angeles–based Erly still derived most of its business from its agricultural side, namely its rice companies. The consulting arm proved helpful in that regard as well. In the mid-1980s, the company leveraged its USAID contacts to secure funding for a port that allowed an Erly subsidiary, Comet Rice, easy access to Iraq's market. Comet's exports to Iraq increased by $100 million from 1987 to 1990. When Iraq invaded Kuwait, however, the US placed the country under an embargo, and Erly's rice sales dried up.

At the same time, opportunities in Haiti were opening up.

Hurricane Hazel not only precipitated Magloire's fall from power, it also devastated Haiti's agricultural sector, which would never fully recover. The lack of a sufficient response from the government or foreign NGOs exacerbated the issue and led to hundreds of thousands of rural families moving to urban areas. During the Duvalier years, especially under François's son, Baby Doc, tens of millions in US and other foreign assistance went to food-for-work programs. Tens of millions more went into direct food aid, which the US purchased from American firms and sent abroad on American ships.

In 1980, Haiti was still largely self-sufficient in the production of its most important dietary staple, rice. Under Murphy's friend, President Ronald Reagan, the US administration began an ambitious effort to increase American agricultural sales abroad. Foreign assistance began to focus more specifically on opening up foreign markets to American goods. But while the US was concerned about an invasion of Haitian migrants in Miami, the result of the policy changes was the invasion of "Miami rice" into Haiti.

Haiti became one of Erly's largest markets. The 1991 military coup presented an opportunity for more. A year later, the Rice Corporation of Haiti, a subsidiary of Erly's Comet Rice, signed a nine-year agreement with the World Bank–trained Marc Bazin, the man the US had believed would defeat Aristide in Haiti's first free election. After the coup, the military junta had placed Bazin in power. When Clinton deployed US military assets to help restore democracy in Haiti, Aristide's return to the presidency relied on his government implementing an International Monetary Fund (IMF) reform program that slashed tariffs on rice from up to 50 percent to just 3 percent. Haiti became a big market for US agricultural producers, which only exacerbated the destruction of rural communities.

Not even the slashing of tariffs was enough for Erly and its various rice-oriented subsidiaries, however. Throughout the 1990s, two of its executives—later indicted under the Foreign Corrupt Practices Act—allegedly bribed Haitian customs and port officials to avoid paying taxes.[12] When the Haitian government confiscated the company in 2000, Republicans in Congress responded by cutting aid.[13] US lawmakers couldn't save Erly, but by the turn of the century, Haiti was producing only 20 percent of the rice it consumed. Around the time of Hurricane Hazel, the population in Port-au-Prince was 150,000. By Reagan's time, it had grown to 732,000. By 2008, it was close to three million, primarily due to the US economic invasion of Haiti, an invasion driven as much by foreign assistance as by military strength.[14]

In March 2010, in testimony before the Senate Foreign Relations Committee, Bill Clinton publicly apologized for his role in the failed policies. "Since 1981, the United States has followed a policy, until the last year or so when we started rethinking it, that we rich countries that produce a lot of food should sell it to poor countries and relieve them of the burden of producing their own food, so, thank goodness, they can leap directly into the industrial era," the former president said. "It has not worked. It may have been good for some of my farmers in Arkansas, but it has not worked. It was a mistake. It was a mistake that I was a party to . . . I have to live every day with the consequences of the lost capacity to produce a rice crop in Haiti to feed those people," Clinton lamented.[15]

IN DECEMBER 1985, in the waning days of Baby Doc Duvalier's presidency, the dictator named a special cabinet to represent the government abroad. Jean-Robert Estimé was among those selected. After being named ambassador to the US and OAS, he arrived in Washington just hours before Baby Doc boarded a US Air Force jet and departed for exile in France. The *Los Angeles Times* reported that Estimé was one of a handful of dictatorship officials who lived in "anonymous splendor in expensive hotels and hideaways" in the US. He stayed at the Four Seasons Hotel in DC.[16] Estimé was out of government work, but he'd soon find a new home in the burgeoning aid industry. In 1991, he took a job with the United Nations Development Programme (UNDP). A year later, he joined a consulting practice working on USAID projects, Chemonics International.

In 1998, Chemonics' parent company, Erly, went into Chapter 11 bankruptcy. But there was one part of the business that seemed primed for growth. The following year, Chemonics International was purchased by a group of investors led by an Arizona businessman and prominent Republican donor, Scott Spangler. In the early 1990s under the Bush administration, Spangler had served in various capacities, including as acting administrator of USAID.[17] He understood what the future of foreign aid had in store. It wasn't just about opening markets for US companies like Comet Rice or Monsanto. With the US increasingly reliant on contractors to implement its assistance programs abroad, the provision of aid itself was becoming the market.

Beginning in the late 1980s but picking up pace throughout the nineties, the neoliberal push to privatize hit the aid industry. USAID became increasingly reliant on private contractors. From 1996 to 2005, the share of funds awarded to for-profit contractors rose from 33 percent to 58 percent, USAID reported.[18] And with the invasion of Iraq and Afghanistan and the long-term nation-building that followed, USAID contractors were increasingly finding themselves working right alongside the military. As the military effort grew, so did the aid effort. As military contractors reaped the benefits, so did aid contractors. A whole new class of businesses started to occupy the corporate high-rises surrounding Washington. The military-industrial complex got a younger sibling, the aid-industrial complex.[19]

The top ten for-profit aid contractors, including Chemonics International, received $5.8 billion from 2004 to 2007, ten times more than they had received in the four years prior. And it was ten times more than the top nonprofits had received over the same period.

But at the same time as USAID was becoming more reliant on these for-profit contractors, its own staff budget was drastically cut. By 2007, USAID's permanent staff had fallen by 24 percent from its 1995 levels, while the amount of money under its responsibility increased by nearly 150 percent to almost $12 billion.[20] One contractor was growing faster than all the rest, Spangler's Chemonics International. Its offices were a few blocks from the White House.

In 2008 and 2009, Chemonics received more than $500 million from USAID, of which $160 million was for work in Afghanistan. But they had operations in more than forty countries, including Haiti, where its former parent company had helped undermine rural families for years.

In 2009, following a devastating series of hurricanes, USAID awarded Chemonics a $130 million contract to revitalize Haiti's agricultural production—the WINNER project that eventually helped distribute Monsanto seeds after the quake. After nearly twenty years working predominantly in Africa, Estimé returned to Haiti to lead the project. In that time, Chemonics had become the largest player in a multibillion-dollar-a-year industry. But helping Haiti was far from the only motivation. This fact isn't hidden. USAID's own mission statement declares its primary function in no uncertain terms: "USAID's work advances US national security and economic prosperity." The mission remains the same today and is still posted clearly on their website, in case there are any doubts about the interests of the agency.

There can be little question that foreign assistance has generally been designed to benefit the US and its corporations both at home and abroad. But that is only half the story. Aid is also political, and that fact had not changed by the time of the earthquake.

7

THE TRANSITION INITIATIVE

———

The United States Congress passed its first foreign aid bill in 1812, providing the modern equivalent of one million dollars to procure food after an earthquake in Venezuela.[1] The South American nation had recently declared independence from Spain and was still embroiled in a civil war. The post-disaster assistance served as a clear message of support in its battle with Spain. No doubt, members of Congress remembered the foreign assistance France had supplied to the colonies in their own independence struggle against the British. It is a story as old as human civilization, and for century after century, nations have provided one another support with the expectation of obtaining something in return, whether it be commercial advantages or a new ally in a broader geopolitical battle. For the United States, a late-emerging imperial power, foreign assistance became a key tool in the advancement of its international agenda.

The modern conception of foreign aid dates to the early post–World War II period. Passed in 1948, the Marshall Plan provided $13.3 billion (some $130 billion in today's dollars) in assistance to Western Europe.[2] It wasn't strictly humanitarian. Seeing the larger fight as one between capitalism and communism, the billions in US support were designed to rebuild nations more in line with the emerging US-led global economic order. The initiative, at least from America's perspective, was perceived as a massive success. Quickly, foreign aid became an integral part of US foreign policy. Already by the mid-1950s, the same agencies that the US created in order to administer funding under the Marshall Plan were providing humanitarian assistance in South Vietnam to build support for the government there.[3]

In 1961, President John F. Kennedy institutionalized foreign assistance. In March, he launched the Alliance for Progress, designed to build economic cooperation between the US and Latin America. In the fall, he created the United States Agency for International Development, or USAID, and the agency's vast deployment in Vietnam began soon thereafter, still a few years before the first combat troops arrived. The US-led aid industry developed in response to real needs on the ground. But it also developed with clear geopolitical interests underpinning it.

In the years since the end of World War II, Kennedy pointed out that there had been at least forty-two newly independent states, representing some one billion people.[4] With colonial regimes of control breaking down and the Cold War in full swing, foreign assistance was another mechanism in ensuring the Third World's allegiance to the First. Though today the term is generally used as an impolite way to describe lower-income countries, its origin has nothing to do with relative poverty levels. In a postcolonial landscape, independent nations in the Third World sought to lead their own futures free from the diktats of Washington or the Soviet Union.[5] Kennedy came into office with idealistic principles guiding his foreign policy. The initial goal of Kennedy's Alliance for Progress in Latin America, for example, had been to use assistance to support the struggles for self-determination taking place across the hemisphere. Quickly, however, the lofty goals were abandoned. The US covertly backed coups in country after country and developed tight relationships with military juntas serving as anti-communist bulwarks.

As had always been the case, there was no divorcing aid from the advancement of national interests. Perhaps nowhere is that historical truth so evident as in Haiti, where, for more than fifty years, the United States had used foreign assistance in an effort to control Haiti's political development.

* * *

THE US SUSPENDED direct financial assistance to the Duvalier dictatorship in the early 1960s, but not direct relations. Haiti is about six hundred miles from Miami but, more important, only ninety miles from
the coast of Cuba, where Fidel Castro had recently taken power.

In 1964, US ambassador Benson E. L. Timmons III summarized his
government's policy goals in a cable to Washington. The US maintained
its diplomatic presence in Haiti despite the actions of Duvalier, "so as to
be able to influence the situation when the inevitable change in regime
occurs . . . and to deny Haiti to Communists," he wrote.[6]

Despite supporting an anti-communist ally, the US still viewed the
fall of Papa Doc as an inevitability. America needed people in-country
it could trust. "Our review of the Haitian situation suggests a need to shift
our tactics in an attempt to build some assets in Haiti," a top diplomat
wrote in a January 1966 cable. "We believe this should be done indirectly
through an expansion of US voluntary agency programs [VSOs]" and
through "the Inter-American Bank."[7] The Bank, known as the IDB,
became a linchpin alongside USAID in America's post–World War II
expansion of global influence, especially in the Western Hemisphere.

Soon thereafter, the CIA drafted a contingency plan in case of Duvalier's death or fall from power. In doing so, the agency drew up a list of
individuals, both inside Haiti and abroad, whom it "deemed suitable for
use in the reconstruction period."[8] These times of transition, these moments of change, are closely linked to the concept of stability. For policymakers, stability means ensuring that whatever change does occur, it
does not mean a transition out of the US-led global economic order. It
took another twenty years, but in the post-1986 Duvalier void, the CIA's
list was finally relevant. The agency stepped up its activities, keeping
military and political leaders on its payroll to help steer the transition.

UNDER PRESIDENT RONALD Reagan, the goals of foreign assistance expanded but maintained their political shading. No longer framed narrowly in terms of economic development, in a 1982 speech made before
the British Parliament, Reagan outlined how aid could promote democratization throughout the Third World. This, he believed, was crucial

to the Western world winning the post–Cold War era. "No, democracy is not a fragile flower; still, it needs cultivating," the president said. "If the rest of this century is to witness the gradual growth of freedom and democratic ideals, we must take actions to assist the campaign for democracy."[9]

The next year, Congress created the National Endowment for Democracy, which, through its closely related partners representing both major parties, the National Democratic Institute and the International Republican Institute, was able to channel foreign assistance without the Cold War–era baggage of the intelligence agency. Though it was funded by the US government, for some reason it was considered a "private" organization.[10] Political aid had been taken out of USAID's hands, but not out of the government's repertoire altogether. "A lot of what we do today was done covertly 25 years ago by the CIA," Allen Weinstein, who had helped to draft the legislation that created the endowment, later told a *Washington Post* reporter.[11]

In the post-Duvalier void, America's support for democratization found new purpose. "Duvalier's departure created a vacuum, or rather exposed one," Andrew S. Levin wrote in 1995. Twenty years later, Levin was elected to Congress representing his home state of Michigan, but at the time, he was a human rights activist and had recently returned from Haiti. "The central government had never provided even the most basic services to Haiti's poor majority. Now the glue that held together the country's repressive structures had loosened . . . and the poor eagerly organized themselves to fill the void left by a government that had always excluded them." Almost overnight, a vast array of civil society groups, referred to as popular organizations in Haiti, was built from scratch.

"In city and town alike, people formed civic organizations at the neighborhood and town level. Almost every city neighborhood had a committee that cleaned up the streets, burned trash, elected leaders, and sought to communicate the neighborhood's demands for change to the government," Levin wrote of the early post-Duvalier days. "Trade unions, women's organizations, youth groups, and organized literacy campaigns sprouted in every part of the country. . . . Meanwhile, Haiti students experienced an awakening, forming new organizations at the high school and university level that became leading actors in post-Duvalier Haitian politics."[12]

These, however, were mostly not the organizations or individuals on the CIA's list, and few were on the receiving end of democratization assistance. Though USAID and the National Endowment for Democracy spent tens of millions of dollars, virtually none of it went to support the emergent peasant organizations in a country that was still 70 percent rural. Instead, the US focused on organizing the local private sector, whose free market interests more closely matched those in Washington.

Kenneth Roth, the executive director of Human Rights Watch, suggested the US stop supporting civil society altogether. It wasn't necessary for outsiders to "build up their own favored groups," he argued. Haiti was producing a vibrant civil society on its own and America should allow that to develop on its own terms. But the strength of these emerging social organizations was most likely the problem, and precisely what to fear, in the eyes of policymakers, as well as the Haitian military and economic elite. Though Duvalierism was in retreat, the US and other foreign donors allied themselves not with democratic governance but with the local elite, creating a powerful new alliance to maintain the dictatorship-era system of extraction.

For years, the US had promoted Haiti as a destination of foreign investment, part of its efforts to encourage the sweatshops that had sprung up in the capital. After Aristide's election, however, the push for investment stopped. Rather, USAID responded by funding the creation of a group of businesses whose primary goal was opposing the policies espoused by the new president, especially his proposal to raise the minimum wage. The US-backed private-sector groups turned into early supporters of the efforts to overthrow Aristide.

Though democracy returned with the help of the US military under Clinton, its parameters had been more narrowly defined since the groundswell of popular organizations brought Aristide to office the first time. After a multiyear embargo, the economy had been eviscerated. Official development assistance for Haiti reached a record $615

million in 1994, growing further to $654 million in 1995.[13] The politics
had changed from the Bush administration's, but not the end goal. The
hundreds of millions in assistance came with caveats, like the slashing
of tariffs on rice and the privatization of state-owned enterprises. The
foreign-led nation-building that began in the midnineties, backed with
hundreds of millions in aid, aimed to ensure Haiti remained firmly
within the US-led global economic order, regardless of who occupied
the National Palace.

BY THE TURN of the century, with another Bush in the White House and
Aristide overwhelmingly elected yet again, America turned the screws.
From its first days in office, the Bush administration sought to lay the
groundwork for the overthrow of Aristide.[14] It cut foreign assistance
and vetoed disbursements from multilateral institutions such as the
IDB, the same bank the US had used to channel support to the Duvalier dictatorship decades before.[15] In 2001, economic growth in Haiti
turned negative for the first time since the embargo. From 2001 to 2003,
during Aristide's first three years back in office, development assistance
dropped by more than 40 percent.[16]

Just like in the 1960s, however, the US didn't cut off *all* its assistance
programs. The International Republican Institute was especially active,
working with opposition leaders and former members of the military
to build resistance to the Aristide government.[17] And USAID provided
direct support to another group of local businessmen, as it had done
during Aristide's first term. In 2004, that group played an instrumental
role in the coup. The US heralded the organization as a beacon of democracy, but it was composed of many business leaders who had backed
the military junta, and who, just ten years earlier, had been under US
sanctions for their antidemocratic stance. The leader of the group was
Andy Apaid Jr., the owner of Haiti's largest garment assembly employer
and a US citizen.[18]

The 2004 deployment of the Blue Helmets was accompanied by another influx of humanitarian aid. The unelected transitional government that took power following the coup received more development

aid than ever before. The US spent millions of dollars in an effort to ensure that the Lavalas movement that had dominated politics for fifteen years would cease to be a threat. The aid was administered through a little-known bureau inside USAID known as the Office of Transition Initiatives, or OTI. In fact, it had been created under Clinton, and one of its first missions had been alongside US troops during their 1994 invasion of Haiti. Ten years later, the agency returned to Haiti alongside the Blue Helmets. Whereas in 1994 the goal had been to provide stability for the Aristide administration, in 2004, the goal was to provide stability for the government that took power following his ouster.

The 2004 coup "created a new environment for collaboration" with the Haitian government, a USAID field manual from the time explained.[19] But protests against the transitional government and the ongoing repression of Aristide's followers presented a problem. The unelected government had little legitimacy, and resistance was growing. While the Blue Helmets initiated violent raids into the capital's red zones, USAID took a different approach, though one that worked toward the same goal.

USAID's internal reports from the time described Petit Place Cazeau as a "stronghold of Lavalas Party presidential candidate Father Gerard Jean-Juste," the man slated to represent Aristide's party in the next elections. OTI wanted to find a way to limit Jean-Juste's support in the community. To do so, the program funded a "Play for Peace" summer camp, which, officials believed, would prevent Lavalas demonstrations "from being larger and giving greater legitimacy to the protesters."[20] In August 2005, at a USAID-financed soccer match in the neighborhood of Martissant, police officers started to fire indiscriminately into the crowd. Armed civilians massacred those attempting to flee.[21] As for Jean-Juste, the transitional government arrested him, preventing him from running in the election at all.

After two coups and twenty years of fighting, Haiti's grassroots were battered. Yet, despite this, each time elections were held, the roots of Haiti's pro-democracy movement showed their enduring strength. Aristide had won in 1990 and 2000; Préval in 1995 and again in 2006. But when Préval took office the second time, the average Haitian's income was 25 percent lower than when Duvalier had fled for exile two decades earlier.[22] The government was more reliant than ever on foreign assistance and foreign political support.

For more than twenty years, the US-led aid industry had used its massive portfolio in Haiti to pick winners and losers, to build up desirable local allies, and to tear down the undesirables—the sources of instability, that, more often than not, represented the poor majority. The times of greatest concern for foreign governments and the local elite are the times of transition, such as Duvalier's fall from power, Aristide's return, his ouster, elections, and, in 2010, the earthquake.

IN THE DAYS following the earthquake, it wasn't just the US Marines and US Army that arrived in Haiti but also USAID's cadre of special forces, the for-profit companies working for OTI.[23] Its website described its mandate as supporting US foreign policy by targeting assistance "at key political transition and stabilization needs." On January 17, this political wing of USAID launched the Haiti Recovery Initiative. Two companies received the contracts, each valued at $50 million; one was Chemonics International. Decades after its founding, the firm was closer than ever to its founder's goal of having his own CIA.

Both companies held standing umbrella contracts that allowed them to rapidly respond to situations across the world without going through a competitive bidding process. OTI used its contracting partners as passthroughs to quickly disburse funds to individuals and entities on the ground. The lack of typical contracting mechanisms allowed near total executive discretion; USAID's special forces are run out of Washington.

The umbrella contract with Chemonics (obtained after a lengthy Freedom of Information Act request) outlined the four "criteria for engagement" in program countries: "Is the country important to US national interests?"; "Is there a window of opportunity?"; "Can OTI's involvement significantly increase the chances of success?"; and "Is the operating environment sufficiently stable?" Put simply, can the US influence the situation to its benefit?

When assessing if there is a "window of opportunity," the contract explained that USAID "cannot create a transition or impose democracy, but it can identify and support key individuals and groups who are committed to peaceful, participatory reform. In short, OTI acts as a catalyst for change where there is sufficient indigenous political will."[24]

By 2010, the little-known USAID agency had also been active in more than thirty-five other countries, from Rwanda, Angola, and Kenya to Iraq, Afghanistan, and Pakistan, and to Bolivia, Cuba, and Venezuela. From 2004 to 2006, the Office of Transition Initiatives implemented a "five-point" plan in Venezuela that was aimed at "Strengthening Democratic Institutions," "Penetrating [Venezuelan president Hugo] Chávez's Political Base," "Dividing Chavismo," "Isolating Chávez internationally," and "Protecting Vital US business," according to confidential diplomatic cables later made public by WikiLeaks. In Bolivia, OTI aided a separatist movement that attempted to destabilize the government. Both countries eventually shut down the USAID programs in response.[25]

These transition programs, at their core, are efforts to tilt the playing field in favor of one actor over another. Unlike in Venezuela or Bolivia, after the earthquake in Haiti, the goal wasn't undermining the government. According to its contract with USAID, the initial objective for Chemonics in Haiti was to "support the Government of Haiti by promoting stability and decreasing the chances of unrest."[26] At the time the contract was written, the Haitian government was considered an ally. Préval, as the former US ambassador had put it, was the "indispensable man." Both Clintons had developed personal relations with the president and his top staff. But Chemonics' contract noted that "program objectives" would likely change "to account for shifts in the political environment."

By the fall of 2010, with elections approaching in November, the political environment had indeed shifted considerably. Préval himself, and the slow pace of relief and reconstruction, were becoming a liability for the internationally led earthquake response.

Chemonics put on hold its plans to build new office space and embed technical advisors within the government. Instead, the company poured millions into get-out-the-vote campaigns, hosted presidential debates, paid for popular musicians to perform pro-election concerts in poor neighborhoods, and created a website to track election-related content. It also provided funding to political organizations on opposing sides.

USAID's political party assistance policy, crafted in 2003, encourages support to political parties as a way to foster "friends and allies" and develop relations with incoming governments. However, US support is allowed only under certain terms, including that all democratic parties receive an equal amount and that the funding not affect election results.[27]

"It was very difficult to be nonpartisan," a technical advisor who worked on the post-quake program explained to me years later. If a candidate from one party asked USAID for support, then we "would ask Chemonics how to help the other party."[28]

Official secrecy remained the norm. When I later used FOIA to obtain documents on the program's local partners, USAID refused. "To release the information in such a way could willfully stir up false allegations . . . and cause strife within target communities," an official wrote, justifying the government's lack of response. The disclosure of the requested information, the letter continued, "would likely instigate demonstrations and create an unsafe environment in which to implement and/or develop programs."[29] USAID's OTI was a stability operation whose activities, if revealed, would cause instability.

The earthquake had shaken the foundation of the nation, and soon, the political aftershocks would crack anew.

8

THE DISPENSABLE MAN

———

In September 2010, René Préval returned to the UN headquarters in New York for the annual General Assembly meeting. When his turn to speak came, he slowly walked to the podium that faced the assembled diplomats and heads of state from across the world. The president wore a black suit, and the 1980s-style shoulder pads highlighted his diminutive frame. His beard was even shorter than normal, and in the nine months since the quake, had skewed even further into full-on gray.

Just over a year earlier, the US ambassador had described René Préval as "Haiti's indispensable man." It had been a mutually beneficial relationship. Préval had utilized US and UN support in his efforts to wield influence in Haiti, to use the foreign-imposed stability to achieve his own vision for his country's future. In managing the nation, there was a long tradition of local politicians and the elite allying with international actors. It had always, however, come with a cost. As Préval stood at the dais, he knew that much had changed since the ambassador had written that cable.

Putting a spotlight on the hypocrisy of the world's rich nations, Préval blasted the trillions spent on wars and noted that, if our collective priorities changed, defense budgets provided more than enough resources to achieve the millennium development goals. He criticized the "incalculable wealth that has simply evaporated in speculation" through the global economic crisis. And the president drew a straight line from yesterday's colonialism to today's globalization.

"In truth," he told the audience of world leaders, "the globalization that began centuries ago, with the colonization and the importation of African captives to work as slaves on sugar-cane and coffee plantations, whose products would then be exported to the West or the North, needs to be reinvented." Préval called for a new kind of economic development, one based on "our common humanity" and "mutual respect."[1]

Ti-René, as many knew the president, grew up in the small rural town of Marmelade in Haiti's agricultural breadbasket, in a region known for its coffee and rice. Under Papa Doc, Préval fled and landed in Belgium, where he studied agronomy. He spent the early 1970s living among the burgeoning diaspora population in Brooklyn, New York, taking odd jobs at restaurants and as a messenger. Préval returned to the nation of his birth in the midseventies, and, soon after the fall of Baby Doc, opened a bakery in the highly impoverished Cité Soleil neighborhood of Port-au-Prince. It was there, in 1987, that Préval first began working alongside Aristide. Préval saw firsthand the vast inequality, the crushing poverty that contrasted with the gilded lives of the country's oligarchs. More than twenty years later, standing on the stage in New York, he harkened back to that formative experience, though now with a wider lens.

"The global village will not be able to maintain forever its fashionable neighborhoods side by side with wretched slums where humanity is dissolving: a socioeconomic North and South—not a geographic one," Préval said. It was like the popular neighborhoods of Haiti's capital and the wealthy enclaves on the surrounding mountainsides, but spread across the entire world.

"South-South cooperation affords new promise," the president said, appealing to his fellow leaders assembled in New York to urgently strengthen those relations. This cooperation had formed the backbone of the Third World movement, consisting predominantly of postcolonial nations that sought to find their own path forward, free from their former imperial authorities. These nations endured additional pain for their desired independence. The Cold War did not result in a conventional military confrontation between the US and the Soviet Union, but tens or even hundreds of thousands of lives were lost in the Third

World, from Brazil to Indonesia.[2] The First World emerged victorious and, with it, so did the US-led global economic order. It makes sense that the term "Third World" has, over time, turned into a pejorative. By the late twentieth century there was really only one acceptable path for economic advancement, a one-size-fits-all template, and countries were either developing or already developed. Countries were either part of the Global North or the Global South, as Préval referenced in his UN speech.

The Haitian president, in connecting twenty-first-century globalization with colonialism, struck at the heart of the development paradigm. The Global North provided a template for nations of the Global South to climb the ladder of development, but the rungs continued to snap on the way up.[3] As Préval pointed out, the roots of the old colonial system still held firm and perpetuated a global power imbalance built on the backs of the enslaved and their descendants. After nearly twenty years of living abroad and twenty years in Haiti's politics, Préval intimately understood this imbalance. After the earthquake, it was greater than it had been in decades. Since its revolution against the French, however, the Haitian people had consistently stood in opposition to the Western-led globalization that viewed human lives as commodities. Two hundred years later, the face of globalization had changed, but Haitian resistance had yet to cease.

In the 1980s and '90s, Latin America was ground zero for the one-size-fits-all development model known as the Washington Consensus. It was Reaganomics in the US, but in the rest of the world, it was referred to as "neoliberalism." At its most basic level, neoliberalism is a hyper-reliance on the free market and private actors at the expense of the public administration. When Aristide returned in 1994 to finish his presidential term, loans from the World Bank and the International Monetary Fund came with conditions that forced the privatization of state-owned entities and the sharp reduction in tariffs on products like rice. This was neoliberalism in the Global South—and it was a massive failure. Not only rural Haiti was decimated. Collectively, per capita economic growth in Latin America was 3.3 percent per year from 1960 to 1980; from 1980 to 2000, it was 0.3 percent—two lost decades.[4]

By the early twenty-first century, Latin America epitomized the global resistance to this neoliberal globalization. The region was a threat to the stability of the global economic order, and a prime target of the Bush administration's neocon cabinet alongside the Middle East. In 1998, in Venezuela, voters elected a charismatic former military officer as president, Hugo Chávez. In 2002, he was briefly overthrown in a coup. The Bush administration quickly recognized the right-wing forces that seized power. However, an outpouring of protests and a counter-coup within the military returned the ousted leader to the Miraflores Palace within days. A US government study later found that the CIA and other agencies had been in direct contact with and provided funding to some of the entities involved in the coup.[5] In 2004, when Aristide was overthrown in Haiti, Chávez was the only president in Latin America who condemned his ouster.

The Venezuelan president advocated a twenty-first-century "Bolívarianism," evoking the history of his nation's independence hero, Simón Bolívar, the revolutionary leader who had received support in Haiti in the early 1800s. Like Bolívar, Chávez was a regionalist. His vision was not only of a new Venezuela; it was for a new continent.

After Venezuela, leftist leaders won election after election throughout Central and South America, upending a region that the US had long considered its backyard. By 2007, the vast majority of the people in South America, from Tierra del Fuego on the southern tip to the Darien Gap in the north, had elected progressive leaders promising to move away from the failures of the neoliberal era.

Most analysts trace the rise of this so-called pink tide—not the red of communism, but the pink of democratic socialism—to the 1998 election of Chávez in Venezuela. But, in reality, Haiti had been the first domino to fall with Aristide's 1990 election. Chávez himself recognized this; there is no clearer example of the damning legacy of colonialism and globalization, the pitfalls of neoliberal thought, than Haiti. Likewise, there is no clearer example of the power of the people than the historic election of Jean-Bertrand Aristide after the end of dictatorship.

After failing to overthrow Chávez in 2002, the Bush administration set their sights on Haiti and Aristide, back in office for the second time. It made sense. Not only did Haiti's now aid-dependent state make for an easy target, but Bush's cabinet of cold warriors included plenty of familiar faces from his father's administration who had helped oust Aristide the first time, including Otto Reich and Roger Noriega. For the US, the Cold War may have ended, but the fight for regional hegemony continued.

Sitting atop the world's largest oil reserves, Chávez began investing heavily throughout the region, especially in the Caribbean through an oil-for-aid program known as PetroCaribe. With allies in South America, Venezuela helped to create the Union of South American Nations. South-South cooperation was beginning to define a continent long dependent on the Global North. Under the Bush administration, turning back this pink tide became official US policy, a twenty-first-century rehash of the Cold War, with Venezuela and Chávez stepping into the role of villain. It was a role the outspoken leader relished. "The devil came here yesterday, and it smells of sulfur still today," Chávez said at the 2006 UN General Assembly, one day after Bush had addressed the audience.[6]

The 2008 election of Barack Obama augured a new paradigm in US–Latin American relations. In April 2009, Chávez and Obama met at the Summit of the Americas. Chávez handed the US president a copy of *Open Veins of Latin America: Five Centuries of the Pillage of a Continent*, Eduardo Galeano's work on the legacy of colonial extraction across South America. The two shook hands and mugged for the cameras. The honeymoon, however, was short-lived.[7]

THREE DAYS AFTER the earthquake, on January 15, 2010, in South Africa, where Aristide remained in exile with his wife, Mildred, the two held a press conference. Journalists crowded inside a meeting room at a hotel next to the Johannesburg airport. The earthquake, Aristide said, is "a tragedy that defies expression, a tragedy that compels all people to the highest levels of human compassion and solidarity." And, he announced to the world, he was ready to return. "As far as we are concerned, we are ready to leave today, tomorrow, at any time to join the people of Haiti, to share in their suffering, help rebuild the country, moving from misery to poverty with dignity." Both he and his wife dabbed at tears as they left the press conference.[8]

For the international community, Aristide remained the embodiment of the populist and anti-market forces that might return to destabilize Haiti if the UN Blue Helmets left, as the former US ambassador had once put it. After his 2004 ouster, both Venezuela and Jamaica had offered asylum, which would have allowed him to maintain a foothold much closer to home. The US flew him to the Central African Republic, then to South Africa in an attempt to ensure that did not happen. In 2006, after Préval was elected for a second time, Edmond Mulet, the Guatemalan diplomat leading the UN mission, convinced the UN secretary-general to personally urge "South African President Mbeki to ensure that Aristide remained in South Africa," the US ambassador later reported to Washington.[9] But that hadn't been enough. Viewing Mbeki as wavering in his determination to keep Aristide in his country, Mulet urged the US to pursue legal action against Aristide to prevent him from gaining further traction among the Haitian population. The former president became the public target of US money-laundering and drug-trafficking investigations, though in the end, he was never personally indicted.

Despite the change in US administrations, the fear of Aristide's return had yet to subside. Seeing Aristide's post-quake press conference, the State Department's top diplomat for the Western Hemisphere emailed the US Embassy in Pretoria.

"As you might imagine," the diplomat wrote, "there is already great concern . . . at State on [the] 7th floor, about [Aristide's] statement and [the] possibility that he might try to return."[10] The concern was coming from the State Department's top floor, the leadership.

On the seventeenth, the embassy staff in Haiti met with representatives of the Vatican to discuss how best to dissuade Aristide from returning. They "agreed emphatically that Aristide's return would be a disaster," the embassy reported.[11] Over the next four days, more than forty emails were sent in response, most heavily redacted when they were eventually released, many years later, as part of a FOIA request.[12]

The diplomatic scramble to ensure that Aristide remained in exile provides deeper context to the international efforts to ensure the stability of the Préval government in the aftermath of the earthquake. And it helps to explain why, precisely, the US viewed Ti-René as Haiti's indispensable man. Préval served as a barrier between the elite and the masses, his hands just enough in both worlds to delicately balance the nation. Aristide's return, diplomats believed, would have upset the equilibrium that, in the years before the earthquake, appeared to have delivered at least modest gains in terms of economic growth and the strengthening of institutions. The relationship between Préval and the donor class, however, had not always been so friendly.

During the 2006 presidential campaign, held under a transitional government and with security and logistics handled by the UN Blue Helmets, Préval had largely remained silent. For more than fifteen years, the soft-spoken agronomist's political capital had been tied to Aristide, and it was that legacy that allowed him to handily win the most votes. But even that was not enough to guarantee he'd be allowed to take office. When partial results were announced, Préval appeared headed to a first-round victory with more than 50 percent of the vote. But as additional votes were processed, Préval's share shrank. International observers had performed their own exit polling and were stunned by the reversal. Two members of the electoral council alleged fraud, pointing the finger at the head of the council, Jacques Bernard, who they claimed was blocking access to the warehouse where votes were being tabulated.[13] "There is an unwholesome manipulation of the data. Nothing is transparent," one of the councilors told the press.[14] After days of demonstrations, a mass of protesters breached the gates of the Hotel Montana in search of electoral officials. They occupied the patio, lounging in cabanas and taking dips in the pool with views of the sprawling capital below. The action constituted a direct rebuke of the stability of the Aid State, which, despite its best efforts, could not eliminate the resistance of the Haitian people. The next day, Préval was declared the winner.

The US and other foreign officials had opposed Préval's candidacy, because, as the president would later explain, they considered him to be a pawn of Aristide—the man they had helped oust just two years earlier. But much had changed since then. Préval had run on his own ticket and with plans to build his own political future. Préval's campaign silence was well calculated. He wanted the support of the masses, especially in the capital's popular neighborhoods, who had remained devoted to Aristide. It was widely presumed that Préval would quickly welcome the ousted leader back from South Africa. Instead, after his victory, Préval had been perfectly content to keep him there. In doing so, he managed to expand his own power base to sectors of the Haitian population that had long been opposed to Lavalas, all while helping secure US and UN diplomatic support.

Préval's first foreign visit as president was across the border to the Dominican Republic, but then he traveled to both France and the United States, where he met with Bush. It was a strategic choice, designed to reassure the Americans spooked by the left's return to power. Préval, however, did not eschew South-South relations entirely. After meeting with Bush, he promptly went to both Cuba and Venezuela, meeting with Castro and Chávez. He quickly brought Haiti into the Venezuelan-led PetroCaribe alliance, the rapidly expanding oil-for-loans program, despite strong pushback from the US Embassy and corporate oil giants like Shell and Exxon.[15] Both domestically and internationally, Préval practiced the art of triangulation, carefully balancing competing powers off one another for his own, and his nation's, benefit. Haiti needed all the help it could get, he believed, and that meant not openly choosing sides between the masses and the elite, nor in the region's larger geopolitical showdown.

Préval was far from the first Haitian leader to practice such a policy with foreign powers. "It would be mere demagoguery for a Haitian president to pretend to be stronger than the Americans, or to engage them in a constant war of words, or to oppose them for opposing's sake," Aristide said in an interview months after Préval's reelection. "The only rational course is to weigh up the relative balance of interests, to figure out what the Americans want, to remember what we want, and to make the most of the available points of convergence." That, Aristide continued, was what had happened in 1994 when Clinton sent troops to help restore him to office. "Clinton needed a foreign policy victory, and a return to democracy in Haiti offered him that opportunity; we needed an instrument to overcome the resistance of the murderous Haitian army, and Clinton offered us that instrument. We never had any illusions that the Americans shared our deeper objectives. But without them we couldn't have restored democracy."[16]

Préval knew perfectly well that he was going to need the support of the donor community if he was going to complete another full term as president. That was why he had been so pleased after his 2007 meeting with Bill Clinton, when the former president pledged his support.

Nevertheless, the US still harbored its doubts and considered him a nationalist who often worked against its larger agenda in Haiti. "Préval clearly believes that he can walk a fine line without losing US or international community support," the US ambassador wrote in the same cable that described the president as the indispensable man.[17]

PRÉVAL TOOK GREAT pride in being the only Haitian president to be elected, complete his term, and hand power to another elected leader. In 2010, he was set to do so again. With the constitution limiting presidents to two nonconsecutive terms, both Préval and Aristide, even if he managed to return from exile, would not be able to run. For the first time in twenty years, the political landscape was wide open. For Ti-René, whose silent machinations had helped stabilize Haiti's nascent democracy, success looked like a retirement back in his rural hometown of Marmelade. To achieve that, however, meant avoiding the fate of so many of his predecessors, exile in a foreign land like Aristide or Baby Doc.

The earthquake destabilized the nation's foundation; it also upset Préval's tenuous triangulation. Rather than rallying behind the president in the face of such a tremendous disaster, the political and economic elite of Haiti almost immediately set their sights on the leader. The quake forced the delay of legislative elections, which had been scheduled for the same month of that devastating blow. His opponents—from both the left and the right—interpreted his silence after the earthquake as absenteeism in the country's time of need and accused him of political interference in the electoral process. They wanted him gone, replaced by a provisional government. On the other hand, many allies wanted elections to be postponed and their mandates extended. To maintain power and the political stability he viewed as necessary for Haiti's development, allying himself with the Aid State appeared as the best option.

Even before the earthquake, the 2010 presidential election was of special importance to the donor community. Political support for the UN mission had been faltering, but foreign officials wanted to stay in Haiti through the 2010 elections. Without Préval or Aristide running, it was an opportunity to ensure, at last, a reliable ally in the presidency. An ally who would cease working against the US agenda in Haiti.

There were worrying signs, however. For Senate elections in 2009, the electoral council had maintained the exclusion of the Fanmi Lavalas political party, which had not been allowed to participate in any election since the coup. The vast majority of Haitians boycotted those elections. Turnout was less than 10 percent. Many blamed Préval, who, in pivoting from his former ally, had embraced much of the oligarchy that had fought Aristide and Préval since their initial triumph in 1990.

Privately, and despite their antagonism toward Aristide and his Lavalas movement, the US and other donors had pushed the council to reverse its decision. But US ambassador Kenneth Merten had recommended that donors, at least publicly, stay quiet. At a December 1, 2009, meeting with other foreign diplomats, Merten suggested announcing donor support for upcoming elections regardless of their concerns. Without it, the presidential succession timeline would be threatened, he said. "The international community has too much invested in Haiti's democracy to walk away from the upcoming elections, despite its imperfections," Merten recounted the EU representative as saying.[18]

That had been the analysis before the earthquake. After, the presidential vote took on even greater importance. The exclusion of Lavalas was maintained, but there were no protests from the US or the UN.

"I think it is important that the political process move forward," Ambassador Merten told the press. "We're going to need some partners here who can make decisions, who have a mandate—a fresh mandate from the Haitian people. And we believe we'll be able to find those partners here."[19] The Aid State needed its local front man.

As the fall of 2010 approached, NGOs and foreign officials looked for someone to blame for the lack of an effective response. The greatest threat to stability was not violence; it was the inability of the relief efforts to respond to the needs on the ground. They were unable or unwilling to comprehend why their best intentions were not enough to address a litany of problems many of them had—wittingly or not—contributed to as part of the global foreign aid industry. The Haitian government, led by Préval, became the designated cause of the effort's woes. Popular anger in Haiti also targeted Préval, criticized either as having sold out to international interests or as having not acted decisively enough in implementing their agenda. Of course, Préval and his government were not the only actors wielding power in Haiti. The aid effort was being driven by the NGOs; it was the Blue Helmets providing security and electoral logistics; and then there was the linchpin of the long-term reconstruction effort, the Bill Clinton–led reconstruction commission. The body had taken on supranational powers due to donors' belief that Haiti was a failed state, but the commission itself seemed to be barely functioning. Had international officials truly supported the government of Haiti? Or, by placing the resource-starved government in the lead, had international officials created a useful scapegoat? It wasn't the "Governor General" on the ballot in November, after all. Regardless of the winner, decisions about how to spend the billions in still unmet aid pledges would continue to be made as much by donors as by the Haitian government or the population it purportedly represented.

Camille Chalmers, executive director of the Platform to Advocate Alternative Development, was skeptical. International actors had taken on an outsized role in the country's reconstruction, he believed. Why have a president, asked Chalmers, "if he is only there to rubber stamp the decisions of [the international community]? . . . How can we have elections when Haiti's national sovereignty has disappeared?"[20] Even Chalmers would soon be surprised at the prescience of his comments.

9

THE ELECTORAL CARNIVAL

At the Corail humanitarian camp, a line had formed outside the make-shift voting center by six A.M. on November 28, 2010, when the sun burst out over the mountains and the nation's 11,181 polling locations were set to open. It was already eighty degrees and it would only get hotter from here. The morning's antecedent reds hung on the horizon, distant warnings of what was to come. The residents hadn't called Corail home for long. The ten thousand who had settled there were among the more than a million people officially displaced by the 7.0 earthquake eleven months earlier.

In April, with a tropical storm threatening further devastation for those with little more than a blue tarp over their heads, the US military and an NGO run by Hollywood actor Sean Penn had relocated many of these families to Corail, part of an expanse of land about fifteen miles north of the capital with pristine views of the Caribbean Sea and the bay of Port-au-Prince. International NGOs provided tents, set up latrines, and handed out food kits with some basic supplies. When the storm came, the new camp flooded anyway.[1] Families had been promised job opportunities and new urban developments to help "build back better," as the post-quake mantra went. By election day, the residents of Corail were still waiting. Waiting, at least, for someone to ask what they might actually need before giving them another handout. The election was a chance to be heard; and they were anxiously awaiting the opportunity.

Unlike many other voting centers throughout the country, the one in Corail opened on time. But there was a bigger problem. One by one those in line failed to find their names on the voter rolls. There were five thousand eligible voters. The voter list contained thirty-nine names.[2] They had lost their homes in the quake and their neighborhoods in the aftermath. Losing their vote was too much. Officials closed the voting center within hours as frustration turned into anger. Those displaced faced systemic barriers to participating in the election, despite tens of millions of dollars spent by donors and the government on preparation. The disorganization at Corail was repeated across the capital, as thousands of voters were turned away at the polls. Twenty-four years after the fall of the dictatorship, it appeared democracy in Haiti remained a dream deferred.

But it wasn't just the Haitian people who had a stake in the outcome of the vote. After the earthquake, donors pledged billions of dollars to assist Haiti in its recovery and spent more than $18 million in support of the electoral process, in support of finding their desired post-quake partner. But what happened on election day was no expression of democratic will. Rather, what transpired revealed the magnitude of foreign power over Haiti's affairs and the real-world implications of prioritizing stability over all else. Over the two decades of foreign-led nation-building, the Aid State had taken over the functions of the state, providing basic services and security. It had also taken over the electoral apparatus.

RICARDO SEITENFUS, A sixty-two-year-old Brazilian diplomat, had come to Haiti in 2008 to serve at the Organization of American States. The hemispheric body had a permanent presence inside Haiti, and Seitenfus, a towering figure with a wispy white mustache, had spent countless hours since the quake trying to get the voter rolls in shape ahead of the day's election. Somewhere between sixty thousand and three hundred thousand Haitians had died. That nobody knew the real number drove home the inherent difficulty in ensuring adequate electoral registration. Hundreds of thousands more were living in camps for the internally displaced, potentially miles from their old neighborhoods.

But Seitenfus was optimistic the hard work had paid off. On the morning of the election, he set off to see for himself how the vote was unfolding.[3]

Seitenfus first traveled to Place Saint-Pierre in the Pétion-Ville neighborhood of the capital. Things seemed to be developing rather normally, he thought. There were no long lines, it was open, and most seemed to be voting without trouble. But he did notice a group of young men causing some disruptions, claiming that their names were not on the voter lists. They were clad in pink, the campaign color of a popular musician running for the presidency, Michel Martelly, still better known by his stage name, Sweet Micky. Opinion polls had shown Martelly in third place. In first, every poll showed, was Mirlande Manigat, a constitutional law professor and the wife of former interim president Leslie Manigat, looking to become Haiti's first woman elected to the highest office. As the leading opposition contender, she drew significant support from the country's elite, including Reginald Boulos. In second was Jude Célestin, the head of the government construction agency and the chosen successor of René Préval, whose political capital had been reduced to rubble by the earthquake. Still, given the party's national reach and perceived control of the electoral apparatus, Célestin was not easily discarded. Overall, eighteen candidates were competing for the chance to lead the quake-battered nation.

Despite the obvious logistical challenges, foreign officials maintained that things were going smoothly. "In general, everything is going well, everything is peaceful," Edmond Mulet told Agence France-Presse around 8:30 A.M., more than two hours after polls had opened. "I see a great passion . . . for democracy in this country. [The UN] is here. There is no reason to be frightened. It's an electoral celebration," the UN diplomat said.[4]

Seitenfus, who had met up with a delegation of visiting Brazilian electoral officials and the Brazilian ambassador, also believed the day was proceeding smoothly. They had traveled outside the capital to get a broader sense of the situation. Clearly there were problems, most obviously the huge portion of voters unable to find their names on the lists, but he was still optimistic. It was, he believed, as good as could have been anticipated given the context.

On the return to Port-au-Prince, the Brazilian ambassador phoned Seitenfus, who was in the car behind him. They had been summoned to an emergency meeting at the private residence of Mulet, the ambassador said. They didn't know what it was about, but they decided to skip lunch and head straight there.

Meanwhile, around noon, while watching the election unfold from his temporary office space, President Préval's cell phone rang. It was Mulet.

"It's no longer an election," the UN chief said. "Mr. President, this is a political problem. We need to get you on a plane and evacuate you."

Préval was stunned.

"Bring your plane, collect me from the palace, handcuff me, everyone will see that it's a kidnapping," Préval remembered responding.[5] He was not going to suffer the same fate as Aristide or Baby Doc.

At nearly the same time, the Martelly campaign began circulating a press release. A massive fraud was underway, the note said, and the campaign was inviting journalists to a press conference at the Hotel Karibe.

ON NOVEMBER 27, the day before the election, a representative of the Martelly team secured a conference room at the Hotel Karibe.[6] Campaign members also drafted a statement denouncing the yet-to-be-held election as a fraud. The stunt had been carefully orchestrated.

The Martelly campaign's text message was followed by another from a different candidate and then another, all calling on supporters to come to the Karibe. Local and international journalists rushed to the scene and waited.

Outside, where the election was still going on, the wind had picked up. But inside, the temperature was rising. It wasn't just press filling the Karibe, but dozens of supporters of the various candidates. It was already an impressive show of political unity, bringing together candidates of the left and the right. At 1:50 P.M., Manigat, the front-runner, strode into the press conference to loud cheers. As others arrived, the cheers turned into an impromptu rendition of the national anthem.

Josette Bijou, a fringe candidate with little hope of the presidency, took her seat in front of a gaggle of microphones and a buzzing audience. "It is clear that the government of René Préval, in agreement with the [electoral council] is putting into execution the plan hatched to tamper with the elections," she read from a statement drafted before a single vote had been cast. The elections, the candidates agreed, should be annulled. "We ask the people to mobilize right now to show their opposition to the election," she concluded.[7] The statement eventually distributed to the press was signed by twelve of the eighteen presidential candidates.

"Arrest Préval," the candidates' supporters chanted in the hotel ballroom.

As Martelly exited, Emily Troutman, a freelance journalist, asked him if his campaign had coordinated the whole event. "You always ask the weirdest questions," he answered, before disappearing into the crowd.[8]

ACROSS TOWN, A diplomatic meeting with just as serious implications was about to begin. When Seitenfus pulled up to the UN chief's residence, he asked John Bevan, the UN's in-country political expert, what was happening. Twelve of the eighteen presidential candidates had just wrapped up a press conference where they denounced the unfolding election as a fraud, demanded its annulment, and called their supporters into the streets, Bevan explained.[9]

The Brazilian diplomat was unsure what to make of the situation, having personally thought the election to be proceeding acceptably, if imperfectly. He approached Mulet.

"I have just finished talking to Préval on the phone informing him that an airplane would be available for him to leave the country. In 48 hours, at the latest—that is, by Tuesday the 30th—Préval will have to leave the presidency and leave Haiti," Mulet told Seitenfus, who struggled to conceal his indignation. The Dominican president, Leonel Fernández, had been contacted to help secure a plane for President Préval's departure.

Seitenfus moved to the living room, which was filling up rapidly with diplomats and their assistants. Officials shared concerns of violent civil unrest in the aftermath of the elections and of the candidates' call for new elections. A representative from France offered his country's support in the effort to pressure Préval into exile.

There was only one Haitian in the residence. And as Prime Minister Bellerive entered the living room, he interrupted the conversation with a simple question.

"I would like to know if President Préval's term is on the negotiation table? Yes or no?" he asked. Were these foreign diplomats plotting a coup? he wanted to know.

The room went silent.

"In 2001, in the Americas, a document entitled the Inter-American Democratic Charter was signed," Seitenfus, making clear he was speaking only for himself, interjected. "This Charter stipulates that any modification to the mandate of a democratically-elected president, outside of the constitutional precepts, should be considered to be a putsch."

He looked to his colleague, the Brazilian ambassador. "I do not know Brazil's position," Seitenfus said.

"Brazil has the same interpretation," the ambassador responded.

Across the room, US ambassador Merten was shaking his head in apparent disappointment. "We are not going to talk about this anymore," he told the gathered diplomats.

The plan to fly the president out of the country was abandoned.

As THE CANDIDATES rushed out of the Hotel Karibe, protests were already growing in downtown Port-au-Prince, and in various cities throughout the country. In Gonaïves, a coastal town a few hours north of the capital, Manigat supporters took to the streets. In Les Cayes, a southern town, angry citizens attacked political establishments affiliated with Célestin and Préval's party. Stoked by the annulment call, those opposed to the election disrupted the final hours of voting and the all-important vote-counting process in many provincial towns. The OAS pulled its observers from the field, unable to ensure their safety. But the largest and most raucous demonstration was in the capital.

After disappearing into the crowd at the press conference, Martelly soon emerged in downtown Port-au-Prince and climbed atop a silver SUV in the midst of a group of hundreds of predominantly young men protesting against the election.

Martelly was a natural performer. After a stilted campaign, he was in his element during the election day spectacle. He was soon joined by another candidate, the industrialist and sweatshop owner Charles Henri Baker, a leading member of the group that had helped oust Aristide in 2004, and by the Grammy-winning star Wyclef Jean, whose own presidential ambitions had been cut down when he was barred from participating. Music blared as they slowly wound through the streets. Martelly, in washed-out jeans and a white button-down, whipped up the crowd with political chants and well-timed hip shakes. Many of those taking the street already referred to Martelly as *Msye Prezidan*—Mr. President—of *konpa*, a distinctly Haitian musical genre. Now, he was declaring himself president of Haiti. But his *rara* performances had always been tinged with politics, and it wasn't the first time he had directly taken on Préval.

Haiti's 1996 carnival was held just a month after Préval's inauguration as president and not long after Martelly's single "Prezidan" hit the airwaves. He had been an outspoken critic of Aristide and Préval for years. Still, the musician, who had been living in Miami, returned to Port-au-Prince for the celebration. Préval watched from outside the National Palace as the procession wound its way through the Champ de Mars, the sprawling plaza outside its gates. "From one president to the other . . . I want to see you dancing," Martelly shouted into the microphone as they approached. Préval had no choice but to shake his hips in response.[10]

Fourteen years later, on election day in 2010, Martelly was once again making Préval dance. Wyclef and Martelly snaked through the streets of the capital for more than three hours, with international media reporting it across the world. At 6 P.M., after the sun had set, the protest finally ended. Martelly finished it off with one more call on citizens to remain mobilized against the election and against Préval. Until late in the night, the streets of the capital held on to the day's carnival-like atmosphere.[11]

As for the election, it had ended in chaos and disorganization. The election that donors had just spent $18 million on and more than a year preparing for, the election that would choose a leader to oversee $10 billion in reconstruction spending, appeared to have been a waste. But the next day, donors would scramble to save the election they had staked so much on, and they would find an ally in Sweet Micky, the man who had just helped to tear it all down. Sometimes it takes a little instability to achieve the desired stability.

MARTELLY AND SOME of his campaign staff returned to the Hotel Karibe the morning after the vote. In the courtyard, the candidate gave an impromptu press conference. "I have a message for Préval and his acolyte," he said, refusing to even mention Célestin by name. "Haiti doesn't want you anymore." As he spoke, hundreds of young protesters clashed with police who dispatched volley after volley of tear gas. "People across the country are waiting to explode. That is why I think it would be fair for all those responsible to act the right way and to make the right decision, which is to listen to the demands of the people," he reasoned.

Missing from Martelly's comments was any call for the elections to be canceled, as he and the other eleven presidential candidates had demanded the day prior. Instead, he would await preliminary results, expected a week later on December 7. Manigat, the front-runner, also reversed her position. "I want to say that I am still in the electoral race, because I have good chances of winning the vote," she said. Despite appearing at the prior day's press conference, Manigat denied she had ever supported the election's annulment. "I played no part in the writing of the text in question. I was surprised when I heard my name," she added.[12]

What had changed?

Later that afternoon, Seitenfus went back to Mulet's residence for another meeting. He was greeted at the building's entrance by Mulet and by Martelly, who appeared to be shaking hands with diplomats as they arrived.

Once Martelly left, Seitenfus asked Mulet why the candidate was at his residence. Manigat, the UN diplomat explained, had just left. He had met with both her and Martelly to explain that they would be the top two candidates in the election's runoff, ahead of Célestin. The candidates' abrupt reversals earlier in the day began to make a lot more sense.[13] Official results were still at least a week away, but the Aid State had already made up its mind on the results.

That afternoon, the OAS election observation mission finally released a statement. After listing a litany of problems that impacted the election and, in an indirect rebuke to the actions of the twelve candidates, noting "deliberate acts of violence and intimidation to derail the electoral process both in Port-au-Prince and the provinces," the mission concluded that the election was valid.

"I think that the concerns and problems we were facing last Sunday are behind us and we'll see what will happen in the next days," Mulet said.[14]

Three days later, on December 3, Mulet called members of Haiti's electoral authority, the CEP by its French acronym, to a meeting at Le Villate, a modest restaurant in Pétion-Ville. In a private room, Mulet addressed the electoral councilors.[15]

"I'm sorry for what I'm going to tell you," he began. "I will not speak on my own behalf, but, in the name of the whole of the international community."

He paused.

"As you know, we are very concerned about the election results . . ."

He paused again.

"We want to tell you that we will not accept that Mr. Jude Célestin is present in the second round of voting, or that he wins in the first round."

The tabulation center had not even received all of the votes from across the country, CEP president Pierre-Louis Opont responded. Further, the electoral councilors themselves were not responsible for tallying the votes.

"Mr. Mulet," he continued, his voice rising, "why don't you ask the two foreign technicians who accompany the CEP . . . to execute your orders?" Opont may have been the man in charge, but it was donors who provided the electoral budget, and it was donors who were overseeing the entire apparatus.

The meeting ended minutes later.

Mulet had told President Préval at noon on November 28, the day of the vote, that whatever was transpiring, it had ceased to be an election. In public, donors projected a democratic façade on what was taking place—they just wanted Haitian voices to be heard, they said. But everything after Mulet's election day phone call "was orchestrated mayhem backed by international meddling," as a former US Embassy employee confided to me years later.[16] Whatever their motives, the international community's attempts to save the election were threatening to destroy a democracy.

And those efforts were just getting started.

10

THE STATISTICAL COUP

The streets of the normally traffic-clogged capital were empty ahead of the announcement of preliminary results on December 7. The protests had waned, but nobody expected that to last. The results came shortly after ten P.M. Mirlande Manigat had come in first place with 31.4 percent of the vote, and ahead of Martelly by less than 1 percentage point was Célestin. With the level of disorganization, the disillusionment, and the disruption from the press conference, only 22 percent of the population had voted—or, more accurately, had had their votes counted.

Within minutes of the official announcement, the US Embassy released its own press statement that cast doubt on the results. A few days earlier, a group of local election observers, themselves funded by international donors, had published an exit poll. The sample was relatively tiny and geographically focused on the capital—the region where Martelly was most popular—and the poll estimated the top two vote getters were Manigat and Martelly. After the announcement of preliminary results, it was used as prima facie evidence that fraud had taken place.

"Like others, the Government of the United States is concerned by the Provisional Electoral Council's announcement of preliminary results . . . that are inconsistent with the published results" of the local observer groups, the embassy's statement read.[1] The US, with the rest of the international community at its back, was publicly turning against the electoral process they had vouched for and funded.

Makeshift barricades went up at main intersections across the capital. Groups, predominantly consisting of young men, charged through the streets chanting anti-Préval slogans, burning tires, and littering the streets with debris. Célestin's party headquarters was set ablaze.[2]

Mulet had been right. This was no longer about an election or about democracy at all. It was a political fight for power. In the West, we often think of democracy as little more than the regular holding of elections. One person, one vote, and voilà, a democracy is maintained. It is rarely so simple. In Haiti, there is election day itself, but, even more important, there is the long, drawn-out process of counting the votes and gaining recognition. Getting the most votes is rarely the most difficult of the two contests.[3]

At these points in time, after votes are cast but before a winner is formally declared, a second campaign begins. But, in these postelection competitions, it is not the support of the Haitian people that politicians court. Rather, it is the support of the international community. By 2010, after nearly two decades of foreign-led nation-building, Haitian politicians had learned a thing or two about how best to secure that support.

The preliminary results had revealed a close election, but they also revealed that Martelly had not received many votes outside Port-au-Prince. The postelection protests had given the impression of a massively popular candidate, but the penchant to view Haiti as nothing more than the capital obscured his lack of a national reach. And there was a larger truth buried in the results as well. None of the candidates had the support of more than about 6 percent of registered voters. Most Haitians had either been prevented from participating or never intended to participate at all.

In the fight for power in the Republic of Port-au-Prince, it was the majority of Haitians who would pay the price, as they had so many times throughout history. And when all that remains is a veneer of democracy, a veneer of sovereignty, new leaders aren't chosen by the ballot box. They are chosen behind closed doors where negotiations are held between diplomats and the Haitian elite.

* * *

THE OFFICIAL RESULTS had been known for only about twelve hours, but already powerful actors were working to remove Célestin from the race altogether. At 9:54 A.M. on December 8, Ambassador Merten sent an email to Cheryl Mills, as well as to Tom Adams and Daniel Restrepo, both key State Department staff involved in the Haiti effort.

"Private sector + Mulet: Célestin should withdraw," the subject line read.[4]

Merten explained to his colleagues in Washington that Reginald Boulos and his private-sector allies had told Préval that Célestin should resign from the race. "This is big," the ambassador wrote.

The barricades were still up in the capital, and protests, even some in the provinces, were turning violent. Merten wrote that he had personally contacted Martelly's campaign team and told them that the candidate needs to "get on radio telling people to not pillage. Peaceful demo OK: pillage is not."

If Célestin were to be removed, it would be Martelly advancing to the second round with Manigat. While the international media focused on the candidate's bawdy stage antics, and presented him as a political outsider just as his foreign campaign team had hoped, the musician's candidacy was being supported by shadowy figures from Haiti's past.

Martelly was advised by former Duvalier officials, including Daniel Supplice, the dictator's social affairs minister in the mid-1980s. Martelly himself had previously acknowledged his at least social relationship with Duvalier's feared Tonton Macoutes, the tips of the dictatorship's spear of repression, who were given membership cards that yielded patronage and privilege for holders. During the 2010 campaign, the Martelly camp sold similar cards for about thirty dollars. Many young men, thinking they would be first in line for jobs in a potential Martelly government, joined the group, which became known as Mouvement Tèt Kale (MTK), the "Bald-Headed Movement," a play on Martelly's shiny shaved head.

MTK was run by George Racine, a businessman who, with some of his friends, created the group in order to "help Martelly" during the campaign, as he later told me. Racine's wife, Magalie, was the daughter of Madame Max Adolphe, a powerful Macoute who ran a notorious torture camp during the dictatorship. "After the first round, it was us in the streets protesting," a member of the group explained.[5] The threat of instability was a powerful force in obtaining international support.

During times of crisis in Haiti, the political and economic elite had often turned to foreign powers to adjudicate their disputes, a legacy of decades of international intervention. This time was no different. After meeting with Boulos and other private-sector representatives, Préval agreed to ask the OAS, the same international body that had observed and continued to back the validity of the election, to form a verification mission to analyze the results. The decision proved fatal.

That evening, Préval met with Mulet alone at his home. "Forget the plane," he told the UN diplomat, the OAS would provide the true accounting of the vote. "René," the diplomat responded, "Martelly is not in the second round. The problem is, we don't want Célestin in the second round . . . we're not talking about elections." Préval called Verret, his advisor who maintained close relations with the State Department and the embassy, to set up a meeting with Merten for the following day.

"Are you a political party or an ambassador?" Préval angrily asked the ambassador at that meeting. "Only parties can contest election results. Are you part of these elections?"

"I'm part of these elections because I'm paying for these elections," Préval remembered Merten responding.

"Okay," Préval said, "what you are saying to me is 'fuck you.'"[6]

IN PUBLIC, DIPLOMATS had played into fears that Préval was trying to steal the election; behind closed doors, they were working to do just that by pushing Célestin out. At the same time, international observers appeared to be agreeing with the disgraced electoral council that the election was satisfactory. The juxtaposition didn't make sense.

If the problems were minor and the election was valid, was the fraud taking place during the processing of the vote at the tabulation center? If so, that process was being overseen by international officials. If, as many had alleged, the election was unfair from the beginning, it was donors who provided the funding and touted its legitimacy. Even if they had changed their assessment over time, they risked undermining it further with their contradictory public and private actions.

When the electoral council website published the individual tally sheets, myself and colleagues at the Center for Economic and Policy Research in Washington assembled a team of researchers. If the results couldn't be trusted, we were going to analyze the 11,181 tally sheets ourselves. As Washington, DC, emptied out for the holiday, we began transcribing the digitized copies by hand, one by one. We worked practically around the clock, inputting each sheet into a database that could then be used to analyze the results for fraud or other irregularities. We finished on Christmas Eve.

The seven-person OAS mission arrived in Haiti less than a week later. Six of its members were American, French, or Canadian. France is not even part of the OAS. It sent a clear message about who was in control. The same day the team landed in Haiti to begin their work, we put out a press release with the initial findings of our review.[7] The irregularities were far more widespread than officials had let on. The UN had claimed only 4 percent of voting centers had been destroyed on election day; we found that the tabulation center was missing tally sheets from 10 percent of voting centers and that many more had been placed in quarantine due to irregularities.

The fact that voters were distributed alphabetically within voting booths allowed us to perform a simple statistical test on the data. Since one's voting preference isn't strongly tied to one's name, the distribution of votes at each booth should be relatively uniform. Put another way, if there are five voting booths in a voting center, and a candidate received twenty votes in four and one hundred and twenty votes in the fifth, there was no statistical explanation for the aberration, and it was likely fraudulent or an error.

When we tested the results, we identified an additional 6 percent of tally sheets that appeared to show fraud or a misrecording of the vote. Taken all together, our research revealed that close to 20 percent of the votes cast were either never counted, fraudulent, or otherwise invalid, a shockingly high figure, especially given the already abysmal level of participation. And while many of the fraudulent sheets did appear to benefit Célestin, he wasn't the only one. Further, the sheets that simply never arrived at the tabulation center came predominantly from rural areas that had voted overwhelmingly for him. If those missing votes had ever been counted, Célestin would have easily come in second place.[8] With an election determined by less than 1 percentage point, it was clear that whatever the OAS mission was going to say, it would be political. There was no way the flawed and partial results could be used to definitively determine a winner. Or so we thought.

While the world waited for the OAS to deliver its recommendations, something even more nefarious was taking place at the tabulation center in the capital.

Before the Haitian government had even approved of the OAS mission, the US had dispatched one of its employees in Washington to Port-au-Prince. The man was Jacques Bernard, the former Haitian electoral official who had been accused of trying to prevent Préval's ascension to the presidency back in 2006. By the time Bernard was called back to the tabulation center four years later, he was working full-time for the US government, as was his wife. The analysis that Bernard conducted in late 2010 was relatively straightforward. With about 450 voters assigned to each voting booth, Bernard decided to exclude any tally sheet where an individual candidate received more than a certain number of votes. He started high and slowly lowered it. He eventually reached a threshold that, if applied, would be enough to change the results and move Martelly into the runoff.[9]

On January 10, 2011, a draft copy of the OAS report was leaked to the press. There had been a parallel fight going on within the regional organization and the team had come up with multiple drafts of their report, only one of which recommended altering the results of the election and placing Martelly into the runoff. That had been the version leaked.

The OAS mission hadn't actually performed a recount of the votes, nor did they analyze all the 10,128 tally sheets that had made it to the tabulation center. The OAS had only reviewed 8 percent of the tally sheets, and, as Fritz Scheuren, the lead statistician for the mission, later told me, they hadn't performed any simulations for the large percentage of tally sheets that were never counted and which came from predominantly pro-Célestin areas.[10] In other words, the OAS report was recommending changing the results of an election without any statistical inference and without a full recount, something never before done in the history of international election observation. The "expert mission" had simply mimicked the work of Bernard and removed all the tally sheets where a candidate received over 150 votes, just the right threshold to replace Célestin with Martelly.

After receiving the leaked report, Jean-Max Bellerive, the prime minister, met with Colin Granderson, a Trinidadian politician and a representative of CARICOM, the Caribbean Community. Granderson had been the head of the OAS electoral observation mission. Bellerive told him the conclusion didn't make sense. How could they change the results without any real analysis? Let alone with such a high portion of votes missing altogether. Granderson agreed. But, he told Bellerive, it was the only result the international community would accept.[11] The question, then, was whether the Préval government would as well. On January 12, 2011, the one-year anniversary of the earthquake, the OAS formally presented its verification mission report to the president.

In Washington, the OAS convened an emergency meeting. According to notes from the meeting, the ministers present agreed that the purpose of the leak was clear: to pressure the government to put Martelly into the runoff.

"I don't have proof," Damian Merlo, an American advisor to the Martelly campaign, later told me, "but I'm sure it was the US embassy."[12]

Its actions did little to dispel that belief. The US offered a full-throated defense of the leaked, and now official, OAS report. "The international community is entirely unified on this point. There is nothing to negotiate in the report," Merten said in mid-January.[13]

For his part, Martelly didn't bother arguing with the specific numbers. "Of course, the numbers that we have seen are not the real numbers. . . . But we say let's just go forward. We will take any numbers that put us in the second round, where we know we are going to win."[14] Since before the first vote had been cast, it seemed this had been the plan.

The US threatened electoral councilors and members of Préval's Unity Party with visa cancellations in an attempt to pressure them to accept the OAS report's recommendations or to preempt the decision by forcing Célestin to withdraw from the race. Other diplomats joined in. On January 20, US ambassador to the United Nations Susan Rice threatened to withhold aid for the earthquake-devastated nation. "Sustained support from the international community, including the United States, will require a credible process that represents the will of the Haitian people," Rice told a UN Security Council debate on Haiti.[15] At this point, international officials had made a determination about what the "will of the Haitian people" had been: anybody but Célestin.

There was little question that the election had been fatally flawed, but in the year since the earthquake, Préval had gone from guarantor of stability to barrier to progress. Allowing his chosen successor to take office was simply untenable, even if it meant overturning the results of an election without any basis.

Foreign officials maintained that their only concern was the protection of democracy. But their actions betrayed the public statements. In late January, under increasing pressure to accept the OAS recommendations, the Haitian government privately offered to hold entirely new elections. Given the problems with the November vote, that would have been the only option that even resembled a democratic solution. It was also precisely what much of Haitian civil society had been demanding for two months and what Martelly and Manigat had called for on the day of the vote.

On January 22, Gabriel Verret, an advisor to Préval, sent an email to Cheryl Mills at the State Department. "Urgent need to talk," the subject line read. Verret wanted to schedule a call with Mills to explain the government's new plan. "It does begin with the cancellation of the Presidential elections of November 28," Verret wrote.[16] In the months after the earthquake, the legislature had approved an emergency law allowing Préval to stay in office until May 14 if the elections were not finished in time. By proposing a redo election, Préval was attempting to save his legacy, and, perhaps, what was left of his nation's sovereignty.

For the US and others in the international community, the priority was to simply move forward. The priority was stability, even if it took months of instability to get there. Donors flatly rejected the proposal. In each of Haiti's four elections since the fall of the Duvalier dictatorship, a left-wing leader had emerged victorious. A second round with Manigat and Martelly, two conservative candidates, was the fresh start donors had been waiting for. It seemed safe, stable.

The US pressure campaign, however, was failing to move the government. On January 28, a full two months after the elections were held, the State Department announced that Secretary Clinton would be traveling to Haiti. In a clear example of the blurred lines between the State Department and the Clinton Foundation, Laura Graham, the longtime aide running the foundation, wrote to Mills, urging a strategy to ensure acceptance of the "mms solution," a reference to the placement of Michel Martelly and Mirlande Manigat into the second round.

"The radio is 24–7 messaging against the current solution, turning [Préval] and [Célestin] from villans [sic] into patriots. Its [sic] unbeliev-able," Graham wrote in a typo-filled email. "The [international com-munity] and USG taking hits and looking like villan [sic]. Nationalism views on rise. [Hillary Clinton] was specifically criticized today for im-posing this solution and pressuring [Préval]," she continued.

Six minutes later, Mills forwarded the email to Secretary of State Clinton with a short note. "Let's discuss this on the plane."

"Bill talked to me about this and is quite worried about what I do and say tomorrow," Clinton wrote back.

"As we all are," Mills responded. She passed along talking points for the following day's trip. "Ask him if he has any thoughts," Mills con-cluded, in reference to Bill Clinton.[17]

The next day, in Haiti, Secretary Clinton met with all three of the leading candidates. She then gave interviews to three different local ra-dio stations. The US fully supported the OAS report and its recommen-dations, she repeated again and again, but this was a Haitian matter for Haitians to decide, she insisted.

"Several political parties and organizations have accused the U.S. Government of exerting unfair pressure" on the government and on the CEP to accept the OAS report, Wendell Theodore of Radio Métropole said. Visas had been revoked, he said, and aid cuts threatened. "Well," Clinton responded, "it's regrettable that for political purposes anyone would make such accusations."[18]

Clinton also had interviews with just about every major Sunday news program, including *Meet the Press, Face the Nation, State of the Union,* and *This Week.* In Egypt, Hosni Mubarak's government was on the verge of collapse and was violently repressing its own uprising. None of the anchors asked the secretary a single question about Haiti.

That night, she met with Bellerive and Préval. If it was up to the Haitian people to decide, she made it quite clear what decision that ought to be. "We tried to resist and did, until the visit of Hillary Clinton," Bellerive later told me. "That was when Préval understood he had no way out and accepted it."

The prime minister accompanied the secretary to the airport after the meeting. On the tarmac, she asked what he expected would come next.

Martelly was going to be president, Bellerive said.[19]

ON FEBRUARY 3, 2011, the electoral council announced that it would accept the OAS report's recommendations and remove Célestin from the race. "It's a great day in Haiti today again," Ambassador Merten, speaking in the State Department's Foggy Bottom pressroom, told reporters.[20] Préval was allowed to stay in office an extra couple of months through the second-round election now scheduled for March and the transition to a new president in May. In the end, he cared more about remaining in Haiti than remaining in power. Meanwhile, those former presidents in exile were making their way back to Haiti.

In mid-January, Baby Doc boarded an Air France flight in Paris, where he had maintained a gilded exile for more than twenty years. With Préval weakened, and two conservative candidates in line to benefit, the former "ruler for life" felt safe enough to return home. Though the arrival had largely been kept private, thousands greeted the former strongman and accompanied him to the Hotel Karibe. He was joined by former allies, including Louis-Jodel Chamblain, a military general and death squad leader who had participated in the insurgency that led to Aristide's 2004 ouster.

Asked about the return of Duvalier, State Department spokesman P. J. Crowley said, "This is a matter for the Government of Haiti and the people of Haiti." But when asked about the possibility of Aristide returning, he said, "Haiti does not need, at this point, any more burdens."[21] While Duvalier's influence appeared to be growing in the midst of the post-electoral political crisis, it was Aristide who scared international officials, as had been the case for more than two decades. But the return of Duvalier, which many believed would have been impossible without at least the acquiescence of US and French intelligence agencies, was a potent symbol of the political changes percolating in the electoral chaos. These changes would shake the foundations of Haiti's fragile democracy as hard as the earthquake itself.

Most assumed that Manigat would be the clear favorite in the second round. The dynamic, however, had shifted. Though Martelly had utterly despised Aristide and the Lavalas movement, he found his greatest support in the popular neighborhoods of the capital. Sweet Micky wasn't famous for his political positions, he was famous for his music. During the campaign, few had taken Martelly seriously and all the ire was directed at Manigat. The two months of protests had transformed the musician from electoral afterthought to the people's champion.

On March 19, the day before the second-round vote, Aristide returned to Haiti, ending his seven-year exile. The US had lobbied hard to prevent his return, and President Obama had personally called South African president Jacob Zuma to urge him to stop the flight.[22] Neither strategy had worked. The former president had good reason to return when he did. Both the Manigat and Martelly camps were actively trying to court the Lavalas vote ahead of the second round, and as news of Aristide's arrival circulated, both voiced their support. But with two conservatives on the precipice of power, the former leader knew those welcoming words wouldn't be long lasting.

"Today, may the Haitian people mark the end of exile and coups d'etat," Aristide told the press that had gathered at the airport. The former president thanked his supporters and finished with a clear message in relation to the election. "Excluding Lavalas, you cut the branches that link the people," he said. "The solution is inclusion of all Haitians as human beings."[23]

The Préval government sent an official vehicle and one of its top emissaries to the airport to greet the former president and return him to his faded residence in Tabarre, just outside the capital. The US and its international partners may have succeeded in ousting Préval's chosen successor from the election. But his support for Aristide's return served as an example of his classically understated political acumen, a way to land one last body blow against the foreign powers who had just relegated him to the political sidelines for the first time in twenty years.

The irony, however, was that while Aristide's return served as an important rebuke of the coups of the past, the statistical coup that had just taken place was about to be consolidated.

JUST AFTER FIVE P.M. on the day of the second round of voting, Cheryl Mills emailed a number of her top staff in Haiti and Washington. "Nice job all," she wrote. "You do great elections." Then she added, "We can discuss how the counting is going! Just kidding. Kinda. :)"[24]

On April 4, the electoral council announced that Martelly won the second-round election with 67.6 percent of the vote.[25] The high share of the vote allowed Martelly to claim a landslide victory and a stunning mandate. But only 21 percent of voters had turned out. He had received the votes of only seven hundred thousand Haitians in a country of more than ten million. It wasn't the first time that power had changed hands undemocratically in Haiti. And while few questioned the legitimacy of Martelly's second-round victory, the entire saga—coming in the aftermath of the earthquake and with foreign embassies and international bodies right in the middle of it—delivered a fatal blow to the illusion of Haiti's sovereignty.

Writing in *Le Nouvelliste* sometime later, the author Lyonel Trouillot described the role of international actors in his nation's democratic process. "The representative of the European Union and the US ambassador have enormous power of decision over what is being done in Haiti," he wrote. "They are the ones who say if there will be an election or if there will not be. And no matter what the wishes of the Haitian people. It is they who validate them, in fact, who decide that, fraud or not fraud, whatever the rate of participation, the result is acceptable."[26]

It had not been the Haitian people who had spoken in the preceding four-month electoral drama, though there was no questioning that Martelly's popularity had grown throughout the course of it. More than a year since the earthquake, the population's anger with the status quo served as a galvanizing force. And Martelly's *tèt kale* slogan served as an apt metaphor for the disparate hopes that many believed he represented. Literally, *tèt kale* translates as "bald head," but it's also a common Kreyòl phrase meaning "until the end." He was the outsider, the celebrity, the change-maker, the future. And he would fight for Haiti until the end. But he owed his mandate to the same foreign powers and local elite that had attempted to dictate Haiti's future for centuries.

Since Aristide's landmark election in 1990, which had brought together the flood, or Lavalas, of the poor majority, international actors and a corrupt local elite had done everything possible to retain their power and keep the floodwaters at bay.[27] Yet each time Haitians had voted, it was Aristide or Préval that had emerged as president. This time, with $10 billion on the line and the ups and downs of such a high-profile aid effort broadcast around the world, it hadn't been left to chance. In May 2011, almost a year and a half after the earthquake, Préval became the first democratically elected president in Haiti's history to hand power to an opposition politician. And the president of *konpa* was now the president of Haiti.

11

THE COMMISSION

Haiti's new president took office in May 2011 with high expectations. Finally, it seemed the long-stalled reconstruction era had begun. But why had the international community turned on its indispensable man, Préval? There was no question that Préval had never been the front man that the Aid State longed for. Still, what had broken his relationship with the donor class? The former president had his suspicions. It all related back to the Interim Haiti Reconstruction Commission, the Clinton-led body held up by donors as the linchpin of the country's reconstruction.[1]

The commission, created ostensibly to strengthen the government and ensure donors acted in support of its goals, ended up being the government's downfall. It fundamentally altered the balance of power. If Préval had been "indispensable" in managing Haiti before the earthquake, the commission made him dispensable.

This changing dynamic makes sense from a foreign perspective. Donors believed the Préval government did not possess the capacity to oversee the billions in aid pledges, that Haitian political instability had undermined their noble efforts to help. The commission's design intended to make those concerns moot. With an eighteen-month mandate, it would outlast Préval. The commission, its proponents believed, would provide the stability that the government could not. Again, following the aid money directly demonstrated this. In the immediate aftermath of the earthquake, USAID's special forces had branded its programs as coming from the government, provided temporary office space to Préval and his ministers, and spent millions in an attempt to stabilize the administration. After the Clinton-led body began operations over the summer, that was where USAID redirected its program support. USAID provided most of the operating budget and paid for technical advisors to help staff up the commission. There was, however, one big problem with this plan. By the time of the 2010 election in November, just eleven months after the earthquake, the commission itself was collapsing under its own internal contradictions.

The Clinton-led body held its fourth official board meeting in December during the height of the postelection uncertainty. With the capital locked down due to protests, the commission held the meeting in the Dominican Republic. Bellerive, the prime minister and cochair, stayed in Haiti and called into the meeting via Skype. Bill Clinton was late to show. The former president attended board meetings but was rarely active in the commission's work, preferring to turn the day-to-day over to his foundation's staff.

The Haitian representatives on the board decided they had had enough. They met in a side room to prepare a statement. Once the meeting got started, Suze Percy Filippini, a former Haitian diplomat, stood to read it. "The twelve Haitian members present here feel completely disconnected" from the commission's activities, Filippini read. The Haitian representatives, she continued, felt like "bit players" and "tokens."

"We consider it our particular responsibility to ensure the proper functioning of the commission in its mission, so that reconstruction of the country is undertaken in the interests of Haiti and Haitians," the statement, signed by all twelve, concluded.[2]

Bellerive and Clinton were furious. But the internal opposition hadn't come out of nowhere. Two months earlier, Jean-Marie Bourjolly, a Haitian-Canadian university professor and one of the Haitian representatives on the commission, wrote a memo for the board making the same points. By "vesting all powers and authority of the Board in the Executive Committee, it is clear that what is expected of us [the rest of the board] is to act as a rubber-stamping body," he had warned. The memo was never included in the board's minutes.[3]

At the end of the December meeting, Clinton approached Bourjolly, whose memo had catalyzed the internal opposition. He put his hand on Bourjolly's shoulder.

"You embarrassed me," the former president said.[4]

A new Haitian president meant new Haitian representatives on the commission. More than that, inside the Clinton camp that was running the show, the commission's problem stemmed from a decision made by Préval during its creation.

AFTER THE MARCH 2010 donor conference, the commission needed specific legal authorizations to begin operating. There had been concern over Bill Clinton's appointment as UN special envoy in 2009. This new framework went much further. Given the role the new institution would play in directing foreign assistance, the Haitian Parliament had to cede its budgetary powers to the commission.

When Bellerive presented the proposal to members of the Haitian Senate, they questioned the extent to which it empowered foreign actors and if it was even constitutional. The document, they said, sounded too "dependent."

"I hope you sense the dependency in this document," the prime minister shot back. "If you don't sense it, you should tear it up!"

Bellerive acknowledged that the government was badly hurting and reliant on outside actors. But he was hopeful it provided a framework for future development. "I am optimistic that in 18 months, yes, we will be autonomous in our decisions," he had told his fellow Haitian political leaders. "But right now, I have to assume, as prime minister, that we are not."[5]

The task of getting the commission off the ground fell to Cheryl Mills, Hillary Clinton's trusted chief of staff. For two hours on April 14, she met with a group of senators opposed to the deal. The next day, they helped pass it. Nobody knew what had changed, only that something had. Merten, the US ambassador, wrote to Mills and other State Department staff. "Hear the Senate approved. Perhaps what you said had a bigger effect than you thought."[6]

That, however, was only one hurdle. Even with the approval from

Parliament, the commission still needed an executive decree from Préval. Mills had worked closely with one of the president's economic advisors, Gabriel Verret, a Columbia University–educated technocrat who had worked in various roles for USAID and other donors for decades. The big fight over the decree, he explained years later, concerned the language around land tenure. "The donors realized this was the big impediment to doing the larger projects which they wanted, and so they wanted the commission to have the power to designate land for public use," he explained. The first draft of the executive decree, written by Mills and the State Department, gave the commission carte blanche over land. Verret took the proposal to Bellerive, who signed off on it. But Préval said no.[7]

Though he had developed close relations with the international community, the president saw this as a step too far. Land and Haitians' struggle for control over their own had inspired the revolution and shaped much of the rest of the nation's history. Préval stripped out the language around land appropriations and published the decree without consulting Mills, who was, predictably, "pissed off," Verret remembered.

"Mills called me and said they needed land for the camps," Préval explained. "They said I was going to have a big problem, and that Bill [Clinton] needed the authority." There were other projects they wanted land for as well, like a new airport and telecom infrastructure, he remembered. "I said it was not possible, that the law doesn't allow it." Eventually, a compromise was reached, and Préval issued a new decree. Rather than handing the power over to the commission directly, the president created a body within the government to review requests and make determinations. Looking back, Préval identified that decision as the turning point in his relations with the US and the Aid State.

"At this moment, I became evil," he said.[8]

PRÉVAL MAY HAVE taken the brunt of the blame for the commission's failures, but the Haitian representatives' critiques at the December board meeting did not come from out of the blue. After so many years of donors working around the government, they had little idea how to do things differently. Part of the problem was that donors didn't even know how to work with one another. Each country or multilateral organization that had pledged $30 million or more earned a seat at the commission. As Paul Collier had suggested in the weeks after the quake, a chair at the table was how to ensure the EU didn't "sulk."

The presence of Bill Clinton atop the commission, however, made clear where the ultimate power rested.

The commission's original office space was a large tent on the grounds of the former US Embassy compound outside the capital. For months it was mostly empty. While Verret, the Préval advisor who had helped assure the commission's creation, became interim executive director, he had little real authority. As Secretary of State Hillary Clinton deputized the Haiti portfolio to Cheryl Mills, Bill Clinton handed the reins to his longtime confidante Laura Graham, the CEO of his eponymous foundation. The thirty-six-year-old had been with the former president since serving as his scheduler at the White House, but she had little experience managing large-scale disaster relief.

Everything about the commission seemed to be connected to the Clintons. At the first board meeting, two representatives of McKinsey & Company, a New York–based consulting firm, gave a presentation "regarding the mission, mandate, structure and operations of the IHRC," according to the meeting minutes.[9] The firm provided its services pro bono, the fulfillment of a pledge it had made with the Clinton Foundation, which seemed ensnared in potential conflicts of interest given Secretary of State Hillary Clinton's official foreign policy role. Next, attorneys from Hogan Lovells, a global law firm headquartered in Washington, DC—and the firm of the attorney who represented Clinton in his impeachment trial—gave a presentation on the commission's bylaws and codes of conduct. The Clinton Foundation even provided the first $1 million of the operating budget.

One former Haitian government official, who worked closely with the Clintons and their staff at the commission, explained years later that, while Haiti had been lucky to get people as high-profile as Bill and Hillary Clinton, their staff "had no idea what Haiti was like and had no sensitivity to the Haitians." "Out of ignorance, there was much arrogance," the official said. "And who pays the price? The Haitian people, as always."[10]

Even at the time, many Haitians were far less sanguine. "The commission is in fact a coup d'état without an army," Mario Joseph, a Haitian lawyer and human rights advocate, told *Democracy Now!* in the summer of 2010. The bourgeois and the foreigners came together to replace the state, he said. "There was a lot of pressure coming from Clinton and others . . . to legalize this coup d'état. But in reality, the Haitian people don't believe in them, because they didn't participate, there wasn't any transparency at all, and they don't have any accountability to anybody."[11]

It wasn't just Haitians who saw the Interim Haiti Reconstruction Commission as a takeover. From the very beginning, the European Union, and especially France, viewed it as a US-led entity. That was why they refused to provide funding. There was also competition between the commission and the World Bank–managed Haiti Reconstruction Fund. The Clinton-led body existed to coordinate and direct the reconstruction. The Haiti Reconstruction Fund, on the other hand, collected donors' aid dollars and, in theory, channeled them toward the projects approved by the commission. It was this complicated, multitiered system that donors had drawn up ahead of the March aid conference. To make it work, donors had to give up control over how, specifically, their $10 billion in pledges were spent.

In July 2010, making good on the Obama administration's commitment at the donor conference, the US Congress approved $1.14 billion in financial assistance for Haiti. Only about 10 percent of that, $120 million, went to the Haiti Reconstruction Fund. Congress refused to cede control even to that entity. In the end, the entire $120 million went to five different projects that USAID had in its pipeline. The Clinton-led commission quickly approved them. All that had changed was that the money would now pass through the World Bank–managed fund, which took a 7 percent management fee off the top.

Once the US earmarked their contribution, other donors did the same. Josef Leitman, the bank official managing the fund, faced a choice. Accept donor preferencing or end up with nothing. "I made a deal with the devil," he later said.[12] Of the first $360 million that the trust fund received, $300 million was earmarked by donors for their own projects. In the end, this suited donors just fine. If any big donor was submitting a project and they weren't requesting funds, the message was "go ahead and approve it," a former commission official explained. "As long as USAID is submitting it, and USAID is paying for it, approve it."[13]

There had, however, been a reason for the multiple layers of bureaucracy and separate functions. In theory, it provided accountability to donors, ensured coordination, and offered a modicum of transparency. After all, it had been donors' stated fear of Haitian government corruption that supposedly necessitated such a supranational framework in the first place. Of course, Haitians did not have a monopoly on corruption.

The decree authorizing the commission mandated regular audits of its work. In response, the commission contracted with the US-based PricewaterhouseCoopers to design a "Performance and Anticorruption Office." When it came time to select a contractor to run the office, PricewaterhouseCoopers was the favorite to win the $2.5 million contract. France's ambassador objected. The deal was "a pure conflict of interest which damages the integrity of the office," he said, according to the meeting minutes.[14]

The firm got the contract anyway.

By December 2010, when the twelve Haitian board members stood up to publicly denounce the commission, they had good reason. Perhaps the reason Bill Clinton found the spectacle so embarrassing was that, in the end, he knew they were right.

By EARLY 2011, as Préval's mandate came to an end, the Interim Haiti Reconstruction Commission remained "not fully operational," a report from the US Government Accountability Office found.[15] Of the thirty-four positions called for in the commission's structure, twenty-two remained unfilled. Further, the report found it had been difficult to convince donors to fund certain priority areas, such as rubble removal. Commission staff admitted to the investigators that "funding for reconstruction projects is unevenly spread among sectors and does not necessarily reflect Haitian government priorities."

Michel Martelly assumed office the same month the report was released. Among donors, hopes were high that their new partner would be more amenable to their plans. After everything they had done to help put him in the National Palace, that was certainly the expectation. Martelly quickly nominated Daniel Rouzier, a local businessman with international ties, to the post of prime minister. However, before he had even been confirmed, Rouzier blasted the commission as dysfunctional and called for an investigation into what the Clinton-led body had done. "I don't mean to crucify the people who came up with the concept," Rouzier said, "but sometimes when something doesn't work, you have to fix it."[16]

The Associated Press ran an article with Rouzier's comments on May 25. That evening, at 5:14, Hillary Clinton forwarded the article to her chief of staff, Mills.[17]

"What's this about? I thought Bill had agreement w[ith] Martelly."

It was unclear, in the redacted emails, what the agreement had been.

Mills responded, writing that she had already spoken to Rouzier, who claimed he had been misquoted.

"He needs to pull back statement asap before it causes damage to [Bill Clinton] and [the commission]," Clinton responded nine minutes later.

Mills reached out to Damian Merlo, the American political consultant who had worked on Martelly's campaign, to figure out what was going on. Merlo assured Mills that he was "drafting a press release to clarify the situation" and would include some of her thoughts. The statement, released that same day, clarified that the Martelly administration remained "very open and willing to begin discussions" over how to make the commission "more efficient."

Rouzier never became prime minister. The Haitian Parliament rejected his nomination. It took months, but the new administration's second choice did manage to get the approval he needed. In October 2011, Garry Conille was sworn in as prime minister. Conille, a Haitian by birth, had long worked for the UN and, after the earthquake, began working with Bill Clinton in the UN Office of the Special Envoy. When Conille received the prime ministerial post, he was a key member of the team that had effectively been running the commission the past year, indicating just how much political sway the Clintons had.

The Aid State was bleeding into the state itself. Even that, however, proved too little, too late. By the time Conille took office, the Clinton-led body's mandate was nearing its end. Despite pressure from donors, this time, the Parliament refused to budge. After eighteen months, the Interim Haiti Reconstruction Commission closed its doors. The entire relief framework, the linchpin of the "building back better" slogan, simply faded away. Donors were free to return to business as usual. Of course, most had never changed. There was little evidence that the experiment had altered much of anything in terms of donor coordination or effectiveness.

The Performance and Anticorruption Office, run by PricewaterhouseCoopers, released only one report. It provided the lone comprehensive accounting of the Clinton-led body's work. Altogether, the commission had approved eighty-seven projects worth a total of $3.2 billion. Many of them were already planned before the earthquake and would have happened regardless of the commission. Of those projects, only four had been completed. Overall, although not all projects provided financial updates, just $117.7 million was reported as disbursed out of the $3.2 billion, a rate of just 3.7 percent.

Things weren't looking much better at the World Bank–managed Haiti Reconstruction Fund, though at least it provided regular board meeting minutes and financial information. The commission had stopped publishing minutes or updating its website after Clinton had been embarrassed at the December meeting. By the fall of 2011, the fund had allocated $270 million for sixteen commission-approved projects. The money went to implementing partners like the UN, the IDB, and the World Bank itself. Together, the three had only spent about 15 percent of the allocation.[18]

Martelly's election had not been enough to save donors' reconstruction framework. Few Haitians were sad to see it go. Few donors seemed to care. Even the US and the Clintons didn't seem to mind. To donors, the early signs from Martelly were encouraging. With a true partner in the presidency and a former employee serving as prime minister, perhaps the commission wasn't necessary at all. With Martelly in office, the lack of a coordination framework ceased to be a concern for donors. The Aid State, it seemed, had finally found their desired front man.

ON APRIL 6, two days after preliminary results of the election had been announced, Ken Merten and the embassy's political counselor met the president-elect. The campaign team was "clearly in a good mood" and "were grateful for U.S. support of the political process," Merten reported. Martelly, the ambassador continued, was "very interested in a strong partnership with the U.S." He "agreed that development was impossible without significant investment, and he seemed particularly interested by our development programs in the north." After the earthquake, major donors had split the country into regions. Canada took the south, and focused its investment there. The US took the northern region, where it had plans for a new industrial park.

"Martelly's gifts of communication will come in handy in the ensuing months and years," Merten concluded.

Mills forwarded the confidential cable to Secretary Clinton. "Nice intro," she wrote. "Pls be sure Bill is briefed on this before his mtg," Clinton responded. "Done," Mills wrote. Martelly would be coming to DC on the twentieth, she added.[19]

In Washington, Martelly met with officials of the IMF, the World Bank, the US Chamber of Commerce, and, of course, with Hillary Clinton and the State Department. It was the first foreign trip he took after winning the election.

In DC, Clinton told the press that she was "very encouraged by the campaign that Mr. Martelly ran." The US, Clinton continued, was behind him. "We have a great deal of enthusiasm. This is not only a goal of our foreign policy, but it is a personal priority for me, my husband, and many of us here in Washington."[20]

With a new government taking office, USAID's special forces were put to work again. After withdrawing funding from the Préval government during the election, Chemonics and USAID's Office of Transition

Initiatives wanted to ensure the success of the incoming Martelly administration. Embassy and OTI staff met with a representative of the
Martelly camp in late April.[21] "They are looking for 'quick wins' to do in
the first 100 days," a USAID staffer wrote to the team.

"I explained OTI's programs and all our experience and investments
to date, emphasizing our support options in technical assistance and
communications," the staffer continued. "He was interested."

Internally, the political arm of USAID reported that it was "actively
engaged in discussions with the new Martelly Administration and US-
AID/Haiti to prioritize activities during the administration's first 100
days to ensure a smooth transition and facilitate quick and notable government successes."

Chemonics was "coordinating with the U.S. Embassy in Haiti to track
and prioritize requests from President Martelly. To date, the administration has requested additional office space on palace grounds, completion
of the palace perimeter wall, an audio-visual studio for presidential use,
and assistance with a press conference hall," emails obtained through the
Freedom of Information Act later revealed.

On May 10, a Chemonics employee emailed USAID staff with a proposal to "partner with Mouvement Tèt Kale (MTK), a social network of
community-based organizations founded by Michel Martelly campaign
members" to "prepare" the capital for the upcoming inauguration. "This
activity will build on the momentum created by the Martelly victory
to recruit community volunteers to remove waste from the streets of
Port-au-Prince in order to ensure that the city will be clean enough to
welcome their new president."

MTK, the Duvalierist-linked organization that had been putting people in the streets over the previous months to support Martelly, received
$100,000 in supplies from Chemonics. In the days before the inaugura-
tion, pink-clad youth swept the streets and piled debris into wheelbar-
rows in a rapid beautification project.

12

THE SLOGAN

———

The grounds of the still-collapsed National Palace were transformed for Martelly's May 14, 2011, inauguration. The cupola remained askew, still sunken into the French renaissance concrete structure. But a large stage had been erected in front, and on a perfectly sunny afternoon, politicians, foreign diplomats, and eager businessmen filed onto the palace lawn for the day's celebration of hope. No longer "Sweet Micky," soon-to-be-president Martelly arrived with his son Olivier, and his wife, Sophia, donning a well-tailored and neatly pressed dark blue suit and a red tie. Bill Clinton arrived shortly thereafter wearing the same.[1]

The showman took to the stage for the first time as president. With thousands of Haitians pressing up against the faded green wrought-iron fence of the palace, Martelly pledged a new era for Haiti, a new image for Haiti. It was not just poverty that Haiti produced. "Haiti is a rich country, we have the most beautiful beaches in the world, the most beautiful sun of the Caribbean and the deepest culture," he said. "We cannot continue with this humiliation of having to extend our hand for help all of the time." Martelly turned to the foreign diplomats in the audience, and, switching to English, addressed them directly. "I ask the international community to have confidence in me," he said. "This is a new Haiti, a new Haiti open for business now."[2]

It was a phrase diplomats and businessmen had been waiting to hear from the government since the earthquake. In reality, the slogan championed by Martelly and foreign investors was simply a continuation of the mantra that had guided US involvement in Haitian affairs for nearly a century, since at least the US occupation of 1915. The "new" Haiti was starting to look more and more like the old.

The US invasion of Haiti had opened the country to American corporations like Standard Fruit Company, the forerunner to Dole, and Haitian American Sugar Company, or HASCO, which obtained massive amounts of land in its attempt to revive the large-scale sugar production of the colonial era. The republic of Haiti had destroyed the institution of slavery more than a hundred years earlier, but the occupation ushered in a modern re-creation of the export-oriented commodity economy. The sugar plantations displaced small-scale farmers, often with violent force. The average wage at HASCO in the early twentieth century was about thirty cents a day, a little more than four dollars in today's currency.[3] Those low wages, and the nation's proximity to the US market, have always made it attractive to foreign investors.

In 1971, Jean-Claude Duvalier took the reins of the regime after his father's death. With a steady flow of rural-urban migration in the years after Hurricane Hazel, the capital had an abundant supply of cheap labor. For the nineteen-year-old president there was an opportunity for tremendous growth in low-wage manufacturing plants. Baby Doc wanted to reestablish relations with the US, which had maintained its freeze on direct foreign assistance. The new face of the dictatorship eliminated tariffs, promised to keep the minimum wage low (and union organizing a deadly proposition), and allowed US firms to bring 100 percent of their profits back to their home country tax free.

"In fact, tiny Haiti—jammed with 6 million people, most of them unemployed—is emerging as the low-wage capital of the world, the Taiwan of the 80's," *The New York Times* reported in 1984.[4] A year earlier, the US had passed the Caribbean Basin Initiative, easing trade restrictions and allowing greater access for goods produced throughout the region, especially in Haiti. Foreign aid flows increased massively, including through the IMF, World Bank, and IDB. Some three hundred American companies had set up shop in Haiti, the *Times* noted, taking advantage of wages "as low as pay anywhere in the world."[5] At the time, nearly every baseball used in the Major Leagues was sewn in Haiti. CBS

Toys produced Bert, Ernie, and Elmo dolls there. Haitians assembled electronics for global firms.

"It's a country where its greatest natural resource is, uh, its man power," Mark Roberts, the local representative of a US company producing textiles in Haiti, explained in an early 1980s interview. "We have chosen to develop a business around Haiti's greatest resource," he said with a wry smile.[6]

Ironically, the largest export from Haiti during the seventies and early eighties was the Haitian people themselves. Despite record aid flows and multinational investments, hundreds of thousands of Haitians fled the country in search of a better life. In a vicious cycle, the increasing number of migrants was then used to justify more aid and the need for more foreign investment, despite the fact that both were deepening an economic model that made success for most Haitians seem impossible. Just as had been the case centuries earlier, the Haitian economy was dominated by merchants, those who controlled the nation's imports and exports. Foreign investors took advantage of low wages to produce goods for export, while those families that controlled the ports and the crucial import of food items came to control the local economy.

Strong relations developed between Haiti's elite, their corporate allies to the north, and the diplomats responsible for advancing and protecting US interests in Port-au-Prince. Since the fall of the dictatorship, it has been this nexus of power and influence that has sought to control the nation through each of its political transitions. The earthquake was no different.

AT THEIR PEAK, the sweatshops of the capital employed more than one hundred thousand. However, by the time of the earthquake, the industry employed just a small fraction of that. Political instability, most claimed, had been the cause of foreign investors' withdrawal. The earthquake had upended the nation, and yet, as exemplified by the Collier Report, it paradoxically had also created an environment conducive to restarting the growth of the export-oriented economy. Echoing what had taken place in the 1970s, foreign assistance was picking up and would go toward building the necessary infrastructure and rewriting legislation to once again make Haiti's manufacturing industry a global leader. Once again, Haiti would place its foot onto the first rung of the development ladder. As Collier had pointed out, the main attraction remained Haiti's incredibly low wages.

"I've been working in factories here for 25 years, and I still don't have my own house," Evelyne Pierre-Paul told a local investigative journalism team after the earthquake.[7] Pierre-Paul had rented a two-room house before the quake for about $250 a year. In Haiti, rents are often paid up front for the entire year. The house had been destroyed, and Pierre-Paul had been unable to save enough for a new rental. She and her three children had been living in a tent for well over a year by the time she spoke with the journalists. How could the answer to Haiti's development woes come from an industry that prevented those like Pierre-Paul from even renting their own home despite more than two decades of work experience?

Pierre-Paul earned about six dollars a day, which was actually above Haiti's minimum wage of $3.75. The money didn't go very far. An analysis of workers in the capital showed that, on average, some 50 percent of wages went toward travel to and from the factory and for lunch. In 2011, the AFL-CIO linked Solidarity Center estimated that a true living wage in Haiti's factories would be $750 per month for a worker with two children.[8] That was nearly five times the actual minimum wage. In a nation with 70 percent unemployment and a majority of the population living on less than two dollars a day, even these substandard wages were enough to attract workers. Still, as the case of Pierre-Paul shows, it was never enough.

Aristide had been reviled by the nation's elite even before his 1990 election. But as much as anything, it had been his attempts to lift the minimum wage that led to his ouster. The US, through USAID and the National Endowment for Democracy, funneled money to organize the private sector in an attempt to halt Aristide's plans to lift wages. Allying with the military, the business elite helped push Aristide out. History repeated itself in 2004, when the main civil society organization advocating for Aristide's second ouster was led by Andy Apaid Jr., an American businessman and one of the largest purveyors of Haiti's sweatshops. By 2008, the minimum wage adjusted for inflation was worth less than one-quarter what it had been when Aristide was overthrown the first time.

By that point, Haiti's garment factories were producing textiles for some of the world's largest brands. Levi's, Hanes, Fruit of the Loom, and many others all sourced from Haiti. In 2009, the Haitian Parliament passed legislation that would nearly triple the minimum wage to about five dollars a day. At the time, foreign donors, led by recently appointed secretary of state Clinton, were making a renewed push to lure large manufacturers to Haiti. But the ongoing fight in Haiti over the long-stagnant minimum wage was putting these plans at risk. USAID and the Association of Industry in Haiti (ADIH), the main private-sector grouping of factory owners, produced studies showing that the wage increase "would make the sector economically unviable and consequently force factories to shut down."[9]

The US ambassador wrote to Washington in the summer of 2009. "A more visible and active engagement by Préval may be critical to resolving the issue of the minimum wage and its protest 'spin-off'—or risk the political environment spiraling out of control," she reported. Less than a week later, protesters marched to the National Palace to urge passage of the law. "Demonstrators paraded placards with slogans such as 'Down with Préval,' 'Down with the Bourgeoisie,' and 'Our Country is not for Sale Either Wholesale or Retail.' Others . . . bore the names of President Préval, Prime Minister Michele Pierre Louis, and UN Special Envoy Bill Clinton with an 'X' drawn through their names," the embassy reported.[10]

In the end, in his typical fashion, Préval facilitated a compromise. The increase would be phased in and he carved out a lower wage level specifically for the garment industry. Even though, under pressure from the US, Préval had worked to limit the increase, he was never the salesman for the garment industry that international officials and local businessmen wanted.

* * *

It is generally believed that, in the earthquake, the single building in which the most Haitians perished was the Palm Apparel factory in Port-au-Prince. The company said that some three hundred workers died when the factory collapsed. The building had just received significant renovations, and USAID, through an American contractor, had spent hundreds of thousands of dollars ostensibly improving the factory. It took less than two weeks for Palm Apparel to begin sewing T-shirts again. A few months later, USAID paid for Palm Apparel's owner, Alain Villard, to fly to Las Vegas for a trade show. While there, he raised $8.5 million in fresh investments for his company.[11]

"I remember somebody saying a crisis is a terrible thing to waste," Georges Sassine, the head of ADIH, said in February 2010. "It is true. The opportunity has been thrust upon us."[12] And it wasn't just the tiny group of Haitian factory owners who leapt at such an opportunity.[13]

In May, Secretary of State Clinton traveled to South Korea. While there, Cheryl Mills called a group of Korean manufacturers to a meeting at the US embassy to pitch them on Haiti. It was a perfect representation of the administration's new concept of business diplomacy and private-sector-led aid. But it would take more to get the companies on board.

Clinton emailed her assistant on June 27 and asked her to add a name to their call list: "Paul Charron about Haiti."[14] Charron had been the CEO of Liz Claiborne, and, besides being a longtime Clinton corporate friend, he maintained strong relations with the garment industry worldwide. He agreed to help.

In late August, Charron called on an old contact of his, Lon Garwood, who was working as an advisor to Sae-A, one of the world's largest garment companies and a producer for global brands like Walmart, Target, and Gap. "Whittle down the list of obstacles because people in D.C. are really serious about making this happen," Charron told his old friend. Sae-A's CEO, Woong-Ki Kim, flew to Washington. In the State Department's treaty room, the Korean textile magnate, the State Department, and the IDB hashed out in broad strokes a deal that would sufficiently entice the company to Haiti.[15]

Sae-A had been one of two companies the Haitian and US governments were courting. Then, in the fall of 2010, the other company dropped out. The US needed a big win to announce on the first anniversary of the earthquake. Officials needed to do whatever it took to lock in Sae-A.

On January 11, 2011, with the US already pressuring Préval to drop his chosen successor from the upcoming runoff election, Bill Clinton made a brief stop in Haiti. At a USAID-financed training center for garment workers, the State Department, the IDB, the Haitian government, and Sae-A signed a deal to build their shiny new industrial park.[16] It was not in Port-au-Prince as initially planned, but in the north, in a small town called Caracol. Finally, the garment industry backers had their long-awaited win. Sae-A's investment, it was announced at the signing, would create up to twenty thousand direct jobs.

But in order to get such an impressive figure, US and IDB officials had made many promises. "We would say, 'We could probably do a factory with about 3,000 to 4,000 people.' They're like, 'Wow. What would you need to make it bigger?'" Garwood told *The New York Times*. "I said, 'If we could get a loan for the machines, we could probably double that.' They said, 'What about 10,000?' We said, 'If we didn't have to worry about purchasing the land, if we didn't have to build the factory shells, then we could double it again.' That's where the 20,000 jobs figure came from."

In the end, the United States agreed to provide $124 million in support of the project, pledging to build a modern port in the north of the country, new housing for the park's employees, and a private power plant. The IDB, at a cost of $100 million, agreed to build the physical infrastructure of the park. And the Haitian government agreed to provide the land, free of charge, as well as a fifteen-year tax holiday. It was costly but necessary, proponents argued. "This will be a match that strikes a fire, and gets things going," Bill Clinton told the *Wall Street Journal*.[17]

On an early January morning, government trucks and bulldozers arrived in Caracol and began to clear the land. Despite what the IDB had reported in their site analysis, the land in the north was not empty. In fact, it had been used for decades by hundreds of small farmers who produced beans, corn, cassava, and other seasonal crops. Those farming the land were given just a few days' notice. They watched in shock as the fences marking their family plots were torn down, and as their bean crops, almost ready for harvest, were ripped from the ground right in front of them. "I farmed my land for 21 years and was then forced to leave for the construction of this park," Elie Josue later told research-ers.[18] He had put all his kids through school off his earnings from the land, and even hired some one hundred workers each planting season. "If we had the support we needed to farm our land, we would be doing well. Now that I've lost my land, I don't have a penny."

Donor and government officials said those displaced would be first in line for the minimum-wage jobs at the new Korean-owned factory producing T-shirts for Walmart, which happened to be headquartered in Bill Clinton's home state of Arkansas.

MICHEL MARTELLY SPENT much of his first year in office flying across the globe to drum up foreign investment for Haiti, to sell the world on the new Haiti. He had plenty of help, including from his longtime friend Laurent Lamothe. In September 2011, the government created an "advisory board" of politicians, business leaders, and bankers that would help promote Haiti as "a more business friendly place and attract foreign investment." Lamothe was made co-chair of the new thirty-two-member entity alongside Bill Clinton.[19] The reconstruction commission was about to close its doors; the formation of this new group served as the definitive transition from "build back better" to "open for business." Joining Clinton and Lamothe was José María Aznar, a conservative for-mer prime minister of Spain who was also a close associate of the public relations firm that had run Martelly's presidential campaign. Right-wing former presidents from Bolivia and Colombia also joined the board.[20]

Later that same month, Martelly attended the annual Clinton Global Initiative event in New York. The musician turned president mingled with A-list celebrities and some of the world's richest businesspeople. Sharing a stage with the Sae-A chairman, Bill Clinton, the president of the IDB, and others, Martelly once again declared Haiti "open for business" as he paced back and forth, commanding the audience as if they had paid to see him perform.

Clinton was thrilled. "Haiti has always needed someone to make a decision," he said. "This man will make a decision." For those paying attention, it was a direct blow to Préval. "He's a great pitchman learning at the knee of the master," the IDB's Luis Moreno, a former US ambassador to Colombia, said in reference to Martelly, his eyes moving to Clinton as he spoke.[21] After functioning as Haiti's hype man for more than a year, Clinton appeared to finally have the wingman he had so desired.

The deal with Sae-A had been wrapped up even before Martelly had taken office. Nevertheless, bringing the project to fruition was going to take significant action on the part of the Haitian government and foreign donors. But, in their rush to secure a public relations victory, the project's backers had overlooked or downplayed a number of red flags.

In December 2010, the AFL-CIO had sent US officials a five-page memo on Sae-A's past labor violations in Guatemala. *The New York Times* noted that the report "accused Sae-A of using bribes, death threats and imprisonment to prevent and break up unions and said a local union suspected company officials of involvement in a union leader's rape never investigated by Guatemalan authorities." The year prior, Gap had stopped sourcing from the Guatemala plant over labor concerns. Sae-A officials had violently crushed a union drive that had begun in 2005. And though it eventually had been allowed to form, by the time Sae-A signed the deal in Haiti, only seven members of the union were still employed in Guatemala.[22]

There were also environmental concerns. When the site had been selected, no real study of the land had been done. But the project's potential environmental impact was clear. The site was just miles from Caracol Bay, home to one of Haiti's only intact coral reefs and a pristine mangrove forest. The area was set to become Haiti's first marine-protected area, and a river ran straight from the proposed industrial park site to the bay. Access to such fresh water was one of the main reasons the site had been rated so highly in the first place. The first environmental analysis of the project didn't occur until mid-2011, months after the signing ceremony. The report suggested it would be best to move, or even outright cancel, the project. But, it added, the park's cancellation "could call into question the reputation of the parties concerned and could harm the reputation of Haiti as a country that welcomes investment."[23]

The project proceeded as planned.

Post-quake Haiti was a time for action, not for due diligence. The needs were too great, the urgency too high. Despite the concerns, the US stepped up its involvement in the project, again utilizing Chemonics International, the company running the overtly political Office of Transition Initiatives program. USAID wasn't just going to build a port, new housing, and a power plant. They were also running PR for the entire project.

USAID financed the industrial park's website. They placed billboards throughout the north of the country, with each declaring, in English, that Haiti was "open for business." USAID built "informational kiosks" and filled them with brochures about the coming jobs, held town hall meetings to assuage environmental and labor concerns, funded "beautification" projects in Caracol and surrounding towns to help build support. Chemonics provided information packets to government officials, local politicians, businessmen.

In November 2011, for Caracol's official groundbreaking, Chemonics funded the travel of Haitian journalists to come to the ceremony, which was attended by Bill Clinton, Mills, Martelly, Moreno of the IDB, and Chairman Kim of Sae-A. Chemonics provided photography for visiting journalists and handed out press kits. They also had selected a number of local residents and provided them access to the event.[24]

Jean-Louis Warnholz, a student of Paul Collier's at Oxford and an early proponent of the Caracol park, had, since the earthquake, begun working full-time for the State Department. After the event, he emailed his new boss, Cheryl Mills. "The event went well. It was big. Way over . . . 1000 members of the community, most in Caracol Park shirts, over 100 press, all the Senators, Deputies, Ministers, Chambers of Commerce, Mayors . . . the Walmart and Kohls executives were very pleased, great images," he wrote. "Spoke to [Bill Clinton]. He though [sic] it was good."[25]

The next day the party moved back to Port-au-Prince, where the

Clinton Foundation and IDB were hosting the Invest in Haiti Forum. More than a thousand companies had apparently registered.[26] Haiti was truly open for business. And it now had to stay that way. Investment is fickle. Earlier that month, citing increasing labor costs and a new investment in Haiti, Sae-A had closed one of its factories in Guatemala. "A Maquila Closes and Goes to Haiti," a local paper reported.[27]

Haiti had not received such a high level of attention from international investors since the Duvalier days. With a charismatic showman in the presidency, perhaps it was no surprise that donors finally had found the leader to restore Haiti's industry to its Duvalier-era heyday. It was always a curious goal, however.

The manufacturing industry provided steady, albeit low-paying, jobs for a population with few alternatives; and it provided steady profits for multinational corporations. But it was as if nobody remembered that the industry had been built on the back of a dictatorship's repression. Thirty years after the industry's nadir, what remained was predominantly a corrupt local elite who had been sanctioned under the Clinton administration for their support of the 1990 coup and had actively worked to thwart the nation's democratic ambitions ever since.

And as foreign diplomats feted Martelly on the international stage, and Haiti received more positive press and celebrity support than it had in decades, perhaps it was no surprise that the increasingly worrying political situation in the nation was hidden further and further from view. But the image of post-quake stability was tearing at the seams like a seven-dollar T-shirt purchased at Walmart with "Made in Haiti" printed on the tag. In attempting to return Haiti to its Duvalier-era economic golden age, the political situation was increasingly characterized by the kleptocracy and political repression of that bygone era.

13

THE MUSICIAN AND HIS BAND

During the campaign and on his international visits, Martelly had sold the image of a post-politics leader, of a man who could bring a divided country together, break with a history of government corruption, and inspire the masses. His own transformation fit perfectly with the public relations effort of the international community, which desperately wanted to portray its post-quake intervention as a success. But Martelly's politics were no secret in Haiti, nor among the foreign embassies that had enthusiastically backed his presidency. He may have been new to politics, but he wasn't new to Haiti's political struggles. He had just waged them from the stage. Nor did he come to office with a clean history of money management. Yet somehow, the story of how Martelly had risen to the presidency was left untold, obscured by the humanitarian emergency, donor conferences, and celebrity appeal.

Michel Martelly was born in 1961, four years into the rule of Papa Doc Duvalier. His father was a Shell oil executive; Michel and his siblings were raised in the relatively well-off Carrefour neighborhood. Martelly attended high school at the prestigious St. Louis de Gonzague, the same institution Duvalier's son, Jean-Claude, attended a few classes before him. After graduating, Martelly enrolled in the Haitian Military Academy. His stay there was short-lived. In 1984 he impregnated the goddaughter of a Haitian general and had to skip town, moving to Colorado and working in a grocery store.[1]

In 1986, Baby Doc fled Haiti, and Martelly reconnected with an old friend, Sophia Saint-Rémy. She had recently endured a romantic breakup and reached out to Martelly. Within months, he returned to Port-au-Prince to be with her. Both families objected to the relationship. Haiti had long been divided among racial lines, and the relatively lighter-skinned Martelly and Saint-Rémy clans believed the union did not do enough to improve the race. The two married anyway and moved to Miami shortly thereafter.[2]

Without familial support, life wasn't easy. To furnish their new apartment, the couple scoured through dumpsters. They shared one car, and Michel would drop Sophia off three hours before her shift as a word processor so that he could get to his job at a construction site. In 1987, the couple had their first child, Michel-Olivier Martelly. It was time for a change, and the three returned to Haiti.

Back home, Martelly learned how to play the keyboard and started playing in a band with some friends. Duvalier was gone, but the country was still being run by a military junta led by General Henri Namphy, whose brother owned a popular hotel and casino called El Rancho. Martelly started playing there regularly. He eventually got a gig at Le Florville, a nightclub in Kenscoff, a wealthy enclave higher up in the hills overlooking Port-au-Prince.[3] His wife, Saint-Rémy, found work as a typist at USAID, the portfolio of which was massively expanding in the post-Duvalier void.

In 1988, with the country in turmoil and Haiti's old guard hanging on to power against a burgeoning pro-democracy movement, many popular musicians were penning paeans to the movement and against the repression, but Martelly was singing a different tune. *Konpa,* and its generally lighthearted lyrics, had been the only music officially allowed under the dictatorship. That same year, he dropped his first single, "Ou La."

"Life is good for me," he sang, "and everything I have is for you." In 1989, Martelly released an album under the same title of his hit song. "Sweet Micky" had arrived.

The musician's ties with the military proved helpful. The night of the 1991 coup, while Sweet Micky was performing in Arcahaie, a town about an hour outside the capital, a military friend approached him onstage. "End the party now because there are some problems in the capital," the friend told Martelly, who listened and had no problem passing through the roadblocks on the way home.[4] After Aristide's ouster, many musicians fled the country amid the military-backed repression, but not Martelly. He and his wife had been relieved to see Aristide sent into exile. During the junta years, Sweet Micky ran the Garage, a bar and club frequented by the military and economic elite.

Martelly also developed a friendship with Colonel Michel François, one of the coup's leaders who, not coincidentally, also went by the nickname Sweet Micky. François was chief of police in the capital and, in 1993, asked Martelly to play at a political rally opposing the arrival of a UN official coming to negotiate the return of Aristide. Martelly agreed, he later explained, not because he was François's friend, but because he would do anything to ensure that Aristide was not able to return.[5]

In October 1994, twenty thousand US soldiers landed with Aristide in tow. Martelly remembered hearing his music playing from some of the American tanks as they rolled through the capital. His older brother, Gerard, had joined the US Army and had been among those invading troops.[6] Martelly and his wife became close with some high-ranking US military officials stationed in Haiti at the time as well as some in the US Embassy, including spokesman Stanley Schrager, who lived in the same neighborhood. By the end of 1995, however, the couple was spending most of their time in self-imposed exile in Miami, where Martelly's tracks were becoming increasingly political.

That same year he released "Prezidan," in which he sang of the need for Haiti's new president to come from *konpa*. "This is Sweet Micky at the army headquarters," he sang. "This is the president at the National Palace." In an interview in the spring, he declared that if he was elected president to replace Aristide, he would "perform nude on top of the National Palace." Martelly even changed his answering machine at his Miami condo. "This is the president," it said. "I'm not here right now. Leave your name. I'll get back to you."[7]

The nickname stuck. He was *Msye Prezidan*, Mr. President—of *konpa*—no matter what country he was in.

* * *

SWEET MICKY DID not compete, let alone win, in the 1995 presidential elections, which saw Préval elected for his first term. Their relationship was no better than Martelly's had been with Aristide. The following September, Martelly flew to Miami and gave a radio interview alleging he had been warned of an assassination plot and that it had been planned by close associates of Préval.[8] The president's rule was tenuous and rumors of a coup led by officials from the former military, which Aristide had disbanded upon his return to power, grew louder throughout his first year in office.

The military, which had run Haiti as a narco-state after the ouster of Aristide, was organizing itself against the new government and stockpiling weapons inside the country. Michel François was arrested in the Dominican Republic on charges of conspiring to overthrow Préval. And in Miami, police arrested two Haitians, Gesner Champagne and Serge Cantave, who were attempting to illegally ship forty-eight handguns to Haiti. Champagne's address, according to the police report, was a Biscayne Bay condo that the Martellys had purchased a few years earlier. Martelly used the condo as collateral to pay Champagne's $150,000 bond.[9]

By 1997, Martelly was living mostly back in Port-au-Prince. In a gated community in Pétion-Ville, the Martellys' neighbors included the Canadian ambassador and the old house of General Raoul Cédras, another of the indicted drug-trafficking coup generals. The US government had since taken over the building.

From his perch, he continued his verbal assault on the Haitian government in music and in print. "In the past ten years Haiti has changed dramatically," Martelly told Elise Ackerman of the *Miami New Times* in a 1997 interview.[10] "It used to be a country under a strong regime. Now it's a jungle. It's like anyone can slap anyone else anywhere, anytime. As a matter a fact, not anyone can slap anyone else. The poor can slap the rich and the rich cannot even slap them back," he said. It was an example from close to home. His wife said she had been slapped by a street vendor after she had accidentally run over some of her products. Saint-Rémy said she had offered to pay the vendor, but instead, the vendor slapped her. She remembered the woman telling her, "I just wanted the satisfaction of having smacked a white woman."

"Everyone is asking for Duvalier," she told Ackerman. Her grand-mother had been detained under Papa Doc and two of her family members executed, but the alternative of Préval and Aristide now seemed even worse. Or maybe someone like her husband, Sweet Micky, could change Haiti for the better? He was happy to entertain the notion.

"First thing, after I establish my power, which would be very strong and necessary, I would close that congress thing. La chambre des deputes. Le senat," Martelly told Ackerman. He said that he would outlaw demonstrations and restore the military, whose poor rights record, he believed, was "greatly exaggerated." He defended his old acquaintance Michel François, who after his arrest was granted political asylum in Honduras and then indicted by the US along with dozens of other military officials for drug trafficking.

"To be honest, one thing I can tell you about the army [is that] if they did kill people, if they did, it was during the coup d'etat," Martelly said. "And I know that a coup d'etat is not like a party. A coup d'etat is a coup d'etat. You will definitely find people who went over the limit. You will find people like that. Just like you find people now doing things they shouldn't be doing. But don't make me say that Michel Francois killed people or the Macoutes killed people, because I wasn't there. Just like nowadays there are people being shot, and I can't tell you who is pulling the trigger."

By 2003, Aristide was back in the National Palace. But no longer were the political divisions quite so clear. During his second term, allegations of human rights violations and public corruption had steadily increased. The economy, partially as a result of an aid blockade imposed by the Bush administration, was flatlining. Aristide faced his usual enemies—both foreign and domestic—but by the end of 2003, as violence increased and political tolerance lessened, even many of his supporters in the middle and intellectual class who had fought the Duvalier dictatorship themselves had become disillusioned with the country's first democratically elected president. Martelly again lent his star power to the anti-Aristide movement.

In December, a group of more than a thousand musicians and artisans organized a free concert to ask for Aristide's resignation. "When I was a student here 20 years ago," Martelly said, "I used to sing against the dictatorship."[11] That part wasn't exactly true. Twenty years earlier, in 1983, Martelly had been enrolled in the Haitian Military Academy. "Twenty years later nothing's changed," he said. Within three months, Aristide had been ousted for a second time. As UN soldiers engaged in a class war with Haiti's popular neighborhoods, bastions of support for the ousted Aristide, Martelly moved the family back to Miami.

After Préval's election for a second term in 2006, Martelly, now in his midforties, decided to give up the concert scene and party life and retire back in Port-au-Prince. As he prepared to leave Miami, the musician sat down with a local journalist for the *Palm Beach Post*, Liz Balmaseda. The president of *konpa* was still entertaining his own political ambitions.

"With the popularity I have and the dedication I have to help my people, you never know how it's going to play out," he told Balmaseda. "I can't wait to go back," he said. "Here, I'm just a number. In Haiti, I am The President."[12]

THE TRANSFORMATION FROM Sweet Micky to President Martelly did not happen overnight. Michel Martelly launched his 2010 presidential campaign not in Haiti, nor even in Miami, but thousands of miles north in Montreal, Canada, home to a thriving Haitian diaspora population. In early August, donning jeans and a white shirt with the top few buttons undone, Sweet Micky stood in front of a friend's camera. It was likely his first campaign speech, though it was unclear who would ever see it.[13]

"Well, switching from being a musician to becoming the head of state is not much of a problem for me," Martelly, the candidate, explained. "First of all, I will tell you that they've been calling me president in my country for the last fifteen years. And with the character that I have, I can lead. I've been in charge of my band for the last twenty-two years and it's like I've been the chief. I've been the chief. I place the orders, I tell them what I want. I tell them what song I want. It's like me telling my government what vision I have for them to follow."

It was a crude beginning. And the press conference that had been scheduled wasn't much of an improvement.

The event had been coordinated by Martelly's friend, the former Fugees member Pras Michel. They had done the musician thing, Pras told Sweet Micky before he entered the small room of foreign journalists; now, it was time to do politics. Beads of sweat were growing on the musician's head. This wasn't like his previous stage performances. He took two fingers, deeply rubbed his eyes, wiped his face with his hands, and walked into the press conference.

After some brief remarks and a few questions, including one journalist asking why he wanted to be president since it was "like wanting to be the captain of the Titanic," Martelly stood up next to Pras for a photo op. It took two attempts after a photographer noticed Martelly's zipper was down.

"Because I have something to show, man," he whispered to Pras with a smile.

Afterward, during a local radio interview, Martelly became irate with a diaspora political analyst, who questioned his ability to lead given his raunchy stage antics.

"I'll answer it simply for you," Martelly responded. "There's the actor, there's the artist, there's the person, and then there's the perception. What you understood is the stupidity because that's all you are able to understand. But in the lyrics of Sweet Micky there was this concerned citizen. A citizen who was aware of the problems in his country. When we speak of the artist . . . you need to completely disassociate the artist with the person. And I'll tell you why . . . if Christopher Reeve was really Superman, he wouldn't be dead like he is. You must absolutely disassociate the actor from the person. Superman would not be dead like Christopher Reeve is."

The interviewer walked out of the studio.

The candidate was going to need some polish.

That fall, with few taking Martelly's candidacy seriously, one of the musician's closest friends, Laurent Lamothe, called on a business associate, a Spanish telecoms executive named Ricardo Olloqui, for some

assistance. Olloqui called in a favor and set up a meeting for the campaign in Miami with Antonio Sola, the principal at Ostos y Sola, a political consultancy with deep ties to the conservative party in Spain.[14]
The firm had a roster of dozens of clients and had run high-profile presidential campaigns, including the 2006 election of Felipe Calderón in
Mexico, which had a reputation for being one of Mexico's dirtiest. Sola
had played a leading role.

At the meeting, Sola brought an American who had recently joined
his firm as executive director, Damian Merlo, who, in his own words,
"couldn't locate Haiti on a map." Merlo had been a foreign policy advisor to John McCain during the 2008 presidential campaign and prior
to that had been employed by the International Republican Institute,
the US-funded organization that actively supported the 2004 coup in
Haiti. He had also worked at Otto Reich Associates, a Washington consultancy. Reich, who worked under both Reagan and the first Bush, had
later served as the State Department's top official for Latin America in
the early 2000s and had been an integral part of the US efforts to undermine Aristide. Reich was also increasingly involved in the telecoms
industry. One of his firm's clients had recently been sold to the Olloquis.

Merlo and Sola agreed to help the Sweet Micky campaign. "They
didn't have an agenda," Merlo explained years later. They didn't have
polling. They didn't have a press office. "They had this notion that you
campaign where people like you. We had to change that."[15]

The Spanish firm hired a local company to conduct focus groups.
"Where would you like to be in four years' time?" "What's the outlook
for the economy?"

The first part of the strategy was changing the perception of Michel
Martelly as nothing more than Sweet Micky. No more undershirts onstage. They would be replaced by the stately blue and red. The second
part was portraying Martelly as a political outsider, despite his well-
established links to the former military regime and public feuding with
Aristide and Préval. The firm wanted Martelly to be "a man who is not
part of the system," Merlo explained.

* * *

MARTELLY'S SIGNATURE CAMPAIGN promise during his 2010 run for the presidency was the restoration of the military. For those familiar with the musician's background, it made perfect sense. But, the Spanish public relations firm that had started managing his campaign largely succeeded in turning Martelly into a political outsider. The press wasn't concerned with Martelly's decades-long dalliance with the loathsome military, but some did start to look into his financial background given that he was ostensibly in line to oversee billions in donor assistance, even if almost all of that would end up bypassing the government altogether.

"He's clean. He's clean. He's clean," Sola told the press after the controversial first round of voting. Sola said his team had done "extensive due diligence" before agreeing to take Martelly on as a client. "Michel doesn't have any mortgages. No debt. Nothing. He doesn't owe anything to anyone."[16]

In March 2011, as Martelly campaigned ahead of the second-round election, the *Miami Herald* reported that banks had foreclosed on three of the candidate's properties in south Florida.[17] Martelly claimed never to have lived in any of them, which he said he had purchased solely as investments. Merlo defended his client. "Every successful businessman has transactions that are not as successful all the time. He is one of the most successful businessmen in Haiti and is hoping to transfer those skills as president of Haiti," he said. "Even Donald Trump went into foreclosure. It doesn't relate to running a country."

According to Florida property records, from 2005 to 2007, Martelly purchased four homes, the most expensive a $910,000, six-thousand-square-foot, five-bedroom home on Wellington View Drive in Royal Palm Beach. He was able to flip his first purchase and nearly double his money, but, by 2007, the market was beginning to turn. He stopped payment on the remaining three Florida properties in 2008. The next year, they went into foreclosure. Court employees couldn't find Martelly to deliver the summons, as he had moved back to Haiti. By late 2010, as Martelly was running for the presidency, court proceedings were underway in Florida to auction off all the foreclosed properties.

But while Martelly had purchased a number of properties in his own name, he also was increasingly involved with a group of diaspora businessmen led by Laurent Lamothe and Patrice Baker, owners of Global Voice Group, a global telecoms firm that sold prepaid phone cards in the States and telephone tracking equipment to governments, mostly in Africa. The front man for the calling card company was Sweet Micky. The foreclosed homes were far from Martelly's only investments.

Beginning in 2002 a series of LLCs and holding companies were registered from Miami to Panama to the British Virgin Islands. In many cases Lamothe and Martelly were listed as directors or managers themselves, along with other closely linked business associates.[18] On January 28, 2002, a British Virgin Islands–based company, Lightfoot Ventures Ltd., was created. A week later, in Miami, lawyer Raul Bajandas signed the paperwork to create Coco Grove Holdings, Inc., another shell company. Between 2002 and 2006, holding companies associated with the businessmen purchased five Florida homes for a total cost of $2.1 million. But the big purchase was still to come.

In May 2010, Coco Grove Holdings purchased a luxury home at 560 Gate Lane in Miami, Florida, for $1.7 million. According to corporate filings, the company was controlled by Lightfoot Ventures, the shell company formed by Michel Martelly, Laurent Lamothe, and Patrice Baker. A real estate advertisement at the time described the home as a "gentle paradise nestled amid perfectly manicured gardens and koi ponds." The home had previously been owned by former Major League Baseball player Livan Hernandez.

Hernandez's agent, Juan Iglesias, who also handled many of the Cuban's real estate transactions, remembered that the buyers had a problem with the financing of the home. The closing was delayed multiple times, he told me years later. Eventually, the buyers agreed to increase their offer by $250,000.

"In one of the documents, they crossed out the entire financing section," Iglesias explained. "At the time, we didn't think twice, Livan [Hernandez] needed the money and they had it."[19] Florida property records indicate the house was purchased without a mortgage. It was purchased in cash. The title was then promptly transferred to yet another corporate shell, obscuring the money trail even further.

In August 2010, two weeks after Martelly launched his presidential campaign, Lamothe signed a $700,000 balloon mortgage on the new property. Using cash to buy a house, then promptly taking out a mortgage on said house is a tried-and-true way to launder money.

Bill Hardin, a real estate expert at Florida International University, described the purchase of the house, transfer to a different corporate entity, and subsequent mortgaging as "atypical" but not necessarily nefarious. It could be to hide the presence of another investor, Hardin speculated, adding that "every transaction is in a legitimate format, but was the actual cash involved obtained in the proper environment? In essence, was that legitimate cash?"[20]

It's unclear if the money from the mortgaging of the Gate Lane mansion went toward Martelly's fledgling presidential bid, but Lamothe did provide financing for the campaign. Martelly was the ideal front man, relishing the limelight and soaking up attention, but few seemed to notice the quiet businessman in the shadows, Laurent Lamothe, or the global telecoms firm he owned with Martelly, Global Voice Group. It had been the two's connections in the telecoms world that had brought the Spanish firm onto the campaign. And it is these relationships, more so than any in Haiti, that help to explain the brash musician's transformation from bawdy musician to internationally feted statesman. But despite his unusual background, the ghosts from Haiti's past were salivating at the opportunity.

14

THE GHOSTS OF THE PAST

In the days before January 12, 2012—the two-year anniversary of the earthquake—the Haitian government built a wooden stage and a grandstand to host the commemoration events in Titanyen. Located about fifteen miles north of the capital, Titanyen is a small community on a hillside overlooking the bay of Port-au-Prince. It's also where tens of thousands of bodies had been buried in the aftermath of the earthquake. The year prior, thousands of small wooden crosses had been placed in the topsoil as a reminder of those lost. It had seemed a natural place for the dead, having served as a mass grave for victims of the Duvalier dictatorship decades prior.

On the day of the two-year anniversary, foreign officials and government representatives filled the newly erected pavilion. In the front row sat Bill Clinton and, a few seats down, Martelly. On one side of the president was Jean-Claude Duvalier, and on the other, Prosper Avril, the head of the military junta that ran Haiti following Duvalier's fall. All together they sat, above the ground that contained the untold horrors of the past. The past, however, seemed to be coming back to life.

When Duvalier had landed in Haiti in the midst of the electoral crisis a year earlier, many expected his imminent arrest, that he would finally face justice for the corruption and human rights abuses that characterized his reign. They were disappointed. Duvalier was represented by a group of Americans, including former Georgia congressman Bob Barr, an ex-CIA officer who had been stationed in Haiti during the 1970s, and a lawyer, Ed Marger, who had been on Papa Doc's payroll as a public relations man in DC. Together they attempted to reshape the former dictator's image, even reminding him to smile at the end of his public remarks.[1]

Facing a litany of corruption and human rights–related charges, Duvalier presented himself before a court upon his return. But, rather than being thrown in jail to await trial, Duvalier was allowed to live in a luxury villa in the hills above the capital. He dined in Pétion-Ville's finest restaurants and met with leading politicians and businesspeople. Meanwhile, his son, Nicolas Duvalier, was named a consultant to Martelly. Louis-Jodel Chamblain,[2] the former paramilitary leader who had accompanied Duvalier to court upon his return to the country, was put in charge of presidential security. Two brothers, Thierry and Gregory Mayard-Paul, with close family links to the Duvalier regime, also received posts in the Martelly government.[3]

In the fall of 2011, Martelly visited Duvalier at his villa. The president also met with Avril, the military junta leader, and Jean-Bertrand Aristide, who had kept a low profile since his return from exile. "It's time for us again to be one nation, stand behind one project," the president said outside Duvalier's home. The project, however, was his own. And while he was touring the world promoting Haiti as "open to business," in Haiti, Martelly was going about living up to his campaign promise, which had been the restoration of the Haitian military. He pledged to move forward despite opposition from those who saw the military as a force for political repression. "I don't want people to think that I won't start without them," Martelly said. "I will start without them if they don't start moving." Like Clinton had said, Martelly was a man of action.

It wasn't time to look back at previous atrocities, but rather, to move forward. The legal proceedings against Duvalier stalled. "He will be cleared of all charges," the former dictator's lawyer said just days after Bill Clinton shook Duvalier's hand at the two-year-anniversary event. "It is almost finished now; the judge is typing up the order to throw it all out."[4] Empowered by Martelly's calls for the restoration of the military, and by the return of Duvalier, former army officials began occupying abandoned bases and other buildings throughout the country.

Despite a long record of human rights abuses, including summary executions, Baby Doc only faced charges related to his financial crimes. When he had fled the country, officials estimated he absconded with at least $300 million that he had stashed away in European bank accounts.[5] It had been a true family kleptocracy. A civil case in Florida determined the total stolen to be just over $500 million, though none of the money awarded to Haitian plaintiffs was ever recovered.[6] By 2012, history appeared to repeat itself in more ways than one.

IN FEBRUARY 2012, Garry Conille, the Clinton staffer-cum–prime minister, resigned. It came as little surprise. He had been feuding with Martelly nearly from his first days in office, when he announced that he would conduct an investigation into a number of multimillion-dollar contracts awarded during the presidential transition in the spring of 2011. Corruption, of course, had been the reason that virtually all donors had decided to entirely bypass the Haitian government with their aid. Well, all donors except for one: Venezuela.

At the 2010 donor conference, Venezuela had pledged more than any other nation to Haiti's recovery. They canceled hundreds of millions in debt, and promised many hundreds more in fresh financing. The money would come from the country's PetroCaribe initiative, a program launched in the mid-2000s whereby Venezuela provided oil to Caribbean governments at preferential prices. The governments could then turn around and sell the oil at market prices, paying only a small portion back to Venezuela and keeping the remainder as a long-term loan with extremely low interest rates. PetroCaribe was different from traditional foreign aid. In theory, it was South-South cooperation at its finest, providing governments with direct influxes of cash to undertake big infrastructure projects and implement new social programs.

Préval had brought Haiti into the program in 2008, against the strong pushback of the US Embassy and multinational oil companies. Though the program would provide very real benefits to Haiti, US officials worried that the program would allow Venezuela to extend its influence throughout the region, while oil giants like Shell and Exxon worried the cheap Venezuelan fuel would displace their own.[7] Once Martelly took office, few expected Haiti to deepen its relationship with Hugo Chávez, whom the US was still trying to isolate and undermine. But that is exactly what happened.

Martelly traveled to Caracas for a regional summit in his first year, and met privately with the Venezuelan president. Laurent Lamothe, the president's longtime business partner who was appointed foreign minister, traveled multiple times to Venezuela. If the US was so influential over the new Haitian government, why did the administration seemingly look the other way when it came to Martelly and Lamothe's friendly relations with the hemisphere's perceived number one enemy? Perhaps post-quake Haiti was actually a time when all nations put their own interests aside and came together for the good of their neighbor. But there is little evidence that was ever the case.

I have a different theory. The US and the rest of the international community understood that Haiti's new government—and perhaps just as important, new political leaders—would need access to money to ensure its continued strength inside Haiti. Nobody, however, wanted to give up control over their own pots of gold. Except Venezuela. While their own aid budgets could continue to support the aid-industrial complex, the influx of cash from Venezuela would keep Martelly off their backs while keeping their new friend in power. When international officials overseeing Haiti's finances realized most of it was being misused, it wasn't really a problem. It wasn't their money. It would also, over time, undermine the case for PetroCaribe in other countries.[8]

By the time Martelly took office, PetroCaribe was pumping hundreds of millions of dollars into state coffers each year. It was money that could be spent with little to no oversight. The PetroCaribe money was never officially part of the government's budget; rather, the council of ministers could directly approve projects without any legislative involvement. Martelly and Lamothe launched new conditional cash transfer social programs, the kind traditional donors had long been loath to support but which had proven tremendously successful in Brazil, Mexico, and across the world. They broke ground on new highway developments that would finally decongest Port-au-Prince's notorious *blokis,* which translates to "traffic jam," but encapsulates so much more. Long rows of multistory concrete residential buildings sprang up on the outskirts of the capital. But from the beginning, allegations of corruption surrounded the Venezuelan-financed projects.

The contracts that Conille wanted to investigate all concerned PetroCaribe funds.[9] It was a family affair. In early 2012, the government approved some $230 million in new PetroCaribe-financed projects. One, a program to build soccer stadiums across the country, was managed by Martelly's son, Olivier. Another, a new social program, would be overseen by the first lady, Sophia Saint-Rémy.

On February 27, not long after Conille's resignation, Laura Graham, the head of the Clinton Foundation, wrote to a top aide of Bill Clinton with an urgent message.[10] Conille's "life has and continues to be threatened by people associated with" Martelly, she wrote. "The US—Cheryl [Mills]—promised him American backed security immediately but when he met with [US ambassador] Merten yesterday Merten was not only in the mind frame of 'well [Martelly] is not such a bad guy and he's better than previous presidents' but he didn't discuss or offer any security. Every day, [Conille's] life and reputation are at risk."

Graham wrote again an hour later after Conille had shared a preliminary version of his report into the questionable contracts. "[Martelly] is saying he will come after [Conille] with everything he's got to prevent the real details (presumably including his take) from coming out."

Conille was also feeding Graham information about the former military officers occupying bases across the country. In a separate email, Graham wrote that she had just seen a UN intelligence report on the occupied military bases. "The evidence is clear as day" that the palace was supporting at least some of the groups, she wrote. Conille had told Graham that he had asked the justice minister three times to act against the occupying forces, but that Martelly had "squashed it because he's backing them financially and with arms."

"He has to act and show he's for democracy or there needs to be consequences," Graham wrote. "Waiting for this truck [without] brakes to hit the bottom of the hill will be too late." Washington, she continued, could "not afford to sit on the sidelines." After all Washington had done to bring Martelly into the presidency, American officials bore a certain responsibility. "They elected him and they need [to] pressure him. He can't go unchecked," Graham concluded.

CONILLE'S RESIGNATION, HOWEVER, opened the door for Martelly to further consolidate his hold on power. Lamothe had served as foreign minister after Martelly's election, but he had always wanted the position of prime minister. Securing the approval of Parliament, where a majority was still allied with former president Préval, seemed impossible. Lamothe, however, had a trick up his sleeve: Global Voice Group.[11] He had managed the company for more than a decade. In recent years the company had secured a number of extremely profitable deals in Africa, allying with some of the continent's most brutal dictators, like Yahya Jammeh in the Gambia. At one point, the coach of the Gambia's national soccer team was being paid by Global Voice.[12]

Basically, the company sold equipment to governments that allowed regulators to collect a small tax on every international phone call. The government would take its share and Global Voice the rest. Lamothe's strategy for getting Parliament's approval was shockingly straightforward: buy it. And to do so, he used his corporate checkbook. "It would probably have been illegal in most countries because of the conflict of interest," Damian Merlo, who helped run the Martelly campaign and then became an advisor to Lamothe, later explained, "but [Global Voice] didn't have business interests in Haiti."[13]

That last part was only partially true. Before his inauguration, Martelly gathered the main cell operators in Haiti, including Digicel, run by one of Bill Clinton's closest associates, the Irish billionaire Denis O'Brien, to explain his plans to impose a five-cent tax on phone calls coming from abroad. The companies agreed. As president, the new tax was one of the first big announcements. The funds would be collected by the government and channeled toward an education initiative. It was exactly the scheme that Global Voice had made millions implementing in Africa.

In order to ease the transition, Martelly had retained Préval's prime minister, Jean-Max Bellerive, who also happened to be Martelly's cousin. Within months of the new president taking office, Lamothe approached Bellerive to ask him to buy the equipment needed for the telephone tax. He said no.[14]

Bellerive only lasted a few months, however, and once he was gone, the government signed a contract with the Swiss-based Société Générale de Surveillance (SGS) to monitor and tax international calls. That same year, SGS entered into an exclusive partnership with Global Voice Group to implement telecom solutions in Africa.[15] The two companies later instituted similar monitoring and tax operations in Rwanda, Tanzania, and a handful of other African nations. SGS received the contract, but also used a subcontractor in Miami. Bellerive was sure that company was somehow connected to Lamothe and Martelly.

In Haiti, the new tax raised tens of millions of dollars in just the first few months after its implementation. At the 2011 Clinton Global Initiative event in New York, Digicel's O'Brien, after praising Martelly, talked up the scheme as a revolutionary new way to raise government revenue and support Haiti's development. But, only a few months later, there was a report that $26 million dedicated to the new education fund was missing. "I've spoken with President Martelly about this, and there will be an audit," O'Brien told The New York Times. "I will make it my business that it will be audited, one way or the other."[16]

Within days, however, O'Brien walked back his comments. The Haitian government then sent a threatening letter to a small diaspora-owned, Florida-based news outlet that had reported on the Digicel CEO's comments, even though they remained in the pages of the Times. "If this smear campaign against the Haitian government or the Free Education initiative continues," the letter warned, "we will have no other choice but to seek redress for injury and assert our legal and equitable rights."[17] The threats worked. Most news outlets dropped the story altogether. There was no audit. Later that month, O'Brien used his private jet to fly Martelly and Lamothe to Davos for the World Economic Forum.[18] It would prove to be a trend; accountability was anathema in a Haiti "open for business."

After returning to Haiti, Martelly named Sean Penn an ambassador-at-large for the country.[19] In June, he bestowed the same title on Czech supermodel Petra Nemcova.[20] Both had been deeply involved in relief efforts after the quake and rekindled their romantic relationship.[21] Haiti wasn't just some politically unstable island in the Caribbean anymore, it wasn't just about earthquake refugees and humanitarian aid, it was sexy. It wasn't just page one articles about devastation, but page six articles about celebrity intrigue. After Lamothe became prime minister, he named Penn as his "special advisor." Within a few months, Nemcova and Penn split and she began dating Lamothe.[22] A world-famous musician and a businessman with a supermodel girlfriend were representing the government, and were getting celebrity backing at every turn. This was a new Haiti.

At the official opening of the Caracol Industrial Park in October 2012, a star-studded cast made the journey to the north of the country. Both Penn and Nemcova gave speeches extolling the virtues of the new government and their focus on development. Richard Branson, the billionaire British airline executive, was in attendance, as were Ben Stiller and New York fashion designer Donna Karan. And of course, Bill and Hillary Clinton attended. Secretary Clinton piled praise on the new president, declaring Martelly Haiti's "chief dreamer and believer."[23]

The next month, at an investor conference held in the capital, Bill Clinton took the stage to heap further praise on Lamothe and Martelly. "In my relatively long experience dealing with this country in one capacity or another, this government is the first I have dealt with that seems more concerned about getting something done every day than with the continuous political wars that have gone on," the former president said. "Everybody on this stage wants prospective investors to make money. We don't think it's a bad thing to make a profit. We just want you to make money in a way that helps the Haitians, too."[24]

Behind the curtain of reconstruction and pro-business progress, however, a fledgling democracy was slowly slipping away. While Lamothe and Martelly were busy parading around the world selling their image of a new Haiti, antidemocratic forces were seizing new ground politically. In 2012, the terms of mayors throughout the country expired, as did those for one-third of the thirty-member Senate. The

Martelly government had failed to organize elections. Instead, the government appointed new mayors by decree. After pushing elections in the immediate aftermath of the earthquake, it appeared international officials no longer cared so much about the electoral timeline and constitutional norms.

With such a high-profile aid effort, and all the US had done to usher Martelly into the presidency, there was little the US administration was willing to do about the democratic slippage of its newest ally. As the third anniversary of the earthquake approached, the foreign aid industry was failing to deliver the results that had been promised. But any criticism was treated as a threat to Haiti's new image, the carefully crafted image embodied by the musician and his band.

15

THE PROMISED LAND

In the fall of 2012, investigative reporter Deborah Sontag of *The New York Times* authored a series of articles highly critical of the international response to the earthquake. The final installment, "In Reviving Haiti, Lofty Hopes and Hard Truths," ran more than five thousand words and got front-page treatment just weeks ahead of the third anniversary. "If you ask what went right and what went wrong, the answer is, most everything went wrong," a former prime minister of Haiti told the reporter.[1] In Washington, questions about the success of the relief efforts grew louder with each new report, as members of Congress asked for greater accountability on the hundreds of millions of US taxpayer dollars spent. "Where did the money go?" everyone wanted to know. It was a question few seemed interested in answering honestly. After years of star-studded events with A-listers and businesspeople jostling for position at the latest aid-financed project, by the time of the third anniversary of the disaster, some of the shine had come off the recovery efforts. In Haiti, the commemoration event would be more subdued than in years past.

The once small town of Titanyen, where thousands lay buried in mass graves, was where the event would be held once again. After navigating the traffic and debris-clogged streets of Port-au-Prince, it's a straight shot out past Cité Soleil and Zoranje, where supermodel Petra Nemcova's charity built a school after the earthquake. Eventually, you come to Route National 1, the main thoroughfare to the country's north, which hugs the coast past beach clubs and banana farms for some forty miles before turning inland.

Titanyen sits on an arid hillside just after the turn onto Route National 1. From downtown Port-au-Prince, it can take hours, especially if traveling in public transportation known as *tap taps,* the small pickup trucks whose beds have been retrofitted to pack in as many riders as possible. But on the back of a friend's *moto,* zigzagging through the metallic mosaic of perpetually congested traffic, we made the fifteen-mile journey in about thirty minutes.

The memorial site was little more than a dusty parking lot with a few dozen SUVs lined up along the side. The actual memorial was a large chunk of rock, like the debris in the capital still visible three years later, set in a circular, black-tiled stand. *"Nou Pap Janm Bliye"*—"We Will Never Forget" in Kreyòl—the small sign read. The grand pavilion that had been built for the prior year's commemoration was gone. In its place stood a small wooden viewing gallery painted white, two unattended matching kiosks, and a neat row of nine porta-potties. Haitian police dotted the perimeter.

As I climbed farther up the hillside to look back across the bay and toward the capital, I noticed the thousands of memorial crosses that had been meticulously placed two years earlier had been burned. Hundreds of yards of charred earth provided a stark, likely not-so-welcome backdrop for the event—and grist for the speculating crowd of journalists. Maybe it was arson; maybe it was a controlled burn gone wrong; maybe it had been a spirit or even an act of God? A few of the small crosses were still standing, persevering on the windswept hillside.

I turned back to see a steady stream of black SUVs turning off Route National 1 into the parking area. Bill Clinton was in the backseat of one. He had flown in that morning. He arrived well before the president or prime minister and remained in the car until they showed up. Once they had, the entire event lasted fewer than thirty minutes. A band played. The president placed a wreath on the memorial. Dozens of journalists, together with diplomats and armed guards making up the vast majority of the onlookers, got photos of the two leaders shaking hands, and as quickly as the motorcades had arrived, they left. The next day, Bill Clinton was in Hollywood on the red carpet at the Golden Globes.[2]

I had spent the previous three years following events in Haiti, mostly from Washington, from a desk on the fourth floor of a Dupont Circle town house where I worked for a small think tank. I scoured official reports, sifted through contracting databases and Excel sheets, and followed the money trail from 1,400 miles away—where, in many ways, it both began and ended. Donors reported spending more than $6 billion in the first three years after the quake. USAID alone had awarded $485 million in contracts and grants. Of that, 1 percent had gone to organizations or companies in Haiti. On the other hand, 67 percent—67 cents out of every dollar of aid—had gone to companies located within a thirty-mile radius of my office in Washington.[3] We had a pretty clear picture of who received the money, but where did it all go? How could the billions in aid have done so little? The numbers only told part of the story.

Looking out from the hillside in Titanyen, I saw blue-tarped settlements dotting the adjacent lands, standing defiant of their surroundings like the few burnt crosses that remained upright. I was standing at the edge of a large stretch of land that the government had declared eminent domain over after the earthquake. It was land for housing developments, for factories, for new communities to take root, land for "building back better," as the post-quake slogan had declared. But as I surveyed the area, I knew that not a single government- or aid-financed house had been built here. There was no electricity, no running water, no paved roads, and no formal jobs—no urban planning whatsoever. Still, I was looking at a stretch of land that was now home to at least 200,000 people. People who were building their own future. The land was called Canaan—the promised land.

THE GAP BETWEEN the rich and poor in Haiti is more expansive than in any other country in the hemisphere. On the other hand, the distribution of land is actually among the more equal.[4] The fight for control of that land has shaped Haitian society for centuries. In the early nineteenth century, in an attempt to break up the big plantations of the colonial era, Haitian president Alexandre Pétion undertook a broad land reform process. Once again, Haiti was a model for the rest of the hemisphere. But like the nation's independence itself, the struggle to consolidate those hard-fought gains has lasted more than two hundred years.

Post-independence land invasions pushed much of the peasant population farther into the mountains. They maintained small plots and passed them down through generations, though rarely with an official land title. After the US invasion, constitutional changes allowed foreign ownership of land for the first time since the revolution. US soldiers then waged a constant battle against the Cacos, a guerrilla front of peasants who fiercely resisted the foreign military presence. During the post-occupation rise of the Haitian military through the 1950s and the Duvalier-family dictatorship, while rural Haiti largely maintained its small-scale landholder model, the elite managed to obtain large tracts in Port-au-Prince.[5]

A handful of families had controlled the Haitian economy for decades. After the earthquake, it was those same families that controlled land in the capital needed for rebuilding projects.[6] And that ground was increasingly occupied by hundreds of thousands of people. In rural Haiti, it was peasant land that had been perpetually invaded by the elite; in the capital, it was the elite's land invaded by the masses.

In March 2010, with the camp population growing and the rainy season approaching, the Haitian government declared eminent domain over a nearly thirty-square-mile stretch of land on the outskirts of Port-au-Prince. As the camps became the center of the humanitarian response, the elites in Port-au-Prince saw a looming disaster. The haphazard construction of the capital had been driven over decades by landless peasants moving there and occupying whatever land they could. A conflict between the landowners and the displaced appeared inevitable. Timothy Schwartz, an anthropologist with more than two decades of experience in Haiti, saw the government's seizure of the land as a way to release the pressure building in the capital. "Without a place to go . . . it would have been civil war in Port-au-Prince," he wrote years later in his book *The Great Haiti Humanitarian Aid Swindle.*

The ground this new city was to be built on, however, was barren. Eventually known as Canaan, the mountainous terrain provided beautiful ocean views, but there was no fresh water. When it rained, the chalky, denuded earth turned into a flowing mass of mud. And, without a *moto* or a car of one's own, it took hours just to get there from downtown Port-au-Prince.

Still, the promise of land of one's own, a promise that had rung out since the revolution, remained a powerful draw. Thousands of families moved there, eventually spreading across the entire thirty-square-mile expanse. But while the population continued to grow, the promised investments from donors and the government never arrived.[7]

JUST PAST THE anniversary site, a four-foot-tall slab of concrete painted bright yellow marked the entrance to a new community. "Welcome to Mozayik village: victims of January 12, 2010," the sign read in Kreyòl. Three years after the families had settled on that soccer pitch in Delmas, they had moved their community to the outskirts of Canaan. At its peak in 2011, the camp population had registered more than 1.5 million. Their tattered tarp roofs, many emblazoned with "USAID: From the American People," were easily recognizable for any international visitor looking out their window on the descent into Port-au-Prince. Stepping off the plane, they would then be greeted by one of the largest camps, which had formed right next to the airport—where international aid had piled up in the days after January 12.

The camps had been the center of the quake response, but eventually, the aid slowed. NGOs stopped showing up. Conditions in the camps, where rains turned floors to mud, where the ratio of residents to toilets often reached more than 100:1, quickly deteriorated. Hundreds of thousands opted to leave the squalor of the camps on their own. Many returned as renters to buildings labeled "red" or "yellow" as unsafe due to structural damage from the quake.

Like Mona Augustin and the residents of Mozayik, not all had the option of leaving on their own. Most of the thousand-plus camps were located on private property; as the temporary shelters became more permanent, landowners began to fight back. The Mozayik camp sat across the street from a construction site, where a local company was building an eleven-story office building. But the 126 families of Mozayik were in the way.[8] All across the capital, the camps' stubborn presence served as a constant reminder of the relief effort's failures and as an impediment to the government's "open for business" slogan.

Violent evictions, carried out with the involvement of local government and police officials, became more common. Some landowners, such as Reginald Boulos, began paying those who had set up camps on their property to leave. He was criticized for essentially "bribing the homeless to participate in their own eviction," as *The New York Times* put it.[9] Nevertheless, in a rush to wash away the stain of the camps, the Martelly government and international donors enshrined the "subsidy" program as an official policy.

The program became known as 16/6—sixteen neighborhoods would be "revitalized" and six of the most publicly noticeable camps would be cleared. As a strategy to reduce the number of camp residents, the return subsidies proved successful. Residents had little choice. Violent evictions were common, and the options seemed to be to take the money and leave or be forcibly evicted with nothing.

From the program's launch to the third anniversary, the official camp population decreased by more than 35 percent. The camp along the airport road closed. The camp that had taken over the Champ de Mars, the public square in front of the National Palace, also closed. More than three hundred camps closed in all. Officials held up the reduction in the camp population as the most apparent evidence that relief and reconstruction efforts were finally taking hold. But the numbers hid a more brutal reality.[10]

On January 25, 2012, with the sun still low in the sky, officials from the mayor's office arrived at Mozayik, then still in Delmas. Each tent was marked. If nobody was inside, it was marked "*elimine.*" Mona tried to keep the camp organized. He went to the offices of the International

Federation of Red Cross and Red Crescent Societies, one of the organizations handing out rental subsidies. The organization said it couldn't help. The Mozayik residents organized a press conference. Sitting at a folding table in front of a few local journalists, housing activists, and a documentary filmmaker from the US, one of the residents slowly read aloud the statement.

"We ask the authorities of the state—the government and the mayor—to have a moratorium with the alleged landowners so that everyone in camp Mozayik can live in peace until the government builds good houses to live in with our families as stated in Article 25 of the Declaration on Human Rights. Long live the rights of all people under tents. Long live the rights of all people."

Residents made handcrafted signs and held a protest. They had nowhere to go but knew that they would be kicked off the land any day. It was happening on each occupied piece of land in Port-au-Prince. "We're under tents. We're not animals," one sign read.[11]

Seeing no alternative, the residents of Mozayik agreed to accept $125 each to leave. The construction company that claimed the land made the payments. It wasn't enough to start over on their own, just enough for a few months' rent. So, the residents of Mozayik decided to stay together. They packed as much as possible into the back of a cargo truck and headed to the promised land of Canaan.

Cut off from the commerce of the capital, the residents of Mozayik attempted to start a new life and build their own community from the ground up. When I visited a few days after the third-year commemoration, Mona showed me around their new land. We sat in a small wooden shelter, open-air, with a view of the bay of Port-au-Prince across the highway. Residents were working to make their own roads and paths to connect their shelters, he explained. One family had purchased an ice chest and was selling cold drinks and packaged foods. Life would be difficult, but the families of Mozayik finally seemed to be in control.[12]

By January 2013, the overall camp population in Haiti had decreased by 1.2 million. But only about 25 percent of that decrease—300,000 people—left because the government or an NGO had provided an alternative like a new home, a repaired old home, a transitional shelter, or a rental subsidy. As for the other 900,000 who had left the camps, some ended up back in damaged houses, in unofficial camps that sprang up out of public view after rental subsidies ran dry, or, like the residents of Mozayik, in Canaan.[13]

TWO WEEKS AFTER catching a glimpse of Bill Clinton, I traveled to Zoranje, where Nemcova's charity had built the school on the road to Titanyen. Zoranje had some of the last remaining public land near the capital and was thus a prime location for post-quake projects. In 2011, the area had hosted a massive housing exposition where local and international companies showcased model homes for the reconstruction era. The Building Back Better Communities project was sponsored by the IDB, the Clinton Foundation, and the Haitian government. It cost $2 million.[14]

At the expo, dozens of companies competed for a cash prize and the possibility of far more if their designs caught donors' attention. "If we do this housing properly," Bill Clinton had said after the March donor conference, "it will lead to whole new industries being started in Haiti, creating thousands and thousands of new jobs and permanent housing."[15]

By the time I traveled to the expo site in early 2013, it was a twilight zone graveyard of empty houses. Some of the houses looked relatively normal, such as the small concrete structures with separate kitchen areas. One looked plucked off the coast of Cape Cod, standing on wooden stilts with clapboard shingles. Another was a faded-pink geodesic dome. All of them were empty. None had been replicated.

At the edge of the expo site, across a wide paved road, stood multiple rows of two-story apartment buildings, their balconies and common spaces full of life. A small plaque at the entrance to the housing development, barely legible from any sort of distance, revealed another interesting fact. The Haitian government had built these houses in 2003, and they had withstood the earthquake. Neighbors barbecued and hung laundry from clotheslines that ran from building to building. A few kids laughed from a balcony as they watched us snap photos of the abandoned "model homes" across the street.

It seemed the real model homes had been here all along. But why hadn't donors seen them? Why hadn't anybody even talked about replicating the apartment buildings across the street from the expo?

I went to see Guilaine Victor, the country director for Miyamoto International, a structural engineering firm that helped evaluate buildings after the earthquake as part of the massive effort to label homes "red" (irreparably damaged), "yellow" (in need of repair), or "green" (safe). "We had a design for two-story and up apartment buildings," Victor explained from her office on the fifth floor of the Hexagon building in Pétion-Ville, once Haiti's tallest building.[16] "But there was no interest because of liability issues." Donors feared being on the hook if their multistory housing projects collapsed in the next disaster. From her office, the sprawling city of Port-au-Prince was visible down the hill. Hundreds of thousands of those homes had been labeled "yellow" or "red" and were now occupied once again.

Miyamoto lobbied hard for donors to fund housing repairs rather than build new single-family homes. "For donors," Victor explained, "yellow housing repairs weren't sexy." Instead, donors wanted greenfield development—to build new houses, "model villages" painted in pastels. NGOs and donors needed output, they needed images to fill brochures and satisfy their funders. But even that process proved far more challenging than most had imagined. In addition to land tenure problems and liability issues, every group wanted to push their own design, which delayed efforts further.

Instead of new homes or repairs, donors instead funneled hundreds of millions of dollars into T-shelters, the "T" being short for "transitional." When the government declared eminent domain over Canaan, donors planned to build 125,000 of these shelters there. The keyword, however, is *transitional*. With a plywood frame, a tarpaulin roof, and, if recipients were lucky, a small cement foundation, the shelters were never meant to last. Worse, renters, who made up the majority of those displaced and upward of 50 percent of the population of Port-au-Prince, were ineligible to receive a T-shelter because they did not have land on which to build it. The UN-led "cluster" system, intended as a forum for coordination, proved to be little more than international groups fighting for contracts to build shelters that were only ever intended to last a few years at most. In the end, upward of $500 million went to these stopgap shelter solutions. Rather than stimulating the local economy, as Clinton had suggested, the international organizations building these shelters imported nearly all the raw materials.

In the end, Miyamoto did convince USAID to provide some funding for housing repairs. Still, that accounted for just a fraction of what the agency was spending on housing. Most of it was earmarked for green-field housing construction, the type of project donors considered sexy. In the months after the earthquake, USAID had developed a plan to build fifteen thousand new houses across the country. It was the most ambitious post-quake housing project.

A few days after speaking with Victor, I found myself driving along a rural highway in the north on my way to a meeting with workers from the newly opened Caracol Industrial Park. Giant billboards declared, in English, the region "Open for Business." Then I saw the houses, symmetrical rows of pastel cinder-block shells—mint green, baby blue, creamsicle orange—in an open and dusty field surrounded by a chain-link fence. Three years after the earthquake, the houses built as part of the signature shelter plan remained empty, and USAID had reduced the goal of 15,000 new homes to 2,600.

IT WAS NO secret that land tenure was going to be an issue after the quake. Donors had spent tens of millions of dollars on studies and analyses of the issue over previous decades. In the rest of the country, addressing land tenure meant confronting small-scale peasants who had informally lived off the soil for decades; in the capital, it meant a confrontation with the elite.[17] Neither the Haitian government nor the international community had much appetite for that.

The composition of the elite had changed significantly since the revolution. At first, the elite were composed predominantly of mulatto families, who held on to large tracts of land and maintained a largely plantation-based economy. By the end of the nineteenth century, as various foreign powers fought for influence, businessmen from across the world moved to Haiti. In 1891, the first contingent of migrants from the Middle East began arriving. During the twentieth-century US occupation and after the breakup of the Ottoman Empire, the US facilitated further migration of merchants from countries such as Syria and Lebanon, placing large parts of the Haitian economy in their hands and creating a parallel, imported bourgeoisie.[18]

The power of this new elite grew tremendously under the Duvalier dictatorship, benefiting from government-granted monopolies over major industries, including the import and export of basic goods like food. By 1986, these families had surpassed the traditional mulatto elite as the most fantastically wealthy and politically influential. They were given an acronym—BAM BAM—standing for the six leading families: the Brandts, Apaids, Mevses, Bigios, Acras, and Madsens. They had come from Israel, Lebanon, Denmark, Jamaica, and across the world. The vast majority of these elite families backed the 1991 military coup and soon found themselves the target of international sanctions. They earned a new nickname: the MREs, Morally Repugnant Elites.

Yet, over the decades, the MREs developed close ties to foreign diplomats, especially from the United States. They became the primary source base for the US ambassador and the embassy's political and economic officers. Haitian elites also had deep personal and business ties with the US. Many owned real estate in Florida or New York or ran companies with US headquarters or subsidiaries. Many had American passports. Some also became prolific donors to the Clinton Foundation. The Acra, Bigio, and Mevs families, three of the BAM BAM namesakes, donated between $170,000 and $361,000 to the foundation.[19]

Fulton Armstrong, a former CIA analyst who worked for Senator John Kerry at the time of the earthquake, recalled meeting with US officials on numerous occasions to urge them to confront the landed elite of the capital more directly—a view espoused by a number of Haiti experts. As the onetime head of the CIA's Haiti branch, he knew all too well what they had done to earn their reputation as the MREs. They had the power to help the country recover from the earthquake, but instead were looking out for their own interests, Armstrong believed. "The Clinton people didn't want to challenge the elites," he explained.

"The US focus was on expanding garment manufacturing, and the State Department's argument was that 'we'll need the elites to support us on these long-term interests,'" he said.[20]

Donors presented the Northern Industrial Park, the flagship reconstruction project, as a commitment to the concept of decentralization. The reconstruction plan had, indeed, called for these so-called growth poles to attract investment outside the capital. But the more significant reason for the factory's placement in the north was that the elite land conflicts of the capital would not be a barrier to development.

It had taken plenty of carrots for major donors to lure the Korean textile giant Sae-A to Haiti. Chief among them was land. The Préval government gave a massive stretch in the north to the company, free of charge. The final piece was housing, and that required even more. Préval balked and said he was unwilling to approve additional giveaways. After Martelly took office, USAID began working with an intermediary in the new administration to obtain the necessary paperwork. USAID even financed surveyors from the government's tax office to go to Caracol and identify potential building sites. USAID got the land and began building neat rows of pastel homes to provide housing for factory workers. Land was always cited as an impediment to progress, but when it became crucial to a key project, those barriers rarely stood in the way.[21]

Perhaps no single issue encapsulates the failures of the reconstruction effort more so than housing—the wasteful spending, the broken promises, the lack of accountability. But whom could Haitians hold accountable anyway? It wasn't their own government, or their own NGOs, or their own companies that had received most of the aid funds. It was foreigners. And those actors are not accountable to the Haitian people; they are responsible to international boardrooms, to wealthy donors, to the foreign aid agencies that awarded their contract or grant. When things went wrong, those international agencies and NGOs blamed the Haitian government for the lack of progress, for not addressing the thorny topic of land tenure. But few could, with a straight face, tell you the Haitian government was really in charge. While the circle of blame turned, good money chased bad. Most of the new houses that eventually did get built went up more than a hundred miles from the capital to shelter workers at the new industrial park. Those were the pastel rows I had driven past in the north. Meanwhile, like the families of Mozayik, others were left to struggle against the barren land of Canaan on their own.

16

THE BATTLE FOR REFORM

———

In mid-January 2013, I sat down with Bill Vastine at his apartment complex in Pétion-Ville.[1] The building, hidden from the street by a tall, thick concrete wall, had been an old hotel. The rooms were primarily full of foreigners who had come to Haiti to work, ironic in a country with 70 percent unemployment. Four days after the earthquake, a former colleague at the US Embassy had given Vastine a call—he had been one of the engineers who helped build the fortress a few years earlier. He had never left. The forty-nine-year-old, an almost stereotypically brash Texan and a self-described disaster capitalist, had been quickly hired as the director of logistics for the US relief mission. The next day, he began work and watched as pallets of relief supplies piled high at the mini green zone at the airport, caught in a bureaucratic maze of overlapping agencies and responsibilities. He watched as US military planes took precedence, and he listened as foreign powers squabbled over the relative priority of their own assistance.

Vastine knew disasters. For more than a decade, he had worked with the Army Corps of Engineers and some of the country's biggest construction companies. He recognized immediately that this was going to be one of the most extensive reconstruction efforts in world history. However, he hadn't stayed in Haiti just for humanitarian reasons. Vastine cares about the places he has worked and the people affected by disasters, but he admits he's motivated by something else, too—the pay is damn good.

In 2009, the Haitian government conducted a study of the industry and found that most foreign aid workers received an "unjustifiable per diem" of $260 on top of their base salary.[2] Most Haitians survived on less than two dollars a day. "You go back to the States and perform essentially the same type of work you do in this country, and you make 40 to 60 percent less," Vastine explained.

Over three years, Vastine had gone from working at the US Embassy to putting together USAID's big housing plan to evaluating projects for the Clinton-led reconstruction commission. From the inside of the Aid State, he had seen it all. He agreed to meet on the condition that I bring a bottle of Barbancourt rum and a bottle of Coke. I diligently complied.

We drank and talked for hours, interrupted only occasionally by younger coed aid workers splashing in the pool behind us. Vastine, a stone-cold realist, had a scathing indictment of the foreign aid system in which he still worked.

"Why has nothing changed?" Vastine asked. "Because it's a money-making enterprise," he answered, his voice rising indignantly. "We don't want to fix it. We want to continue to come back here and make money attempting to fix it. . . . The whole world is asking, where did the money go? Where is all this money?" The answer was pretty straightforward. It's not that the billions had simply been stolen or never spent. Rather, the money went to the wrong places for the wrong reasons and was handled by the wrong people. A significant amount of it simply went to organizational expenses and staff salaries.

It is about more than waste and inefficiency, though. In the aftermath of the earthquake, the priority for the international community, as it had been for years, was stability. That response was driven by fear. Fear of unrest, fear of chaos, fear of change. Emergency aid functioned as a Band-Aid, soothing and buying time for a real recovery that the aid itself could never provide. Stability implies a lack of change, and the aid industry delivered just that. It provided basic necessities while consolidating power, money, and influence in the hands of actors unable or unwilling to change. Whether or not that was the goal is irrelevant. That is what happened.

* * *

VASTINE MAY HAVE been blunter than most of his colleagues, but his basic analysis wasn't controversial. Hillary Clinton had admitted as much during her 2009 nomination hearing for secretary of state, when she declared that "it's fair to say that USAID, our premier aid agency, has been decimated." She noted its staff had been cut in half even as its budget increased. "It's turned into more of a contracting agency than an operational agency with the ability to deliver," Clinton said.[3] Once in office, she had designated Cheryl Mills to oversee a total aid rethink in Haiti. She had also begun a process of reforming US foreign assistance more broadly. The effort was formally launched in the fall of 2010; it was called USAID Forward.

The reform program called for breaking up the big contracts the agency relied upon; it mandated greater transparency and accountability and prioritized working *with* local institutions and organizations instead of around them. Even if everyone recognized the problems, changing the foreign aid system was going to be a battle.

In the fall of 2011, I sat down with a USAID official at the Parc Historique de la Canne à Sucre, a former sugar plantation turned historical site and restaurant located just 750 feet from the US Embassy.[4] The outdoor tables were full of US officials and aid workers enjoying the lunch buffet. The official had been tasked with implementing and ensuring compliance with USAID's ambitious new reform program. A year in, however, little appeared to have changed.

The official explained that foreign aid has to comply with US regulations and laws, making it challenging to partner with local groups, most of which would not be compliant with rules mandating five years of audited financial statements, for example. There was also a language barrier, which often created divisions between local and international actors. But he was optimistic. USAID was going to hold trainings for local groups and was adding local procurement requirements into new contracts.

It was relatively easy to ascertain the first level of transparency in USAID funding. Government contracting databases and fact sheets regularly report the initial recipient of US taxpayer funds. But what happens after? How much goes to local subcontractors? How much goes back to the Beltway in the form of overhead? How much is spent on employee salaries and housing?

"You need hard data . . . and I need that hard data, too," the official told me.

Chemonics, which received more than $100 million and was the largest recipient of USAID funding, had done exceptionally well for themselves, the official acknowledged. "You know, no organization is going to go in and not have self-interest." But he pushed back on the idea that aid funds channeled into US organizations and for-profit companies didn't benefit the local economy. "It's a myth," he said. While the headquarters may profit, he explained that the amount of money spent in-country is far more significant. "For every international person you have," he continued, "it could cost you up to $250,000 a year to maintain that—housing, security, support." Yes, he acknowledged, many Americans were benefiting, but they have "to live here, eat here, dance here, whatever. . . . To rent a three-bedroom house costs six thousand a month." And donors pay it because the worst thing that could happen is a US citizen gets kidnapped. "You can't make them live with the people—they're not Peace Corps volunteers," he said. "They are professionals—masters. You can't put them under a tent."

You could call it the trickle-down aid theory. Forget whether the assistance is well administered, in other words, or whether the loss in efficiency of paying high-priced salaries makes funneling all your donor money into foreign NGOs seem wasteful; those high salaries support the local economy.

AS RECONSTRUCTION EFFORTS faltered and the billions in pledges evaporated with little progress to show, aid accountability became the topic du jour in Washington. The question "where did the money go?" wasn't just a slogan. It was a critical issue. Local procurement is a proven and sustainable way to improve the local economy; channeling aid through local businesses creates jobs, develops capacity, and reduces the need for more aid down the line.[5] To judge how effectively US taxpayer money was being spent in Haiti, it was necessary to know what actually got spent in Haiti and what got funneled back to the US. For the most part, the reasons offered by foreign officials for why aid continued to bypass Haitians were that local companies and even the government didn't have the capacity. It seemed to me, however, that the real barriers to reform were in Washington, DC.

Together with a coalition of other organizations and researchers, I made the rounds in Congress, meeting with staffers and preaching the need for greater transparency. The only way it seemed the aid system would ever be reformed was if the public, and members of Congress, understood where the relief money was actually going. In late 2011, the coalition began working with some members of Congress on a bill that would mandate greater levels of transparency in US foreign assistance to Haiti, which became known as the Assessing Progress in Haiti Act. But we weren't the only ones making the rounds in Congress.

In January 2012, a congressional staffer reached out to say that Chemonics had requested a meeting. The firm wanted to talk about the critical role American companies play in global relief efforts. In fact, months earlier, the world's largest for-profit development companies had banded together to form the Council of International Development Companies (CIDC). The group put up $300,000 and hired the Podesta Group, a lobbying and public relations firm whose cofounder, John Podesta, had been Bill Clinton's former chief of staff and had run the Obama administration's transition team.[6]

The Beltway bandits wanted nothing to do with USAID Forward, which, if implemented, would have eroded their fiefdoms. In Haiti, CIDC members had received more than 70 percent of all USAID funds by the end of 2012. USAID was funding organizations that then turned around and lobbied against USAID's own reforms.

The talking points were pretty simple in Congress, which controls the purse strings of USAID. American dollars should be supporting American business, the group argued. Foreign aid was a multibillion-dollar industry, and for-profit contractors employed tens of thousands of residents in the greater Washington, DC, area. If members of Congress were concerned about waste, fraud, and abuse, it would be easier to hold US companies accountable than those in poor countries.

But that assumed that the US government was actually in the business of holding its contractors and grantees accountable. It wasn't.

Audit after audit showed that US contractors failed to live up to their obligations, yet not a single one had faced any legal repercussions. And rather than fostering greater transparency, NGOs and firms steadfastly refused to provide any data on where the money was going.

I obtained Chemonics' USAID contract after a multiyear FOIA battle with the agency, but all the financial information was redacted. The amount a company charges the government in overhead is considered a protected trade secret. When the Associated Press asked a large health NGO for detailed budget data, the organization initially said they would turn it over before telling the reporter that USAID prevented it from doing so.[7] And it wasn't just lobbyists who pushed back on the demand for greater accountability and transparency.

Efforts to reform food assistance also faced entrenched political and economic interests inside Washington. The program itself, like the reliance on for-profit aid contractors, mainly served US business interests. A 2010 study found that it wasn't the needs on the ground that determined a country's level of food assistance; it was the quantity of excess agricultural products that US companies had in stock. USAID was purchasing around a billion dollars of agricultural products a year, a massive subsidy for US farmers. But USAID was also spending around a billion dollars a year to ship the goods, and Congress had legally required USAID to use US-flagged vessels.[8]

Together with NGOs that distributed food aid on the ground, shipping lines and agricultural producers formed an "iron triangle" that served as an effective lobby against any effort to increase local production or procurement of agricultural goods.[9] The reality is that our foreign aid system is not geared toward actual development. It serves as a jobs program in congressional districts across the country. Despite former president Clinton's public apology for past policies, little changed after the earthquake.

Poll after poll shows that Americans have little sense of the size of our foreign aid budget.[10] Most think it is massive. It is not. It's just a fraction of 1 percent of our overall budget. But the only way to justify continuing even those tiny aid flows to a US-centric public is to make it benefit the US. The blame for USAID's failures to serve the needs of Haiti and other countries overseas is "not the fault of the long-suffering staff of US aid agencies, who can deliver very effective programs if given the chance," Charles Kenny, a development expert at the Washington-based Center for Global Development, wrote in a 2013 opinion piece for *Bloomberg*.[11] "The blame, instead, lies largely with members of Congress who complain that aid is wasted because it doesn't lead to development, and then turn around and ensure hardly any assistance is designed or delivered with development as the primary goal."

CORRUPTION DOES PERMEATE life in Haiti. The country consistently ranks in the bottom 10 percent on Transparency International's Corruption Perceptions Index. In Haiti, corruption can occur in plain sight; everyone sees and recognizes it, like having to slip a little something extra to renew a driver's license or even obtain a birth certificate. In the US and other rich countries, corruption manifests itself in different but no less maleficent ways. We have simply legalized corruption. The US economic and political system adapted to formalize corruption, not eliminate it. For-profit development contractors, for example, hire a politically connected lobbyist to ensure US foreign assistance still primarily benefits them over the populations they claim to help. That is legal; it is also corrupt.

In the first three years after the earthquake, donors reported spending $6.4 billion in Haiti. Less than 10 percent had gone to the government in the form of budget support.[12] The vast majority of the funds flowed not through Haitian companies or organizations but the aid-industrial complex just as it had before the earthquake. For Haitians, what looked corrupt was a bunch of young foreigners driving around in brand-new SUVs and moving into the hills of Pétion-Ville. How could Haitians be the corrupt benefactors in this equation when foreigners seemed to be controlling all the money?

The pay had been good enough to draw Vastine to Haiti and good enough to keep him there. To incentivize working in Haiti, the US and other donors gave contractors both "danger pay" and "hardship pay," which is what allowed Vastine to make more in Haiti than he could back home in Texas.

Vastine had particularly harsh words for Cheryl Mills, Secretary Clinton's chief of staff. "Mills marched into Haiti and basically took over; she came in here and fired a bunch of people, then she pretty much started commanding." The problem with that, Vastine explained, was that while Mills was supremely talented and intelligent, she had no experience in disaster relief or large-scale reconstruction efforts. "She was making decisions she was not qualified to make, and we didn't have much choice other than to say, 'Yes, ma'am.'"

Vastine worked under Mills when he was putting together the initial plan for USAID's post-quake shelter plan. He remembered that Mills wanted a groundbreaking by the fall of 2010, within months of the project's start. He found the request absurd, but he understood it. "They've got to have something to put in the media and sell to Congress; the big thing is Congress because every year they go battle for a budget," Vastine explained. "The fiscal year ends in September, so every year around that time, we've got to do some marketing to claim some of the good things that we've done."

The results are rushed projects with little community involvement, which makes perverse sense since it is not the Haitian people to whom donors are accountable, but politicians in their own country. "We come in, and we push everyone out of the way and say we're working over here, have a ribbon cutting, cameras flash, say this community of four thousand people is better off. Come back in three years," Vastine said. Just as often, however, the person who made that initial decision is no longer there three years later.

With Jean-Louis Warnholz, another State Department employee, Mills played a crucial role in negotiations that brought the South Korean company Sae-A to the Caracol Industrial Park. The deal required donors to come up with more than $300 million in subsidies to close the deal, and Mills managed to get it all for Sae-A. In late 2013, Secretary of State Clinton stepped down from the position, and Mills left the State Department. The following year, with Warnholz, she started a consulting firm called BlackIvy to promote industrial parks in Africa. Part of the initial financing for their private venture came from Chairman Kim, the CEO of the South Korean company they had helped bring to Haiti.[13]

DESPITE THE APPARENT imperfections, with so many dollars flooding the country from 2011 to 2014, Haiti experienced the longest and largest sustained period of economic growth in thirty years. Where that growth occurred, however, is especially revealing. Given the post-quake rhetoric around building public institutions and supporting agriculture, one might think that those sectors would have seen significant increases. In fact, the agricultural sector grew more slowly than almost any other branch of the economy. Public administration, education, health care, and other such services did experience some growth. Still, those sectors were not among the top performers. Rather, more than 50 percent of the total growth over those three years came from two sectors: the service industry, which includes hotels and restaurants, and the real estate/banking sector.[14]

Most of the billions in aid were in the hands of foreigners, and the so-called trickle-down aid economy was leading the recovery in Haiti. Restaurants and nightclubs were full, and the real estate market was doing great. Haiti, or at least the capital of Port-au-Prince, was going through a gentrification-like process familiar to many communities in the US. The services, however, were not really for most Haitians but for the many thousands of foreigners who had come to Haiti after the earthquake. The foreigners who wanted to live, eat, and dance, as the USAID official had told me years prior.

Vastine's apartment was roughly 320 square feet, the size of a small hotel suite. The owners of the complex realized quickly they could make more money on aid workers than tourists. "It's $1,500 a month to rent this thing," Vastine explained. "I can almost rent in New York City for that." According to Vastine, the housing budget for US personnel ranges from $25,000 to $50,000 per year. "You know why this apartment is $1,500?" he asked. "It's because it's the UN's maximum rate for lodging in the country—so everyone jacked their rates up to it."

While housing for Haitians lagged, new high-priced apartments for foreigners did get built—along with new hotels. The Clinton Bush Haiti Fund, the entity created by the two former presidents to raise money after the quake, made a $2 million investment in the Oasis Hotel, a long-stalled project backed by some of Haiti's most well-known elite families.[15] The World Bank's investment arm chipped in another $7.5 million. The Clinton Foundation helped facilitate another deal, to bring a Marriott hotel to Haiti.[16] The World Bank contributed $26.5 million to make that a reality.[17]

The new hotels were in the capital, which made sense. As thousands of aid organizations arrived in Haiti, almost all set up their operations there. The concentration of aid in the capital provided a reverse incentive to the decentralization that had occurred naturally after the quake, as those who initially fled were pulled back by the provision of basic goods in the camps. But, in the most unequal nation in the hemisphere, the concentration of aid in the capital also further concentrated wealth in the capital. The elite owned the hotels, the car dealerships, the gas stations, the restaurants, and the homes whose rents shot up to thousands of dollars per month.

In 2012, inequality in Haiti was unchanged from before the earthquake, according to the World Bank.[18] For billions in foreign aid to have not made any dent in Haiti's entrenched inequality is as damning a finding as anything related to the post-quake relief and reconstruction effort. Aid bypassed local organizations and local governments because of fears over accountability and waste, over fears that Haiti was a failed state with a corrupt oligarchy blocking progress. Instead, assistance went to foreign organizations that fought tooth and nail against the common-sense reforms that could have actually changed the aid system. The money that stayed in Haiti predominantly enriched the elite, which empowered them even further, preventing a change in Haiti. Aid wasn't leading to change; it was further consolidating the status quo.

To VASTINE, THE solution was simple if unlikely. The kingdoms that rule the aid industry, he said, have to be broken apart. "Everyone has a kingdom," he said. "The NGOs, the different bureaucracies, they all have their kingdoms, and I don't know if it can ever be done because it's so entrenched."

With little staff of their own, when things went wrong, USAID ended up needing to rely on the same contractors that had created the problems in the first place. Contractors and NGOs obtain such large portfolios, "it's almost like [USAID] thinks of them as part of their bureaucracy," Vastine explained. The system, he believes, repurposing a familiar take on US corporate structures, had become too big to fail. "They're running their own game."

"To my knowledge," Vastine continued further, "nobody has even gotten a suspension" for any shoddy work in Haiti, and there had been plenty of that.

In Washington, however, calls for accountability and aid reform were treated as dangerous criticism of the high-profile aid effort. But the drumbeat for accountability was too loud to block it out entirely. On the ground, the lack of progress was palpable. And in Washington, audit after audit provided fodder for advocates of aid reform.[19] In the summer of 2014, after more than three years, Congress passed the Assessing Progress in Haiti Act on a bipartisan basis.[20] USAID Forward remained stuck in neutral, but at the very least, the State Department would be required to provide some semblance of transparency over where the money really went. For the first time, the State Department had to report contract information concerning a program's actual goals and objectives. For the first time, the State Department had to report data on subcontractors. It was too little, too late. By the time the first report was released, the politics in the US had shifted. Transparency is one thing, but accountability is another matter entirely.

With a presidential election coming, few Democrats in Congress were willing to criticize Barack Obama, or his former secretary of state and what seemed his likely successor, Hillary Clinton. The lack of accountability in Washington—and in Brussels or Quebec or Caracas—showed up on the ground in Haiti in disparate ways. By intervening in the 2010 election, donors had done more than the Haitian people to put Martelly into the National Palace, but how could they ask for government accountability when they refused to hold themselves or their proxies accountable?

As 2014 came to a close, the stakes were higher than ever—in Haiti and the US. By the time of the earthquake's fifth anniversary, in January 2015, Hillary Clinton's presidential run was an open secret, and her record in Haiti was becoming a liability.[21] Major media outlets broke stories on the Clinton Foundation's Haiti kingdom and alleged a widespread "pay for play" system where donors to the foundation benefited from the reconstruction effort. Inside the State Department, ABC News later revealed, staff had a special designation for when they received an offer of assistance or a meeting request from Clinton Foundation allies. They called them "FOBs," friends of Bill.[22] The allegations were weaponized by partisans on one side and fiercely fought by those on the other.

Aid accountability was no longer about helping Haiti or other countries; it was just about US politics. Democratic lawmakers and government officials attempted to deflect blame for the failures of the reconstruction period in an attempt to protect the legacy of Clinton, her State Department, and her husband. But in their attempts to resist criticism, officials in Washington provided cover for the political situation on the ground in Haiti, which was quietly becoming the most damning legacy of their interventions. Five years after the earthquake, the democratic façade of post-quake stability was in tatters, just like the blue and gray tarps that still colored the capital.

17

THE DIPLOMAT'S JOB

As the fifth anniversary of the quake approached, there was a real question of whether or not Martelly would be able to hang on to the presidency. Protesters filled the streets of the capital daily, often led by a former senator, Moïse Jean-Charles, who used imagery of the revolutionary hero Jean-Jacques Dessalines and would appear on horseback in the midst of the throngs of demonstrators. Calls for Martelly's ouster were growing louder by the day.

In late October, the United States dispatched its top diplomat, Tom Shannon, to help save Martelly's mandate. "Unfortunately, the political impasse over the long overdue legislative and local elections has worsened and elections will not occur in 2014," the US Embassy wrote in a "scene-setter" cable. In an attempt to sideline those politically undesirable to Washington, Moïse Jean-Charles and a group of opposition senators, whom diplomats had labeled the "radical opposition," were to have no role in the solution. "If consultations are to bear any fruit the moderate opposition and the Executive will need to urgently engage in dialogue with a defined and agreed upon agenda," the cable noted.[1]

Despite the democratic erosion taking place under Martelly, he was, diplomats and the local elite believed, better than the alternative. After meeting with business leaders, Shannon reported to Washington that "several participants described the government under President Martelly and Prime Minister Lamothe as pro-business and pro-investment, while others noted that the administration had been an improvement over its recent predecessors for simply 'not being against business.'" In other words, at least Martelly wasn't Aristide or Préval. And, in order to ensure those former leaders and their heirs remained on the sidelines, Martelly would need to be saved.

In November, Ambassador Pamela White traveled to Washington, where she got an earful from congressional Democrats. A crisis in Haiti was the last thing anybody wanted in the run-up to the US presidential election. The next week, back in Haiti, White met with a handful of politicians belonging to the "moderate opposition." At the meeting, Evans Paul, a former Lavalas mayor of Port-au-Prince who had later turned against Aristide, proposed an advisory commission that would meet with stakeholders and propose a path forward.[2] When the commission formed in early December, Paul was placed in one of the top spots along with Reginald Boulos.

Shannon and the State Department's Haiti coordinator, Tom Adams, returned in early December to ensure the commission's recommendations would be accepted. The panel called for a new electoral council, for political prisoners to be released from jail, and, perhaps most important, for the resignation of Prime Minister Lamothe and the formation of a consensus government. Within days of the report's release, with protesters still flooding the streets of the capital, Martelly's old friend and longtime business partner acquiesced and resigned from office.[3] Without electoral stability, donors and the local elite had opted for manufactured stability; they believed sacrificing Lamothe would convince enough of the opposition to come to the table.

In Haiti, a diplomat's job is akin to holding a lid on a pot of boiling water. The task at hand is to prevent any of the water from spilling over the edges. In other words, the job is making sure the situation on the ground in Haiti does not spiral out of control and cause blowback at home, either in the form of waves of migration or political liability. To do so, American diplomats exercised tremendous influence over the country's political developments.

*   *   *

THE SUN HAD already set over the bay of Port-au-Prince, but in the halls of Parliament diplomats and politicians were still scrambling to hold a vote. In just a few hours, at midnight on January 12, 2015, the five-year anniversary of the quake, the terms of the remaining members of Parliament were set to expire. If they didn't act, President Martelly would be ruling by decree, the checks and balances nominally provided for in the constitution stripped away. For four years, the international community's reconstruction front man had failed to organize a vote. The veneer of democratic legitimacy atop the Aid State was wearing thin. The pot was boiling over.

From a friend's couch in the Christ Roi neighborhood of the capital, we watched pixelated coverage of the scene in Parliament. Would legislators show up and vote? There had been a tentative agreement reached to extend the terms of Parliament and to approve the long-delayed and much-maligned electoral law, the first step in the march to a vote. Still, we weren't terribly optimistic. It would take only a few senators staying home to prevent a quorum.

Then, we caught sight of US ambassador Pamela White. She wasn't alone. The Canadian ambassador and the OAS special representative were right there also. At the height of Haiti's political crisis, these international diplomats were in the building whipping votes—on camera.

Still, their efforts failed. At ten P.M., unable to obtain a quorum, the Senate president announced that the session was over. In two hours, Parliament would be dissolved.

Ambassador White was shocked. She had spent weeks carefully assembling the deal and had personally gone door-to-door to meet with senators and deputies to ensure the vote would take place. For months the Haitian government and foreign diplomats had blamed the impending crisis on a group of opposition senators. But privately, they understood that Martelly would be happy to dissolve Parliament and rule by decree. Ambassador White had pleaded with the president, telling him that if he wanted to run for the presidency again in the future, he would have to look good in the eyes of the West. Allowing Parliament's dissolution, she had warned, wasn't a good look.[4]

In the end, a group of pro-Martelly senators never showed up.

Instead, they spent the evening at Martelly's house, watching the scene unfold on their televisions just like I had. White had been betrayed by her sources and by the president. The year 2015, which began in Haiti with the dissolution of Parliament, marked the one-hundred-year commemoration of the US occupation of Haiti. And, after all those years, the US Embassy and American diplomats were still hard at work attempting to manage Haiti's affairs and protect US interests.

AMBASSADOR WHITE HAD known Martelly and his wife, Sophia, for more than two decades by the time she arrived at her new post in 2012. It was her second stint in Haiti, after living in Port-au-Prince from 1985 to 1991 through the fall of Baby Doc and the first election of Aristide. White and her husband both held posts with USAID. White worked in an administrative role and got to know Sophia, who worked as a typist. By the time White returned twenty years later, her old friend was First Lady.

She had another personal connection with Laurent Lamothe, who was ratified as prime minister just two months before her own arrival in Haiti. Lamothe's business partner in Global Voice Group, François Dugué, had been a technologist at USAID in the late eighties. His career eventually took him to Africa, where he remained close with White. As ambassador, White deepened her relationship with the Martelly family and with Lamothe, with whom the US had invested tremendous political capital.

White became so close with the government that many in the opposition began referring to her as Pamela Pink, a play on the color of Martelly's political party, Parti Haïtien Tèt Kale (PHTK). But White sought to downplay the influence of the embassy.

"There is no doubt that we have had a long history of intervening in Haiti, starting with the Marines . . . 'Here we come, whether you like it or not,'" White said in August 2013. "So there is a perception that the US is involved in every decision that is made within the Haitian government, which is just not true, nor do I want it to be true. We try to stay away as much as we can so Haitians can make decisions for Haitians.

But you have to be very careful that you are not saying something that someone is going to perceive as leaning to one side or the other."[5]

Then, White added, immediately undercutting her earlier argument, "I do try to support the Martelly administration because I think that they care about their people, but also because any change in government here destabilizes the country and throws us five years backwards. We just can't afford to keep doing that in Haiti."

White had failed to get Parliament to extend their terms, but the diplomat did have a backup plan. On January 11, the day before the vote, the embassy gathered more than a dozen political parties inside the Kinam Hotel. Around four P.M., twenty-six "parties" signed the Kinam Agreement, named for the hotel where it was signed, agreeing to support the Martelly administration and join a consensus government.[6] Most of those parties, however, had only recently been formed and had scant representation in Parliament or support among the population.

After the signing of the accord, the US Embassy released a terse statement encouraging Haiti's lawmakers to act. But, the embassy continued, if "a solution cannot be reached by January 12, the US will continue to work with President Martelly and whatever legitimate Haitian government institutions remain to safeguard the significant gains we have achieved together since the January 12, 2010 earthquake."[7] The message was clear. The US would stand by Martelly regardless of whether Parliament voted to extend their terms. Martelly was not the perfect ally, but, diplomats believed, he was the best option they had. They were choosing stability over democracy as they had so many times throughout history. But that choice would only make instability inevitable.

MORE THAN A year later, in the summer of 2016, I met Pamela White at a hotel lobby bar in Crystal City, Virginia. The ambassador had retired in the midst of the 2015 electoral cycle, which had yet to be resolved by the time we sat down for a drink. White, like myself, had grown up in Maine. I still think that's the main reason she agreed to speak with me. But maybe there was something else. A diplomat's job is a job like any other. Speak out, and you probably won't get the next promotion.

White had hoped to land a job with the Clinton campaign after leaving Haiti. The US election was heating up just as Haiti's was and White was a fan. "OH wow wow wow . . . You tell the most Marvelous Secretary of State EVER that I humbly accept," she had responded when told of her nomination for ambassador.[8] For most of her tenure in Haiti, she had certainly done her job, doing her best to protect her former boss's reputation, manage Martelly, and keep a lid on things. But, I suspected that her departure from Haiti in the middle of exactly the type of crisis Clinton had desperately tried to avoid had made her hoped-for transition less than likely. White was at the end of her career in the foreign service. Maybe she'd be willing to open up.

She ordered a double scotch on the rocks. I followed her lead.[9]

"It's so frustrating because for so many years—and not just my time—we've tried to get a semi-decent election to happen in Haiti," the ambassador began. "Truthfully, you can go back almost to Duvalier and you can see . . . It, it leads me to believe that maybe, in a lot of countries, not just Haiti, our style of democracy is just not going to happen. . . . You can't just have an election," she said. "As much as our diplomats say it, an election is not democracy in many ways they think it is."

But, I asked, doesn't the international community, and the US in particular, keep making that same mistake? Each time, it's just "we need an election."

"Yes," she said. "I do believe that, I gotta tell you, I do."

And, I continued, "the more often you do that . . . you just engender this same pattern."

"At this point, I'm not even sure who wants [elections] more," the ambassador responded. "Frankly, I'd say the international community wants it more."

For the local political and economic elite, elections are a means to extract—protection, wealth, status. But international actors are more than willing partners, funding and approving of elections that exclude a majority of the population in a macabre attempt to provide a fig leaf of legitimacy to a system that they themselves know is no longer legitimate.

And what about the influence of drug money? I asked. The DEA had made some arrests, I acknowledged, but little seemed to change. A number of well-known traffickers were on the verge of winning political office.

"Some of these bad guys, are they with us or against us?" she asked. "I don't know."

That's certainly what helps feed theories about US protecting certain players, I pointed out.

"Oh, honey," she said. "Let me tell you, that's the underbelly of Haiti. I don't think any of us get to see it. . . ."

What had transpired that forced the ambassador's reckoning with this legacy?

The 2015 elections, which hung over our hotel bar meeting unresolved.

18

THE PARTY

———

On January 16, 2015, four days after the expiration of Parliament's terms, Martelly swore in a new prime minister. Of course, there was no legislature to confirm the appointment, but Evans Paul, the man who led the commission that had saved Martelly months earlier, could count on a "consensus" of parties—the same parties that had signed the US-brokered accord on the eve of the expiry of Parliament's terms. Months earlier, international consultants had drafted a new law on political parties, which lowered the barrier to creating a new party.[1] All it now took were twenty signatures.[2] The number of parties ballooned, which proved quite helpful in selling the "consensus" as larger than it truly was.

That night, Martelly made a live address to the nation. He struck a conciliatory tone in his remarks, pledging to work with the opposition and not to abuse his freshly consolidated power.

The next morning, I sat down with Jean-Max Bellerive, the former prime minister under both Préval and Martelly. "His speech last night reminded me of when two brothers are fighting and their parents tell one of them to apologize to the other," he told me.[3] In the analogy, the parent was the United States.

"When Martelly took office, he was a president without actors," Bellerive said. He had few allies in Parliament and no real political party. Bellerive figured the only way forward was to form a political consensus, to include different parties because he barely had one of his own. But, Bellerive explained, Martelly "was a prisoner of his campaign—which was all about ousting the political class—and he remains one to this day." Certainly, the population broadly loathed the political class; it was compelling. After four years of that, however, Haiti had arrived at a situation where it was "only one guy." That, Bellerive believed, was "exactly what he wanted. . . . Haiti has never consolidated political parties, so it still is very personal," he explained. Many, however, are at ease with that dynamic. "Inside, everything is possible," he said. The instability, the chaos, these were opportunities for Haiti's elite. With the formation of a new government, "you've got big contractors calling people asking if they want to be ministers . . . people we all thought were dead. . . . Perhaps this is no accident," Bellerive opined. "There are many actors working underground that know politics better than Martelly and can take advantage." And while Martelly had consolidated power, his plans for the upcoming election were being tested. Parliament's terms had lapsed without an election, but his own term was coming to an end soon as well. By imposing Evans Paul as prime minister, the government—and its foreign allies—believed it would be able to maintain its control over the political system regardless.

A population atomized by the Aid State made the path for consolidation easier. It doesn't take a conspiracy theory to understand how. By focusing on the interests and needs of disparate groups, by picking winners and losers, the system undermines grassroots organizing and domestic civil society, thereby inherently reinforcing the ability of foreign actors and their local allies to shape domestic politics. Occasionally, foreign assistance played a more direct role, and if one thing was clear in the run-up to the 2015 vote, it was that Martelly was no longer a man without a party.

By 2015, Martelly's PHTK had become the most well-funded and organized party in the country, thanks in no small part to its international connections. For the previous twenty-five years, there had been no political movement that could compete with Lavalas and its descendants.

After more than two decades of outsourcing of elections, together with the consolidation of the PHTK, that dynamic had finally shifted.

In April 2015, my friend Ti Mo—*moto* driver, savant, and longtime collaborator—and I showed up unannounced at the party's headquarters, a multistory home in a residential neighborhood of the capital. A towering canopy of trees shaded the driveway and courtyard.

After about thirty minutes, we were led up a flight of stairs and into a dark office, decorated with black leather furniture. The AC unit in the window buzzed loudly, working to turn the humid Caribbean air into an artificial cool breeze. I sat in one of the leather chairs and introduced myself to a man with an ear-to-ear smile who sat on the other side of the desk.[4]

"My name is Roudy Choute. I used to work for the International Republican Institute and lived in Washington—so I'm familiar with 'think tanks,'" he said, inspecting my business card. Choute was Haitian American, short, probably somewhere in his forties, with a shaved head, a neatly trimmed beard, and a small gap between his two front teeth, which he continued to show off.

Martelly had run in the 2010 elections under the banner of a small party, but once in office, he went to work consolidating his own movement. The upcoming vote would be PHTK's first as an official party. The marathon electoral season would span more than five months, beginning in August with a vote to elect twenty senators and the entirety of the lower house, then culminating in the election of a new president in December. As the party "close to power," as Choute described it, everyone expected them to do well.

The day I met with Choute was the final day for candidates to register for the legislative races. "We are submitting our list of candidates today," he explained. "Over one hundred for deputy and fifteen for the Senate." Those numbers meant the party was running a candidate in virtually every race across the country. Few, if any, others could field such a roster. The long campaign, spread out over three rounds of elections, meant only a handful of parties would have the resources to compete.

I asked how the party remained funded. The opposition had long accused it of benefiting from state resources.

"Funding for political parties is not like the US where you have a middle class and can get smaller donations that add up," he responded. It's mostly the upper class, he said. "They say this person will fund these candidates, another these, etc." The party also received some support from outside the country, Choute acknowledged. "They are subject to different laws," he noted, without commenting on the potential conflicts of interest such support might imply.

As a former staffer at the International Republican Institute—the same organization that had worked with key organizers of the 2004 coup against Aristide—Choute was well aware of the role that international organizations played in local politics.

"International organizations also provide support," he acknowledged. "They control lots in Haiti and also they control the political parties. Yes, they're involved."

PHTK was no different. And Choute wasn't the only international connection inside the party. Two of the founding board members were Danielle Saint-Lôt[5] and Ann Valérie Timothée Milfort,[6] who founded Femmes en Démocratie (Women in Democracy) in 1998.[7] The organization was inspired by the Vital Voices Democracy Initiative, itself launched the year prior by then First Lady Hillary Clinton and then secretary of state Madeleine Albright. The Vital Voices Global Partnership, a nonprofit entity based in DC and run by one of Clinton's former aides, began operating in 1999 and incorporated the Haitian entity as an affiliate. Timothée eventually started working as an accountant for Sophia Saint-Rémy, and when her husband ascended to the presidency, Timothée was named his representative to the Bill Clinton–led reconstruction commission and the chief of his cabinet. Saint-Lôt was named an ambassador-at-large.[8] Ahead of the 2015 election, her brother was put in charge of the PetroCaribe aid funds.

Few in Haiti questioned the closeness of Martelly with the Clintons and the international community in general after the 2010 election—but few understood just how thoroughly that closeness had manifested itself in the years following the election. This new party was built to compete in the Aid State's outsourced democracy. It was no coincidence that one of the party's top officials was Line Balthazar. He had worked with the UN and other agencies supporting Haiti's elections for years. He was even part of a small team of experts that conducted an evaluation of the UN's support for the 2010 electoral process.[9] Nobody knew the system better than he did.

In consolidating PHTK, however, Martelly had not simply relied on the support of the international community. Over his first four years, the musician and his band had assembled a broad tent under which they played. They quickly and easily had co-opted much of the entrenched political elite, the senators and deputies who would tie themselves to whoever was in power. His "pro-business" rhetoric had won over much of the private sector. And of course, there were still the ghosts of Haiti's Duvalierist past that lurked behind the showman. There was also a younger generation of the private-sector elite. The first names had changed even if the last had not. These new, old elite formed a group, Haiti Cherie, in the run-up to the 2015 elections.[10] The group was led by another Haitian American, Pierre Antoine Louis, who had worked at the US Embassy during the 2010 election. He had joined the Martelly administration while still on the US payroll.[11]

Legislative elections were scheduled for August 9, 2015, with the presidential vote to find Martelly's replacement coming a few months later. After decades of coups, of foreign intervention, of overturned results and ever-declining turnout, it was unclear what would transpire. But the foreign-drafted electoral law contained a worrying change. No longer were candidates required to receive a criminal background check before registering.

"One thing is certain," Marie Yolène Gilles, program director for RNDDH, a national human rights network, said. "These elections will unleash a post-electoral crisis." Gilles's organization released a report ahead of the vote revealing that at least thirty-one candidates approved to participate in the upcoming elections had criminal records. Two days before the election, the *Miami Herald*, the only US paper to provide regular Haiti coverage, ran a headline: "'Legal Bandits' Could Take Charge in Haiti's Parliament." Jacqueline Charles, the *Herald*'s award-winning Caribbean reporter, was making a play on a popular 2008 Sweet Micky song by the same name, "Bandi Legal."[12]

19

THE LEGAL BANDITS

Amid the 2015 electoral process, Martelly's PHTK party set up an informal campaign office in a second-floor suite at the 1950s art deco–style El Rancho Hotel. During the country's tourism heyday, the El Rancho had provided exclusive revelry to the world's rich and famous. Richard Burton, Jackie Kennedy, Nelson Rockefeller, and Elizabeth Taylor were among the many visitors. After decades of neglect and significant damage in the earthquake, it reopened in 2013 following a multimillion-dollar renovation, part of the reconstruction-era hotel bonanza. It was a fitting location. Like Martelly's presidential campaign, the hotel was managed by a Spanish firm. The investors in the new renovation were led by three individuals: Reginald Boulos, Sherif Abdallah, and Marc-Antoine Acra, all of whom were financial backers of PHTK.[1] And Martelly had his own history with the hotel.

In the late eighties, the El Rancho was where a young Sweet Micky first started performing. By then, the foreign A-listers had largely been replaced by high-ranking officials in the Haitian military and others among the country's post-Duvalier elite. The El Rancho was also, at the time, an incredibly efficient money-laundering operation for Pablo Escobar's Medellín cartel. The hotel's casino was, according to US law enforcement, run by Fernando Burgos-Martinez, who had been sent to Haiti by Escobar in 1987 to establish a local foothold.[2]

In the 1970s, the emergence of the drug trade sent political ripples to all corners of the hemisphere. The demand for cocaine has always come from the north; in nearly every nation from the Andes through Central America, the Caribbean, and Mexico, the cocaine trade has been inexorably linked with political developments. Equally as ubiquitous has been the response, the US-led War on Drugs.

While white Americans seem to now be reckoning with the legacy of criminalized poverty and institutionalized racism at home, there has been a corresponding political and social effect of those long-standing practices throughout the region. The devastating impact on human rights has been well established. And abroad, just like at home, rarely did combating drug trafficking deter the political objectives of US leaders. Manuel Noriega had been "our man" in Panama before he was indicted on drug-trafficking charges in 1988.[3] US troops invaded and overthrew him a year later. Perhaps most notorious is the Reagan-era Iran-Contra scandal, in which US intelligence agencies facilitated the cocaine trade as a way to fund the Contras' war against the Sandinista government in Nicaragua.

Interestingly, it was partially as a result of the US congressional inquiry into Iran-Contra that information concerning the trade's hold in Haiti made international headlines. Burgos-Martinez, Escobar's representative, had made fast friends with leadership in the Haitian security forces. He operated openly and lived lavishly, with the casino at the El Rancho Hotel turning over an estimated $50 million a week.[4] At the same time, the CIA was looking for information as well as allies in the military to help steer the post-Duvalier political transition.

While official military financing was prevented by Congress, the agency financed the creation of a Haitian intelligence agency, run entirely by the military.[5] The stated purpose was to combat drug trafficking. However, it was later revealed that the intelligence agency was heavily involved in the drug trade—all while using its newfound equipment and training to repress political opponents.

After Aristide's 1990 election, the president sought to combat traffickers but was virtually powerless to do so. Préval later recalled his first meeting with the US Embassy upon his becoming prime minister that year.[6]

"The US ambassador came to me," he explained. "He said, 'Do you know Fernando Burgos?'" Préval said no.

"He is the head of the Medellín cartel in Haiti," Préval remembered the ambassador telling him. "If you arrest him, you will die, and they'll have a replacement tomorrow."

The new administration certainly couldn't count on any support from within the military or the police.[7] At the time, one of the Medellín cartel's greatest assets in Haiti, according to US court documents, was the head of police in Port-au-Prince, Michel François—a personal friend of Martelly.[8] Certainly, Aristide faced the ire of the country's economic elite, the oligarchs who had gotten fantastically wealthy under Duvalier, but it may have been his efforts to replace François as much as anything else that precipitated his ouster in September 1991, the "Cocaine Coup." The junta that took power ran the country as a de facto narco-state.

Ironically, some ten years later, it was Aristide on the receiving end of US allegations of drug trafficking. Though Escobar was dead, and Aristide had disbanded the Haitian military upon his return to power in 1994, the country was still serving as a significant transshipment point for Colombian cocaine. And still, the US government's stated antidrug objectives seemed to have more to do with political objectives than anything else.

In the early 2000s, the charges against Aristide were weaponized in the multiyear effort to overthrow him for a second time. Nevertheless, in June 2003, Aristide turned over to the US Haiti's most-wanted trafficker, Jacques Kétant. The heir to Burgos's Haiti operation, Kétant had been just as untouchable, living a life of open luxury. Kétant's sentencing hearing took place in February 2004. He was already cooperating with US prosecutors and pled guilty. At the hearing he spoke for twenty-five minutes, lashing out at Aristide. "The man is a drug lord," he said. "He controlled the drug trade in Haiti. He turned the country into a narco-country."[9] That, of course, had not been Aristide's doing; the drug trade was long established before he took office. Still, Kétant's charges made for effective propaganda.

Within a week, Aristide was gone. "You have to look at the declarations of Kétant to understand a lot of things, to explain a lot of things," a European diplomat said at the time. "It was a way to help the negotiation [along]."[10] Though the allegations continued to hang over him, Aristide has never been charged with drug trafficking.

The group of paramilitaries that had been spreading terror across the country and receiving US support in their efforts to force Aristide from power, however, did include a former police chief later indicted on drug-trafficking and money-laundering charges—Guy Philippe. Though public focus on Haiti's drug trade dwindled after the 2004 coup and supply chains shifted, there is no doubt that it remained a significant force in Haitian politics.

Traffickers have "more power than the government," Préval told me, some twenty-five years after he was first told of Burgos-Martinez. "They have more money, and they don't want good people to be in power," he said.[11]

For international officials and their allies among the Haitian elite, the 2015 electoral process was a necessary step in consolidating the Aid State, or, at the very least, in preventing its collapse. But Haiti's outsourced elections had long stopped representing any notion of legitimate democracy. They did, however, offer a path to protection for the country's most corrupt, who were best placed to compete in a low-turnout vote. And once again, the US appeared perfectly content to look the other way on drug trafficking to ensure its political objectives.

AMID THE INFLUX of billions in post-quake reconstruction funds, there was little focus on the lingering influence of the drug trade. But some people were paying attention. After Martelly took office, a number of former police officers who had been removed for their ties to traffickers were reincorporated into the force. There were also questions about his close associates, including his brother-in-law, Charles "Kiko" Saint-Rémy, and longtime bandmate RoRo Nelson, and their own ties to the drug trade.

In 2012, a DEA sting operation resulted in the seizure of some 270 kilos of Colombian cocaine in a house on the outskirts of Port-au-Prince. The deal ensnared at least two Colombians and a high-ranking Haitian police officer.[12] The next year, the wealthy Haitian businessman

Rodolphe Jaar was arrested in the Dominican Republic. He owned a company in Florida with a relative of Martelly.[13] It later emerged in court that Jaar had been working as a DEA informant, and had stolen five kilos from that 2012 bust to fuel his own illicit activity.[14]

The same year as Jaar's arrest, the owner of a popular beachfront hotel frequented by the president was arrested after he reported "finding" more than twenty-three pounds of marijuana floating off the coast. Kiko, the president's brother-in-law, intervened. The government prosecutor who had ordered the arrest was charged with abuse of authority and later fled the country fearing for his life. For good reason, it turned out, as just months later Evinx Daniel, the hotelier, disappeared.[15] His body was never found. According to an individual who has long worked as an informant for the DEA, the disappearance took place right after Daniel had flown to Miami to meet with DEA officials.[16]

"Kiko is a known, documented drug trafficker," Keith McNichols, a DEA agent who spent years in Haiti, told me.[17] But it likely wasn't just the president who was protecting his brother-in-law. During Martelly's time in office, Kiko had free rein and met frequently with the DEA's Haiti section chief, prompting many to assume that he was an informant, or being shielded from scrutiny for some other reason. McNichols, who would eventually blow the whistle on his colleagues, alleged corruption and blamed the local station chief and other DEA officials for thwarting an investigation into what was one of Haiti's largest drug busts ever.

In early April 2015, a Panamanian-flagged cargo vessel docked at the Varreaux terminal, a private port on the outskirts of Cité Soleil that is owned by the Mevs family, one of the wealthiest in Haiti. The ship, carrying 650 tons of sugar from Colombia that belonged to Acra Industries, a conglomerate owned by another of Haiti's wealthiest families and the same one that had a stake in the El Rancho Hotel, had been delayed when crossing the Panama Canal and then spent another three days in the bay of Port-au-Prince before docking.

When longshoremen began off-loading the cargo, however, they stumbled upon several packages of cocaine among the tons of sugar. The workers started scrambling, jostling with one another to get ahold of the drugs.[18] Before law enforcement had even been summoned, a series of vehicles sped into the port. One was a white Toyota Land Cruiser, which witnesses later said was driven by Dimitri Hérard, a Haitian police officer assigned to the National Palace and one of Martelly's top security officers. Another package allegedly wound up in the trunk of a car belonging to a local judge from Cité Soleil.

By the time the DEA and Haitian antidrug agents arrived at the scene, drugs were nowhere to be found. However, a twenty-eight-day search conducted by the US Coast Guard did eventually discover 107.6 kilos of cocaine and 12.8 kilos of heroin stowed away among the tons of sugar. The DEA estimated that the full load was likely closer to 800 kilos of cocaine and 300 kilos of heroin, with a street value of more than $100 million. Most of the drugs had been siphoned off before any police arrived. It was a stark reminder of the role that drug trafficking plays in the country's politics—and its economy.

"Two-thirds of the richest families in Haiti are drug traffickers," McNichols explained, exasperated. "You don't get rich selling rice and sugar," he added.

Well, when your family has a monopoly on imports of basic goods, maybe you do. The Acra family, as well as the Mevses, both supported the 1991 military coup and found themselves on the US sanction lists. Despite the international embargo imposed on the military junta, Haiti's elite soaked up profits as prices for basic goods skyrocketed. They did indeed get rich on rice and sugar. But while the DEA agent may have been exaggerating, there was little question that many among Haiti's elite were awash in drug money.

"Everyone knows," the former agent continued. They all have legitimate businesses as fronts, "but they're known traffickers." The elite, however, can rely on their closeness to political power to avoid any repercussions.

After the bust in the spring of 2015, the Acra and Mevs families categorically denied any implication in the drug seizure. A local judge did issue an indictment against members of both families but it was quickly dropped. The judge later acknowledged, in an interview with the DEA, that he had received multiple "favors" from the Mevs family.

In the end, only one individual, a longshoreman, was arrested. Marc-Antoine Acra, who had taken over the family business along with his brother, traveled to Florida—where he and his family own millions of dollars' worth of real estate—and hired two high-profile lawyers who began reaching out to the US embassy in an attempt to clear his family's name. It would take years for more details to emerge about what really happened on that sugar boat and about the network of corruption that worked to cover it up. But, on the eve of elections, it served as a stark reminder about what was at stake in the coming vote.

Guy Philippe, still on the list of the DEA's most-wanted fugitives, emerged from hiding and announced his intention to run for the Senate. As did two others allegedly tied to the drug trade: Hervé Fourcand, a former military man from Martelly's hometown, and Ralph Féthière, himself a onetime military official and police commissioner. And they all were running under the banner of PHTK, or for parties closely aligned with the Martelly administration. One of those parties was Bouclier; ironically, given the immunity at stake, it was French for "shield." The party was rumored to be led by Kiko.

"The legal bandits take to the streets. Can't wait. The entire team is going to prepare itself. Yes, they're legalizing," Sweet Micky had sung in his 2008 track. The *bandi legal* were ready for the elections. The international community was ready for the elections. But was the country?

History shows that when Haitians have faith in their electoral process, they will turn out. As the outsourcing of elections deepened, however, participation rates have plummeted. Part of this has been due to conscious efforts to break the grassroots movements that had brought Aristide and then Préval to the presidency, but it also reflects a growing disappointment with electoral politics among Haitians. The 2010 election made it abundantly clear who the real powers behind Haiti's democracy were. In 2008, an already low 36.6 percent of Haitians reported having trust in elections. By 2015, that figure had fallen below 20 percent—the lowest for any country in the region.[19]

20

THE ELECTORAL TEST

————

The polls were late to open, but before they had officially closed, it was clear the election had been a disaster. I pulled into the Damien voting center, one of the nation's largest, just as a plainclothed man with an automatic weapon casually got into a crowded SUV and left the premises. Inside the gate, three Haitian National Police officers sat in the shade. All fifty-one voting booths had been destroyed, and lunch-pail-like ballot boxes and the thousands of ballots that had once filled them littered the courtyard. The ballots themselves looked like the board in a game of Guess Who? In Cité Soleil, where the Damien center was located, more than two dozen candidates were competing for the position of deputy, including Vladimir Jean Louis for PHTK, whom local residents blamed for the violence. Of the 17,000-plus votes that were counted in Cité Soleil, he officially received 373.

Reports from all over the country made clear that polling center violence and intimidation was a problem not confined to the capital. In Chansolme, in Haiti's rural northwest, a polling place supervisor was forced to hide under a bed for hours after being threatened by armed individuals. They needed his signature to officially endorse the stack of already filled-in ballots they had brought. In the Nippes department, another supervisor was held at gunpoint and forced to sign a document canceling the election for an entire voting center. In the small town of Desdunes in the Artibonite, all five voting centers were shut down by midday.

As word spread over local radio, many potential voters stayed home. The expected crowds that often form after church lets out never materialized. There were structural barriers as well. In the promised land of Canaan, the sprawling informal suburb of Port-au-Prince where more than three hundred thousand had moved since the earthquake, there wasn't even a single voting center. *Tap taps, motos,* and other transportation were banned on election day. Many residents of the capital, when they discovered where they had been assigned to vote, simply had no way of getting there. Hundreds of thousands across the country never even had election cards; the national ID system that donors had spent tens of millions reforming still contained untold numbers of those killed in the earthquake, while remaining out of reach for far too many of the living.

Soon after polls officially closed, however, the president of the electoral council announced that the day had been a success. A local coalition of observers, led by Rosny Desroches and funded by the US and other donors, offered up a largely positive assessment as well. The verdict from the OAS was clear. While noting "some incidents of violence," the observer mission hailed the election as "a step forward for Haitian democracy."[1] Soon thereafter, the EU agreed. Yes, there were some problems, the EU noted, but nothing that would undermine the legitimacy of the vote itself. Official results were still more than a week away.

If the first leg of the electoral marathon had been a test, it failed any reasonable democratic standard. But it had worked just fine for those inside the system. PHTK was defiant. After the vote, the party denounced a "smear campaign" on the part of its political adversaries.[2] To prove their point, PHTK pointed to the statements from international observer groups claiming the vote had been a success.

I caught up with Roudy Choute, the former International Republican Institute employee who was now working with PHTK. The election had done little to take the smile off his face; the gap between his two front teeth was visible as ever.

"From the beginning the opposition wanted to start over," he explained.[3] "When you're a loser, that's what you do." But the opposition "forgot it's a democracy," Choute continued. "Even if there are three votes, the one with two goes on. You can't cancel the vote." After thirty years in power, he believed, the opposition still had nothing to campaign on. "That's how we got the international community on our side." He wasn't ashamed of that fact. He was proud of it.

Choute, however, did acknowledge that some of the government's allies were causing a public relations problem. He singled out Bouclier as "the party with the worst drug connections." Little was known about this new upstart party that had caused so many problems on the day of the vote. I wanted to find out for myself.

THE PARTY HEADQUARTERS was located in the old Ministry of Defense building in Delmas 60. There was something fitting about this mysterious new party occupying the military's old building. When Ti Mo and I showed up on his *moto* unannounced, we had no idea if we'd even be able to get into the building.

Outside, a handful of young men sat in the shade leaning against the building's façade. Most wore dark sunglasses, name-brand shirts, and awkwardly set baseball hats. The door was locked, but Ti Mo convinced one of the guys outside to make a call. Before long, we were led into the building, up a narrow flight of stairs, and into a small room with a large wooden desk and papers piled high. A tall man, clean cut, in a slim-fitting navy blue suit, entered the room, sat down behind the desk, and introduced himself. His name was Pierre Antoine Louis, he said. The name rang a bell. He was the director of Haiti Cherie, the private-sector association made up of the younger generation of Haiti's elite families that had been backing Martelly. He was a lawyer by trade, licensed in New York—an American citizen, in fact. He had worked for the United Nations, for the US Embassy, and been an advisor to President Martelly. He introduced himself as the chief of staff to Bouclier's presidential candidate Steeve Khawly, a member of Haiti Cherie.

The Khawlys were a well-known family in Haiti, but a regional one. Compared to the national presence of the Mevs, Acra, Boulos, and Vorbe families, the Khawlys' influence was felt most acutely in the south of Haiti. The Khawlys, whose palatial residences and flashy cars were well known along the southern coast, had accumulated their wealth amid allegations of drug trafficking; but they had plenty of legitimate businesses. The family owned car dealerships, for a time was Chevron's sole fuel distributor, and had multiple hotels and resorts.[4] Perhaps the biggest family business was flour. They owned a milling operation in Guyana and controlled much of the distribution in Haiti.[5] Steeve Khawly and Martelly had been friends since they were children.

Antoine Louis asked a few pointed questions and googled my name. He had to do his due diligence, he said. But he was nonplussed when I said that I was interested in Kiko's role within the party and alleged ties to drug traffickers. Being a *blan* in Haiti provides a level of access that is unrecognizable to most Haitians. Ti Mo always got a kick out of it. Antoine Louis graciously led us into the room next door, where Khawly waited.

"Elections happened on Sunday like the [electoral council] said they would happen," Khawly said after a brief round of introductions.[6] The government and international observers are saying it was acceptable, he pointed out. He acknowledged problems, but denied that Bouclier had benefited. "Bouclier was a victim in the elections," he countered. Khawly recognized that some parties would benefit from the low turnout and violence. "We did fairly well," he stated, still more than a week before any official results would be known. I asked about the party's perceived closeness with PHTK and Martelly.

"I have a special relationship with Martelly," he said. "I've known him all my life but we are fighting for the same place." Khawly graduated high school in 1986, just months after Duvalier's exile to France. "Haiti was a beautiful place," he recalled, "but thirty years later, it's worse than ever." It was a common refrain from those who had opposed the alternating Préval and Aristide governments for the previous twenty-five years. Haiti's failures since the fall of Duvalier reflected the failures of Aristide and Préval alone.

I asked if things had continued to get worse under Martelly. Was that why he was running for president?

Khawly started rattling off a list of Martelly's accomplishments before his chief of staff interrupted. "We're not here to talk about how great our competitor is," Antoine Louis said.

And what about the party's finances? They were one of the only parties that had run candidates in all ten departments, I noted.

"It's just an impression that Bouclier has money," Khawly responded. "We have friends, and we are using money we received"—his chief of staff interrupted again with "raised"—"from the private sector," Khawly finished, less confidently than he had begun.

And what about the president's brother-in-law, Kiko? Was he involved with the party?

"We have a board of nineteen members," Khawly shot back. "And Kiko is not one of them." I asked for a list of their board members. Antoine Louis called in a few other aides, and the four of them started whispering among themselves. On a single sheet of lined paper Antoine Louis wrote the board members' names down for me. I slipped the note into my bag, thanked them for their time, and said I'd be in touch. Once outside, I unfolded the piece of paper and began to inspect the names. Kiko wasn't listed, but one name immediately jumped out: Marc-Antoine Acra. Bouclier's party treasurer was the man implicated in the sugar boat drug bust, and one of the investors in the newly renovated El Rancho Hotel.

A few months later, with the next president still up in the air, Martelly appointed Acra as a goodwill ambassador to the Dominican Republic, providing the businessman with state-backed immunity.

IT TOOK ELEVEN days for the electoral council, CEP by its French acronym, to publish the official results. The national participation rate was a paltry 18 percent, and in the West department, home to the capital and 41 percent of registered voters, participation hadn't reached double digits. But even many of those who did turn up to vote never had their ballots counted. In fact, almost a quarter of all the tally sheets from across the country were never even collected. The electoral authorities did, at least partially, acknowledge the scale of the problem, announcing that deputy races would be rerun in those areas where less than 70 percent of the votes had been counted due to fraud or violence. The decision meant that in some areas, the results would stand despite more than a quarter of the votes never being counted.[7]

In such a fractured field, there were only a handful of winners in the first round, but PHTK was advancing more candidates to the October runoff than any other party for both deputy and senator. Bouclier had also done well. Overall, the *bandi legal* had thrived. Hervé Fourcand was advancing in the Senate, as was Ralph Féthière. In the Grand'Anse, Guy Philippe qualified for the vote's second round.

It was impossible not to be struck by the brazenness, seeing it all unfold in real time. Everyone knew the donors would sign off on the election regardless of what happened. Candidates understood they could get away with just about anything. The vast majority of the population had given up on their internationally managed elections altogether, or been excluded from participating in the first place. Before the election, an international official had told me that the credibility of the process hinged on the first step. But even after the chaos of election day, there was simply no turning back now, and donors would do everything imaginable to ensure the electoral train continued to push forward, regardless of the flaws—and who stood to benefit from them.

21

THE MOST VOTES MONEY CAN BUY

The presidential election was scheduled for late October 2015. With Martelly constitutionally barred from running, his party selected Jovenel Moïse, a businessman from the north, as its presidential candidate. Martelly's plan B seemed to be Khawly, the Bouclier candidate. But in total, fifty-four candidates were on the ballot. Lavalas was finally back, for the first time since the 2004 coup, with Dr. Maryse Narcisse. Moïse Jean-Charles, who had risen to national prominence leading protests against Lamothe and Martelly on horseback the previous year, was the candidate for Petit Dessaline. And Jude Célestin, the man left out of the 2010 runoff in favor of Martelly, was once again in the race, running for a new party, LAPEH. Préval had a different candidate in mind this time: Jacky Lumarque, the rector of a local university. There was just one problem: the electoral council had barred him from participating.

If August had been a test of the electoral system, October was the main event. Martelly's term was ending in February 2016; with another botched election, the succession timeline would be thrown into doubt, raising the possibility of a transitional government. Martelly's desire to hand power to an ally was no secret. "If there is continuity, I can come back," he said.[1] But it wasn't just the next president and Parliament on the line. After the billions of dollars and pledges to "build back better" after the 2010 quake, the legitimacy of the Aid State rested on a successful political transition from Martelly. That's what passed for stability, defined, as it always had been, by foreign powers and Haiti's tiny elite. And, with

Hillary Clinton running for president, failure—instability, waves of migrants showing up in the US, and uncomfortable questions of her own role in the situation—also meant real danger of political blowback in the campaign.

While the failure of the reconstruction effort dogged Clinton in the US, in Haiti, it was her intervention in the 2010 election that continued to reverberate. Préval had tentatively backed Martelly's efforts to hold the elections, but after the exclusion of his party's candidate and the violence in August getting an international check mark of legitimacy, his party threatened to boycott the presidential vote. "The international community has their own agenda," Fritz Longchamp, a former minister under Préval and an official in his party, told me. "They see money was wasted [on the August vote], but they want to do what is good for Martelly. . . . It's 2010 all over again but instead of against Préval, it's for Martelly."[2]

Doing little to dispel those memories, the United States named Ken Merten, the ambassador when the US forced Martelly into the runoff election, as its new Haiti special coordinator.[3] Pamela White was sent into retirement, and the policy reins in Port-au-Prince returned to the man who had helped set this chain of events off in the first place. The message was just as clear in Washington, where a growing chorus in Congress was warning about the perils of the US continuing its failed policies in Haiti. The appointment of Merten meant more of the same. He and others in the Core Group did all they could to salvage the electoral process, and with it Martelly's presidency and their own legacy.

THE OCTOBER VOTE came and went without a repeat of the August violence. There "was no black smoke," as one diplomat put it.[4] No evidence of burning tires, which can reliably be spotted from the bird's-eye view afforded by Pétion-Ville hotels and embassy residences. A clear view was the measure of success for many in the diplomatic corps. With no public exit polls and the long process of tabulating votes ahead, the only thing clear was that the real political fight was just beginning. As 2010 had shown, elections weren't just about turning out voters, but also turning out the international community. And the lack of violence did not mean a clean election.

I had first heard rumors that parties were selling their observer cards in the days before the October vote. Each party was legally entitled to have an observer at each of the more than thirteen thousand voting bureaus across the country. With more than 120 parties—inflated by the lower threshold to form—the electoral council distributed 916,000 passes. They had value because the holder would be allowed to vote "off-list" wherever they were observing, regardless of whether they were registered at that particular center. Apparently, the passes were going for as much as thirty dollars apiece.[5]

In the capital, the problem was evident before the doors to the polls opened. I arrived at the Ecole Horace Etheard voting center in Solino just after six in the morning. Inside, poll workers were still setting up. They explained that only six of the party observers—*mandataires*—would be allowed in at a time, and that they would rotate throughout the day to ensure all parties had access. Outside, more than twenty Haitian antidrug agents were standing guard, and a few sought to organize the large crowd getting increasingly impatient. They separated those with the observer passes from those without. I counted 160 in the *mandataire* line. There were just a handful in the other.

It was a scene repeated at center after center in the capital and, local observers reported, in provincial cities across the country. As the day wore on, I noticed that, in many instances, those voting with their *mandataire* cards were only asked to write their name on a blank piece of paper before poll workers handed them a ballot to fill. Normally, a voter would need to be registered at that particular bureau, have their ID checked against a voter registry list, and then sign said list, in order to get a ballot. With a *mandataire* pass, it was as if a ghost had voted.

If the indelible ink used on voters' thumbs had worked, it would still have been visible when parties began questioning the results the next day. And more individuals began speaking out about the "silent" fraud that had occurred on election day. Steven Benoit, a former senator from the West, denounced his own party for having pocketed the public funds destined for his campaign and selling a majority of the party's observer credentials for about twenty dollars each. "There was no violence," he told the press, it was the "perfect crime." Many of those questioning the results began calling it the "Sola election," a reference to the Spanish political consultant who had run Martelly's 2010 campaign and had recently returned to Haiti.

Even some of those close to PHTK privately acknowledged the problem with the observers. "This may be a case of where there's smoke, there's fire," Antoine Louis, Khawly's campaign manager, told me.[6] "Elections are a way to make money," he said. "It's like Black Friday in the US." It was rational behavior, he explained, and everyone played their part. "The international community has their particular way, the NGOs have their way, it's all rent-seeking to profit from Haiti," he said. "The only ones not to profit are the Haitian people."

Still, Antoine Louis saw the political games as theater. "Everyone is manipulating everyone," he said. It reminded him of the 2010 election. "They are trying to manipulate the *blan,* the US."

There was a saying in Haiti: everyone in the elite had "their *blan.*" Haitian politicians knew the vote was as much about convincing the international community as anything else, and *blan* certainly could help. I knew part of the reason I had access was that some wanted me to be their *blan.* While the manipulation of foreigners was real, it appeared the manipulation of the election was, too. I needed an opinion that wasn't tainted by politics, that couldn't be cast aside as the denouncements of a sore loser. I called Rosny Desroches.

"There was definitely concern over control of *mandataires,*" Desroches told me.[7] He was the head of a consortium of local organizations that observed the election, financed with some of the millions that donors had spent on the process. Over the many years that he had been a vocal member of Haiti's civil society, he rarely bucked the line of the embassy class. But it was obvious he was concerned now. His organization estimated turnout of about 25 percent, meaning only about a million and half votes in a country of eleven million. Desroches believed upward of half may have been from those with *mandataire* cards. "Those who would do that are those with money," and they could see beforehand how to use it to their advantage, he said.

Finally, on November 5, officials announced that the top two fin-
ishers were PHTK's Moïse (32.8 percent) and LAPEH's Célestin (25.3
percent). Moïse Jean-Charles finished third (14.3 percent), and Fanmi
Lavalas' Dr. Narcisse came in fourth (7.1 percent). Célestin and Moïse,
it appeared, would be headed for a runoff election.[8] But by the time the
results had been announced, opposition to the election had reached a
boiling point. LAPEH, despite their candidate's placement in the runoff,
pledged to contest the results, which it deemed a product of fraud. In a
joint statement, eight presidential candidates—the G8—termed the announced results "unacceptable," and called for an independent commission to investigate fraud. The group characterized the current process as
a "dangerous return to the past" when dictators organized elections and
reinforced the perception that "those who vote decide nothing."[9]

Five years earlier, it had been Martelly leading protests in the capital
against the Préval government and its alleged fraud. The international
community eventually intervened in his favor. In the late fall of 2015,
however, it was Martelly and his chosen successor, Jovenel Moïse, who
were the target of protesters' ire. But PHTK could still count on the
support of the international community. Regardless of the election's
flaws, the most important thing was to simply move forward. It wasn't a
flawed election that threatened stability; it was no election, as had been
the case in 2010.

IN EARLY DECEMBER I met Ken Merten in the cafeteria of the Rayburn
House Office Building in Washington. He was about to leave for Haiti.
"We will see what Jude will do," Merten said.[10] The two had faced off five
years earlier; they knew each other well. Merten thought Célestin's opposition was a bluff, a way to extract concessions from the government.
"His public posture is he's not going to the second round and is standing
with the G8. Personally, I think this is a rash decision. . . . Our position
is that there was a process and rules and everyone agreed to them and
it needs to be stuck to," he told me. If there was any further delay to the
runoff, Haiti would quickly find itself running up against the end of
Martelly's constitutional mandate on February 7. "We definitely don't

want to see a transitional government that has no democratic legitimacy," the diplomat said.

As for the claims of widespread fraud, Merten thought it was little more than sore losers. "Our understanding is that both the UN and OAS think the [official] results were close to their quick counts," he said. I pointed out that while that may be true, a quick count tells us nothing about the legitimacy of the votes themselves. "I don't disagree with that," he said. "But I don't think there is any way to prove that. We'll probably never know." He discarded the calls for an audit as too time-consuming and too political. "We need to be careful not to let the perfect be the enemy of the good."

It was *tèt dwat*—straight ahead—for the second round. It made sense. A verification commission, some international actors worried, could end up sanctioning the PHTK candidate for fraud, opening the door to the runoff for Moïse Jean-Charles or someone else associated with Lavalas, "whom they dread," as one diplomat told *Le Nouvelliste*.[11]

And, as the conflict dragged out, it threatened to more intimately impact the unfolding presidential race in the United States. "Since Mrs. Clinton was well involved in the 2010–2011 decisions, if we started badly, we must end well," Ricardo Seitenfus, who had blown the whistle on international interference in the 2010 election, told a local radio station. The US, he said, just wanted a clean power transfer. An end to the crisis that didn't threaten to blow up in their face.[12]

There was good reason to suspect the legitimacy of the results, but there was no denying that the opposition had shown strength. Célestin, Jean-Charles, and Narcisse, representing three strains of Haiti's center-left pro-democracy movement, had combined to receive more votes than Moïse even with possibly hundreds of thousands of ghost votes. Still, a low turnout, a divided opposition, and the support of the international community had indeed created the space for PHTK to move on. Keeping the opposition divided had been the government's strategy, but breaking Haiti's grassroots movements had been the goal of retrograde forces in Haiti and the international community for decades, ever since Aristide's first election in 1990. Now, in an attempt to consolidate their ill-gotten gains, the government and international push to blindly march forward with the elections served as a unifying force among opposition political parties and, more broadly, Haiti's long-repressed civil society organizations. Organizations that had been on opposite sides of the 2004 coup, and on opposite sides of just about everything since, began collaborating.

Pressure was building, and a united opposition together with a united civil society was a potent force. There was fear; fear of the "radical" opposition taking power, fear of a transitional government, fear of the unknown. Above all, there was fear that international actors were losing control.

As THE GOVERNMENT continued to push forward, with the US at its back, opposition to the runoff election only hardened. Two of the nine electoral councilors resigned, then another and another. Local observers, including Desroches's outfit, backed out and pledged not to participate. Private-sector groups, which had largely supported the government, reversed themselves and called for serious reforms before moving forward. There were even signs of dissent in the international community. Celso Amorim, the Brazilian diplomat heading the OAS electoral observer mission, issued a statement expressing concern about pushing forward without further dialogue.[13]

On the Thursday before the Sunday vote, Martelly defiantly took to the airwaves. He again fell back on his foreign support. The international community, he said, would not accept a transitional government. "The country will be under embargo," he warned.

On Friday, another electoral councilor threatened to resign. It would have left the institution without a quorum, rendering it unable to legally sign off on election results. In the meantime, a massive protest—the largest Port-au-Prince had seen in years—began the long march from the popular neighborhoods at the base of the hill, past the hotels of Pétion-Ville, and to the headquarters of the electoral council. For diplomats in their homes high among the hills, the flood of people sent a clear message. "A few days ago, some diplomats questioned the capacity of the opposition to mobilize," an international electoral official told me. "Obviously it does not look good now that they are on the streets."[14]

That afternoon, with thousands protesting outside their office, the electoral council announced that the runoff vote would be canceled. There would be no democratic transfer of power on February 7. For the last dozen years, Haitian poet Lyonel Trouillot said at the time, "all Haitian political decisions are made practically under the diktat of this nebula that is called the international community."[15] Since the 2004 coup and establishment of the UN Blue Helmets, donors had rarely not gotten their way. This time, the historic mobilization—itself largely the result of blowback to the international community's earlier intervention in favor of Martelly—knocked the electoral train off its tracks and represented a historic shift in Haiti's relationship with the international community. It was a stunning victory over the desires of the donor class and local elite. For the first time since the coup, it seemed, at least for a moment, that change was coming.

But while the opposition and a burgeoning civil society had come together, it was clear there would be more fights ahead. Most directly, was Martelly going to relinquish power on February 7? Would his Duvalierist allies let him? Either way, foreign actors and ghosts from the past were mobilizing to maintain their influence regardless of the outcome.

In the Grand'Anse, a sparsely populated department in southwestern Haiti, former paramilitary death squad leader Guy Philippe, expected to secure a seat in the Senate, had pledged, "We are ready for war. . . . We will divide the country."[16] Philippe had helped lead the 2004 coup against Aristide and had long hinted of his relationship with US intelligence agencies. By 2015, however, he was listed as a fugitive by the DEA, wanted on drug-trafficking and money-laundering charges. Philippe had endorsed Jovenel Moïse and appeared at a campaign rally in his home region.[17]

While Martelly and his international allies had failed at the presidential level, the ill-gotten gains from August at the legislative level were consolidated. The presidential results were pushed aside, but donors brokered an agreement to allow the legislative results to stand. In January, on the sixth anniversary of the earthquake and with dozens of members of the international community in attendance, Haiti swore in a new Parliament. The legislative body was politically fractured, but PHTK and its allies were going to hold a clear majority. The bandits were legal.

Over three decades, the creation of the Aid State had severely constrained Haiti's fledgling democracy. The state had been hollowed out, distributed to foreign NGOs and the private-sector elite. The influx of cash and international attention post-earthquake had helped accomplish what the elite and their foreign backers had long failed to do: divide the population and consolidate a pro-US, pro–free market political regime. The Haitian population's rejection of the election, however, appeared to provide Haiti with an off-ramp from its constricted democratic path. A new transition, like the one that followed the end of the dictatorship, offered hope, a chance at a new beginning. A chance at a new, freer road forward. But the next nine months would reveal just how resistant to change the Aid State had become.

22

THE TRANSITION

As February 7, 2016, approached, there was still no clear successor to Martelly. As tensions heightened, the OAS—whose intervention in 2010 had put Martelly into the presidency—sent a diplomatic mission to facilitate a smooth transition.[1] While negotiations took place in private homes high above the city center, the fight for power was increasingly being waged in the streets below.

Early in the morning on February 5, a local radio station reported that pickup trucks with their beds filled with groups of men in olive-green uniforms were circulating in the capital. Former troops and hopeful recruits had been occupying old military outposts in the countryside for years, waiting for the call to action. With the end of his mandate less than forty-eight hours away, it appeared Martelly was activating these informal groups as a show of force. But, with so many protesting in the streets, the early-morning report portended a dangerous escalation.

Ti Mo picked me up around one. He handed me a bag with his video equipment and I hopped on the back of the *moto*. Protests generally started in La Saline, outside the St. Jean Bosco church where Aristide had delivered sermons against Baby Doc in the eighties. We were late, though, and so instead we went straight to a small side street in Delmas 2. A concrete rooftop there overlooks a small ravine and the street on the other side, which climbs a steep hill. We had been on this rooftop before. Ti Mo wasn't just my driver and friend; he was a videographer and loved the angle from this rooftop. As the first of the day's crowd came into view, he readied his camera. I tried to take it all in.

Tensions were obviously high, but as the crowds wound through the narrow streets, so was the mood. Across the trash-clogged ravine, on a concrete balcony above a small shop, a young girl in a khaki dress danced and shook her fists to the beat. Protesters carried signs, faces of opposition presidential candidates, slogans against Martelly and in support of a transitional government. Toward the rear, there was a sound truck with stacks of speakers blaring music and a few guys hanging on the back. Still, all I could think about was whether we'd see those olive-green uniforms.

We followed along the protest route, driving ahead on the *moto,* parking, and waiting as the wave approached and surrounded us. As we neared the Champ de Mars, the mood had changed. There were more police, and they were responding more aggressively than usual. A volley of tear gas split the remaining protesters into smaller crowds surrounding the main square. In the chaos, I noticed two pickup trucks heading right toward us, their beds full of men in olive green. Guns were slung over some shoulders.

As the trucks turned the corner in front of us, someone threw a rock. It clanged off the cab, or maybe it hit a metal barricade. Brakes screeched. *Pop, pop, pop*—gunfire. Everyone scattered, or most everyone. Some of the protesters charged straight at the men in olive green. Those on the truck had weapons, but they were vastly outnumbered. The driver of the second truck slammed on the gas; one of those in the bed jerked backward and fell to the ground. The two trucks disappeared, leaving the man to the incoming crowd. He staggered to his feet. He was older than I expected; he looked frail. His black combat boots were faded and his clothes hung loose over his frame. He wasn't fighting, he was pleading for his life.

The man fell to the ground not more than five feet from me; the kicks started immediately. I lunged forward to do something, I don't know what, but was stopped short. A local journalist, a photographer I had seen at countless protests over the years, had pulled me back. He shot me a look that made me realize he had likely saved me, and then he steadied his camera. The man on the ground was already bleeding badly; he appeared to be unconscious. His motionless head rested on the curb. Then, a young man raised a chunk of concrete high over his head, extending both arms upward. When I close my eyes, I can still hear the sound of its crash against the sidewalk and the man's skull.

From the first shot to the death of the old man at my feet, less than a minute had passed. I stood on the corner with Ti Mo in silence. Neither of us knew what to say, we just kept shaking our heads.

Later that day, we learned his name: Neroce Ciceron, a seventy-something former captain in the armed forces. He was not part of some high-powered paramilitary force; he was a relic, used, in this case, as a pawn in a political game, a desperate attempt to show force on the eve of February 7. "The [ex] military in the streets was a clear warning," Pascale Roussy, the EU electoral mission's political analyst, explained the next morning. "If there is no deal, this is what can happen." What had happened, she continued, was "controlled violence." She paused. "A sacrifice even."[2]

But a deal had been reached.

Around two in the morning of February 6, the OAS announced an agreement with the president and with the partially seated Parliament on a transfer of power.[3] Martelly had relented—or had gotten what he had asked for in return for his departure. Thirty years to the day after Baby Doc's departure, on February 7, 2016, Martelly let go of the presidential sash.

That afternoon, protesters once again took to the streets. They were more jubilant than in days past, however. Even if few trusted Martelly, it was a celebration and a show of their strength and determination in the face of threats and violence. But, as had occurred every day prior, when protesters approached the Champ de Mars, they were met with tear gas. I was on foot in the middle of the crowd; we all scattered. After the clouds cleared, at my feet, on the side of the street, was a spent tear gas canister. I picked it up. "RIOT CS SMOKE PROJECTILE," it read. The company was Combined Systems Inc., based in Jamestown, Pennsylvania. "Made in U.S.A." was printed on the opposite side. Even as political change, at last, seemed possible, it served as a reminder that powerful forces still worked to manage the situation.

MICHEL MARTELLY, THE Aid State front man, was gone, but the agreement that pushed him out kicked the decision about his replacement to the newly installed Parliament. The head of the body was the president of the Senate, Jocelerme Privert. He was one of ten senators whose mandates had not expired the year prior, meaning his position had not come as a result of the most recent electoral debacle. Privert had been in or around government since the midnineties: a tax official, a minister under Aristide, a political prisoner. The last transition had taken place following Aristide's ouster in 2004, when the UN Blue Helmets first arrived. For nearly the entire two-year period, Privert had sat in a jail cell in Port-au-Prince.[4]

Prior to the coup, he had served as Aristide's interior minister. In the final weeks and months, state security forces had largely abandoned the government. At the same time, Guy Philippe and his paramilitary band of ex-soldiers were marching through the countryside, terrorizing populations on their way to the capital. In Gonaïves, a seaside town in the Artibonite department, armed opposition groups began mobilizing, seizing control of significant chunks of the city and surrounding towns. Privert traveled to the region and called for calm. But, in the government's subsequent efforts to retake control of the city, the few state security agents still loyal to Aristide appeared to operate together with armed civilians under their own control. Initial news reports indicated that five people had been killed in the clashes. Within days, however, a local human rights group alleged a "genocide" had taken place, and that pro-government gangs had massacred dozens of people.[5] Within three weeks, Aristide was on a plane to the Central African Republic. Soon thereafter, Privert was thrown in jail, where he languished until the end of the US-backed transitional government.[6]

Nearly ten years after his release from prison, on February 14, 2016, the Haitian Parliament voted Jocelerme Privert "interim" president of Haiti. The last transitional government had jailed him; now, he would be leading the transition. The last transition had swept Lavalas from power, but in the eyes of some, his rise to the presidency represented Lavalas' return.

At the inauguration celebration, held in the temporary offices of the National Palace, Lavalas presidential candidate Dr. Maryse Narcisse could be seen toasting Mildred Aristide, the former First Lady. It was a sight few could have predicted just weeks earlier. "The last time I came to the palace was in 2003 when President Aristide was in power," Ores Nixon, a street activist, told Reuters.[7] "Now look at me, inside the national palace with a glass of champagne, celebrating the inauguration of our President Jocelerme Privert." The photo must have sent shivers up the spines of just about every member of the diplomatic corps. Had they really lost that much control of the situation?

For thirty years, whenever Haiti's democracy threatened elite interests, those forces were able to secure their protection—through coups, UN missions, and tightly managed political negotiations. Though Privert had not won an election, his ascension and vocal support for an investigation into the 2015 election was a victory for Democracy—capital "D"—just not the kind favored by foreign actors or much of the Haitian elite. But reform wasn't as simple as swapping one man for another.

As Ken Merten had told me the previous fall, the US was categorically opposed to a transitional government, but, once it was an inevitability, the priority became limiting its scope and duration. The deal that ushered Privert to the presidency gave the interim leader just 120 days to finish the electoral process and hand power over to an elected president. An advisor to the electoral council described the 120-day timeline as "fantastical" and "unrealistic." He despaired that Haiti's political class was trapping itself by agreeing to foreign demands. "Once again, the pressure of the international community is pushing us to make bad choices," he said.[8]

There was also internal pressure. On February 29, the twelve-year anniversary of Aristide's ouster, Guy Philippe took to the airwaves. "Today is an important day," he began. "Not only is it my birthday, but what's more important is that it's the day—in 2004—where Haitian men and women put their heads together to say 'no' to a dictatorship. And they stood before a bloody regime that Jean Bertrand Aristide put in place to end it and give Haiti rest, to give the country another chance." Philippe warned that there was a plan—"a Machiavellian plan to bring the country directly into a civil war." And he had a warning for the interim president. "There's an election that needs to happen, and it will happen. And if it doesn't happen, neither Parliamentarians, nor the provisional president, nor anyone with any repressive force they know and have in their service, no one will be able to hold back this people, no one will be able to hold back these honest citizens, no one will be able to hold me, Guy Philippe, back."[9]

PHTK and its allies like Guy Philippe, together with the international community, were clear that they simply wanted to move forward with a second round. Yet Privert did not cave to the pressure. In April, the interim leader announced the creation of a verification commission that would fully analyze the presidential vote.[10] The 120-day timeline for handing over power to an elected president had passed, but, at long last, it seemed there might be a true accounting of what transpired.

The 2016 transition was far from Haiti's first, but it appeared different from those traversed in earlier years. The 2004 transition was a way to straighten the leftward tilt of Haiti's political arc, and ushered in a UN peacekeeping occupation expressly designed to prevent any future shift. On its surface, the 2016 transition appeared to be a homegrown course correction. But while it was a rebuke to the status quo, to the dictates of foreign actors, the retrograde guardrails running alongside Haiti's road to democracy made any new path nearly impossible to forge.

IN LATE MAY, the commission released its findings. The results were devastating and laid bare the farcical nature of the previous October's vote. The commission explained that the results had been badly distorted by "zombie votes," that is, votes that could not be traced to any living voter, the number of which "exceeded the legitimate votes acquired by politicians." On the whole, the commission found 628,000 untraceable votes, accounting for 40 percent of those cast, and recommended starting the electoral process over, meaning a new first round, precisely what the international actors and PHTK had feared.[11]

On June 8, State Department spokesperson Mark Toner told the press that the US "regretted" the decision by Haiti's electoral council.[12] "The Haitian people deserve to have their voices heard, not deferred," Toner told journalists.

"Right. Well, on Haiti, just—I mean, is it—what's more important?" a journalist asked in response. "For them to have a president that was elected under suspect circumstances, or for them to have a president that was elected in a clean and—"

Toner interrupted. They weren't mutually exclusive, he said. Another spokesperson was even more direct. A week earlier, they had warned of the consequences. "The longer it takes for Haiti to have a democratically elected president, the longer it's going to take for the United States to consider new elements of partnership in helping Haiti confront the mounting economic, climate, and health challenges that they continue to face today," he said.[13] In other words, so long as Privert moved forward with a new first round, the US would withhold financial and political assistance.

On June 14, the day his mandate was supposed to end, many thousands turned out in support of Privert and in support of the new electoral process. Still, the Parliament, full of legal bandits who remained untouched by the verification commission, refused to vote on a bill extending Privert's mandate. While his mandate ended, Privert's interim leadership continued.

The US was once again forced to retreat. On the sixteenth, Merten told the press that, "at this moment," the US recognized Privert as interim president.[14] But bucking demands from the international community came with a cost.

For more than a decade, Haiti's elections had been predominantly financed by donors. But not this time. In July, the US pulled $2 million from the election's internationally managed budget.[15] It wasn't only the US that pulled funding, however, and it wasn't just money for elections. The UN warned that future humanitarian aid was in jeopardy. The IMF, World Bank, and Inter-American Development Bank all either reduced outlays or delayed funding decisions with Privert in office.[16] It stood in stark contrast to the 2004 transitional government, which had always counted on international financial support even as elections were delayed again and again. While the donor community hid behind appeals for "democracy," it remained steadfastly opposed to the actual democratic process unfolding. As Haiti's civil society had been saying for months, there could be no moving forward without looking back.

Still to be determined was if PHTK was even going to be allowed to participate in the new election. After the revelation of widespread fraud, Privert was under immense pressure to exclude Jovenel Moïse from the race. Many believed he would. In September, the government's anti-corruption watchdog released a report accusing Moïse of money laundering. A court issued summonses to former electoral officials and high-ranking Martelly officials, barring many from leaving the country. Justified or not, to some it all smacked of political retribution. But Privert never really went against PHTK. The idea that Privert was a political radical, or hell-bent on damaging PHTK, was a ruse. The opposition may have had the ear of the president, but Privert was also responsive to the same elite groups that had controlled Haiti's political and economic life for years.

In late summer, Jean Marie Vorbe called his old friend Privert. The Vorbe family is one of the wealthiest in Haiti, involved in virtually every sector of the economy and political life. The Vorbe clan included supporters of Lavalas, as well as the most retrograde forces that had spent decades fighting Lavalas. Jean Marie, the family patriarch, had been fielding worried calls from PHTK and its allies for weeks. They were sure Moïse would be excluded.

"I got a call," Jean Marie recalled to me years later. "He said, 'You are the only one who can help me.'" The person, whose identity Vorbe did not disclose, asked for a favor. "I called Privert," Vorbe continued. "He said, 'Let me guess, you are calling about Jovenel.'" The interim president had been fielding a steady diet of such calls. He had said no to all of them. "I told him, 'Privert, you have to [let him participate].'" He eventually set up a meeting for the PHTK candidate to meet with Privert. After, it was clear that Moïse would remain in the race.[17]

The election was on. Then, on October 4, just five days before the vote, everything changed. Just as the sun was setting, Hurricane Matthew, following a similar path to Hurricane Hazel fifty years earlier, made landfall near Les Anglais on Haiti's southern peninsula. One hundred fifty mile per hour winds lashed all night. Some areas received upward of forty inches of rain. The interim presidency of Privert had been fraught, no doubt, but it had also been a time of hope for many. As the storm clouds receded the next morning, so, too, would the remaining hope for change.

23

THE BANANA MAN

————

Martelly's choice of Jovenel Moïse as his successor surprised many in Haiti and the international community. He had never even run for political office, focusing instead on his various business ventures in the country's North-West department, where he was born. He owned an auto parts store, ran a water distribution company, and, the year before launching his presidential campaign, broke ground on a large state-backed banana plantation. The country had once exported plantains and bananas, but that had ended decades earlier after Hurricane Hazel devastated the crops. During the campaign Moïse spoke with lofty rhetoric about restoring the nation's agricultural production and once again exporting produce around the world.

"He was president of the North-West chamber of commerce when I became president of the West," Reginald Boulos, one of Haiti's richest men, told me.[1] Each of the chambers functioned independently, he explained, sort of like little kingdoms. "Jovenel was king of the North, me of the West," Boulos said. He had known Moïse since 2004, and when his old friend told him that he had Martelly's support, he was ecstatic. "If someone knows this country, it is Jovenel," Boulos said. "He's traveled all over." Unlike most of the political elite, with their narrow focus on the Republic of Port-au-Prince, Moïse presented himself as a man of rural Haiti, the forgotten Haiti. But as his long-standing friendship with Boulos demonstrates, he also had important relationships with the nation's political power brokers.

Standing over six feet tall and rail thin, the forty-eight-year-old's candidacy also got a boost from Martelly's family, especially his wife and brother-in-law, Sophia and Kiko Saint-Rémy. Another one of Moïse's business ventures was a cracker company, Mariella Food Products, which he ran with his partner, Evinx Daniel, the hotelier who had been accused of drug trafficking and went missing in 2014. During Martelly's presidency, Moïse also got increasingly involved with Kiko in a business exporting eels, a practice that had long been rumored as a front for laundering money and illicit goods.[2]

Initially, Moïse's lack of political experience showed. In one meeting with an international diplomat, he showed up in a suit so large it appeared to hang on his slim frame like a sail.[3] But his campaign quickly got into shape thanks to the support from Ostos y Sola, the Spanish PR firm that had run Martelly's campaign back in 2010. Enter Neg Bannan Nan ("The Banana Man" in Kreyòl). Moïse's banana plantation officially opened in the fall of 2015, just as the campaign got underway. Quickly, billboards and posters plastered the country with a picture of Moïse and his new moniker, all in the classic PHTK pink.

It was clever public relations, but his message of decentralization, of finally supporting the Haiti outside Port-au-Prince, resonated—even if not all believed the hype. "We are going to use the people, the sun, the land and water to develop the country," he often said on the campaign trail. But never had his message resonated more than in the aftermath of Hurricane Matthew.

HAITI'S 1987 CONSTITUTION, drafted in the aftermath of the Duvalier dictatorship, enshrined the principle of decentralization within the structure of the state. For centuries, Haitian society had been stratified by race, class, and geography. It wasn't until the early nineties, during the first Aristide administration, that all Haitians received the same birth certificate. Prior to that, those born in rural areas, like Moïse, were officially marked as "peasant," denoting their status as second-class citizens, or *moun andeyo* in Kreyòl.[4] But the hopes of a truly decentralized state faded as foreign aid and trade policies decimated rural livelihoods and political power remained concentrated in the Republic of Port-au-Prince. The reconstruction period served as a second chance to achieve the lofty goals contained in the nation's charter. But, by 2016, while the political fights still raged in the capital, so, too, had the neglect of the provinces.

Despite their near total exclusion from political power, Haiti's rural population has always formed a critical part of society, both politically and economically. Politicians focused on the electoral importance of the capital's teeming seaside neighborhoods, but the country remained majority rural. While rural Haiti had long ago learned to survive on its own without any state or outside support, the capital itself remained dependent on the food produced in the provinces. In 2010, rural Haiti was largely spared from the destruction of the earthquake. But, as Hurricane Matthew and its hundred-plus mile an hour winds approached land in October 2016, it was rural Haiti in the eye of the storm.

Jamesky Blaise's family is from Abricots, an isolated and rural community in the Grand'Anse department at the tip of Haiti's southern peninsula.[5] On their property were three modest houses, one occupied by Jamesky's mother, another by his grandmother, and a small church. They had a garden, where the family grew beans, cassava, corn, yams, and plantains. Like roughly 60 percent of the population, the Blaises relied on subsistence agriculture to survive—and sometimes would have enough to sell at the local market, where *Madan Sara* might buy it and bring it to feed the capital. On October 4, 2016, the outer bands of Hurricane Matthew brought the first rains. Over the next twelve hours, up to three feet more would fall.

The Blaises had nowhere to go. When the winds came later that night, and the seas surged, both houses were completely destroyed. They moved to the church. Soon after, its roof was completely torn off. The eye of the storm made landfall around four in the morning. The family huddled close and prayed.

THE STORM CLOSED the international airport, but I was on one of the first commercial planes available. Ti Mo's *moto* wouldn't get us to the

Grand'Anse, where the worst of the damage was, so we both hopped in a friend's beat-up SUV, whose chances of making it may not have been much better. We popped a tire before we had made it out of Port-au-Prince. The Grand'Anse is perhaps Haiti's most isolated department. Foreign media crews and aid organizations were able to charter flights that took less than an hour from the capital. Haitians can choose from either a nine-hour-plus bus ride or an even longer journey by boat. In our old SUV, the drive, through overflowing rivers and atop treacherous mountain passes, lasted at least six hours—and took yet another tire change. The final stretch of road before the descent into Jérémie, under construction for years, remained as unfinished as Haiti's plans to reverse urban migration through decentralization.

We arrived in Jérémie, the largest city in the southwest and one of the few places still accessible by car, less than a week after the storm had caused billions in damages and displaced hundreds of thousands, including the Blaises. From the vantage point of a small concrete foundation perched on the mountain that cradles the city, the insides of those houses that still stood were visible below. Their corrugated aluminum roofs ripped off and turned into deadly projectiles. The burnt-red cathedral downtown was knocked back to the nineteenth century when its construction began. The elegantly tiled roof was gone, its tower toppled. The trees that still stood were bare. Privert, who flew over the devastation a few days after we had made the drive, later told me it reminded him of photos of Hiroshima.[6]

But the storm's impact went far beyond the jarringly visible. Nearly 100 percent of crops were damaged or destroyed. More than 60,000 tons of plantains were lost. Across the country, two million chickens, 75,000 sheep, 160,000 pigs, and more than 100,000 cows were killed. Coming just before harvest time, food stocks meant to last through lean months were gone by the time the skies cleared.

Downtown in Jérémie, I noticed a fleet of dump trucks rumbling through the streets, picking up the wreckage and clearing blocked roads. The trucks bore the logo of V&F—Vorbe et Fils—one of the country's largest construction companies. Each truck was also adorned with a campaign photo of Jovenel Moïse, Neg Bannan Nan. The storm had forced the election to be delayed yet again, but it also provided candidates with an opportunity. Moïse himself had been in Jérémie the night before.

I met Bette Gebrian on the grounds of the municipal office building in Jérémie, which had morphed into a makeshift emergency response center. Gebrian, an American anthropologist, had lived in the area since 1987. She had been at the meeting with Moïse. He promised to bring a boat with supplies to isolated communities along the coast, she said. "He's trying," but, she added, what the community really needed was a ship full of seeds so they could replant.[7]

A few days after I left Jérémie, the ship Moïse had promised arrived, stocked with materials provided by the campaign's private-sector backers—but no seeds. While other campaigns ran out of money, Moïse had been able to basically continue uninterrupted for the entirety of the transition, though to be sure he was far from the only candidate to put their face on a hurricane relief kit. "He was the one who supported us," Blaise remembered. "That is when the community began talking about Moïse as president."

The hurricane provided PHTK with a perfect opening. The besieged and broke interim government looked feckless in the face of the storm. Their candidate, on the other hand, was a rural agricultural expert who ran a banana plantation. Though they had fought it tooth and nail, the long transition ended up suiting PHTK just fine. With Martelly out of office, Moïse was able to recast himself as an opposition figure, fighting a tyrannical Lavalasian president unable to respond to a crisis.

I met Roudy Choute, the PHTK representative, back in the capital. "Absolutely, it is to contrast with the government," he explained, in reference to the aid ship. His candidate was the one able to do things. The storm had rendered countless voting centers useless, but Choute was not concerned with the logistics of the election or the need to prioritize relief. "If there are not elections by the end of October, we are ready to take to the street," he told me. "The people in power are not legitimate," he continued. "They can't negotiate with the international community."[8] Once again, six years after the earthquake, the need for continued aid flows appeared to be trumping the need for a legitimate electoral process.

Few people I had spoken with in Jérémie or on the drives there and back had expressed any concern at all for the election. "We're not even thinking about that now," one middle-aged man told me, taking a break from hammering a piece of mangled zinc back onto his ramshackle home. Port-au-Prince may have been obsessed with the election, but rural Haiti had bigger concerns. And no government had ever really done much for them anyway.

Nevertheless, it quickly became clear that, despite the damage, elections would only be delayed a short time. That would be the only way to have a transfer of power before another February 7 came and went. It seemed the date itself was the only one with any real power.

I met a foreign diplomat on the veranda of the Hotel Montana. Set high above the sprawling city, with twenty-five-dollar burgers and fifteen-dollar cocktails on the menu and panoramic Caribbean views, the hotel felt a world away from the lives below and even further from the devastation in the Grand'Anse. Over a round of Prestige, the diplomat crassly explained the stakes.

"If they mess this one up, you can stick a banana republic in your . . ." I could finish the sentence.[9] Donors had refused to fund the election, but the interim government managed to cobble together the funds on its own. With the storm, everything was in doubt, and the message from the diplomat was clear: if Haitians couldn't pick a president on their own, the international community would do it for them.

The hurricane had changed everything. Funding the elections domestically had been a source of pride for the interim government, but with the scale of the devastation coming into focus, there was simply no way the government would be able to respond without international assistance. The entire transitional period had been a blow to the international community, and they had spent the next nine months attempting to claw back some of their lost influence. The hurricane gave it all back overnight.

Less than a week after the hurricane hit, the head of MINUSTAH, Sandra Honoré, addressed the UN Security Council. The mission had been expected to end after the 2015 electoral process, which was now dragging into the fall of 2016. The election was supposed to have happened by the time Honoré addressed the council, its "successful" completion her, and the mission's, final act. No longer. Honoré said that the impact of the storm "on the political process and on stability in the country could only serve to reconfirm" the need for an extension of the troops' mandate.[10] They got it. The Blue Helmets would be around for another year. The guardrails on Haiti's road to democracy weren't going to come down anytime soon.

BACK IN THE capital, meeting with politicians and bankers, diplomats and aid workers, human rights activists and local journalists, one thing kept coming up over and over again. Everyone wanted to talk about the US election. "Is Donald Trump really going to be president?" they wanted to know. The US election was less than a month away, and virtually every single poll showed Hillary Clinton winning. "There's no way," I reassured each who asked me. But in Haiti, nobody seemed to believe it. It was totally reasonable that someone like Trump would win the election, especially after seeing Martelly, a man who used to don a diaper during his stage performances, wearing the presidential sash. It didn't hurt that the Clintons' post-quake involvement had left a sour taste with many Haitians, and who trusts polls anyway?

In contrast, few expressed much care over who might be the next president in Haiti. I took it as indifference, and to an extent, that was likely true. After a year of transition, a year of political fights, threats of civil war, an opposition failing to unite, a steadily declining economy, and then the worst hurricane in fifty years, indifference was understandable. But the constant discussion of the US election revealed something deeper. I was reminded of a common refrain I had heard over the years: that political change in Haiti followed political change in the US. It wasn't crazy to think that the US election might have a more direct impact on Haitians than their own.

On November 8, 2016, Donald Trump surprised the world—or, most of the world outside of Haiti—winning the electoral college and defeating Hillary Clinton. Haiti itself had played an outsized role in the election. Republicans had weaponized the Clintons' Haiti failures, and turned them into another in a laundry list of alleged corrupt Clinton misdeeds. In the last months of the campaign, Trump had even gone to Little Haiti in Miami in an attempt at winning over the diaspora, which had always voted by overwhelming majorities for Democrats. He ended up winning Florida by just over a hundred thousand votes. Many think that depressed turnout among the diaspora was a key reason why.

Two weeks later, I was back in Haiti for their presidential election. I traveled throughout the southern peninsula on election day, visiting more than a dozen polling places. All were virtually empty. Across the street from one, just a few yards from the Caribbean Sea, I spoke with a group of a dozen or so who were busy chopping debris from the storm and rebuilding their shelters. None of them had voted, even though we could see the voting center from where we stood. Maybe if they paid us, someone said with a laugh. They had work to do. And as always, they were on their own. The election wasn't going to change that.

A few weeks later, the electoral council announced the official results. Moïse had won, and he had secured the win in the first round with more than 50 percent of the vote. Turnout was a historic low of 18 percent. Moïse had received less than six hundred thousand votes in a country of eleven million.[11] Perhaps it was naïve to have been hopeful, to have imagined something else was possible. The election had finally happened, but it was clear it wouldn't bring change—or the stability that donors craved. Much of the opposition rejected the official results, convinced the race had been stolen again. Maybe they were right, as they had been the year prior. But there would be no investigation this time, not with the devastation from Hurricane Matthew necessitating fresh donor funds.

On February 7, Privert passed the presidential sash to Neg Bannan Nan. After securing the presidency, Moïse, smiling, posed for a picture holding a T-shirt promoting Haitian tourism.

"Banana Republic" was printed across the chest.[12]

* * *

NINE MONTHS LATER, about the time it takes a banana tree to go from planting to harvest, I returned to Haiti to see if the Banana Man was beginning to bear fruit.[13] The carefully cultivated image of a rural agro-businessman created by Moïse's handlers was as much about selling overbearing foreign embassies as it was about selling bananas. At least on that front, it appeared to have succeeded. But the agricultural development represented by Moïse, and megaprojects like his plantation, have generated displacement and disruption, not a more stable food supply.

It is just 130 miles from the capital to Trou-du-Nord, Moïse's hometown and where the plantation that gave him his nickname is located. On a good day the drive will take seven hours. The road north hugs the coast, then inland past the rice fields of the Artibonite Valley and back to the port city of Gonaïves, and up and over Morne Puilboreau's narrow muddy crossing to the north coast and the city of Cap-Haïtien—the site of Haiti's decisive battle against the French.

Eventually, we reached Trou-du-Nord, where a bamboo-and-barbed-wire fence shields the president's 2,500-acre banana plantation, eight times the size of the National Mall in Washington, DC, from the road.

In 2014, the Haitian government seized the land on the other side of this fence as part of its first-ever agricultural free trade zone. Agritrans, a new company created by Moïse, was granted a twenty-five-year lease and fifteen years free from taxes. The government provided a $6 million loan. Anonymous investors chipped in $10 million. But the agro-industrial banana plantation in the north appears to have been more successful at securing political power in Port-au-Prince than exporting its harvest or feeding the country's people.

In addition to his catchy nickname, the plantation gave Moïse a national platform. In a large public ceremony less than twenty-four hours before the campaign officially opened, Agritrans exported its first container of bananas to Germany. By the time I arrived at his farm, Moïse was president, but no bananas had been shipped since the Banana Man's election.

"We had just 2 shipments and it seems that due to unknown reasons Agritrans was not in a position to establish the relationship we wanted," a spokesperson for Port International, the German company that signed a multiyear deal with Agritrans, told me via email. They added: "We lost contact during and after elections."[14]

The bamboo fence eventually gives way to Agritrans' entrance, where two uniformed guards greeted our car. There was no office. Just land as far as the eye could see. The guards let us enter on foot.

A dozen or so farmers tended one of the few remaining productive fields. A handful of workers—some chatting in Spanish with their Dominican colleagues—watched as the engine on a new-looking Hyundai excavator fired up and it began slowly poking at the fertile land, now largely overgrown with grass.

Erlin Tijerino, a Costa Rican agronomist and banana specialist, was perched on a conveyor belt in Agritrans' processing area, his head and back curled forward in order to reach his laptop. Tijerino didn't have an office but this worked for him. The belt hadn't moved in more than a year, since he had been hired.

When he showed up for work, soon after Moïse won the election, Agritrans had "lost all of their plants," he said. None of the employees I spoke with knew exactly what had happened. But Tijerino provided one possible answer.

"The soil is not right," he explained. "It's very acidic, which makes it difficult to grow bananas."[15]

A year after the crop loss, less than a hundred acres had been replanted—about 5 percent of the total land. The soil, said Tijerino, was better suited for small-scale production of foods such as peanuts, corn, and beans. That is precisely what thousands of families had grown on the land for decades.

I met Nadia Joseph in the yard of her mother's house across the street from Agritrans' fenced-off land, land that she had lived and farmed on for some thirty years. Within fifteen minutes, more than a dozen others joined us. All claimed to have used what was now Agritrans' land.

"Everything was wrecked," a man yelled out from the crowd. "We lost it all."

"We used to sell our goods at the market to buy local produce," Joseph explained once things had calmed down.[16] Now, she said, "it is mostly imported rice we eat." The best hope for their kids' employment is the neighboring sweatshop—the construction of which also displaced many hundreds of families. The three thousand jobs that Moïse promised Agritrans would create had yet to materialize.

None of those I spoke to had worked a day on the Agritran land once the fence went up. Employees at Agritrans said only a few dozen worked there full-time. For the few farmers lucky enough to get rotational shifts preparing fields, the daily pay is about three dollars. It's the same rate offered down the road at the Korean garment factory.

Jennifer Vansteenkiste is a Canadian anthropologist who was doing fieldwork around Trou-du-Nord when Agritrans took over the land. Her work provides a rare glimpse into the actual impact on those communities displaced by megaprojects.

Her before-and-after study, published in May 2017, showed a drastic change in diet and a significant loss of income.[17] On average, each person lost about $1,400 a year, she found. Some families received a small onetime payment as compensation. But nobody I spoke with had received more than about $800.

"There is a lot of talk [about promoting agriculture], and I listen, but what I see is this," Jean Edmond, who had farmed the land since 1992, told me, motioning down the street to the largely barren fields.[18]

But even if the plantation someday succeeds, like the T-shirts produced down the road, the Banana Man's harvest isn't meant for local consumption. It doesn't take a natural disaster to rob Haiti's rural population of their livelihood. The fight for power in the Republic of Port-au-Prince and a foreign-imposed development model have done that all on their own.

AFTER THE HURRICANE, Jamesky Blaise coordinated efforts in his hometown of Abricots to conduct a local census to determine the needs of the community. The purpose, he explained, "was to determine what we could do to ensure effective international intervention."[19]

Though Moïse had sent a ship with supplies ahead of the election, little governmental support had shown up since. Instead, the response in the storm-impacted rural communities of the southern peninsula had, once again, largely been outsourced to foreign NGOs. Blaise's study fell on indifferent ears.

Three months after the hurricane, the World Food Programme reported that residents of the Grand'Anse were actually consuming more calories than before as a result of free food distributions.[20] But Blaise said what the people really had needed were seeds. It was exactly what I had heard ten years earlier, after the earthquake. All these years later, precious little had changed.

Donors spent hundreds of millions after the hurricane, but the appeal for food security was less than 50 percent funded.[21] Instead, the aid that did come largely arrived in the form of emergency food assistance like rice, the vast majority of which was still imported. "There are still many who do not eat," Blaise told me when we caught up in the fall of 2017. By then, food insecurity in the Grand'Anse and other impacted regions had reached an "acute" level. The NGO-led food distributions had mostly stopped.

Many families, he said, moved to Jérémie, the regional capital, or even to Port-au-Prince seeking aid or employment, once again echoing the long-term impacts of Hurricane Hazel and exacerbating the urbanization that has hampered Haiti's development.

The Blaises were able to replant their family garden, but there is less variety and it's smaller. Plantains started growing again, but strong winds and rain in 2017 left the still vulnerable trees naked once again. Breadfruit, the tree for which the Grand'Anse is most known, fared better. Unlike plantains, breadfruit—known as *lam veritab* in Kreyòl—regenerates. "They are our guardian angel," Blaise told me.

But Haiti's president was not Neg Lam Veritab, he was Neg Banann. And Blaise wasn't holding his breath for any government support to reach Abricots. "After the campaign, when presidents come to power, they don't leave Port-au-Prince," he said.

Of course, Moïse did physically leave Port-au-Prince. But Blaise was making a deeper point. Once a candidate becomes president, they become politically trapped in the hinge of the claw, the Republic of Port-au-Prince, where, despite decades of discussion around decentralization, political power in the Aid State continues to reside. So long as that re-mains the case, more and more rural families like the Blaises are left with a devastating and destabilizing choice: to give up their land and hope for a job in the capital, or give up on their country in the hopes of more opportunity elsewhere. Increasingly, more and more had been opting for the latter.

24

THE SEARCH FOR LIFE

A few minutes' drive down the road from the new president's defunct banana plantation, I met Philomise Pierre on the front steps of her modest cement home. We had met once before, years earlier. She was one of thousands displaced by the construction of the Caracol Industrial Park. The flagship project of the reconstruction era had been fast-tracked and the internationally funded construction broke ground before there had even been an environmental and social impact assessment. The IDB, along with the US as the main financier, had described the land as "devoid of habitation." Pierre was living proof that had been a lie.

"They tricked us," Pierre told me, her voice rising.[1] Officials had promised Pierre and the hundreds of other families that had farmed the land for decades that they would make them whole. Many received a few small payments, but nothing that would replace what they had lost. After the last payment, they were told not to continue protesting at the industrial park or they would be arrested. "It's not even enough to feed my kids," she said, years after those payments had ceased. Pierre used to grow a variety of local foods—papayas, peppers, beans. "Now we have to buy imported food," she said. By the time we reconnected in late 2017, inflation had reached double digits and food prices were soaring.

Pierre explained that she no longer would have enough money saved to send her kids to college, something she had been preparing for her entire lifetime. "My kids will have to work at Caracol for two hundred gourdes a day," she said, clearly frustrated. It was the equivalent of about three dollars.

After the earthquake there had been some hope, as communities came together to think about what a better future could look like, and as donors pledged to promote decentralization, reverse the rural-to-urban migration, and stem the flow of those seeking a better life outside the country. But, in the end, the nation's economic future was staked on low-wage garment manufacturing. In nearly eight years, the sector had indeed added thousands of new jobs—though still a far cry from the sixty thousand the industrial park's backers had promised.

As the UN economist Paul Collier wrote in his infamous report, and as American businessmen had gushed decades earlier, what set Haiti apart was its incredibly low wages. The displacement of families from the land in Caracol or down the street at Agritrans fit neatly into this development model. Forced from their land and their livelihoods, rural families would be pushed to seek employment at Caracol or one of the factories in the capital. That, or they would decide to leave the country altogether.

Though the elite-owned sweatshops that provide cheap T-shirts for Walmart, Hanes, Gildan, and other international brands were Haiti's top source of jobs, the irony is that the economy overall remained far more reliant on Haitians packing up and leaving. Stopping migration may have been on the tops of minds in Washington, DC, but economic stability in Haiti was being purchased with remittances. In 2017, Haitians living elsewhere sent a record $2.6 billion back home, reaching nearly 20 percent of the country's GDP.[2] It was a higher share than almost any other country in the world. The Aid State's viability depended on continued migration.

Haitians first began moving to the United States in large numbers during the late fifties and early sixties. Many from the middle class moved to the US as repression grew under François Duvalier. In 1969, then New York governor Nelson Rockefeller traveled to Haiti on behalf of President Nixon and reached a deal with the dictator. In exchange for renewed financial assistance, Haiti would open its doors to US foreign investors. Dozens of companies moved their operations to Haiti, seeking to take advantage of the lowest labor costs in the Western Hemisphere. Multilateral development banks poured hundreds of millions into new infrastructure to support their operations. Foreign investment did nothing to stem the flow of migration, however. In fact, it only increased. The new investment displaced farmers while repression and starvation wages in the sweatshops of the capital forced more to search for life outside their borders.

As Baby Doc took power and began promoting Haiti as the "Taiwan of the Caribbean" throughout the seventies and eighties, some five hundred thousand Haitians migrated to the US, forming thriving diaspora communities in New York, Boston, and, of course, Miami.[3] Mass migration had continued in fits and starts ever since. By the middle of the 2010s, the Haitian diaspora numbered in the millions. Perhaps it comes as little surprise that the two periods of greatest migration—the seventies/eighties and the post-quake period—coincided with massive increases in foreign money entering Haiti.

In the US, there is rarely focus on the root causes of migration, especially when those causes include national policy itself. From its support of the Duvalier dictatorship, myriad coups, and the imposition of trade and aid policies that decimated rural livelihoods, to the consolidation of the Aid State after the quake, the US has a direct responsibility in creating the conditions from which Haitians flee. Despite this dynamic, once Haitians arrive at our border, they have always been treated abysmally.

WHEN A CONTACT called Guerline Jozef in late 2015 to tell her that dozens of Haitians had just been released by the US Border Patrol in San Diego, she didn't believe it. Haitian migration was nothing new to Jozef, who had left Haiti and settled with family in Queens, New York, as an adolescent in the early nineties.[4] That was meant to be a short trip to visit relatives, but, while there, the military overthrew Aristide and began its campaign of terror. So, Jozef stayed. She was lucky to have already been here when the US government began detaining the resulting wave of Haitian asylum seekers at its naval base on Guantánamo Bay.

Migration to the US from Haiti had generally followed along one of two paths. Those with family or friends already in the States, and enough money, would fly to cities like New York and Boston. Many more attempted to make the trip to Florida by boat, a six-hundred-mile voyage across extremely dangerous waters that had claimed an untold number of lives over the years. But Haitians showing up at the US-Mexico border? That would be a new development entirely.

Jozef, living comfortably in Orange County, California, decided to travel to San Diego and see what was happening for herself.[5] On that first trip, she met twelve Haitians. Their phones had been taken by Border Patrol and they had no way to contact waiting family members. They were shocked to learn how far they were from Florida or New York, their ultimate destinations. But getting there would be nothing compared to the journey they had just completed. Through the Amazon rain forest, across the treacherous Darien Gap from Colombia into Panama, and then up Central America crossing another five borders, it had been more than ten thousand miles, by foot, boat, car, or train. It had taken everything they had, financially, emotionally, physically. Negotiating with smugglers, avoiding violent drug cartels, they had arrived at the US southern border in search of asylum, knowing that returning to their home country was no longer a possibility. They hadn't stepped foot in Haiti for years.

American fears of migrants showing up on Miami Beach after the earthquake, the fear that ostensibly motivated the overly militaristic initial response, never materialized; but as reconstruction stalled and hope was met with stasis, more and more had left Haiti. Most, however, did not come to the US. Rather, they went to the Dominican Republic, or to Brazil, Ecuador, Chile, and other destinations in South America. After the global financial crisis, the economies in Latin America were achieving far more rapid growth than the US and obtaining a visa was far easier. Brazil, for example, was experiencing a massive construction boom as it prepared to host both the 2014 World Cup and the 2016 Summer Olympics. Tens of thousands of Haitians left their country to seek work on one of the megaprojects.

From 2010 to 2015, more than 340,000 Haitians officially took up residence in a foreign country, according to United Nations data, about 3.5 percent of the population.[6] And that is certainly a massive underestimate. Hundreds of thousands more had found work in the informal economies of other countries. Few officials wanted to talk about the record number of people leaving Haiti, an obvious indication of the reconstruction era's failures. In fact, it was a necessity. The Aid State couldn't provide for those who stayed, let alone hundreds of thousands more.

By the middle of the decade, however, the economies of South America entered a recession. Progressive leaders were replaced by conservatives. Jobs began to dry up, and anti-immigrant sentiment soared. Having fled their country once before, Haitians now fled their adopted homelands. Seeing no other choice, they packed up what they could carry, collected their life savings, and set off for America's southern border. The dozen asylum seekers Jozef met on her trip to the border were some of the first to make it. Jozef contacted friends and colleagues and together they provided temporary housing, helped locate family members, and even paid airfare to help get them there. "I thought that was it," Jozef told me. "It wasn't."

From October 2015 to May 2016, about fifteen hundred Haitians requested asylum at the US-Mexico border, more than from any country other than Mexico and Guatemala.[7] Many more settled in Tijuana, waiting to navigate the complexities of the border. Jozef, who began making more regular trips, recognized there was a massive need and sprang into action. With the network she had helped cobble together, she created the Haitian Bridge Alliance to provide services and legal advice to the Haitians arriving at the border. By October 2016, another five thousand Haitians had shown up.

Though a drop in the bucket of overall migration trends—hundreds of thousands had arrived at the border during the same time period—the "wave" of Haitians generated a political backlash. In the months ahead of the 2016 US election, headline after headline blared about the flood of migrants from Haiti showing up in Mexico. That fed right into the narrative of Donald Trump, who was on the campaign trail demonizing migrants and lambasting Democrats as weak on the border.

Among the root causes that had pushed so many thousands to leave Haiti was, of course, US policy. But, once they arrived at the border, Haitians were not considered refugees; rather, US officials viewed them as a political liability.

After granting legal status to tens of thousands of Haitians already living in the US in 2010, the Obama administration had largely made things easier for Haitians to migrate. That changed two months before the 2016 election. In September, the Obama administration announced a change in policy, clearing the way to immediately deport Haitian asylum seekers.[8] In parallel, the administration implemented a new "metering" policy specifically targeting Haitians, which required those arriving in Tijuana to wait there until their number was called by border agents, allowing them to officially request asylum.[9] At first, according to Jozef, it actually worked pretty well and provided some order. But it quickly fell apart. Democrats lost the election anyway.

As election season came and went, Jozef noticed the narrative on the border changing. The majority of those trying to cross into San Diego were Black; in addition to Haitians, who constituted the majority, there were also people from all across Africa arriving after traveling along the same route. At first, Mexico had been welcoming. They saw Haitians as hardworking and professional, she explained. "They were young people looking for jobs," she said. But with anti-immigrant fervor taking over the campaign trail and Democrats caving to political priorities, everything shifted. "It went from 'Haitians are model immigrants' to 'we don't want them here at all,'" Jozef remembered. When Trump took the White House in early 2017, anti-Black racism on the border burst into the open.

IN JUNE 2017, President Trump stormed into a meeting in the White House. On the campaign trail, he had pledged to crack down on immigration, but, now in office, he worried the continued steady influx was making him look bad. He carried a piece of paper showing that fifteen thousand Haitian immigrants had received visas to enter the United States. "They all have AIDS," the president reportedly said.[10]

The association of Haitians with AIDS, and the explicit racism of Trump's hard-line immigration platform, served as a clear reminder about the roots of the United States' carceral response to those coming here in search of a better life—and a clear reminder of Haiti's centrality to that story. While Trump said the quiet parts out loud, the racist mistreatment of Haitian asylum seekers had been bipartisan for decades, and always saturated with crass domestic political motivations. That mistreatment had served as the leading edge of US immigration policy.

Congress codified the disparate treatment of Haitian migrants in 1966, with the passage of the Cuban Adjustment Act. The new law labeled Cubans seeking to migrate as "political refugees" fleeing the Castro dictatorship, and allowed them a relatively quick and easy path to US citizenship. At the same time, however, many thousands of Haitians began arriving in the US. Though they, too, were fleeing a dictatorship—and a much more violent one at that—Duvalier maintained US political support. Haitians were labeled "economic refugees," which, under US law, does not allow for the granting of asylum.[11]

Through the middle of the twentieth century, the US had rarely bothered detaining immigrants, instead letting most stay on parole while they attempted to obtain legal status. In the summer of 1980, some one hundred thousand Cubans and fifteen thousand Haitians arrived in Florida. Facing a local political backlash, and with a presidential election just a few months away, the Carter administration began to hold new arrivals in detention centers.[12] One of the first was the Krome Avenue Detention Center in Miami, which had been used to store old missiles since its time as a Cold War military base.[13] Some forty years later, Krome continues to house immigrants from all over the world, including Haiti.

Carter lost the election, and, while most Cubans eventually were allowed into the United States, many Haitians remained behind bars. The incoming Reagan administration took the precedent and went further. In 1981, the new administration began detaining all Haitian immigrants without documentation.[14] The same year, the administration signed an agreement with Baby Doc that allowed the US to intercept

Haitian asylum seekers at sea and forcibly return them to Haiti. That policy continues today.[15]

The disparate treatment of Cuban and Haitian asylum seekers was about more than different skin color and political regimes. Anti-Haitian racism was especially vile. In 1982, the CDC included Haitians among four groups at "high risk" for the recently identified "acquired immuno-deficiency syndrome," or AIDS. For years, Haitians were banned even from donating blood. For the more than one hundred thousand Haitians already living in the United States, it was a source of near constant discrimination and heartache. For the tens of thousands more in search of life outside a brutal dictatorship, it was practically a death sentence.

The jailing of Haitian asylum seekers or their interception at sea, soaked in overt racism, was meant to send a clear signal to others thinking about attempting the journey: don't. It was the beginning of the United States' immigration policy of detention as deterrent, which every president since has perpetuated.[16]

It wasn't until 1985 that the CDC removed Haitians from its "high risk" designation for AIDS, finally acknowledging that there was no science to back it up.[17] In the late eighties, after the fall of the dictatorship, migration from Haiti began to slow. After the September 1990 election of Aristide, a time of such tremendous hope, migration ground to a halt. That changed after the military coup that followed. With the reign of terror following Aristide's ouster, thousands again took to the seas.

After initially allowing those intercepted to come to the US and request asylum, the George H. W. Bush administration quickly changed course and restarted the forced repatriations that had begun under Reagan. Legal advocates in Miami, who had organized to fight the racist treatment of Haitian asylum seekers in the early eighties, again sprang into action and obtained a court injunction blocking the returns. Thousands remained in limbo; rather than allowing them entry into the United States, Bush made use of the US Naval base at Guantánamo Bay, a way to keep the problem out of sight, out of US constitutional jurisdiction, and out of the way of his reelection campaign that was already underway.

At Guantánamo, the legacy of stigmatization of Haitians continued. All those brought to the US military base were screened for HIV, and, if positive, individuals were held in a separate detention site. It was "the world's first and only detention camp for refugees with HIV," wrote Michael Ratner, a lawyer who fought the administration's policy at the time.[18]

During the 1992 presidential campaign, Clinton pledged to reverse Bush's policies. Once in office, however, he reversed himself. Clinton's team was fearful that the president's inauguration would be marred by the arrival of "boat people" on the beaches of Miami. Rather than opening our borders to the victims of a military coup, a coup that at least some parts of the US government appeared to have supported, Clinton followed the path of his predecessors and continued to detain Haitians at Guantánamo Bay.[19] Haitians didn't stop taking to the open ocean as their best chance for survival until 1994, when their ousted president was finally restored to office. Clinton later expressed regret for detaining Haitians at Guantánamo, not because it was inhumane but because, with the "problem" out of sight, public opinion turned against his decision to use the US military to bring Aristide back to power.[20]

Given this history, the Obama administration's actions in the fall of 2016 were well grounded in US political history and echoed those of his predecessors. Once again, domestic political objectives trumped international law and morality. And, in another historical parallel, it was a Democratic administration's immigration policy targeting Haitians that ended up paving the way for a Republican's most hard-line policies. Trump eventually instituted a controversial new policy called Remain in Mexico, which required all migrants to wait in Mexico until they were allowed to request asylum at the border. It was the Obama administration's "metering" of Haitians, but applied across the board. And while it was Trump who had deported a record number of Haitians, many of those had been detained under the Obama administration, left to wait in inhumane immigration detention centers like Krome. Trump was the one to call Haiti a "shithole,"[21] but in doing so, he was acting in line with a long tradition of US politicians who had demonized Haiti and Haitians for political gain.

Despite the policies in the US, Haitians would not stop *chèche lavi*—searching for life. In 2017, Jovenel Moïse's first year in office, more than one hundred thousand Haitians, about 1 percent of the population, left to go to just one country in South America: Chile.[22] That fall, a conservative won the presidency of Chile and imposed new restrictions on migration, especially from Haiti. And tens of thousands more left again, starting the dangerous journey by land to the US-Mexico border.

THE ECONOMIC MODEL of low-wage exports is, in many ways, a modern replication of the plantation economy of the colonial era. Rural families are pushed into working in the elite- and foreign-controlled factories as they were once confined to the elite- and foreign-run plantations. Philomise Pierre certainly understood this historical parallelism, reminding me that the body of Charlemagne Péralte, the leader of the Cacos who had fiercely resisted the US occupation, had been buried in the land now being used for the Caracol Industrial Park.[23] Péralte was killed in 1919 by US Marines, who infiltrated his camp reportedly by dressing in blackface. The soldiers were awarded Congressional Medals of Honor.

Nearly one hundred years later, Pierre was organizing in resistance to the continued profiting off the backs of the peasantry. She and hundreds of others displaced from the land formed a collective in 2014. Then, in January 2017, they filed a formal complaint with the IDB, asking for new land and legal titles to be provided so they could once again farm. Noting that the bank remained a major funder of the industrial park, the collective (receiving support from two international NGOs, Action-Aid and the Accountability Counsel) asserted that years of promises of compensation and restitution had been broken.[24]

The collective's efforts also got support from AREDE, a grassroots peasant organization working to protect the environment, support farmers, and fight land grabs, led by Milostene Castin. The fact that the industrial park had received so much international funding opened a door toward accountability. Rural families had long been neglected by the Haitian state; by themselves, the farmers had little hope of negotiating directly with their government. The appeal to the IDB was about creating the conditions for an actual dialogue with all those involved. One year after filing their complaint, the collective, the IDB, and the Haitian government signed an agreement to provide new land to the most vulnerable families, technical assistance for new agricultural activities, access to financing, and education opportunities for children. One member of each family was also promised a job at the Caracol Industrial Park.

"Finally, today, we have written a page in the history of Haiti," Castin said in a press release at the time. "This is the first time that Haitian farmers have stood up and been listened to."[25] But the historic victory was the exception that proved the rule: accountability was anathema in the Aid State. And while the tremendous organizing in Haiti began to bear fruit, ensuring those promises became a reality would be another challenge entirely.

I started working with Castin not long after he had helped broker the agreement with the bank. We spent time in DC together, attending meetings in Congress, briefing the State Department's Haiti desk, strategizing with allies. But few in Washington could comprehend the importance of their work and how it connected to what Washington did ostensibly care about: stability in Haiti and preventing migration. Stability for the economic elite meant continued instability for farmers like Philomise Pierre and Castin, and in turn, that meant that more and more Haitians would continue to *chèche lavi* elsewhere. Years later, the farmers have yet to receive the compensation promised in their historic agreement.

25

THE $80,000 HOUSE

———————

It wasn't until November 2017 that I finally walked through the streets of the Caracol-EKAM village in northern Haiti, the site of the United States' largest post-quake housing project. What started in the months after the earthquake with an ambitious plan to build fifteen thousand "culturally appropriate" homes for those displaced by the earthquake had concluded with just over nine hundred constructed, seven hundred and fifty of them at the EKAM village. After following the housing program's development for nearly seven years, the village felt familiar. The blueprints made real; the scandal come to life.

A new drainage canal at the edge of the manufactured town trickled with muddy water. A power grid, connected to a US-funded plant built to support the industrial park a few miles down the road, provided homes with steady electricity and steady bills. A blue bus bearing the name "Sae-A," the largest employer at the park, picked up passengers—employees, or children attending the Sae-A school nearby.

I had driven past the houses once before, in 2013, when the development was just symmetrical rows of empty, pastel cinder-block shells. At the time, a small billboard just off the main road declared that for security reasons, only those with identification badges from Thor Construction or CEEPCO could enter the grounds. As I stood in the morning's light rain four-plus years later, both firms were barred from receiving USAID funds because of their faulty work on the houses.

The US shelter team's ambitious plan to build $8,000 homes with local materials, the plan that Bill Vastine had helped put together in the immediate aftermath of the quake, had transformed into an epic boondoggle, resulting in a $20 million cover-up and a stalled criminal case. And it had all started with a no-bid contract given to a childhood friend of Michel Martelly.

On April 19, 2011, two days before official elections results would confirm Michel Martelly's presidential victory, the musician and a group of advisors traveled to Washington, DC. They met with the president of the World Bank and that of the IMF, with Secretary Clinton and other high-level officials. The mission was to "promote a new Haiti," a Haiti that was, in the familiar slogan, open for business. One of the advisors accompanying him was Harold Charles.[1]

In September 2011, while USAID was making a final decision on who the first big contracts for the housing program would go to, Charles spoke at a State Department–sponsored event about doing business with the US government in Haiti. "I worked for the federal government for nineteen years prior to starting my company," Charles told the audience. "I know how the system works. . . . I know the acronyms. When we meet with the federal government, we can speak their language. . . . That's part of our success."[2]

Charles, a Haitian American and a resident of Maryland, was speaking as the CEO of a construction company, CEEPCO. "I must also point out that I am one of the six [reconstruction commission] board members that represent the [Martelly] government" on the Clinton commission, Charles said. He acknowledged being a "reconstruction advisor" to the newly elected president, with whom he had been childhood friends.

"There is no conflict of interest. All the contracts that I've had and that I'm still having were way before the President was sworn in, and there is no connection between what I'm doing to help my government as well as what I'm doing as a U.S. contractor," Charles added.

But he wasn't exactly telling the truth. The first contract CEEPCO received from USAID came in April 2011, just two weeks before Charles accompanied Martelly on the president's trip to DC. In June, two months after Martelly was sworn in, CEEPCO received $475,000 to begin work preparing the EKAM shelter site.[3]

Soon after his remarks at the State Department event, USAID awarded CEEPCO its largest federal contract ever: $9 million to continue its work on the EKAM village and to perform an environmental assessment for the overall housing program. There was no bidding process. The USAID engineer in charge of the project justified that lack of competition by pointing to the urgency of the housing crisis in Port-au-Prince, 150 miles from the site. He did not mention that the contractor was a childhood friend of the new Haitian president. "This was seen as a deal that would please Martelly," a former Haitian government official later told me.[4]

Meanwhile, NGOs did their own analyses of the land and the plans. In March 2012, a group of American architects issued what would prove to be a prophetic warning.[5] "[The] housing project design is substandard, inadequate and anything but 'culturally appropriate,'" the architects wrote. The location of the housing development, they pointed out, was in a floodplain. The sewage systems appeared unsustainable. The roofs were poorly designed. "We are convinced that, however urgent the need for housing, the Caracol EKAM project will only worsen the excruciating homeless problem," the architects wrote. "We are appalled that USAID touts this project as a 'model' for replication in multiple locations."

The review concluded with a clear warning: "We strongly recommend that USAID not award the contract to build the Caracol EKAM housing project as designed and that a complete redesign be initiated immediately."

The next month, USAID awarded two contracts to build more than a thousand houses. The design remained unchanged and the contracts ended up going not to small local companies as originally called for, but to large international ones. CEMEX, a Mexican company, got over $7 million. Thor Construction, based in Minnesota, received $13 million for the 750 EKAM houses. Thor was already the largest minority-owned construction firm in the country at the time, but it had never done any international work or received a federal government contract for anything like this project.

In October 2012, just before the star-studded inauguration of the Caracol Industrial Park down the road, then secretary of state Hillary Clinton toured the EKAM site. During the brief visit, Clinton spoke of "affordable homes with clean running water, flush toilets, and reliable electricity ... built to resist hurricanes and earthquakes." Harold Charles was by her side, as was Richard Copeland, the founder of Thor Construction.[6]

Back at the housing site, delays and cost overruns were piling up. USAID increased Thor's contract twice, in June and July 2012, by a total of $4 million. That September, they upped CEEPCO's by $3 million. Nobody should have been surprised; cost overruns are an intrinsic part of the foreign aid system we have created.

"OUR MISSION WAS to go out and figure out how to build as many houses" as possible, Bill Vastine had recalled when I met him in January 2013.[7] The plan the experts came back with was simple and meant to be implemented quickly. Jerry Erbach, another member of the team, told me that "there was a good deal of pressure to develop a series of projects very quickly and at low cost in order to meet the needs of those households who became homeless after the earthquake."[8] The plan was to build homes that were simple, modest, and small, but that could be expanded over time.

The shelter team homed in on the area the government had declared eminent domain over, the promised land of Canaan. But the plans ran up against America's bigger priority, the Caracol Industrial Park, and the promise to build housing for workers that lured Sae-A to Haiti.

"I was working on how to be able to focus on areas affected by the earthquake," Erbach explained, but "Cheryl Mills took over and wanted to do a greenfield project around Caracol, building houses for workers." And so, the geographical focus of the housing plan shifted from an area thirty minutes outside the capital to land six hours north of the capital.

"Every agency has its own little fiefdom, their own little budgets to protect and their own cadre of people they protect," Vastine explained. "There is no cohesiveness with our own internal bureaucracy in the United States." The shelter team working for USAID on the ground in Haiti had submitted their plan, but the seventh floor at the State Department in DC had other priorities. And the plan itself was about to enter the foreign aid bureaucracy, a black box of contracting officers and politically connected firms. When it came out the other side, it showed little resemblance to the original.

"They told us, 'You need to get the houses down to around $8,000,'" Vastine said, but now "they tell us, 'Oh [the Caracol houses are] costing $17,000 a house.' Well, no, it's not, it's probably costing more like $25,000," he explained. "They don't want you to see the true cost because if the American people saw the true cost of this, the American people would be like, 'You've got to be out of your mind!'"

IN JUNE 2013, the Government Accountability Office (GAO) published an investigation into US reconstruction programs in Haiti, with a particular focus on the housing plan.[9] The problems were not just at EKAM. In fact, those were almost the only houses that USAID had built at all. By December 2012, when the entire project was originally set to be finished, USAID had constructed only nine hundred homes. Seven hundred and fifty of them were the pastel rows at the EKAM site, and they were still empty.

Further, the total cost per house had risen from $8,000 to over $33,000. USAID increased the original $53 million budget to $90 million, the GAO report revealed. As Vastine had predicted, many congressional staffers on Capitol Hill did indeed say, "You've got to be out of your mind," when they found out what these houses were costing.

Eliot Engel, the ranking member on the House Foreign Affairs Committee, demanded answers. "This report shows a significant and sobering disconnect between what was originally promised for the Haitian people, and what it appears USAID is now prepared to deliver," he said.[10] "The Haitian people, as well as the US taxpayer, deserve better answers about our assistance than we have received to date." A bipartisan group of lawmakers organized a hearing to castigate USAID for its apparent failures.

Speaking before Engel's committee in October 2013, Beth Hogan, an assistant administrator at USAID, justified the skyrocketing costs of the housing plan by pointing to the rigorous federal standards that ensured the homes would be "disaster- and hurricane-proof." Hogan added that she was "very happy with the quality" of the houses. The author of the GAO report echoed Hogan's remarks, telling Congress that "they are excellent homes that are built to a very high standard."[11]

Nevertheless, Hogan conceded that "what we realized as we were going into this . . . is that new homes isn't [sic] the solution for Haiti." Building permanent shelters was just too difficult, Hogan explained, and instead, USAID was shifting its resources toward rental support and other market-based housing solutions. The permanent shelter program was finished.

Meanwhile, on the ground in Caracol, most of the houses that the US contractors built remained empty. The industrial park had only just opened and the promises of tens of thousands of jobs remained only that. Shutters flapped in the wind, banging against concrete walls in an empty field.

Global Communities, a US-based NGO, helped with the process of finding tenants for the new homes. Jerry Erbach, who had helped come up with the original USAID shelter plan, had taken a job with the organization. Pressure from State, he explained, led to a "significant amount of time and effort being wasted on identifying and vetting workers from the industrial park who were not [families whose homes had been destroyed by the quake]."[12]

The signature post-quake housing program of the US government wasn't actually going to benefit those who lost their livelihoods in the earthquake, at least not predominantly. And the few residents who had moved in were sounding the alarm.

* * *

Yvon St-Martin moved into one of the EKAM houses in August 2014. Residents would pay rent, and eventually receive a deed to the house (though not for the land on which it was built). A friend of St-Martin had been chosen as a beneficiary, but the friend had another house, and so let St-Martin stay there.

"The drainage system was a big problem," he told me.[13] Houses were flooding each time it rained. "You couldn't even flush the toilet" without the house filling with water, he said. Because of the problems, many of those initially selected as beneficiaries ended up renting their houses out to local university students or to friends without better options, like St-Martin.

USAID often met with residents, he recalled. "They were always saying something was going to happen, that USAID would send someone." People were still happy to have a place to live, even with the problems, but they were being asked to invest in their future. By the time they actually owned the house, would it even be livable?

St-Martin worked for a local NGO involved in the sanitation sector and had worked on a number of post-quake projects. To him, the problem was obvious. "This is what happened with a lot of projects after the earthquake. When you don't have anybody to supervise, the contractor will try to save as much money as possible," he said. A USAID Inspector General audit reached the same conclusion.

In August 2014, as St-Martin was moving into his friend's house at EKAM, the US Army Corps of Engineers had sent a team to review the houses. Their report, which USAID did not release publicly or share with residents, made clear that the problems of the EKAM houses did not stem just from some missing nails or inexperienced contractors struggling in Haiti.[14] From the very beginning, the contractors had ignored International Building Code standards. The report "found no evidence that a formal internal or external review" of the housing design was conducted and further, that "the project was designed with inconsistent application of code and latest design criteria," thereby violating the tenets of the contract.

"Seismic design of the housing units is deficient for construction within an area with high seismic activity. The design does not provide special reinforced masonry shear walls as required for seismic design classification," the report found, adding, "Combined with a lack of masonry joint reinforcement, omitted by the contractor, the walls are vulnerable to shear failure and step cracking in a seismic event."

In simpler terms, the US government's largest post-earthquake housing project was not built to withstand an earthquake. What Hogan, the USAID official, had told Congress to justify the rising costs was way off base.

Months later, USAID brought another company in to review the sanitation systems, the systems that St-Martin told me backed up and flooded the houses when he flushed the toilet. They found that household water pipes "were buried in the same trench with sewer pipes," creating "serious contamination potential." The assessment also said "overall poor construction quality" had caused a number of leaks. But the "most critical issue" was the poor-quality piping used in the sewage system, which was collapsing and causing "sewer water backing up into the home." The report remained hidden from the public.[15]

While study after study showed the structural deficiencies, US special agent Marvin Burgos was on the ground investigating and preparing possible criminal charges against the contractors responsible. But at the time, nobody—not members of Congress, not the public, and certainly not the residents of the EKAM houses—had any idea of the scope of the failure.

St-Martin moved out of the EKAM houses in December 2014. "By the time I left, nothing had been done to fix the problems," he said.

THE FIRST PUBLIC hint that anything was structurally wrong with the EKAM houses came in October 2014, when USAID awarded a $4.5 million no-bid contract to yet another US-based company, Tetra Tech, for remediation work.[16] The justification document, required when USAID does not follow normal bidding procedures, explained that an independent assessment had "revealed numerous deficiencies," including "missing roof fasteners, sub-specification roof materials and concrete reinforcement, and other structural and drainage issues." The document went on to explain that given the location's susceptibility to hurricanes and other extreme weather events, the repairs must be "carried out immediately in order to prevent possible harm to residents."

In December, members of Congress called for another hearing with USAID administrator Hogan. At the hearing, Representative Jim McGovern held up a copy of a blog post I had written on the issue. "I am just looking at an article here entitled 'USAID Houses Found to Be of Poor Quality, Will Cost Millions to Repair,' talking about 750 houses built by USAID. . . . Maybe you could address that as well."[17]

"I would be happy to," Hogan responded. "In fact, we have an active investigation underway to look at that." As part of a normal review, USAID had determined that "some of these materials are subpar," she explained, adding that they had called the contractors back to fix things. "We will not tolerate anything less than what we have contracted for in terms of quality and safety," she said. That was the first public disclosure of any type of investigation. Hogan did not mention the Army Corps of Engineers study nor the sanitation system study.

On February 3, 2015, Thor Construction was suspended from receiving government contracts because of its work on the EKAM houses. Seven weeks later, when CEEPCO finished work on its other project, it was suspended as well.[18] They were the only two US contractors who faced any repercussions for their actions in Haiti, but they would end up getting off easy.

MARVIN BURGOS HAD been a special agent assigned to USAID's Office of the Inspector General since 2005. He won commendations for his work uncovering a kickback scheme on a multibillion-dollar infrastructure project in Afghanistan, which, in 2009, led to an indictment and arrest warrant against two executives. In 2009, *Parade* magazine and the International Association of Chiefs of Police honored Burgos as one of the top twelve cops of the year.[19]

While members of Congress were grilling USAID officials over the EKAM houses, Burgos was assembling a case very similar to the one in

Afghanistan. The problems with the EKAM houses, it appeared to him, involved more than mere incompetence.

Burgos had obtained email records confirming that Thor, its local subcontractor, and CEEPCO altered project requirements to save money. They pocketed at least $400,000 on that deal alone, according to a source familiar with Burgos's investigation. But fixing those mistakes would prove far costlier, and Burgos wasn't about to receive a host of awards for his work.

The US government had acknowledged some problems with the houses, and the existence of a legal investigation, but withheld the most damning revelations from the public and called in some friends to make sure the depth of the problems would remain hidden. Tetra Tech, which received the no-bid contract to oversee the remediation work, was one of the biggest USAID contractors in the world, and at the time was working on a number of other projects for the US in Haiti. In other words, Tetra Tech executives could be trusted.

This was a "can you keep it on the q.t. type of thing," a source involved with the EKAM houses later told me.[20] Though the contract was awarded without a bidding process due to the urgency of the repairs, Tetra Tech didn't do any work to fix the houses. Instead, they performed yet another evaluation.[21] It was a smoke screen, the source said, and "Tetra Tech provided the smoke." Its employees sat largely idle on the ground in Haiti.

It wasn't until September 2015, more than a year after Tetra Tech had received its contract, that any actual remediation work on the houses began. USAID awarded $7.9 million to another US company, Virginia-based DFS Construction, to fix the houses.

As the repairs finally began in Haiti, in Maryland it looked possible that criminal charges could be brought against the contractors responsible. Investigators had obtained emails in which the companies were arguing over how to split the money they had saved. Prosecutors, it seemed, had a strong case.

Then, in October, CEEPCO issued a press release saying any problems had been fixed and that "both parties have come to a resolution to ensure optimal outcomes going forward" and that it was "thrilled to continue its work with USAID."[22] None of the agencies, or the contractors, commented further on the "voluntary exclusion agreement," whereby both Thor and CEEPCO agreed to a temporary placement on the contractor blacklist. But for the source involved in the project, the purpose was obvious. "It was about nipping this in the bud," they said. Burgos, the federal agent investigating the housing program, was reassigned to Frankfurt, Germany.

But could the legal case focusing on CEEPCO in Maryland have continued? The US Attorney's Office for the Maryland district told me that they could not confirm or deny an investigation. USAID's legal department offered the same generic response. Charles, the CEEPCO CEO, and Copeland, the Thor founder, offered no comment when I asked, in mid-2016, on the status of any legal cases.

When I asked USAID if the voluntary exclusion agreement prevented the government from bringing legal charges, a spokesperson demurred: "USAID works hard to ensure US tax dollars are spent wisely and that our implementing partners are held to the highest standards." At the time of writing, no charges have been brought against CEEPCO, Thor, or either of the company's directors.

WHEN I FINALLY walked the streets of the EKAM village in November 2017, the remediation work was still ongoing. The next month, DFS Construction's contract was extended further, and USAID awarded the company another $2.8 million. Tetra Tech received another million on the same day. Together, the work that Tetra Tech and DFS did, all to fix the earlier problems of Thor and CEEPCO, cost US taxpayers $20 million.

When USAID's shelter team first came up with the post-quake housing plan, it called for at least ten thousand homes, located predominantly in the greater Port-au-Prince area. They were supposed to cost $8,000 each. The entire program's budget was initially set at $53 million. When I met Vastine in January 2013, he estimated the houses would cost somewhere around $25,000 each. By the time I showed up on the ground, the 750 EKAM houses alone had cost $57.8 million, or more than $77,000 per house. When all was said and done, the total per house would reach $88,000.

It is easy to blame locals for corruption in foreign aid projects, but just as often, it is the American or other foreign companies involved that are the primary culprits. An ineffectual judicial system allows local corruption to continue, as almost all development experts would agree. The same is true for the United States.

At the EKAM village, life was going on as normal. Nobody I spoke to had any idea about the US contractors' suspension and the multi-year scandal in the United States. It may have cost $20 million to fix the houses, but in the end, residents were just happy to have a house that did not flood anymore. These houses had opened my eyes. In many ways, they were the perfect encapsulation of everything wrong with our foreign aid system: the favoritism and corruption, the reliance on expensive foreign "experts," the lack of community consultation. Most of all, the houses stood as proof of how difficult it was to hold anybody accountable for their actions in Haiti.

26

THE APOLOGY

———

In the fall of 2017, the United Nations Security Council officially ended its peacekeeping mission in Haiti, MINUSTAH. After arriving in the aftermath of the 2004 coup, the UN spent more than $7 billion over the mission's thirteen-year mandate. "The departure of MINUSTAH represents, on the one hand, that the stabilization mandate entrusted to the Mission by the Security Council has been met," Sandra Honoré, the Trinidadian politician leading the mission since 2013, said on the date of its withdrawal.[1]

The UN, Honoré said, had helped to professionalize and train the Haitian National Police, building its numbers to more than fourteen thousand. And the Blue Helmets had helped manage three presidential handovers—culminating in the swearing in of Jovenel Moïse. "The fact that the democratic process has started to become stronger, to consolidate itself," Honoré said, "I think [this is] the legacy of MINUSTAH."

To many Haitians, however, the legacy of the UN mission looked much different. In its early years, there had been the dozens of violent raids into Cité Soleil and other neighborhoods of the capital, resulting in scores of civilian deaths. And there had been innumerable cases of sexual abuse and exploitation. From 2004 to 2007, more than a hundred Sri Lankan soldiers ran a child sex ring, abusing kids as young as ten years old who were often lured into military bases with the prospect of a cookie or a small piece of food. None were ever jailed. In 2011, a teenage boy was gang-raped by a contingent of Uruguayan peacekeepers.[2]

One independent investigator, traveling around the country and interviewing communities surrounding UN bases, estimated there had been more than 550 individuals abused by UN troops—and given the limitations of the study's scope, that was certainly an underestimate.[3]

Another team of researchers interviewed more than 2,500 Haitians about their experience with UN troops. They found that 10 percent of those they spoke with knew someone who had had a child with a UN soldier. In one case, the girl was fourteen when she started a relationship with a Brazilian soldier, who would give her food and money. But, when she told him she was pregnant, he was sent back to Brazil and stopped responding to her messages. "MINUSTAH gave us many children without fathers," one study participant told researchers.[4]

Even against this history, there was another legacy more damning than all the rest: cholera. Since the UN had introduced the disease into Haiti in the fall of 2010 through its faulty sanitation practices, it had spread across every department. Conservatively, the disease killed ten thousand and sickened close to a million—some 10 percent of the population. Realistically, those figures are likely at least eight times higher, according to a French scientist who has long studied the epidemic.[5] A study by Doctors Without Borders found that the real toll was as much as ten times higher than the official data in some areas.[6] Cholera, which had never been recorded in Haiti before, ravaged rural communities and the urban poor, tearing apart families and instilling terror in the population.

After thirteen years, the foreign troops were finally leaving. But it wasn't just because UN officials had declared their mission complete. Between cholera, extrajudicial killings, and rape, pressure had been building to end the troops' presence for years—both inside Haiti and in those countries sending soldiers. Many Haitians considered the Blue Helmets' presence just another in a long line of foreign occupations of their country. It wasn't just the scandals. It was also the fact that the UN had done precious little to hold itself or its troops accountable.

Throughout the life of the Aid State, foreign donors had spent billions ostensibly to help strengthen the rule of law, likely more than on any other single issue. It was one of MINUSTAH's foremost objectives, and the phrase "rule of law" was attached to countless multimillion-dollar USAID projects. There is little question that a lack of justice and accountability severely affects Haitians, but, as the Blue Helmets show, those problems were certainly not confined to Haitians or Haitian institutions. Which made what the UN did next all the more absurd.

The foreign troops might have been withdrawing, but the UN wasn't about to leave Haiti. The same resolution authorizing the end of MINUSTAH also created its successor mission, MINUJUSTH—the United Nations Mission for Justice Support in Haiti.[7] The new peacekeeping operation would be composed of more than a thousand police officers and would maintain the political mission of its predecessor. Its mandate was "to assist the Government of Haiti to strengthen rule of law institutions." But how could the UN have anything to offer on the rule of law when it couldn't—or wouldn't—do anything to hold itself accountable?

In August 2016, after more than five years of denials, UN Secretary-General Ban Ki-moon finally acknowledged the UN's role in the introduction and spread of the deadly disease. The UN stopped short of taking direct responsibility, but Ban's spokesperson told *The New York Times* that "over the past year, the UN has become convinced that it needs to do much more regarding its own involvement in the initial outbreak and the suffering of those affected by cholera."[8] Ban announced that, within two months, the UN would launch a "new response" to the outbreak that, all those years later, continued to kill people in Haiti. The UN, however, was quick to point out that this did not change its legal position: that it was immune from any claims by individuals affected by the epidemic.

In December, Ban went further. "On behalf of the United Nations, I want to say very clearly: we apologize to the Haitian people," the secretary-general said, before outlining an ambitious two-track program to help eliminate the disease from Haiti and provide compensation to victims.[9] At the time, the outbreak in Haiti remained one of the most severe in the world and was increasing again in the aftermath of Hurricane Matthew. Ban spoke of the UN's "moral responsibility" to act and urged the world to step up and provide funding for the new initiative.

The UN simply could no longer ignore its own role. The final straw that had prompted the reckoning was an internal report, prepared by Philip Alston, a UN special rapporteur and a professor at New York University. In the report, echoing what activists, legal representatives, and dozens of members of Congress had been saying for years, he had castigated the UN's cholera policy as "morally unconscionable, legally indefensible and politically self-defeating." The UN's refusal to accept responsibility, he wrote, "upholds a double standard according to which the UN insists that member states respect human rights, while rejecting any such responsibility for itself." The arguments from the UN Office of Legal Affairs, refusing to be held legally liable, "trumped the rule of law," Alston wrote.

Indeed, by the time of the secretary-general's apology, legal efforts to seek compensation had been ongoing for five years. In the fall of 2011, the Boston-based Institute for Justice and Democracy in Haiti (IJDH), together with its Haitian partner organization, the Bureau des Avocats Internationaux (BAI), filed a claim with the United Nations on behalf of some five thousand cholera victims.[10] The UN and its various peace-keeping missions enjoy immunity from suit. That said, each mission is required to establish a formal dispute resolution mechanism in the countries where they operate. In theory, such an institution would be able to hear complaints concerning the force's history of extrajudicial killings, sexual abuse, and even cholera. Nowhere, including Haiti, had the UN ever actually set up such a mechanism.

After the UN rejected the claims, the lawyers and their Haitian clients filed a civil suit in New York federal court in October 2013. The case was against the United Nations as an institution, but also the head of its mission at the time of the outbreak, the Guatemalan diplomat Edmond Mulet, and Ban himself. I showed up at the federal courthouse on a rainy day almost exactly one year later to hear oral arguments on whether the case would be able to move forward or if the UN's immunity would continue to trump the rule of law.

"Haitian people are all too familiar with the court expressing sympathy to their plight but closing doors to them," Muneer Ahmad, a clinical professor of law at Yale, told the court. "That need not be the case here," he said. Though UN officials still refused to admit their own role in the disease's introduction into Haiti, myriad scientific studies had come out establishing a concrete link between Nepalese troops and the emergence of cholera. "It is not seriously disputed that the UN is responsible for causing this devastating epidemic," said Beatrice Lindstrom, the attorney for IJDH spearheading the case.[11] Still, no UN officials even showed up in court. The job of defending the UN's immunity instead fell to US Department of Justice lawyers, who said they had a duty to do so as the institution's host nation.

Mario Joseph, the managing attorney of the BAI, noted in a press release after the hearing that "the UN spends lots of time and money telling our officials and citizens to respect the rule of law. Then it refuses to have the law apply to itself after killing thousands of Haitians. Does the UN think Haitians do not notice the double standard?"

Everyone could see it.

Less than three months later, the judge dismissed the case and upheld the inviolability of the UN's immunity. In 2015, a federal appeals court once again opened its doors to Haitians. Once again, the Obama Department of Justice intervened in support of the UN. In the summer of 2016, with the case still pending, 158 members of the US Congress wrote to the Obama administration, criticizing the lack of a meaningful response to the cholera epidemic and urging the State Department to do more to ensure the UN provide meaningful reparations to victims. "The UN continues to refuse to even discuss providing compensation for the losses incurred by those killed and sickened by the cholera it brought to Haiti," the letter stated.[12] Two months later, the appeals court dismissed the suit, and the case ended.

The years of advocacy did pay off, however. "The lawsuit became a rallying point for advocates in Haiti and around the world to call for justice," Lindstrom, who worked the case from the beginning, later explained. "Though we lost in US court, the case helped us win in the court of public opinion and pressure the UN into finally promising action."[13]

After apologizing for the UN's role in bringing cholera to Haiti in late 2016, Ban Ki-moon also announced a $400 million two-track plan to compensate victims and invest in the infrastructure needed to eradicate the disease. The UN created a trust fund to pool resources. The UN had avoided any legal responsibility, but, at the very least, the years of public pressure had forced some action. There was just one problem: nobody wanted to fund it.

At first, UN officials sought to incorporate the funding into the peacekeeping budget. Member states, however, rejected that proposal as too costly. Then, in an attempt to at least get *some* money, the UN tried to reallocate unspent money from MINUSTAH's budget. Even that effort was thwarted by member states, including the US, now led by Trump.[14] By the time MINUSTAH officially closed its doors in the fall of 2017, the trust fund had just $2.6 million and only $23,000 had actually been spent.[15] To this day, not a single Haitian victim has received compensation.

Nevertheless, be it Martelly or Moïse, no Haitian government intervened to push for UN accountability. It was, quite simply, impossible to go against the managers of the Aid State. Everyone knew what could happen if you tried. In 2003, President Aristide had launched a national campaign for reparations. France, he said, owed more than $20 billion for the ransom Haiti was forced to pay for its freedom two hundred years earlier. It was an "explosive," the French ambassador at the time, Yves Gaudeul, later said. "We had to try to defuse it." Just like Department of Justice lawyers had argued in the cholera case, such a demand would open the floodgates to others asking for the same. The next year, Aristide was overthrown in a coup. It was "probably a bit about" Aristide's call for reparations, the French ambassador later acknowledged.[16]

AT 6:30 A.M. on November 13, 2017, Armand Louis received a phone call from the school he had directed for the last thirty years.[17] At the Maranatha Evangelical College campus in Grand Ravine, a tree-lined oasis in the middle of the city's sprawling concrete, dozens of police had arrived and something terrible was happening. That morning, more than two hundred police officers had launched an anti-gang raid in the neighborhood and the operation had spilled onto the school's campus, a mishmash of buildings set back off the bustle of the street and guarded by a low retaining wall.

By the time Louis arrived at the school a few hours later, the courtyard was already full of tear gas. But it appeared things had calmed down. Then, the school's guard approached Louis and told him that a number of armed men had shown up on the campus that morning and had threatened him. They were hiding in a supply shed on campus. Louis told the officers. When police opened the door to the storage facility, the armed men inside opened fire, killing two.

The anti-gang raid had been planned with the support of the new UN mission, MINUJUSTH. After the shots fired, UN police from Jordan and Senegal responded to the scene, administering first aid to the injured officers and securing the perimeter of the school. But, as UN police stood guard, the surviving Haitian officers took revenge on the school employees.

First, witnesses said, the officers shot and killed the guard who had told them about the armed men. The police blamed Louis, the director, for setting them up. They dragged him into the courtyard and beat him with a chair. A teacher tried to intervene. He was shot five times, once in the head. When police left the campus, shortly after eleven A.M., nine individuals lay dead in the courtyard. Human rights investigators reported that five of the dead had received shots in the head, indicating summary executions. When I arrived at the campus a few days later, the courtyard was still stained with blood.

Residents believed the death toll was likely much higher, not just at the school but in the surrounding neighborhood. At the local morgue, the director told me they had received eight bodies the day after the killings, more than the police had initially acknowledged. "Maybe the police moved some bodies," he said, "because we had five or six people come here to ask if we had their relatives." But none of them were among the bodies they had received.

Rovelsond Apollon, an observer with Justice and Peace, a local human rights organization that was one of the first to investigate, said they had confirmed twelve dead, but that the real total was unlikely to ever be known. Not that many people are paying attention to what happens in Grand Ravine, he said. "A hundred or even two hundred could die there and nobody would know."

It took more than a month for the United Nations to even acknowledge that its police had been present while the massacre took place. An internal inquiry found that no UN police had fired their weapons, and that they had simply secured the perimeter of the school. "None of the [UN police] unit proceeded to the location at Maranatha College where the alleged killings took place," a spokesperson told me.

The operation was one of the first under the auspices of the new UN mission. Less than a month into its new mandate, however, and already its officers had been involved in a massacre. Apollon noted that Haiti had seen many international missions throughout its history. "They all failed," he said, because they do not understand the Haitian reality. In Haiti, he said, impunity reigns.

The head of the scaled-down UN mission at the time was Susan D. Page, a career diplomat with the US State Department with decades of experience, predominantly in Africa. She had first taken a position in Haiti in early 2017, before the troop withdrawal and transition to the new justice-focused mission. After the massacre, Page began to privately push the Haitian authorities to investigate what had happened, and also encouraged the government—futilely—to look more into the corruption allegations surrounding PetroCaribe.[18] But it wasn't only the Haitian government that didn't want to hear it.

In early 2018, private citizens filed lawsuits related to both the PetroCaribe corruption allegations as well as the Grand Ravine massacre. Page thought the time had come to go public. In late February, she issued a press release welcoming the assignment of investigating judges to both cases and noting the importance of justice and accountability. Predictably, the Haitian government was furious. The foreign minister denounced Page for overstepping her authority. "The country is fighting to defend its image," Moïse said. "People have to speak well of the country."[19]

The government pulled its ambassador from the UN and called on

Page to face consequences. The UN, heavily influenced by the Trump administration, sided with the Haitian government over its own staff. Page was recalled to New York and never returned to Haiti.

"I was running a justice support mission," Page later recounted. "Am I not supposed to call for justice?"[20]

Apparently not if doing so threatened the hard-earned "stability" of the Aid State. The UN wasn't in Haiti to push for justice; rather, it was there to support the president. Neither case went anywhere.

The UN, given its own lack of accountability for the introduction of cholera, myriad sexual abuse cases, and involvement in the police massacre itself, was never a credible vector to push for justice in Haiti. What credibility does any international actor have to lecture Haiti about justice when they cannot accept accountability themselves? Nevertheless, the rapid jettisoning of Page for what amounted to a statement welcoming progress on investigations into high-profile corruption and human rights abuse cases sent a clear message. The international community's support for the rule of law in Haiti was mere rhetoric. Perhaps that was a product of the White House's new occupant, but for those who had watched the situation deteriorate under Democrats as well as Republicans, it was a sign of continuity, not change.

The only person ever to spend time in jail for Grand Ravine was Armand Louis, the school's director. After being beaten, he was thrown into a cell in the national penitentiary for more than a week. As for the police officers accused of perpetrating a cold-blooded massacre, an Inspector General report did accuse a number of them of wrongdoing and recommended they be punished.[21] The leader of the unit was an officer named Jimmy Cherizier. I had heard his name once before. After the 2015 sugar boat drug bust, a key informant had barely survived an assassination attempt. He claimed it had been a Haitian police officer who tried to kill him: Cherizier.[22] When police attempted to apprehend him for questioning related to Grand Ravine, he barricaded himself in his neighborhood home in Delmas 2 and engaged in a protracted shootout. He continued receiving a police paycheck for at least another year.

27

THE TWEET

On August 14, 2018, Haitian Canadian filmmaker and writer Gilbert Mirambeau Jr. tweeted a photo of himself, blindfolded, holding a sign with a message scrawled in black sharpie. *"Kot Kòb Petwo Karibe a?"* the sign asked—"Where is the PetroCaribe money?" A few days later, a popular Haitian singer tweeted a similar picture, this time with the hashtag #PetrocaribeChallenge. The next day, a group of young Haitians who had been organizing themselves through social media decided to promote the hashtag. From that innocuous first tweet, a movement was born, one that threatened to upend the fragile status quo of the Aid State.[1]

From 2008 to 2017, the Venezuela-led PetroCaribe initiative provided more than $2 billion in budget support to the Haitian government. The activists' focus on the fund made perfect sense. Donors had spent more than $10 billion since the quake, but the Haitian people had little recourse to hold any of those actors accountable. PetroCaribe was different because the money actually reached the Haitian government. That provided at least the possibility for some accountability, and many Haitians had been demanding that for years.

In 2012, two lawyers filed a civil suit against First Lady Sophia Saint-Rémy and her son, Olivier Martelly. After taking office, President Martelly had placed both in charge of PetroCaribe-funded programs. The lawyers accused the First Family of massive corruption. Judge Jean Serge Joseph accepted the case and began an investigation.[2] On July 11, 2013, Joseph was called to a meeting with the minister of justice. According to the judge, he was confronted by Prime Minister Lamothe, President Martelly, as well as the justice minister, who not so subtly pressured him to drop the case. Martelly became so angry that spittle flew into Judge Joseph's face, according to testimony later received by Senate investigators.[3]

Two days later, Joseph was dead, the result of cardiac arrest. The government officials allegedly present at the meeting all denied it had ever taken place. But Samuel Madistin, a former senator and presidential candidate who counted Judge Joseph as his friend, told me that he believed the pressure from the president was what killed him.[4] Some opposition senators launched an impeachment process against Martelly, accusing the president of obstruction of justice, but were unable to achieve a quorum to hold a vote. The investigation went nowhere.

Martelly dismissed the case as nothing more than fake news from political opponents, but it wasn't only the opposition making noise about PetroCaribe. In December 2013, Mary Barton-Dock, the World Bank's special envoy to Haiti, addressed about fifteen reporters in French outside her office in Port-au-Prince. "You need a wise use of PetroCaribe funding in the economy," she cautioned. At the time, the program was contributing more than $200 million a year to the government. "For state funding, what I'm suggesting first is more transparency," she continued.[5] While more critical than donors generally are in public, the rather innocuous comments received a furious response.

The envoy's comments are "out of touch and in complete disregard of what this administration is and has been doing," an advisor to Lamothe told the press.[6] "This is simply insolent," the Venezuelan ambassador said.[7]

"It was clear I had hit a nerve," Barton-Dock explained to me years later. "It didn't make sense, so I started to look into it." The more she looked, the more she came to believe that money was being misallocated.[8]

Meanwhile, the First Family appeared to be accumulating wealth, and quickly. A member of one of Haiti's wealthiest families recalled Martelly telling him, around this time, "I came to office with nothing, now, I'm richer than you."[9]

Martelly purchased an ostentatious mansion along the Haitian coast. The president claimed to have received a multimillion-dollar loan from a local bank to pay for it. In 2015, the government issued a decree redrawing the boundaries of the municipality where it was located, creating an entirely new town. "I told him to sell it, to pay back the loan and present the whole thing as a business investment," Damian Merlo, Martelly's former advisor, told me. Martelly's response, according to Merlo, was "I'm never selling that house."

By that time, Martelly was ruling by decree without any oversight. "It was a perfect storm for corruption," according to Barton-Dock. The PetroCaribe spending is not part of the regular budget, rather it is handled by the government's Bureau of Monetization of Development Aid Programs (BMPAD), which handles oil imports and authorizes the actual PetroCaribe disbursements from an account held at the central bank.

Merlo told me that there had been a big fight within the government about replacing the head of BMPAD. "They tried to replace the guy with a crony to funnel money to them," he explained.[10] In early 2015, with Martelly ruling by decree, he named Eustache Saint-Lôt the new head of BMPAD. He is the brother of Danielle Saint-Lôt, one of the founders of Martelly's PHTK party. A few years later, Eustache's son married the daughter of Kiko Saint-Rémy, the president's brother-in-law.

In November 2017, the Senate's anti-corruption commission released a 650-page report detailing nearly a decade of PetroCaribe-related spending.[11] The report identified overbilling, ghost companies, contracts for uncompleted work, and a host of other financial improprieties. The report generated widespread discontent and a brief period of sporadic protests, but many criticized the commission for selectively publishing information for political purposes. Though it included some former allies of President Moïse, the commission was largely associated with the opposition. Not only that, it consisted of a number of politicians who themselves had faced allegations of corruption for years. Momentum fizzled.

By 2018, cheap oil from Venezuela had dried up. The Venezuelan economy was in shambles, partially the result of wide-ranging sanctions implemented by the Trump administration. In Haiti, which had relied on the discount oil program for nearly a decade, the declining shipments forced the government to privatize the fuel import industry. In early July, during a World Cup match between Brazil and Belgium, when the government assumed the population would be glued to their TV sets, the Moïse administration announced that it was ending fuel subsidies. Without the PetroCaribe money, the Haitian government wanted to reach a deal with the IMF for fresh funding, and ending the fuel subsidies was a precondition. But the government miscalculated. Within hours, the streets were full of black smoke. Businesses were ransacked. Three days of rioting closed the international airport and shut down the capital.

The government was forced to backtrack, but the attempt focused attention on how the government was managing its meager resources. Rather than taxing the elite, the budget gap would be closed by hitting the population where it hurt the most. Then, a month later, Mirambeau sent his viral tweet, effectively taking the PetroCaribe dossier out of the hands of the political class and placing it with the people. Momentum began building for a national day of protest to be held on October 17, 2018—the date marking the death of the revolutionary hero Jean-Jacques Dessalines.

On October 15, more than a half dozen political activists held a press conference in La Saline, a popular neighborhood in Port-au-Prince that is home to St. Jean Bosco, the church where Aristide made his name. The neighborhood has remained a fount of support for the former president, but rival armed community groups have fought for control of the area for years. Outside a youth foundation associated with one of the groups, Project La Saline, the activists announced their support for the upcoming day of protest.

On the seventeenth, a group of demonstrators began assembling outside St. Jean Bosco. They eventually joined up with groups from other neighborhoods throughout the capital. The protest was massive and echoed throughout the country. It wasn't just Port-au-Prince in the streets but the entire country. The social media campaign had come to life, and it sent shockwaves through the political establishment. President Moïse responded by firing a handful of his closest advisors and promising an investigation. "No one will escape justice," he tweeted.[12] Activists called for another day of action on November 18, another holiday, this time celebrating the Battle of Vertières, the decisive fight against the French.

But the situation in La Saline deteriorated. Threatening WhatsApp messages circulated warning the population of reprisals for their participation in the growing anti-corruption movement. Around four o'clock on the afternoon of November 13, some two hundred heavily armed individuals descended on La Saline.[13] Many of them wore police uniforms, sending project members scrambling. In their absence, the police-disguised group indiscriminately terrorized the neighborhood, ransacking more than 150 homes, pulling men and women into the street to be executed, beheaded, cut into pieces, left charred. Women "were raped in the presence of their powerless husbands or partners, and sometimes even in the presence of their children," police investigators found. The gunmen allegedly killed seventy-one people, including children as young as three years old, according to RNDDH, a local human rights organization.

At five P.M., according to an investigation prepared by UN human rights monitors, Joseph Pierre Richard Duplan, the president's personally appointed delegate to the region that includes La Saline, appeared outside the youth foundation associated with Project La Saline. Three police officers and the leaders of a number of neighboring *baz* allegedly accompanied him. "You killed too many people," eyewitnesses reported him as saying. "That was not your mission."[14]

"They wanted to control the area because of what La Saline represents in terms of its ability to mobilize," Pierre Esperance, the head of RNDDH, told the *Miami Herald*.[15] "They didn't kill them because they were in the opposition. They did it because . . . they wanted to break the mobilization."

Action started early on November 18, as disparate groups slowly wound through lower Port-au-Prince and eventually amassed at the overpass, a single-arch viaduct funded by PetroCaribe and inaugurated in 2015 as a step toward a modern transportation system. Instead, it had become a $21 million concrete symbol of government waste, and a rallying point for anti-corruption protesters.[16]

From there, the ever-growing assemblage began the long ascent up Route Delmas to Pétion-Ville. Over the four-mile stretch, demonstrators climbed more than a thousand feet, about the equivalent of scaling the Washington Monument—twice. As they hit the steepest section, in front of the Canadian embassy, the sun was directly overhead. Music was blaring and the throng of people seemed to be moving in unison all around me. I looked to my left and saw Mirambeau with a small group all wearing black shirts. *"Kot Kòb Petrocaribe a?"* they asked in white block lettering.

After walking another five miles, up to Pétion-Ville and then back down the hill to the National Palace, where we were dispersed by tear gas, I sat down with Samuel Madistin at his law offices tucked down a narrow alley off Avenue John Brown. "The momentum today around PetroCaribe is the continuation of Judge Joseph's legacy," Madistin explained, sitting behind his desk where a Lady Justice statue was collecting dust. "Impunity breeds further impunity," he said.

"This is bigger than PetroCaribe," Madistin continued. It's about moving toward a new system.[17] "But we can't go anywhere if we don't stop corruption." The lawyer, however, was not optimistic that his country's justice system had the independence and skills necessary on its own.

"Normally, if a country wants a good process they can ask [the international community] for technical support," Madistin noted. But, he continued, there is a trust deficit. Many see the current Haitian government as supported by the same international actors whose support would be needed. First, he said, the decision has to be made locally. "If we show them that we have the will, the international community will follow." The protesters were not just targeting their own political class, but also sending a message to the Aid State's foreign managers: the status quo must end.

"It is easy to blame Haitians," a diplomatic source explained, "but there is blame on all of us."[18] For more than a decade, donors had focused narrowly on the concept of "stability," but that stability locked in an unsustainable system that excluded the majority of the population. "We are looking at the end of a system—the final stretch," the diplomat said. "We just don't know if it has ten more years, ten more months, or ten more days."

As for an investigation into PetroCaribe, the diplomat was clear. "For sure, PHTK received money from PetroCaribe. . . . [The government] doesn't want an investigation." But, the source added, "the international ramifications of PetroCaribe are far greater than we know."

And so, it wasn't just the Haitian government that didn't want an investigation, which would be sure to ensnare politically connected firms in the Dominican Republic, as well as diaspora-owned businesses in Miami, according to the diplomatic source. State Department officials privately indicated their reluctance to aggressively pursue corruption allegations out of fear of being seen as picking political winners and losers. But that fear had never appeared to impact US policy in the past, nor had it stopped the Trump administration from deepening its involvement in Haiti.

AFTER THE FUEL price riots and the PetroCaribe protests, President Moïse noticeably changed his rhetoric. He began speaking openly about the power of the elite and the entrenched interests that blocked reform. He also tasked the Court of Auditors, the nation's highest oversight body, to undertake an investigation into PetroCaribe. Few outside his strongest supporters trusted his sincerity, however. For starters, while he did pick high-profile fights with a few elite families, he relied on the support of many others. But there was something more going on. Though it remained out of public view, not long after the November protest I obtained internal government financial documents showing that Moïse himself had received at least a million dollars in PetroCaribe funding.

There was a certain irony in it all. Venezuelan oil money was financing the political consolidation of the party the US had helped to put in power. At the time, I asked the Venezuelan ambassador to the United States, Bernardo Álvarez, about exactly this.[19] Did the Venezuelan government understand what was happening in Haiti? Álvarez did, but there was nothing to do about it, he said. The ambassador there was corrupt, he explained, and had made lots of money. He was also connected in Caracas, meaning he was protected. When I finally found proof of Moïse benefiting from the PetroCaribe funds, it came as little surprise.

In May 2015, when Jovenel Moïse arrived at the electoral council to register as the PHTK candidate in the upcoming presidential elections, the rural businessman was largely a political unknown. But already his business was finding success and receiving a healthy dose of government largesse. Of course, there was Agritrans, the banana plantation that received a $6 million government loan and became the centerpiece of his political campaign. But that wasn't all.

Five days after registering as a presidential candidate, the government disbursed more than $1 million in PetroCaribe funds to Agritrans, as well as another company also belonging to Moïse. The funds, however, were not for growing bananas but to build a road near the town of Port-de-Paix in Haiti's North-West department.

Melius Hyppolite, a former senator from the region and a personal friend of Moïse, said that millions were awarded for Agritrans' work on the road project. "The North-West does not receive attention from the government," Hyppolite explained.[20] Residents believed this was finally the time that changed. "We supported Jovenel, he was from here and his wife was born in Port-de-Paix." Government budget documents show more than $7 million of PetroCaribe funds allocated to the road project in fiscal year 2014–2015.

In December 2015, the country representative of the IDB sent a letter to the Haitian government. The letter revealed that some $800,000 had gone to Agritrans through a subcontract on a road building contract, and that an internal audit discovered unjustified expenses far beyond what was expected. The IDB asked to be reimbursed for the expenses.[21] Moïse and Agritrans adamantly denied any wrongdoing.

In the fall of 2016, the government's anti–money laundering entity, the Central Financial Intelligence Unit (UCREF), released an investigation into Moïse's finances. The report identified a number of suspicious bank accounts (including some in the name of Agritrans) and transactions that appeared to indicate involvement in money laundering.

Another investigation, this one from the government's anti-corruption unit, found that Moïse had received two personal loans totaling hundreds of thousands of dollars in 2011 and 2013 from a state-run bank now on the verge of bankruptcy.[22] Moïse labeled both reports as nothing more than politically motivated hit jobs. But, once he took office, Moïse illegally fired the head of the anti–money laundering office. Then, Parliament passed legislation consolidating the executive branch's control over the anti-corruption institutions.[23] In 2017, the body did not forward a single case to the judicial system.

After the election, the banana plantation never made another export of bananas. And the PetroCaribe-funded road project that Agritrans was working on fell by the wayside as well. "There was a lot of hope," Hyppolite, the former senator, told me, "but it has not materialized." In early 2019, another former senator from the region, Jean-Baptiste Bien-Aime, confirmed that the road had yet to be completed.[24]

In April 2019, the judge investigating the anti-corruption and anti–money laundering reports into Moïse returned his final judgment, clearing Moïse of any wrongdoing. But the ruling did little to assuage the activists in the streets. They were still waiting for the full Court of Auditors report on PetroCaribe.

In late May, the auditors released a 600-page report detailing nearly a decade of mismanagement in the PetroCaribe program. What perhaps received the greatest attention, however, was the revelation from the documents I had obtained months earlier: that two firms controlled by Moïse had received more than a million dollars for those road building contracts.[25] It appeared both companies had received money for the same project. "For the court, giving a second contract for the same project . . . is nothing less than a scheme to embezzle funds," the report read.

The next week, protesters were again in the streets across the country. This time, however, they were specifically targeting Moïse, calling for him to resign and face justice. It had been nearly a year since the fuel price riots. Moïse had cycled through two prime ministers, the economy had entered a recession, and prices of basic goods, especially food, were skyrocketing. It was an explosive combination.

For Mirambeau, the struggle for accountability had taken on a much broader meaning from when he sent his initial tweet. This wasn't just about Moïse or his party or even PetroCaribe, he told me later that year. This was about challenging the status quo of corruption that has strangled Haiti's development, he said. I had been spending time in Haiti only since the earthquake, but, at least in that relatively short period of time, it seemed different to me, too, like something had shifted.

I had walked in dozens of Port-au-Prince protests; they were led and organized by people I had come to recognize. The manifestations were a ritual, and, at times, a job. They ebbed and flowed. Now, those same people, largely from the popular neighborhoods, were being joined by the artists and academics in Pacot and Pétion-Ville. Women made up an ever-increasing portion and took leadership roles in many of the burgeoning social organizations that were popping up. People I had come to know within the upper classes started whispering things privately that sounded like what my grassroots activist friends had been chanting openly for years. The Core Group, and more specifically the US, had lost such credibility over the years that even many who once would have put their trust in foreign intervention began to wonder if street action was actually the only way for anything to change. Civil society leaders who had fought over the past for more than a decade instead discussed the way forward together. There was a wholesale rejection of the Aid State and that was a potent force for change.[26]

But, as the massacre in La Saline showed, challenging Haiti's entrenched interests came with real danger. And, perceiving the threat to his mandate, Moïse did what Haiti's political elite were accustomed to doing: he turned to the United States.

IRONICALLY, WHILE IT was corruption in the Venezuelan-led PetroCaribe program causing him so many problems, Venezuela also provided Jovenel Moïse with his best chance for ensuring Washington's continued support. In 1964, an embassy employee sent a cable to Washington explaining why it was important to maintain diplomatic relations with Papa Doc, despite mounting evidence of gross human rights violations and rampant corruption. One reason, the official wrote, was that it helped to ensure Haiti would continue to vote with the US in forums such as the UN and OAS.[27] In 1962, Duvalier's representative voted to kick Castro's Cuba out of the OAS. The next year, the dictator declared himself president for life—and remained a voting member of the OAS.

More than fifty years later, shockingly little had changed. For the Trump administration, in addition to being a "shithole" that produced immigrants, Haiti was a vote, and an important one at that. And while Cuba had been allowed to rejoin the OAS in 2009, there was a new hoped-for regional pariah in Venezuela. Washington had long sought to isolate Venezuela, and both the OAS and PetroCaribe related closely to those efforts.

The Bush administration had backed the brief coup against Hugo Chávez in 2002, and then lobbied regional governments aggressively, including Préval in Haiti, not to join the PetroCaribe initiative despite the obvious monetary benefits available to those who did. It was worried about losing influence, not fiscal mismanagement. The Caribbean holds a special importance for US foreign policy objectives in the hemisphere, which have long been advanced through the OAS. The regional body has thirty-five members, and a measure needs majority support to pass through its Permanent Council. Fourteen of those votes belong to Caribbean nations, and they have long voted as a bloc, turning the individually diplomatically weak countries into a significant force, the Caribbean Community or CARICOM.

Under the Obama administration, the US was the only country in the region that didn't quickly recognize the 2013 election of Nicolás Maduro following the death of Chávez.[28] The next year, the US launched the Caribbean Energy Security Initiative, which was touted as an "antidote" to the Venezuelan-led oil program.[29] In early 2015, Obama declared Venezuela to be an "extraordinary threat to the national security" of the United States.[30] However absurd the designation's merits, it had the effect of authorizing the Department of Treasury to impose sanctions on Venezuelan officials, and, eventually under Trump, on Venezuela's oil industry and entire economy.[31] Trump used the authority given to him by Obama and expanded the sanctions while talking openly about wanting to overthrow the government.[32] Haiti would prove critical in those efforts.

Haiti, like the rest of CARICOM, had traditionally voted against or abstained from US-backed OAS resolutions condemning or denouncing Venezuela. Even the Martelly government, despite its reliance on US political support, had maintained strong relations with Venezuela. Many saw the Caribbean's voting record as old-fashioned aid diplomacy given the billions of dollars in PetroCaribe resources flowing throughout the region. That is certainly how the US had always viewed, and secured, multilateral votes. But, even as the PetroCaribe resources dried up, most didn't change their voting behavior. While the financial support no doubt helped, as small, mostly island nations, international law and the principle of sovereignty were all they had in terms of territorial defense. US efforts to sanction or oust a government ran entirely counter to that.

The US had failed to advance its regime change agenda through the OAS, largely because of opposition from CARICOM.[33] But that changed in June 2018, when the OAS passed a resolution paving the way for Venezuela's suspension from the organization.[34] Five CARICOM countries voted in favor. Haiti, which had traditionally voted against such efforts, abstained. As the protest movement in Haiti gained steam in the fall of 2018, and the allegations of corruption reached high-level government officials including the president, the Moïse administration understood it would need to go further. In January 2019, Haiti broke precedent and voted in favor of an OAS resolution kicking Venezuela out of the body. The effort succeeded. Then, a few weeks later, Haiti joined the Trump administration in recognizing Juan Guaidó, a Venezuelan national assemblyman, as the president of Venezuela.[35]

"Poor Haiti. They can't withstand the pressure," Ralph Gonsalves, the prime minister of Saint Vincent and the Grenadines, told the *Miami Herald* after the vote. "The current president of Haiti is just craving for US protection. That's all."[36]

The Haitian government had hoped its vote at the OAS would result in more than just political support. In March, Moïse was among a hand-ful of Caribbean leaders—all of whom had voted against Venezuela at the OAS—who received an invitation to Mar-a-Lago to sit down with Trump.[37] There, the US talked about billions in new funding and invest-ment for the region. The Moïse administration, which had hired a DC public relations firm after Trump's "shithole" comments the year prior, brought on another consultant, and then hired one of DC's most prom-inent firms, Dentons, for $25,000 a month. By the summer of 2019, the cash-strapped government was spending close to $40,000 a month on its roster of lobbyists.[38] Moïse had the diplomatic support of the Trump administration as he sought to hang on to power, yet had next to noth-ing concrete to show for his government's vote at the OAS outside of a photo op with Donald Trump. Or, perhaps, the support had come in a more indirect manner.

28

THE MERCENARIES

———

At 4:59 A.M. on Saturday, February 16, 2019, a private plane registered to a South Florida charter company touched down in Port-au-Prince. For the previous nine days, large parts of the country had been shut down by barricades and street protests pushing for the president's resignation.[1]

The night before, Moïse had spoken multiple times with the head of the airport and with a former minister of state security under Martelly, Fritz Jean-Louis. Preparations had been made; along with Jean-Louis, two businessmen with close ties to the PHTK ruling party arrived at the airport before the sun rose to meet the plane. "I can tell you, the government of Haiti was welcoming these people," the owner of the plane explained when I reached him by phone. "I can tell you that authorities at the airport were very helpful."[2]

The charter flight arrived direct from Baltimore/Washington International Airport (BWI). On it were a handful of American security contractors, including highly trained special operations officers with military experience in Iraq and Afghanistan and with private firms like Blackwater. In Haiti, they became "the mercenaries."

The next day, at least some of them attempted to enter the central bank, the Banque de la République d'Haiti. A security guard on-site denied access and alerted high-level bank officials. Publicly, the bank denied it had any role in bringing them into the country. Phone records I obtained, however, show that Jean-Louis and another of the men who met the contractors at the airport had been in contact with the central bank governor over the previous two weeks. But the contractors apparently never entered the bank, and someone tipped off the police.

That afternoon, police detained seven contractors and their driver—five Americans, two Serbians, and a Haitian national—just a few blocks from the bank. Inside their unmarked vehicles, agents found six semi-automatic rifles, six pistols, two drones, satellite phones, and other tactical equipment. The group was on a government mission, they told the police. "Their boss will call our boss," one of the police officers recalled being told. The government publicly denied any role.

Some speculated they were there to take out political opponents;[3] others claimed it was about destroying records implicating the president and other powerful figures in the PetroCaribe scandal. *The Intercept,* citing someone with firsthand knowledge of the mission, reported the team had been part of an effort to move $80 million from the central bank to the president's personal accounts.[4] The full truth has never come out.

Four days later, when the group was supposed to make their first appearance before a Haitian judge, multiple tinted-out SUVs loaded with armed US security personnel pulled up to the front door of the jail where the mercenaries were being held. Inside their cell, the detained contractors saw someone from the US Embassy approach the bars. Don't make a scene, the man explained to them. When these doors open, walk out quietly and quickly, he said. They did.[5] When the contractors were supposed to be appearing in court, they were in fact on their way to the airport under the custody of the US Embassy. There, they were escorted onto an American Airlines flight bound for Miami. Once in Florida, all the contractors were released. They were never charged with a crime.

Two days later, one of the contractors broke the silence and posted on Instagram. "We were not released we were in fact rescued," Chris Osman wrote. "To the men who risked their lives to do so: you boys are getting some serious care packages!!! We owe you our lives." Osman, who was one of the first US Special Forces on the ground in Afghanistan after September 11, thanked the US government, State Department, and US Embassy in Haiti, specifically the ambassador. "It's been a long time since I have seen the weight of the US government at work and it's a glorious thing," he wrote.

We may never know exactly what those heavily armed men were doing in Port-au-Prince, or who, precisely, they were working for. But their arrest and prompt release under US and Haitian government pressure did make one thing crystal clear. There was a serious rift developing both within the police and between the police and the Moïse administration. The National Police, the embodiment of the Aid State, was on the verge of collapse.

MARIO ANDRESOL WAS living in New York when he got a call in 2005 asking him to come back to Haiti and take the job of police chief. He had fled three years earlier, fearing for his life. He answered the call and ended up serving in the position for the next seven years until he was forced out about a year into Martelly's term, after he refused a presidential request to collect intelligence on political opponents. He understood a thing or two about politicization of the police.

"The mercenaries' detention [and release] exposed deep divisions within the police," Andresol told me when we caught up shortly thereafter.[6] If foreign security contractors were really on a government mission, it undermined the role of the police, he explained. Their release from prison had been a slap in the face to the officers who had just been doing their jobs. Resentment among officers had been rising for some time. The pay, if it ever came, was abysmal. Officers were overworked controlling protests and protecting businesses during the unrest. A few months prior to the mercenaries' arrest, foreign-looking security agents were seen embedded within the president's security detail, fueling additional anger among the rank and file.

President Moïse came to power with a police chief, Michel-Ange Gedeon, freshly installed during the transitional government. They had never seen eye to eye. Just over a year into his term, Moïse issued a decree modifying the law that had created the Police Nationale d'Haiti. Rather than allowing the police chief to control budget allocations and internal promotions, those decisions would have to be approved by the president's ministers.[7] Moïse also furthered his predecessor's efforts to reinstate the armed forces. He formally did just that in the fall of 2017.[8] The government announced plans to begin training an initial class of recruits and establish a formal budget.[9] It was still a long way from becoming the repressive force it once had been, but it did send a clear message to the extremely under-resourced police: you would not be the priority.

Then came the fuel-price rioting in July and the launch of the nationwide anti-corruption movement in November. That same month, the Palace Guard—a distinct unit that answers to the president and not the police chief—appeared in the streets to repress the demonstrations, donning brand-new gear and driving in new trucks, some mounted with .50-caliber machine guns. Gedeon and Andresol both spoke out publicly denouncing the president's illegal use of the Palace Guard.[10] While the president's men paraded through the streets with their shiny toys, most police officers lacked even basic equipment and were being asked to go into neighborhoods increasingly under the control of groups armed with higher-powered weapons and seemingly endless ammunition.

Some police started working private security; some even formed their own companies—including the head of the Palace Guard, Dimitri Hérard, who had risen in the ranks since his implication in the sugar boat drug bust of 2015.[11] Some, like Jimmy Cherizier, the officer implicated in the Grand Ravine school massacre, absconded and began working with the increasingly powerful armed groups in the capital's popular neighborhoods. Some started openly talking about forming a union.

When the foreign security contractors were arrested in early 2019, Gedeon received multiple phone calls from individuals close to the executive, pleading for him to release them. He had refused. The government was furious.

In August 2019, Moïse replaced Gedeon as police chief. At his successor's swearing-in ceremony, Gedeon delivered a blistering message to the police corps.[12] "Be aware that the real bandits to be feared are not those known to all, but those who go around in suits and white shirts, cruising in big cars," he said. "We have a PNH that politics has been trying to divide," he continued, urging officers to "stay united" and to stay apolitical. "You will defeat and overcome any attempt at division and implosion," he assured the assembled officers.

The next month, opposition politicians and anti-corruption activists called for another general strike. In what became known as *peyi lok* or "country blocked," the capital was virtually shut down for nearly three months. Businesses shuttered, schools closed. Hospitals remained out of reach. Those not risking their lives attending protests remained boarded up in their homes, waiting for brief reprieves to run outside and gather supplies as quickly as possible. Barricades went up in neighborhood after neighborhood, blocking transportation further, and protecting communities from attacks by police or other armed groups.

Since the beginning of the nationwide protest movement in the fall of 2018, police tactics had become increasingly repressive. Overall, local rights groups documented 187 deaths, including more than 40 who died from single bullets to the head.[13] During the *peyi lok* period, things got even worse. Amnesty International documented multiple instances of state security forces using live ammunition, tear-gassing civilians at close range from moving vehicles, and a host of other blatant human rights abuses. In one instance, members of the Palace Guard disrupted a funeral held for slain protesters, firing live ammunition and injuring at least three.[14]

In October, officers announced their intention to form a union, the SPNH, and started issuing communiqués demanding greater pay, proper equipment, and appropriate support from their government. They marched in the streets to ensure their voices wouldn't be silenced.[15] Another group of officers, including some who had already left the force, later formed Fantom 509 and began taking to the streets with their weapons, faces covered. Most believed them to be receiving support from some within the opposition. It was an open revolt. The government branded them "terrorists."[16]

The disintegration of the Haitian National Police may not have been a surprise after nearly a decade of overt politicization. Yet, in another sense, it came as a true shock. Over the prior twenty-plus years, foreign donors had spent billions of dollars building up the force. Now, like the rest of the Aid State, it was falling apart in dramatic fashion.

The police were intended to be the spine of stability in Haiti. The question is: Stability for whom? As had been the case for more than two hundred years, on the lips of the local elite and their foreign allies, stability in Haiti meant the protection of the highly unequal status quo, the protection of capital and profit over the needs of the majority.

SINCE HAITI'S 1804 revolution, the local elite and foreign powers had formed a durable alliance in their attempts to manage the nation and ensure the continuation of an economic system based on the exploitation of the peasantry. The repressive armed forces—themselves created during the US occupation—had been their bulwark against the masses for decades, the chosen means of political and economic control. But, when Aristide returned to office in 1994, one of his first acts was disbanding the military. Instead, he focused on building a modern police force, something international donors were more than happy to support.

During the Cold War, the US had channeled significant resources into the Third World to train and equip—"professionalize"—local security forces. With the breakup of the colonial order after World War II, new nations were sprouting up, and the mechanisms global powers had relied on for centuries of control were unwinding. Meanwhile, new ones were emerging. As Stuart Schrader outlines in his book, *Badges Without Borders: How Global Counterinsurgency Transformed American Policing,* the security assistance offered by the US was expressly designed to help replace these methods of colonial control with domestic security forces.[17] US officials recognized that it was no longer feasible to openly occupy these countries (exceptional circumstances notwithstanding, of course). It would be easier to exert influence through a local force that "looked" like the population they were controlling. The Duvalier dictatorship provided a bulwark against communism, rendering this assistance mostly moot at the time. But that changed after Aristide's dismantling of the armed forces.

Haiti's national police force is, for all intents and purposes, a creation of the international community. The US and UN vetted new recruits, provided training, and supplied the bulk of the new forces' budget. They also, against the desires of Aristide, forced the government to reincorporate more than a thousand former soldiers into the police. Donors sank hundreds of millions into the new force while each successive UN mission was mandated with increasing capacity and "professionalizing" the police. Of course, like the rest of the Aid State, foreign support for Haiti's police had largely been outsourced. Big defense contractors like DynCorp received huge contracts, as did many of USAID's darlings, like Tetra Tech and Chemonics.[18]

Still, even after all that, the police had remained a work in progress— which is one big reason why the Blue Helmets had stuck around for as long as they had. That mission, however, had come to an end in late 2017. Though some foreign police remained, it was a far cry from the ten thousand foreign troops who had been on the ground. Without those troops, and with the police force disintegrating, Haiti's political and economic elite turned elsewhere.

DURING THE DUVALIER era, the dictatorship relied on the paramilitary Tonton Macoutes to repress dissent and protect father, then son, from a military coup, the fate that had met so many of their predecessors. Even after Baby Doc's exile in 1986, Haiti's military leaders relied on such extra-official paramilitary actors to enforce their will—though now with a different name. The elite's reliance on paramilitary violence intensified after the 1991 coup against Aristide. The FRAPH death squad, led by a former Macoute, Louis-Jodel Chamblain, and receiving support from the CIA, killed an estimated four thousand and sent many times that number searching for safety outside Haiti.[19]

When Aristide returned to the presidency in 2001, the elite once again turned to paramilitary violence. Chamblain again took the lead, working with former military officers, Macoutes, and active members of the police—including some of those military men incorporated into the force under international pressure—to overthrow the government.

In December 2001, this paramilitary force attacked the National Palace in an attempt to dislodge Aristide for a second time.

Unable to rely on state security, Aristide had turned to the *baz*. In 2004, with the paramilitaries marching to the capital, Aristide was ousted again. With the president gone, the paramilitaries disbanded. With ten thousand foreign troops coming to Haiti in the form of the Blue Helmets, the elite had little use for them. The Blue Helmets didn't come to Haiti to dismantle the paramilitary units, however; they came to dismantle the *baz*, criminalized by the local and foreign elite as bandits and *chimères*.[20] For the better part of two years, the UN waged battle against these groups, which were fighting to restore their ousted leader, Aristide.

The Blue Helmets killed or jailed countless *baz* leaders throughout Port-au-Prince. While responsible for their share of violence, the *baz* had functioned to a large extent as the de facto political representation of the masses. Their destruction only furthered the political and economic exclusion of the popular class. But the UN troops were not just in Haiti to fight armed Aristide loyalists. They were also there to "professionalize" the local police force and to increase its numbers exponentially. In a tragic repeat from the nineties, UN and US officials oversaw the incorporation of many of the paramilitaries who had just been marching on the capital into the police force.

By 2010, the police force had tripled its size to more than ten thousand. And rates of violent crime had dropped significantly. There was a reason UN troops began referring to their mission as a beach-keeping operation. Though its history is punctuated with periods of extreme brutality, the vast majority of Haiti is, and almost always has been, overwhelmingly peaceful. But even in periods of calm, another deeper kind of violence had continued. Haiti remains, functionally, an apartheid state controlled by the political and economic elite. There is daily violence imposed on the urban poor, not in the form of homicides or theft but through a lack of basic rights and dignity. This structural violence is pervasive and manifests in various ways, including outbursts of physical violence.

A police force, no matter how many officers it counted among its ranks, was never going to be able to address the nonexistent social contract undergirding the insecurity. Neither could thousands of foreign troops. Like democracy and development, perhaps security never could truly be imposed by outside powers—at least not in the long run. But the police—and the foreign efforts to train, equip, and professionalize them—eventually failed even in their own narrow role as protectors of the status quo, as protectors of stability. Over the roughly thirty-year consolidation of the Aid State that had mirrored the creation of the national police, civil society and what was once the "popular movement" were systematically weakened. In turn, the apartheid-like undercurrent had only hardened. And that reality made instability and violence inevitable.

The 2018 uprising represented the greatest threat to the elite and their tightly managed status quo since the ouster of Aristide. And, as they had so many times throughout Haiti's history, the political and economic elite turned to paramilitarism. But the dynamics had shifted over the prior decade. The *baz* of the capital's popular neighborhoods had maintained something of a fragile peace for years, working together to resist being used as pawns in the political machinations of the elite. That began to change during the Moïse administration, as the economy began sinking, inflation spiraled, and daily life for millions got even harder—and the fight for political power hit the streets.

While the streets were demanding systemic change, the system responded the only way it knew how: with paramilitary violence. Though they had developed practically in opposition to one another, Haiti's *baz* culture began to blend with the paramilitary. Long criminalized by the elite, even many Haitians once sympathetic to their goals started to refer to these armed groups as gangs, indicating the straight criminality that increasingly characterized their actions.[21] Though many *baz* leaders maintained their community ties, the vast majority had become disassociated with the popular class, uprooted from the needs of their long-excluded communities. They, too, had become mercenaries for the political and economic elite.

* * *

ALL SIDES OF the political class, each with their own faction of elite financial backers, utilized the capital's gangs in their fight for power. In October 2019, government officials tried to persuade community leaders in Bel Air, a bastion of opposition support, to remove the *peyi lok* barricades. They refused. On October 31, the secretary of state for public security approached Cherizier, the former police officer, and asked for help. Days later, Cherizier, two other gang leaders, and at least forty heavily armed men attacked the Bel Air neighborhood. Over the course of four days, the siege killed twenty-four people. Cherizier reportedly received a large sum of money and a fleet of new *motos* in return. Bel Air is surrounded by four police stations. Yet, during the sustained attack, the police never responded. At least three officers wearing civilian clothes were witnessed participating in the attack alongside Cherizier.[22]

Throughout it all, the US continued to financially support the police, though not in the form of higher wages. In November 2019, the Trump administration awarded a $73,000 contract for the provision of "riot control kits." The contract went to X-International, a security firm based in Florida and run by Carl Frédéric Martin, a former Haitian American US military officer and a business partner of Dimitri Hérard, the head of the Palace Guard. Martin had been one of the foreign-looking mercenaries embedded within Hérard's unit during the protests the year before. The two were on their way to becoming some of the largest arms dealers in the country. And some of those weapons would make its way into the hands of the capital's mercenaries.[23]

As the ten-year anniversary of the earthquake approached, the Aid State was crumbling. As it did, and the hope for a brighter future percolated in the streets, powerful actors resorted to violence to ensure that whatever came next, their place in the system would not be affected. But the demands for change were getting louder and louder. It wasn't just the streets calling for Moïse to resign; they were joined by the Catholic and Protestant churches, members of the private-sector elite, university professors, the Port-au-Prince bar association, and myriad others. The feeling in Port-au-Prince was that Moïse would be forced to resign any day; that the only thing keeping him in power was the support of the United States.

But, while there is no doubt that the elite had attempted to co-opt the anti-corruption movement and were waging their fight alongside the popular uprising, the demands for change were about more than just replacing a president. They were about overthrowing the Aid State. While officials in Washington, Paris, Quebec, and New York threw their hands up in exasperation at yet another "political crisis" in Haiti, Haitians understood that it was those same officials' representatives perpetuating the violence and instability. Protesters held signs denouncing the Core Group, the US ambassador, and the head of the UN mission, itself led by a former US diplomat. And, as they had time and time again, those same foreign officials would intervene to try keep in place the inherently unsustainable system they had helped create.

29

THE ONGOING REVOLUTION

———

I hitched a ride to Titanyen for the earthquake's tenth anniversary with an Al Jazeera reporter and her videography crew. Given the deteriorating security situation, I had, begrudgingly, mostly stopped riding around on the back of Ti Mo's *moto*. As we made the turn from Route National 9 to National 1, the sprawl of Canaan was on full display. It looked so much more permanent than the first time I had seen it, nearly a decade earlier. The blue tarps gradually had been replaced by gray concrete shells, one block at a time.

Turning into the memorial site, I noticed the once-deserted location now encircled by new homes. The large cross on the crest of the mountain still stood, though the thousands of smaller ones that had burned five years earlier were never replaced. Police blocked the entrance with some of the Palace Guard's new toys—camouflaged pickup trucks with heavy artillery mounted in the bed. The masked officers opened each bag while two dogs sniffed their way through our belongings. Inside, most of the diplomatic corps were already there, standing beside the memorial rock and waiting for the president.

When Moïse arrived, he greeted the diplomats, then, accompanied by the UN mission's number two, placed a wreath at the memorial. The US ambassador, Michele Sison, followed with a wreath of her own. Then, one by one, each diplomat placed one flower. A few minutes later, we started to hear voices getting louder. I walked to the edge of the retaining wall to see what was happening. A group of ten to twenty people had arrived, fists raised and chanting something—I couldn't quite make out what. The police had blocked their entrance and seemed to be pushing them out of the way. By the time I looked back at the ceremony, it had come to a prompt close. Black SUVs churned dust in the parking lot and sped away. Within a few minutes, the only ones left were the small group of protesters, journalists, and a handful of people who lived nearby and had gathered on the edge of the parking lot.

The protesters had come with their own flowers. They entered the site, pushed the wreaths placed just minutes earlier to the ground, and delicately laid their own. They gathered into a tight circle, held their hands together overhead, and began chanting. *Fos, fos, fos.* Strength, strength, strength. The trombone player from the official ceremony stuck around and provided a soundtrack. Then they, too, left. Soon, all the white lace, wreaths, and other decorations were loaded into the back of a van. Within an hour from its start, it was as if nothing had ever happened.

A young man among the crowd sitting in the shade of the lone tree in the lot approached us. "Every year the president comes here," he said. "But we still don't have services. There's no school and there's no water."[1] Indeed, while many more continued to move to the promised land of Canaan, others had already left. Just down the road, the stone marking the entrance to Mozayik was still there. But nearly all those families, who had been displaced in the 2010 quake, then displaced again in the rush to close the camps, had been pushed out of Canaan as well. The title they thought they obtained legitimately was contested; the land was on the edge of two municipalities and each mayor wanted the land for their own. Few were satisfied in their new surroundings anyway.

When I reconnected with Mona Augustin, the musician who had barely survived the quake and then done everything he could to support the families of Mozayik, he told me that the land in Canaan had once been used as a dumping ground for medical waste. On more than one occasion, kids playing would step on a dirty syringe sticking out of the ground, he said. Rather than fighting to stay, they received some resources from friends in the US and purchased a plot of land in the Central Plateau a few hours from Port-au-Prince. By the time we spoke, they had built nine modest homes, a small classroom for the children, a guesthouse for visitors, and a music studio. It was a work in progress, but unlike the desolation of Canaan, the ground was lush and green and the land was, at last, truly theirs. Ten years after the earthquake, that's where most of the Mozayik families were living. Mona, however, was living in Wisconsin with his American wife. He was still playing music, and still using the connections he had to raise funds in support of his old neighbors from Delmas 30.[2]

As for those who remained in Canaan, they continued to survive without any formal services or infrastructure. A city of hundreds of thousands, with homes built from scratch brick by brick without oversight, sitting on a deforested hillside surrounded by a floodplain. Was this what everyone meant when they had pledged to build back better? No, this was precisely what experts said must be avoided. More haphazard construction in a location extremely vulnerable to another natural disaster. Ten years after the earthquake, the promised land of Canaan stood as a living monument both to the failures of the Aid State and to the eternal hope of the Haitian people.

AT 12:02 A.M. on January 13, 2020, Moïse sent a tweet, noting the end of the legislature's term and the "institutional void" that it would cause.[3] For the second time in five years, the terms of Parliament had expired without an election to replace them. There had been some speculation that Haiti could be kicked out of the OAS itself, just as it had helped do to Venezuela, because of the lack of democratic institutions. Moïse, however, wasn't worried.

Less than a week earlier, the secretary-general of the OAS, Luis Almagro, had personally traveled to Port-au-Prince.[4] Almagro, however, was in the middle of his own political fight, competing for reelection as head of the OAS. He was facing opposition due to his—and the organization's—role in a military coup that had taken place in Bolivia just months earlier.[5] Interestingly, it had been the first time the OAS performed an electoral audit since it had done so in Haiti in the fall of 2010, ushering Martelly into the presidency. Now, the two leaders needed each other. If the quid pro quo wasn't explicit during their private conversations, Almagro's public comments spoke for themselves. "Today I reiterated to President [Moïse] our staunch support for good governance & political stability in Haiti," he tweeted. Almagro made no reference to the fact that the president would be in office without a functioning parliament in just five days' time.

Without legislative oversight, Moïse was free to rule by decree. Already on his third prime minister, and with discussions ongoing over their replacement, Parliament had proven to be a barrier to Moïse's interests despite what on paper showed a majority of members allied with the president. His first priority, he declared within days, was to overhaul the country's constitution.[6] He blamed his ongoing political troubles on the text, which had placed too much power with Parliament. That, of course, had been no accident given the memories of the Duvalier dictatorship. Checks on the executive were of paramount importance, and the constitution ceded many executive functions to the prime minister, whose position came and went at the behest of Parliament, not the presidency. But Moïse wasn't alone in wanting reform. It had long been a desire of the US and other donors. The elite, too, had long wanted changes. The diaspora, an increasingly influential actor in Haiti's politics, was perhaps most motivated as they sought to enshrine their right to vote and hold political office, something the 1987 text had not allowed.

"The constitution is made of paper, bayonets are made of steel," a famous Kreyòl saying goes. The problem isn't what is written on the paper, in other words; it's that governments ignored those words and ruled by steel. How could Moïse oversee constitutional reform when he was ruling entirely outside the bounds of the constitution that already existed? The concept of a referendum wasn't even contemplated in the 1987 text. Nevertheless, the OAS and the UN both provided material and financial assistance to the effort.

It was hard not to recognize the parallels to previous reform efforts: how the US had disbanded a recalcitrant parliament and reformed the constitution through a vote held under Marine occupation; or how Baby Doc had sought to reform the document through a referendum in 1985.[7] It had passed with, officially, 99.98 percent of the vote, though the population rejected the results and the dictator was living in France within a year. In the streets of Port-au-Prince, few believed Moïse would make it to the end of the month, let alone stick around to see through a referendum.[8]

Two hundred years after the revolution, and the struggle was incomplete, the resistance ongoing. Thirty years after Haiti's first free and fair election, the nation's democracy had ceased to function; sixteen years after the arrival of the Blue Helmets, the security forces had been hollowed out from the inside and the wheels of justice had ground to a halt; ten years after the earthquake, after donors had spent more than $10 billion, after celebrities and political leaders from across the globe pledged this time would be different, Haiti's public institutions had practically disappeared. So, was Haiti a "failed state"?

Jean Casimir, the Haitian sociologist, has long argued the question is itself flawed. What do we mean by "state"? For Casimir, the Haitian state is about far more than public institutions. It is also the state of community among Haitians, it is the *lakou,* the *Madan Sara,* the various ways in which Haitians themselves have survived in spite of constant attacks from the State—capital "S."[9] And this broader state hasn't failed. Rather, it has endured and continued to stand as a beacon for freedom, despite the unceasing efforts to control it by the Aid State and the elite.

I think the question, at least when asked about Haiti, is flawed for another reason. Even if we talk only about the state as public institutions, had "Haiti" failed? No doubt a select few Haitians had played leading roles, but the state created over the previous thirty years reflected the intervention and interference of foreign actors and the local elite more so than it did the Haitian people. Haiti wasn't a failed state, it was an Aid State. Haiti never even had the opportunity to fail on its own.

Of course, the failure of the Aid State was an inevitability. No Haitian state that excluded the majority of the population was going to last forever, as the revolution had shown the world. But, by the ten-year quake anniversary, the Aid State had failed even on the terms of its managers. There had never been stability for the masses, but now there wasn't even stability for the elite. Far from stopping migration, more Haitians had left Haiti in the decade after the earthquake than during any ten-year period in modern history. Haiti had even plausibly cost Democrats a presidential election. Like the US occupation, the dictatorship, and these earlier incarnations of the Haitian state, the Aid State *was* failing. But was this even an inherently bad thing?

For Haitians to build their own state, their own sovereign democracy, the collapse of the Aid State is a necessity. And while insecurity and violence were reaching new heights throughout the country, so, too, was the grassroots organizing—in rural communities, some still recovering from Hurricane Matthew years earlier; in the popular neighborhoods of the capital, many once again "red zones"; in universities, high schools, and even middle schools. At the ten-year anniversary, few saw beyond the failure to see the bigger picture. In failure there was hope, and across the country, citizens were taking action to build something new. If I had learned one thing over the decade I'd been coming to Haiti, it was that a state imposed on the population was never going to work. The resistance was winning, just as it had in 1804.

None of that meant change would be easy or would happen overnight. After the collapse of the Duvalierist system, it had taken more than four years for a legitimate election and the rise of Aristide. Now, the next incarnation was collapsing, and whatever followed it—for better or for worse—would only happen after a long and likely violent struggle.

A FEW DAYS after the anniversary event, I went to the historic Hotel Oloffson to meet the owner, a renowned musician and friend, Richard Morse.[10] He had taken over the building, set back off a main road and surrounded by lush palms, in the late eighties when he was just thirty years old. The hotel had been shuttered for a couple of years already, everything inside stripped out in the chaotic aftermath of Duvalier's exile and the collapse of tourism that occurred following the spurious linking of Haitians with AIDS. Morse had deep ties in Haiti. His mother and grandfather were both famous singers, while another wing of the family were direct descendants of Demosthenes Sam, whose cousin, Vilbrun Guillaume Sam, lived in the residence during his presidency until he was killed by an angry mob on the eve of the US Marines' early twentieth-century invasion.

During the occupation, the home served as a private hospital for the occupying forces, but, after they left, it was turned into a hotel. The twenty-one-room gingerbread castle received worldwide fame in the 1950s and '60s, when it was known as the "Greenwich Village of the tropics," and everyone from Mick Jagger to Barbara Walters came to take in the culture—and the rum punches. In the early sixties, Graham Greene, who had first been brought there by his friend Truman Capote, used it as the setting for his novel *The Comedians,* which chronicles a foreign hotelier during the Duvalier dictatorship.[11] Richard Burton and Elizabeth Taylor starred in the big-screen adaptation, which had to be filmed in Africa due to the mounting repression under Duvalier.

"With its towers and balconies and wooden fretwork decorations it had the air at night of a Charles Addams house in a number of the *New Yorker,*" Greene wrote. "You expected a witch to open the door to you or a maniac butler, with a bat dangling from the chandelier behind him. . . . But in sunlight, or when the lights went on among the palms, it seemed fragile and period and pretty and absurd, an illustration from a book of fairy tales."[12] When I sat down on the massive wraparound porch some fifty years later, the building remained practically unchanged from when Greene had stayed there.

The Oloffson is both everything that is Haiti and a window into everything that Haiti is not. A reminder of the deep artistic culture that, for decades, travelers have come to appreciate and learn from, of the Afro-inspired beats that provide a soundtrack of daily life and connect two centuries of Haitians, and of the architecture that, even today, boggles the mind. Richard, with his band, RAM, still played at the hotel most Thursday nights. At least until recently.

While we sat in the shade and drank overly sugared Haitian coffee, there was only one other table with guests. That was no surprise. Ever since the July 2018 fuel riots, the State Department had a Level 4 travel warning in place. Tourism, the little that had existed before, disappeared entirely. Street protests and long periods of *peyi lok* had made even reaching the hotel, which sits on a small hillside just a few blocks from downtown, nearly impossible. It felt like an oasis. But Richard hadn't simply watched the Aid State collapse from his hotel.

He had been one of the leading artists who pushed for Aristide's overthrow in the early 2000s. All these years later, Richard regretted his role in that coup. Then, after the earthquake, his cousin Michel Martelly reached the presidency. Caught up in the moment and feeling a sense of duty, he joined the new administration. That's when I first had met Richard, in the halls of Congress in DC, with his long gray hair, glasses, and top hat. He was hard to miss amid the drab suits and ties. He served as Martelly's special envoy to DC.

"Yeah, I fucked up," he said, looking back. He left the administration in December 2012. He saw where things were headed.

All these years later and the *peyi lok,* the protests, none of it surprised Richard—he didn't even seem upset, even though it had virtually closed his hotel. There were no legitimate ministers, no parliament, and no elections. "It's no longer a democracy." He saw the streets as the only possible way forward, the only way to disrupt the game and change the system. "Shut the motherfucker down," he said. "Hit everyone."

Yes, he acknowledged, life was getting harder for everyone and no doubt there were elites trying to manipulate the situation, to use the streets for their advantage. But, he asked, if all demonstrations take is money, "where are the pro-Moïse protests?"

In so many ways, Morse saw what was transpiring in Haiti as a continuation of a revolution that had begun more than two hundred years earlier. "This is an apartheid state," he said. "Jovenel is a front man for an imported elite and the US State Department." In that regard, Moïse wasn't unique, just the latest manifestation. The Haitian people, Richard believed, would never accept it.

After we had been talking for nearly an hour, Richard looked past me into the distance. "How do you know the revolution here is still on?" he asked with a smirk. He stood. "You can stand here and still have a clear view of the ocean."

We walked to the edge of the balcony. It was like looking into a postcard come to life, the leafy palms in the foreground seemingly reaching out and touching the Caribbean blue of the Port-au-Prince bay. "There are no buildings," he said. "Where are the businesses? Where are the hotels? . . . Haiti hasn't bought in and they're still pissed," he said with some finality. "I know it's true."

EPILOGUE

THE ASSASSINATION

President Moïse spent the evening of Tuesday, July 6, 2021, in front of his TV, watching the Copa América semifinal match between Colombia and Argentina.[1] His wife, Martine, and two of his children were also there, at the home the family had moved into shortly after Moïse assumed the presidency. Moïse had barely left the residence in over a week, refusing to make the trip downtown to the National Palace. A number of his staff had recently fallen ill with coronavirus. More important, he was scared for his life.

Around midnight, the soccer match ended in dramatic fashion, with Argentina defeating Colombia in penalty kicks and advancing to the final. Along with the Brazilian squad, Haitians root for Argentina's national team nearly as hard as their own. It was a night of distraction. The president was often up late on the phone, and this night was no exception. He finally hung up around one A.M. on the morning of July 7. Then, just before 1:30, gunfire rang out through the Pelerin 5 neighborhood surrounding the first family's home.

The gunshots were getting closer and closer to the president. At 1:34, Moïse spoke with one of the police officials in charge of his security detail and asked for urgent backup. Two minutes later, he called the chief of police. There was shooting everywhere. He needed help. Next, he spoke with Dimitri Hérard, the head of the presidential guard.[2]

The gunfire continued. He called the police chief again, who said he had dispatched a trusted official and a friend of the president, who was already on their way. At 1:46, the president called that friend. It lasted twenty seconds.

"Where are you?" he screamed. "I need your assistance. Now! My life is in danger. Come quick. Come save my life!"[3]

The friend could hear shots in the background.

Outside the residence, at least twenty-one former Colombian soldiers; a recently fired official from the ministry of justice; three local police officers; and two Haitian Americans, one a former DEA informant, were quickly approaching. They disabled the team at the first security checkpoint, telling them it was an official operation backed by the US antidrug agency. As they neared, one of the Haitian Americans got on a loudspeaker. "This is a DEA operation," he shouted in both English and Kreyòl. "Don't shoot . . . everybody stand down."

He repeated it over and over and over.

It took Hérard only about twenty minutes from the time the president called to get there. But, he later told investigators, he couldn't reach the house due to the presence of more than a dozen armed men. He could hear someone speaking in perfect English, saying it was a DEA operation.

When the president's most trusted security officials did eventually make it to the house, around 2:20 A.M., they found the president's wife in a pool of blood at the top of the staircase. She was alive. Their two children were by her side, unharmed. Inside the bedroom, they discovered the president. He was on his back, his once-white Hugo Boss button-down and jeans soaked in blood. Shot twelve times seemingly at close range, his body had been ripped apart. His arm was shattered, one eye was missing. Jovenel Moïse, the president of Haiti, was dead.[4]

At a predawn press conference, the acting prime minister, Claude Joseph, solemnly confirmed to the nation, and the world, that the president had just been assassinated by a group of armed "foreigners," who were heard speaking English and Spanish. "Stay calm, the nation is secure, let's look for harmony," he said. Nobody knew what had just happened, or, as important, what would happen next. An eerie calm hung over the capital as the nation held its collective breath.[5]

The president's death was shocking, but not necessarily surprising. In the one and a half years since the ten-year earthquake anniversary, the situation on the ground had deteriorated quickly. The writing was on the wall; the Aid State had collapsed and in the battle for control of Haiti, nobody was safe.

WHEN, ON THE ten-year quake anniversary, Parliament's terms expired, it had left Moïse to rule by himself. But the legal justification used to disband the Senate set a dangerous precedent for the president's own mandate. Some senators' terms had been measured not from when they took office but from when they should have taken office if the elections did not have to be rerun. Applied to Moïse, it meant his mandate would end not on February 7, 2022—five years after he took office—but on February 7, 2021—five years after he should have taken office.

As always, he could still count on the support of the international community. The UN and OAS both publicly declared that Moïse should remain in office until 2022.[6] Still, few believed he'd be able to. Daily life had simply become too precarious for things to continue as is. The economy was in near free fall, inflation higher than it had been in decades. Armed groups had expanded their territorial control over the capital and spread throughout the country. Kidnappings were becoming commonplace. And the president pushed forward alone, amid ever-growing opposition.

Meanwhile, in the halls of the Congress in Washington, DC, pressure was building for a change in US policy. Led by Representative Andy Levin, a freshman Democrat from Michigan, who had been a human rights worker in Haiti during the early nineties military junta and spoke Kreyòl, Congress held its first hearing dedicated to Haiti in nearly six years. Members peppered the Trump administration with letters warning of Moïse's authoritarian turn. They fell, predictably, on deaf ears.

Trump had stood by Moïse through it all, a clear quid pro quo for Moïse's support in the US campaign to overthrow the Venezuelan government. But once again, a US presidential election portended political changes in Haiti. Joe Biden, the Democratic nominee running against

Trump, campaigned in Little Haiti and ran targeted radio spots in Kreyòl. In the end, Biden still lost Florida, but he did win the presidency.

In December, Levin and other members issued a statement noting Moïse's actions were "reminiscent of past anti-democratic abuses the Haitian people have endured, including the run-up to the Duvalier dictatorship." They promised to work with the incoming Biden administration to "develop a U.S. policy that prioritizes the rights and aspirations of the Haitian people and supports a credible, Haitian-led transition back to democratic order."[7] Still, those hoping for a change in US-Haiti policy were left wanting.

On February 5, with the potential expiry of Moïse's mandate just days away, the newly inaugurated Biden administration offered its stamp of approval for the embattled president. "[A] new elected president should succeed President Moïse when his term ends on February [7], 2022," a State Department spokesperson told the press.[8] The US and the rest of the Core Group declared their support for fresh elections to be held as quickly as possible. But most Haitians had given up on the country's outsourced electoral process as a viable path for change. Few saw another low turnout election held under the eyes of the same old foreign actors as a positive development.

At 2:59 A.M. on February 7, 2021, Haitian police officers raided an apartment complex known as the Petit Bois residences in Port-au-Prince's Tabarre neighborhood. Altogether, eighteen individuals were arrested, including a sitting Supreme Court judge, a high-level police inspector, and a former government minister, all accused of organizing a violent coup d'état.[9]

"There was an attempt on my life," President Jovenel Moïse told reporters a few hours later. He personally thanked the head of the presidential security unit (USGPN), Dimitri Hérard, for thwarting this nefarious plot. The president turned the mic over to his prime minister, who explained that some of those arrested "had contacted the official in charge of security for the national palace," and had been planning on arresting the president and swearing in new leadership to oversee a transitional government. There was apparently an arrest warrant signed by a local judge.

Soon thereafter, the government released audio recordings it claimed proved the seriousness of the matter. They were of conversations between Hérard, the man the president had just personally thanked for stopping the plot, and a few different individuals discussing plans to arrest the president.

In one of the recordings, a female voice tells Hérard, "Listen, I received an order from the State Department."

"Yes, they contacted me, too," Hérard responds.

The government promptly identified the alleged State Department officer as Daniel Whitman, a retired member of the US Foreign Service, who had briefly served in Haiti in the early 2000s.

AFTER THIRTY YEARS of tightly managed democracy in the Aid State of Haiti, foreign support had become politically deterministic, or, at the very least, perceived as such. Within that context, a cottage industry had emerged of individuals with real (or claimed) access to US government officials or policymakers. There was official US policy, that discussed at State Department podiums and in press releases, and then there was the unofficial side. Given the history of coups, overturned elections, and political subterfuge, one could argue the unofficial side was just as important.

True or not, the references to US support for the Petit Bois coup attempt therefore came as little surprise; it is unlikely that anybody in Haiti's political class would think their plans could ultimately succeed without a wink and a nod from the State Department. Everyone had adapted to the realities of the Aid State.

In the fall of 2019, I had spoken with a Haitian American pastor and businessman, Christian Emmanuel Sanon. He explained that he and a group of allies were planning a transitional government to help get Haiti back on the right track. "We're putting a group together and getting ready for if there is US support."[10]

I asked what sort of connections he had with the US government.

"We are trying to make connections with people that can help us," he vaguely explained, before adding that he had access to individuals in both the State Department and the Trump White House. Sanon assured me that Moïse would be willing to resign. "The president is just waiting for someone to tell him to go," he said.

Eventually, Sanon and his team began to target February 7, 2021, as the opportune time for a change, the date many believed the president's mandate would officially end. But his own efforts had been displaced by the plan coming together at the Petit Bois housing complex. They, too, believed they had US support, and had convinced many of that fact. Daniel Whitman, the former diplomat, had been reaching out to actors in Haiti for months. The rental agreement for the Petit Bois apartments was even made under his name.

We met on an unseasonably warm mid-February afternoon at the Bishop's Garden in the shadow of the National Cathedral in Washington. Whitman, seventy-five years old with thinning white hair, showed up wearing a trench coat. "It makes for a better movie opening than a parking garage in Arlington," he said with a wry smile that seemed to rarely leave his face. It was a reference to "Deep Throat," the anonymous source who drove the *Washington Post*'s Watergate coverage. Deep Throat he was not, but Whitman did hold the key to identifying the person using his name in Haiti.[11]

In early October 2020, Whitman received a phone call from someone he had not seen in nearly twenty years, a man named Philippe Markington. They had last met in the aftermath of the April 2000 assassination of Haiti's most prominent journalist, Jean Léopold Dominique, when Whitman was still at the US Embassy. Markington presented himself to the police as a witness. He quickly became a suspect and was arrested. Nevertheless, police allowed Markington to meet Whitman at his embassy office. It wasn't their first encounter. Markington, portraying himself as a government insider, had been coming to the office frequently with tales of "hit lists" and other supposed evidence of government misdeeds.

After a brief stint in prison, Markington managed to escape to Argentina, where he lived until his extradition back to Haiti in 2014. For the next seven years, he sat in a jail cell in the National Penitentiary. Jean Sénat Fleury, a former judge and prosecutor who had worked on the assassination case, long wondered how exactly Markington had managed to get to Argentina, even suggesting that he believed US intelligence had provided a helping hand. "Markington is someone very well connected," he told me. But, he added, Markington was a talker. "With his speech, he can drive you anywhere. If something is white, he will tell you it is black—and you will believe it."[12]

When Markington called, he told Whitman that he and others in Haiti were planning a transitional government. He wanted Whitman to come to Haiti for the inauguration in early 2021. He said they had rented a house near the US Embassy and invited Whitman there. Whitman told me he declined, and put the issue behind him. Regardless of what he said, it was clear that, from his jail cell, Markington had continued using Whitman's name to drum up support for this "transitional government."

I spent the next few months investigating the Petit Bois coup attempt, trying to get to the bottom of Markington's role in the entire saga. As time passed, the investigation in Haiti had fallen by the wayside. By the spring, all eighteen of those arrested had been released from prison. Instead of the judicial police taking the lead in the investigation, Moïse gave the task to his own security forces, mainly to Hérard. It made little sense. Though the president had publicly praised Hérard, phone records show Hérard had communicated directly with Markington in his jail cell. If the Petit Bois plan ever represented a real threat to the president, it would only have been because Hérard was a part of it.

The fact that a man in jail for his role in an assassination twenty years earlier was now involved in an attempt against the head of state passed without public exposure. It would have been an easy connection to make; the police had phone records documenting Markington's role in the monthslong ruse. If authorities did make the connection, they never acted on it. Impunity continued to reign. But if anyone had looked closer, they would have discovered that, months later, Markington submitted a formal complaint to the nation's anti-corruption agency. He alleged that a longtime government official, a close confidant of high-level politicians, including the police chief and the minister of justice, had solicited a $30,000 bribe with a promise to get Markington out of jail. Could that help explain why Markington had been impersonating Whitman? The official, Joseph Felix Badio, would soon be the most wanted fugitive in Haiti.[13]

Despite the government's high-profile crackdown on dissent, real or manufactured, Haitians continued to organize in opposition to the government, and still with the explicit intent of replacing the president with a transitional government. In the spring of 2021, hundreds of civil society organizations, including the human rights sector, peasant associations, unions of factory workers, and popular organizations, met under the banner of the Commission for a Haitian Solution to the Crisis. For too long, foreign powers had dictated the nation's political realities. No longer. It was a wholesale rejection of what politics had become in the Aid State of Haiti.

Sanon, the Haitian American pastor I had spoken with years earlier, had yet to give up on his plans to take power. His team had continued to work in the aftermath of the Petit Bois arrests, even hiring a team of former Colombian soldiers to provide security for him as he cobbled together support. The first group arrived in Haiti in May; the rest joined in early June. The Colombians had been recruited by an active FBI informant, a partner in a South Florida private security company. He had assured everyone that their actions had the blessing of the United States government.

On June 12, Jovenel Moïse wrote a short reminder in his personal notebook. "To verify Pastor Sanon's full name and phone number on an attempted coup," it read.[14] But, by then, it wasn't just the president's ostensible political opponents moving against him.

BY THE SUMMER of 2021, Moïse and his one-man rule had become an impediment to those who had placed—and kept—him in the presidency. Moïse was a product of the system, but he had also become an increasingly vocal critic of it. "Today I take the decision of breaking that system in your name. Why? Because it didn't start today. That is the same system that took us from Africa and kept us in slavery for over three hundred years," the president thundered in an early February speech in front of hundreds of supporters.[15] Those who pushed against the system had been assassinated, exiled, or jailed, he continued. "You will not be able to kill this one," he said, referring to himself. "He is stuck in your throat."

Ironically, he most aggressively targeted two elite families—the Vorbe and Boulos clans—that had financed his campaign and done perhaps more than anybody else to ensure he became president. Engulfed by corruption allegations of his own and accused of giving political allies and friends sweetheart commercial deals, few trusted the sincerity of his efforts to attack elite control. Nevertheless, it had become clear he was no longer the hoped-for guarantor of the status quo. He had become a threat to the system.

Moïse also found himself at odds with his predecessor, Michel Martelly, who hoped to return to office. Moïse had run under Martelly's PHTK party, but, like so many before him, he went about creating his own movement once in power. In May, Moïse had even picked his successor—and it wasn't Martelly. The former president was furious.[16]

Further, while foreign support had helped to keep Moïse in office, the president's insistence on prioritizing his controversial constitutional reform effort over elections was putting the international community's core objective in jeopardy. Bucking the Aid State's foreign managers came with a cost. Moïse was desperate for greater support on the security front. But his traditional allies were hesitant to offer much of anything in terms of financial or technical assistance. Some close advisors began reaching out to the Russian government seeking help, and accredited a new Russian ambassador in early June.[17]

And then there was Dimitri Hérard and the president's Palace Guard—the elite unit tasked with keeping the president alive. I had been investigating Hérard even before the Petit Bois "coup" attempt, after he and his business partner had created a private security firm in early 2020. After I wrote an article alleging that Hérard had become one of Haiti's biggest arms traffickers, I became the target of anonymous threats made through a newly created website pretending to be a news portal. One of the site's first articles included my name and photo, alleging I had been paid vast amounts of money to destabilize the government.[18]

"The government decided to press charges for 'complot contre la sureté de l'état' against . . . the American subpar writer, Jake Johnston," the article claimed, citing government sources. The charge was the same as leveled against those arrested at Petit Bois, a charge that had only ever previously been used under the Duvalier dictatorship. The article ended with an explicit threat. "Coming back to Haiti to further destabilize a democratically elected government will prove to be harder for time to come . . ."

I did return, however, with no legal trouble in late June 2021. I met with two individuals who had been arrested at Petit Bois. They were clear that there was never any plan to violently overthrow the government. They believed they were negotiating with those close to the president over a transitional government. The key, they said, was the involvement of Hérard. Without his involvement, there simply was no plan, or, at least, no ability to actually carry one out.

The thirty-five-year-old Dimitri Hérard, slim, fit, with a chiseled jawline, and enough ambition for five men, made for an interesting co-conspirator in the Petit Bois affairs. He had studied at an elite Ecuadorian military university and had been trained in intelligence. He also had developed a close relationship to Martelly, who met the young cadet on a trip to Ecuador early in his term. Moïse elevated Hérard to the head of his security team at the explicit request of Martelly.

In the months since Petit Bois, Hérard had parlayed his role in the arrests into even greater influence within the president's inner circle. But by June, it seemed like things were shifting. Multiple US law enforcement sources had told me that investigators were looking into Hérard's drug-trafficking ties and his role in the country's vibrant arms-trafficking network.[19]

In Haiti, I met with a high-ranking police official, someone with direct access to the president. They said Moïse was aware of the US law enforcement attention on Hérard. They claimed to have supplied the FBI with evidence of Hérard's role in providing weapons to the capital's armed groups. But the president wasn't going to make a move against someone so close to Martelly. Rather, he was "waiting for the US to make a move," the police official said.[20]

On the eve of his assassination, Moïse was embroiled in an all-out internal battle for control of Haiti—protected by an elite security unit that had largely abandoned its mission. Of course, it was impossible to know at the time, but in just two short weeks, Hérard would find himself in the National Penitentiary for his alleged involvement in a conspiracy to assassinate the president.

Keith McNichols, the DEA whistleblower who had investigated Hérard's role in the 2015 sugar boat drug bust, saw a direct line from the failure to properly investigate that case to the assassination of the president six years later. "It is the same network," he said, noting the involvement of Hérard and, he alleged, Kiko Saint-Rémy.[21] *The New York Times* later reported that, at the time of his death, Moïse had also been considering handing Saint-Rémy over to US authorities to face justice for his role in drug trafficking.[22] Could the assassination have actually been related to a fight between narcos for control of a key transshipment point? Given the legal bandits in power, it wouldn't have shocked many. "I would be a fool to think that narco trafficking and arms trafficking didn't play a role in the assassination," Daniel Foote, who was appointed US special envoy to Haiti in the aftermath of the president's death, told the paper.

THE SPECIFICS OF what happened in the early morning hours of July 7 that resulted in the president's assassination remain shrouded in mystery. Testimony is incomplete and contradictory. But, in the days following Moïse's killing, Haitian police arrested nineteen former Colombian soldiers and issued arrest warrants for dozens of others allegedly implicated in the plot, including Joseph Felix Badio. Eventually, authorities detained more than a dozen police officers and members of the Palace Guard, including Dimitri Hérard. Not a single security officer had been injured in the attack. They also arrested Christian Emmanuel Sanon, the man I had spoken with nearly two years earlier, presenting him as the mastermind of the assassination plot. The authorities' prompt action, they claimed, had prevented Sanon and his team of Colombian mercenaries from completing their attempted coup d'état. But few believed the official narrative.

There was no question that Sanon had plans to take over the government—he had made that much clear to anyone he spoke with. Still, it was also clear that he had largely lost control of the plot in the final weeks leading up to July 7. The infrastructure had been set up by Sanon and his team, but, at some point, a plot to arrest the president and install a transitional government had been usurped—and turned into an assassination. Had a coup been prevented? Or could things actually have gone just as the real masterminds anticipated? Given the paper trail on Sanon and the Colombians, whoever was actually behind it knew they'd have a useful fall guy.

While media outlets across the world ran constant headlines with the latest developments in the international whodunit, behind closed doors in Port-au-Prince, the nation's political future was again being worked out by foreigners and the local elite.

In the days before the assassination, Moïse had been in negotiations over the nomination of a new prime minister—another desperate attempt, at the urging of the UN and others in the Core Group, to cobble together enough support for fresh elections. On July 5, Moïse issued a decree naming Dr. Ariel Henry as his choice for prime minister. Though close to parts of the political opposition, Henry was a strategic choice. He had served on the "council of sages," a group backed by the international community in the aftermath of the 2004 coup that helped choose a transitional government. He was also the preferred choice of Martelly.

At the time of the assassination, however, Henry had yet to officially take office or form a government. Instead, the acting prime minister, Claude Joseph, stepped into the role of chief executive. Less than a week later, a high-level delegation of US officials traveled to Port-au-Prince to meet with Joseph, Henry, and the president of what remained of the Senate, who also was making a claim for the throne, to broker an agreement.[23] Left out of the discussions entirely was the recently formed Commission for a Haitian Solution to the Crisis. The last sitting head of state to have been assassinated in Haiti was Vilbrun Guillaume Sam in 1915; US Marines had landed the same day. More than a hundred years later, foreign powers were not going to sit on the sidelines and wait for Haitians to take the lead.[24]

After initially backing Joseph, the Core Group issued a statement on Saturday, July 17, calling for the creation of an "inclusive" government. And, in case that wasn't clear, the diplomats added: "To this end, it strongly encourages the designated Prime Minister Ariel Henry to continue the mission entrusted to him to form such a government."[25] Just like that, the power dynamics had shifted. Three days later, Henry was sworn in as prime minister. With no functioning parliament or judiciary and no president, Henry assumed near total political power, and he had done so largely based on a press release from foreign diplomats.

Still, the question of who ultimately was behind the assassination remained a mystery. And it was likely to stay that way with Henry in power.

At 7:17 P.M. on June 24, two weeks before the assassination, Henry placed a phone call to Badio, the man swirling around the center of both the Petit Bois coup attempt and the president's death five months later.[26] The call wasn't random; they had known each other for years. On June 28, phone records show six calls between the two. There were calls again on July 1 and July 4. Most damning, however, were two calls from Badio to Henry on the night of the assassination. At 4:03 in the morning, barely two hours after the murder, Badio called Henry. They spoke for three minutes. At 4:20, Badio called again. This time, the call lasted for four minutes.

Henry categorically denied any involvement in the assassination and claimed to have no memory of speaking to Badio, either on the night of the president's death or in the weeks before. But Rodolphe Jaar, a former DEA informant turned convicted trafficker, whose house was used as a staging ground on the night of the assassination, has told a different story. He claims that, days ahead of the assassination, Badio told him the newly named prime minister would be an important ally. "He is my good friend, I have full control of him," Badio allegedly told Jaar.[27] Further, Jaar said that the phone calls on the night of the crime were because they were trapped and needed help. Henry had promised to "make some calls," he said.

Not only the phone calls, however, connect Henry to the assassination. Before heading to the president's residence that night, the Colombians, two Haitian Americans, Jaar, Badio, and certainly others were at a home high up in the hills waiting for the final go-ahead. No exact address has ever been identified, but cell phone data shows the principal suspects' calls all routing through the same cell tower in the neighborhood of Thomassin 31. Interestingly, it is the same cell tower that pinged when Henry first called Badio on June 24. Could Henry's presence in the same location be a coincidence?

The first time that Badio's phone pinged the tower in Thomassin 31 was the morning of June 24. Cell records show that, around the same time, both Jaar and Joseph Vincent, another former DEA informant implicated in the plot, pinged there as well. That phone record is a first for Vincent, but Jaar appears to have a long history in the neighborhood, which makes sense, as everyone claims to have been at his house that night. After June 24, both Badio and Vincent began to ping from that location more frequently, and they weren't alone—so did Henry. On June 26, at 9:30 P.M., Henry's cell phone records show him in the same location, then again on July 2. The cell phone data is far from definitive. There are plausible explanations for why Henry could have been in that general vicinity. Still, it is hard to simply cast it aside as a coincidence.

Months after the assassination, when the prime minister's phone calls with Badio emerged publicly, the chief prosecutor called Henry in for questioning. Henry refused and called the justice minister, a holdover from the Moïse era, and told him to fire the prosecutor. He said no. Days later, Henry fired both.[28] Soon after, audio leaked of a private conversation with the judge on the case.

"Ariel (Henry) is connected and friends with the mastermind of the assassination. They planned it with him. Ariel is a prime suspect of Jovenel Moïse's assassination, and he knows it," the judge can be heard saying. Someone asks why he hasn't pursued any legal action against the prime minister. "Do you think I can touch Ariel (Henry) now? How can I do that? I won't be able to give (any order to indict him), it won't see the light of day," the judge answers.

"Henry is at the center of everything," one investigator explained after the leak. "All he has done since taking over as PM is obstruct (the investigation) and fuck us over."[29]

After firing the minister of justice, Henry replaced him with Berto Dorcé, who had facilitated the bribing of a judge to drop charges against key actors in the sugar boat case, according to testimony collected by the DEA. "He was put there to help cover the whole thing up," McNichols, the former agent, believed.

With the inquiry stalled in Haiti, many turned their hopes to the United States, where the Department of Justice was slowly building a parallel criminal case based on a number of the alleged participants' ties to South Florida. But, at least to me, the Stateside investigation seemed little worthier of hope than the one in Haiti. One of the key participants, the man who had recruited the Colombians, was an active FBI informant.[30] Joseph Vincent and Rodolphe Jaar had both been DEA informants.[31] And there were additional characters who had claimed to be working for the US government, including at least two who had been deeply involved with Sanon. None of it meant the US had just assassinated the president of Haiti, but it did mean that any public disclosures from a criminal investigation would likely be a massive embarrassment. Eventually, the US placed much of the case under seal in order to protect national security.

As of the time of this writing, we are no closer to solving the question of who ultimately masterminded the assassination of President Jovenel Moïse. One reason why is that it is clear that everyone—from his political opponents, to his political patrons, his security detail, and the United States and Core Group—all have blood on their hands. But while we may not yet, or ever, know the true mastermind, we can try to understand why it happened. In many ways, this book itself is an explanation. The collapse of the Aid State was inevitable, though few foresaw this as the final act.

ACKNOWLEDGMENTS

Acknowledging everyone who contributed to this book is a daunting task, and one in which I will surely come up short. It is made that much harder by the situation in Haiti today. Too many friends, colleagues, sources, and collaborators find themselves under constant threat. Printing their names here feels like burdening them with an even greater risk. Though their names may not appear, needless to say, I will forever be indebted to all those in Haiti who shared their stories, their experiences, their contacts, their vehicles, their dinner tables, their homes, their country, and so much more with me. Writing a book can feel like a lonely endeavor at times, but it truly takes a village. I am fortunate to have had the support of such an amazing village.

There are two people whose names deserve to be on the cover of this book as much as my own: Etant Dupain and Ti Mo (an alias). I owe them everything. Over twelve years, I have rarely stepped foot in Haiti without one, the other, or both by my side. They are two of the most talented, generous people I have met, and this book—and all my work in Haiti—would not have been possible without their patience, dedication, and support over the years.

I am especially grateful to Naomi Klein and Edwidge Danticat, two authors who have been inspirations for many, many years. Their early words of encouragement and support were deeply humbling and meant the world to me. They gave me the confidence, and perhaps more important, courage, to actually see this project through.

Countless friends and colleagues have read portions of this book over the course of the drafting process, offering their feedback and expertise. Jessica, Natalie, Andréa, Sean, and Robert stand out as non-family members who were always willing to read (and tell me when I was being stupid and needed to go back to the drawing board). The book is much stronger because of the support from all of them—and everyone who read chapters along the way. I also owe a special thanks to Matt Mahoney for fact-checking the manuscript. He caught plenty of potentially embarrassing errors, and any mistakes that remain are all on me.

When I started working on Haiti and US policy in 2010, I knew little about Haiti or its history. I never imagined I would write a book. One reason I stayed with it for so many years was because of the amazing group of people I worked with within the broader Haiti advocacy community. Spanning the US, Haiti, and the world, these are just some of the colleagues whose work inspired, informed, and challenged me over the years: Brian, Melinda, Ellie, Jess, Sasha(s), Kira, Erica, Nicole, Guerline, Marleine, Paul, Pierre, Mark(s), Bea, Sienna, Gabrielle, Vijaya, Alan, Steve, Bob, Amber, Ryan, Alex, Nixon, Emma, Ian, and so many more.

This book, quite literally, would not have been possible without the steadfast support and commitment of my employer, the Center for Economic and Policy Research, and all my CEPRista family. It's hard to imagine it was more than thirteen years ago that my colleagues tasked me—a recently hired junior researcher—with helping out on our newly formed blog to monitor the earthquake relief efforts in Haiti. When, a few years later, I gave up on the econ path and said I wanted to write (even) more about Haiti, my boss, Mark Weisbrot, could have told me to find a new job; he didn't—and I am eternally grateful to have worked alongside him for as long as I have. I will never forget my first trip to Haiti with Alex Main—and am looking forward to our next. I've been lucky to learn from the best. And I want to express my deepest gratitude to Dan Beeton, who has read and edited just about every single piece

I've written on Haiti for more than a decade. I wouldn't be half the writer (or know half as much about Haiti) without his guidance and support.

It is no coincidence that writing a book went from a theoretical to a reality while I was enrolled in the Johns Hopkins University writing program. I had just planned on taking one class to help me get over the hump on a long-form investigation I had been banging my head against a wall about for months. I will never forget my first professor, Baynard Woods, whose own work and passion for storytelling inspired me to actually enroll in the program and see it through. I owe a tremendous debt to David Taylor and Ron Cassie, who read oh so many chapter drafts and who undoubtedly made the book infinitely better by pulling me, repeatedly, out of the weeds—even if I like the weeds. My appreciation for the art of writing, and the power of the sentence, can be traced straight to Ed Pearlman. Most especially, I do not have enough thanks to give to Karen Houppert, who has always had my back with this project. Be it editing, pitching, making contacts, or just providing a necessary sounding board . . . I owe Karen as much as anyone for making *Aid State* a reality. Finally, a huge thank-you to all my classmates who, semester after semester, read story after story about Haiti. David, Rachel, and Garret, I am so grateful for our writing group.

Writing the book was one thing, finding it a home was another, and it wouldn't have been possible without Eileen Cope and Julie Checkoway at Mark Creative Management. They jumped headfirst into the project and held my hand through it all. I owe a tremendous thanks to George Witte, Brigitte Dale, and the entire team at St. Martin's Press for believing in the project and working tirelessly to make it the best book possible.

I am often highly critical of the international press and especially of its coverage of Haiti. But, make no mistake, in writing this book I relied on the work of many, many talented journalists who have covered Haiti over the years. Thank you all for all you do: Ansel Herz, Amelie Baron, Jacqueline Charles, Jonathan Katz, Trenton Daniel, Jessica Desvarieux, Sebastian Walker, Teresa Bo (and everyone at Al Jazeera), Amy Wilentz, Pooja Bhatia, Jeb Sprague, Deborah Sontag, David Adams, Maria Abi-Habib, Natalie Kitreoff, and so many others whose work informed my own. Azam Ahmed is deserving of a special shout-out for pushing me to actually go out and pitch this thing.

But while all of us, as foreign writers or journalists, could come and go, I owe a special thanks to all the Haitian journalists I've worked with throughout the years. Courageous and talented individuals who put their lives on the line every day and who, despite it all, continue to shine light on their country. I am especially grateful to Widlore Merancourt, Jetry Dumont, Ralph Thomassin, and the entire Ayibopost team; to Frantz Duval, Roberson Alphonse, and all the journalists at *Le Nouvelliste;* and to Gotson Pierre and the wonderful folks behind Alterpresse. I've been honored to have my work translated and published in all three outlets over the years. Jane Regan, Milo Milfort, and the amazing team behind Haiti Grassroots Watch, whose investigations into the post-quake period are among the finest out there, are also deserving of a special thank-you.

I would have been lost without the work of academics and writers, including: Robert Maguire, Marlene Daut, Laurent Dubois, Gina Athena Ulysses, Laura Wagner, Claire Payton, Jemima Pierre, Mamyrah Dougé-Prosper, Greg Becket, Peter Hallward, Robert Fatton, Chelsey Kivland, Mark Schuller, Régine Michelle Jean-Charles, Jean Casimir, the late Michel-Rolph Trouillot, and myriad more.

Finally, to my family. I wouldn't be here without you. I feel so lucky to have grown up in a home full of creativity, art, and love—even if it took me a few decades to appreciate the former two. I am so thankful to my parents for encouraging me to keep at it, even when I felt totally lost, and especially my mom, for reading everything. I'll never get tired of my mom complimenting my writing, even if I know it's basically a motherly obligation. I promised Meryl, my wife, I'd have this book done by the time our daughter was born. Well, Simone is sixteen months old as I write this. But, I don't think I could have done it without both of them. It's been almost six years since I first started saying, "I'm writing a book," and Meryl has been my first reader and the project's biggest supporter ever since (even if her comments are generally way harsher than those from friends, colleagues, and especially my mom). Somehow, I got some of my best writing done with Simone sleeping in my lap. A book can be all-consuming, but Simone gave me (er, demanded of me) a balance that, in the end, was what allowed me to get across the finish line.

I might be the author, but I hope all those I've crossed paths with in this work over the past decade see a bit of themselves in the text as well. And last, but certainly not least—thank you for reading this through until the end.

NOTES

PROLOGUE

1. Jonathan M. Katz, "The Disasters in Afghanistan and Haiti Share the Same Twisted Root," *The New Republic,* August 20, 2021, https://newrepublic.com/article/163329/afghanistan-withdrawal-haiti-earthquake-crisis.

2. Portions of the prologue are drawn from: Jake Johnston, "La bataille d'Haïti n'est pas finie," *Le Monde Diplomatique,* December 2021, https://www.monde-diplomatique.fr/2021/12/JOHNSTON/64136.

3. I use the terms "America" and "American" in this book for shorthand, but want to acknowledge the problematic aspects of this construction. "America" is a region, not a country, and "Americans" applies to anybody from the Americas (North or South America). For ease, in this text, "America" refers to the United States of America, and "American" refers to citizens of the United States of America.

4. Emma Graham-Harrison, "Ghani Declared Winner of Afghan Election—but Opponent Rejects Result," *The Guardian*, February 18, 2020, https://www.theguardian.com/world/2020/feb/18/ashraf-ghani-wins-afghan-presidential-election.

5. Anonymous foreign official, discussion with the author, January 2022, virtual.

6. Aamer Madhani, "States Learning How Many Afghan Evacuees Coming Their Way," Associated Press, September 15, 2021, https://apnews.com/article/us-afghanistan-evacuees-262203820a617808f4a40a130e2d179a. By 2023, the Biden administration had resettled more than seventy thousand Afghans in the United States. The policy, however, has faced scrutiny from a variety of actors. In late 2022, the administration changed the policy to focus on reuniting family members. Still, the administration even gave a name to its new policy: Enduring Welcome.

7. In 2022, *The New York Times* dedicated an entire special edition to a Haiti-focused project it called "The Ransom." The multipart series focused on the long-term implications of the funds Haiti was forced to pay France for its independence and freedom. As the United States reckons with its own problems with systemic racism, there are some indications that the general US public is becoming more aware of Haitian history. See "Haiti 'Ransom' Project," article series, *New York Times,* 2022, https://www.nytimes.com/spotlight/haiti.

8. Much of Joseph's and his family's experience is documented in a lawsuit brought against President Biden, the Department of Homeland Security, as well as other agencies and officials of the US government for their treatment of migrants in Del Rio. Haitian Bridge Alliance et al. v. Biden et al., 21–3317 (Washington, DC, December 20, 2021), http://justiceactioncenter.org/wp-content/uploads/2021/12 /Stamped-Complaint-HBA-v-Biden.pdf.

9. Under the Trump administration, the American Civil Liberties Union and others filed a lawsuit seeking to halt the Title 42 policy. For more information on the policy, see Leonardo Castañeda and Katie Hoeppner, "Five Things to Know About the Title 42 Immigrant Expulsion Policy," American Civil Liberties Union, March 22, 2022, https://www.aclu.org/news/immigrants-rights/five-things-to-know-about-the -title-42-immigrant-expulsion-policy.

10. Nick Miroff and Sean Sullivan, "As Immigration Heats Up, Biden Struggles for a Clear Plan," *Washington Post,* July 17, 2021, https://www.washingtonpost.com /national/biden-immigration-policy-struggle/2021/07/17/5e8bb9b6-e67c-11eb -8aa5-5662858b696e_story.html.

11. Sabrina Rodriguez, "Biden Administration Renews Title 42 Order, as ACLU Fights Back," *Politico,* August 2, 2021, https://www.politico.com/news/2021/08/02/biden -administration-sued-aclu-migrant-expulsions-502140.

12. John Otis, "Thousands of Haitians Prepare to Trek Through Panama's Jungle and on to the U.S.," NPR, September 29, 2021, https://www.npr.org/2021/09/27 /1040829977/haitian-migrants-inundate-a-colombia-town-on-the-way-to-u-s -border.

13. Jasmine Aguilera and Harold Isaac, "A Haitian Man's Brutal Experience with U.S. Border Agents Sparked Outrage. Now He's Telling His Story," *Time*, March 16, 2022, https://time.com/6144970/mirard-joseph-haitian-migrants-del-rio-border/.

14. I used public flight-tracking databases such as Flight Aware to monitor US expulsion flights to Haiti. The full database of flights is available here and continues to be updated at the time of publication: "ICE Air to Haiti—Mass Expulsion Flight Data," https://docs.google.com/spreadsheets/d/1mvPiOvISRYTNEg7Mzk7nmZsk3PG0 _jw4y8XVJ3oDMms/edit#gid=0.

15. Tom Ricker, "Biden Has Deported Nearly as Many Haitians in His First Year as the Last Three Presidents—Combined," Quixote Center, February 18, 2022, https:// quixote.org/biden-has-deported-nearly-as-many-haitians-in-his-first-year-as-the -last-three-presidents-combined.

16. Jake Johnston, "US Envoy to Haiti Resigns, Citing Political Intervention and 'Inhumane' Deportation Policy," Center for Economic and Policy Research, September 23, 2021, https://cepr.net/us-envoy-to-haiti-resigns-citing-political-intervention -and-inhumane-deportation-policy/.

17. In October 2021, seventeen foreign missionaries, sixteen of whom were US citizens, were kidnapped in Haiti. They were eventually all released in December.

18. Daniel Foote, discussion with author, September 2022, Washington, DC.

19. Jake Johnston, "De Facto Haitian Authorities Call for (Another) Foreign Military Intervention," Center for Economic and Policy Research, October 14, 2022, https:// www.cepr.net/de-facto-haitian-authorities-call-for-another-foreign-military -intervention/.

20. A few examples available in English include: Michel-Rolph Trouillot, *Haiti: State*

Against Nation: The Origins and Legacy of Duvalierism (New York: Monthly Review Press, 2000); Robert Fatton Jr., *Haiti's Predatory Republic: The Unending Transition to Democracy* (Boulder, CO: Lynne Rienner Publishers, 2002); Jean Casimir, *The Haitians: A Decolonial History*, translated by Laurent Dubois (Chapel Hill: University of North Carolina Press, 2020).

1. THE "COMPASSIONATE INVASION"

1. Jacqueline Charles and Lydia Martin, "Without Even a Shirt, Préval Stayed Focused in Aftermath of Earthquake in Haiti," *Miami Herald,* January 20, 2010, https://www.miamiherald.com/news/nation-world/world/americas/haiti/article136304303.html.

2. Friedemann Freund, "Rocks That Crackle and Sparkle and Glow: Strange Pre-Earthquake Phenomena," *Journal of Scientific Exploration* 17, no. 1 (March 2003).

3. Charles and Martin, "Without Even a Shirt."

4. US Department of State and US Agency for International Development, "FY 2010: Haiti Supplemental Budget Justification," April 28, 2010, https://2009-2017.state.gov/documents/organization/141243.pdf.

5. René Préval, "Interviews: René Préval," *Frontline,* PBS, March 16, 2010, http://www.pbs.org:80/wgbh/pages/frontline/haiti/interviews/preval.html.

6. Only two individuals, Aristide and Préval, reached the presidency through an election. The others were military leaders and/or the heads of transitional governments.

7. US Embassy Port-au-Prince, "Deconstructing Preval," June 16, 2009, in Public Library of US Diplomacy, WikiLeaks Cable: 09PORTAUPRINCE575_a, https://wikileaks.org/plusd/cables/09PORTAUPRINCE575_a.html.

8. Amy Wilentz, "René Préval: The Unassuming President Who Wanted to Save Haiti," *Politico,* December 28, 2017, https://www.politico.com/magazine/story/2017/12/28/rene-preval-obituary-216191/.

9. René Préval, discussion with author, 2015, Washington, DC.

10. Joe Mozingo, "Haitian Quake Shook Leader to His Core," *Los Angeles Times,* August 15, 2010, https://www.latimes.com/archives/la-xpm-2010-aug-15-la-fg-haiti-preval-20100815-story.html.

11. Jay Newton-Small, "Can America's Top Gun in Haiti Keep the Relief Effort in Order?," *Time*, January 25, 2010, http://content.time.com/time/specials/packages/article/0,28804,1953379_1953494_1956342,00.html.

12. "First-Hand Account of Tragedy," *McLean (Virginia) Connection,* February 11, 2010, http://www.connectionnewspapers.com/news/2010/feb/11/first-hand-account-of-tragedy/.

13. Ibid.

14. Kenneth H. Merten and Ken Keen, "Haiti 2010 Earthquake: 40 Seconds That Changed Haiti Forever. Ambassador Merten and Lt. General Keen on Leading the U.S. Relief Effort and US Interests Today," podcast audio interview by Deborah McCarthy, *The General and the Ambassador,* American Academy of Diplomacy, June 11, 2018, https://generalambassadorpodcast.org/007.

15. David R. DiOrio, *Operation Unified Response—Haiti Earthquake 2010* (Norfolk, VA: Joint Forces Staff College, November 2010), https://jfsc.ndu.edu/Portals/72/Documents/JC2IOS/Additional_Reading/4A_Haiti_HADR_Case_Study_revNov10.pdf.

16. Barack Obama, "Statement by the President on the Earthquake in Haiti," Office of the Press Secretary, White House, January 12, 2010, https://obamawhitehouse .archives.gov/the-press-office/statement-president-earthquake-haiti.

17. DiOrio, *Operation Unified Response.*

18. Gary Cecchine, Forrest E. Morgan, Michael A. Wermuth, Timothy Jackson, Agnes Gereben Schaefer, and Matthew Stafford, *The U.S. Military Response to the 2010 Haiti Earthquake: Considerations for Army Leaders* (Santa Monica, CA: RAND Corporation, 2013), https://www.rand.org/content/dam/rand/pubs/research_reports /RR300/RR304/RAND_RR304.pdf.

19. Cheryl Mills, "Situation Report No. 1—Haiti Earthquake," email to Hillary Clinton, January 12, 2010, in Hillary Clinton Email Archive (Email-ID 3999), WikiLeaks, https://wikileaks.org/clinton-emails/emailid/3999.

20. The intelligence briefs were obtained as part of a FOIA request by researcher Jeremy Bigwood and shared with the author.

21. *Operation UNIFIED RESPONSE—Haiti Earthquake Response* (Joint Center for Operational Analysis, US Joint Forces Command, May 15, 2010).

22. Timothy Schwartz, *The Great Haiti Humanitarian Aid Swindle* (CreateSpace Independent Publishing Platform, 2017).

23. Mona Augustin, interview with author, January 2021, virtual.

24. Barack Obama, "Text of President Obama's Remarks," transcript of remarks, *New York Times,* January 13, 2010, https://www.nytimes.com/2010/01/14/world /americas/14obamatext.html.

25. Douglas Fraser, "General Douglas Fraser (USAF) Holds a Defense Department News Briefing on the Haiti Earthquake," Political Transcript Wire, January 13, 2010, accessed via Lexis Academic. (Video aired on January 13, 2010, on C-SPAN, https://www.c-span.org/video/?291295-2/haiti-earthquake-relief-efforts.)

26. CNN, "CNN Newsroom," January 13, 2010, transcript accessed via Nexis Uni.

27. Mike Mount and Larry Shaughnessy, "First U.S. Military Aid Reaches Quake-Stricken Haiti," CNN, January 13, 2010, http://www.cnn.com/2010/US/01/13/haiti .us.coast.guard/index.html.

28. U.S. Embassy Port-au-Prince, "TFHA01: Embassy Port au Prince Earthquake SitRep as of 1800 Day 4," January 16, 2010, in Public Library of U.S. Diplomacy, WikiLeaks Cable: 10PORTAUPRINCE50_a, https://wikileaks.org/plusd/cables /10PORTAUPRINCE50_a.html.

29. Mark Thompson, "The U.S. Military in Haiti: A Compassionate Invasion," *Time,* January 16, 2010, http://content.time.com/time/specials/packages/article/0,28804, 1953379_1953494_1954326,00.html.

2. THE FEAR

1. Cecchine et al., *The U.S. Military Response to the 2010 Haiti Earthquake.*

2. Ibid.

3. US Agency for International Development, *FY 2010 Fact Sheet #58: Haiti—Earthquake* (USAID, June 11, 2010), https://pdf.usaid.gov/pdf_docs/PA00J27V.pdf.

4. Jake Johnston, "Blacklisted Contractor Continues Receiving Government Money Through Haiti Contracts," Center for Economic and Policy Research, December 2, 2011, http://cepr.net/ blacklisted-contractor-continues-receiving-government -money-through-haiti-contracts. Shorter version published in *The Hill,* December

2, 2011, https://thehill.com/blogs/congress-blog/foreign-policy/180297-blacklisted-contractor-continues-receiving-government-money-through-haiti-contracts/.

5. Mike M. Ahlers and Mike Mount, "Radio Station in the Sky Warns Haitians Not to Attempt Boat Voyage," CNN, January 19, 2010, http://www.cnn.com/2010/WORLD/americas/01/19/haiti.broadcast.warning/index.html.

6. Rebecca Solnit, "In Haiti, Words Can Kill," *TomDispatch*, January 21, 2010, http://www.tomdispatch.com/blog/175194/tomgram:_rebecca_solnit,_in_haiti,_words_can_kill/.

7. Jonathan M. Katz, *The Big Truck That Went By: How the World Came to Save Haiti and Left Behind a Disaster* (New York: St. Martin's Press, 2013).

8. "The American Public Response to the Earthquake in Haiti," KRC Research, January 22, 2010, preserved in Internet Archive, August 31, 2010, https://web.archive.org/web/20100831010244/http:/www.krcresearch.com/news_americanPublicResponse_012210.html.

9. Doug Gross, "Red Cross Text Donations Pass $21 Million," CNN, January 18, 2010, https://www.cnn.com/2010/TECH/01/18/redcross.texts/index.html.

10. Marc Lacey, "An 'Uphill Battle' to Polish Haiti's Image," *International Herald Tribune*, February 15, 2007, https://www.nytimes.com/2007/02/15/world/americas/15iht-haiti.4609127.html.

11. David Brooks, "The Underlying Tragedy," *New York Times*, January 14, 2010, https://www.nytimes.com/2010/01/15/opinion/15brooks.html.

12. Frank James, "Pat Robertson Blames Haitian Devil Pact for Earthquake," *The Two-Way*, NPR, January 13, 2010, https://www.npr.org/sections/thetwo-way/2010/01/pat_robertson_blames_haitian_d.html.

13. Astra Taylor, "Rebecca Solnit," *Bomb Magazine*, Fall 2009, https://web.archive.org/web/20091124114626/https://bombsite.com/issues/109/articles/3327.

14. Ibid.

15. Laurent Dubois, *Haiti: The Aftershocks of History* (New York: Metropolitan Books, 2012).

16. Jean Casimir, *The Haitians: A Decolonial History*, translated by Laurent Dubois (Chapel Hill: University of North Carolina Press, 2020).

17. Julia Gaffield, ed., *The Haitian Declaration of Independence: Creation, Context, and Legacy* (Charlottesville: University of Virginia Press, 2016).

18. See, for example: C. L. R. James, *The Black Jacobins: Toussaint L'Ouverture and the San Domingo Revolution* (London: Secker & Warburg, 1938).

19. *New York Times*, "Haiti 'Ransom' Project," article series, 2022, https://www.nytimes.com/spotlight/haiti.

20. Bolívar emancipated those enslaved on his properties, but the liberated countries did not immediately abolish slavery. Further, Bolívar betrayed Haiti by siding with the US and excluding the newly independent nation from the first hemispheric summit, held in Panama.

21. Casimir, *The Haitians*.

3. THE BLUE HELMETS

1. CNN, "Haiti Halts Flights into Overburdened Airport," January 14, 2010, https://www.cnn.com/2010/TRAVEL/01/14/faa.haiti.flights/index.html.

2. Edmond Mulet, "Interview with Edmond Mulet, Former Special Representative of

the Secretary-General in Haiti and Head of MINUSTAH," by UN News Centre, July 11, 2011, preserved in internet archive, November 11, 2012, https://web.archive.org /web/20121111103129/http://www.un.org/apps/news/newsmakers.asp?NewsID=34.

3. US Embassy Port-au-Prince, "Why We Need Continuing MINUSTAH Presence in Haiti," October 1, 2008, in Public Library of U.S. Diplomacy, WikiLeaks Cable: 08 PORTAUPRINCE1381_a, https://wikileaks.org/plusd/cables/08PORTAUPRINCE1381 _a.html.

4. Lawrence A. Yates, *The US Military's Experience in Stability Operations, 1789–2005,* Global War on Terrorism Occasional Paper 15 (Fort Leavenworth, KS: Combat Studies Institute Press, 2006), https://usacac.army.mil/sites/default/files/documents /cace/CSI/CSIPubs/yates.pdf.

5. Colin Powell, "The Situation Room: Haiti in Ruins," interview by Wolf Blitzer, *Situation Room,* CNN, January 14, 2010, http://edition.cnn.com/TRANSCRIPTS/1001 /14/sitroom.03.html.

6. US Embassy Port-au-Prince, "Why We Need Continuing MINUSTAH Presence in Haiti."

7. For an account of this time period, see Amy Wilentz, *The Rainy Season: Haiti Since Duvalier* (New York: Simon & Schuster, 1990).

8. Stephen Engelberg, Howard W. French, and Tim Weiner, "C.I.A. Formed Haitian Unit Later Tied to Narcotics Trade," *New York Times,* November 14, 1993, https:// www.nytimes.com/1993/11/14/world/cia-formed-haitian-unit-later-tied-to -narcotics-trade.html.

9. Susanne Schafer, "Pentagon Puts Together Plans for Haiti Aid," Associated Press, April 12, 1993, accessed via Lexis Academic.

10. Susanne Schafer, "UNKNOWN," Associated Press, April 13, 1993, accessed via Lexis Academic.

11. *New York Times,* "The 2000 Campaign; 2nd Presidential Debate Between Gov. Bush and Vice President Gore," October 12, 2000, https://www.nytimes.com/2000/10/12 /us/2000-campaign-2nd-presidential-debate-between-gov-bush-vice-president -gore.html.

12. Fulton Armstrong, in discussion with the author, February 2023, virtual.

13. *Democracy Now!,* "Exclusive Breaking News: President Aristide Says 'I Was Kid-napped' 'Tell the World It Is a Coup,'" March 1, 2004, https://www.democracynow .org/2004/3/1/exclusive_breaking_news_br_president_aristide.

14. UN News, "Security Council Authorizes Three-Month Multinational Interim Force for Haiti," February 29, 2004, https://news.un.org/en/story/2004/02/95652.

15. Edward Keane, "Nation Building in Haiti: Can We Do Better This Time?," Center for American Progress, April 12, 2004, https://www.americanprogress.org/issues /security/news/2004/04/12/725/nation-building-in-haiti-can-we-do-better-this -time/.

16. Lydia Polgreen, "New Haitian Prime Minister Arrives, Vowing to Restore Unity," *New York Times,* March 11, 2004, https://www.nytimes.com/2004/03/11/world/new -haitian-prime-minister-arrives-vowing-to-restore-unity.html.

17. The densely populated slums of Port-au-Prince are referred to as "popular neigh-borhoods," which I use throughout the text.

18. For a more detailed discussion of the role of *baz* in Haiti, see Chelsey L. Kivland, "Based in Respect: Street Politics and the Workings of an Informal Rule of Law in

Haiti," in *Rule of Law: Cases, Strategies, and Interpretations*, ed. Barbara Faedda (Dueville, Italy: Ronzani Edizioni Scientifiche, 2021), https://static1.squarespace.com /static/5efa3e4eb1788c3251bc5750/t/62028a89d16b89059fe12276/1644333708077 /Based+in+Respect_Rule+of+Law_Kivland_off+print.pdf. For an even more thorough accounting of this important and complex history, see Chelsey L. Kivland, *Street Sovereigns: Young Men and the Makeshift State in Urban Haiti* (Ithaca, NY: Cornell University Press, 2020).

19. Siobhán Wills, Cahal McLaughlin, and Ilionor Louis, "Sent to Haiti to Keep the Peace, Departing UN Troops Leave a Damaged Nation in Their Wake," *The Conversation,* October 13, 2017, https://theconversation.com/sent-to-haiti-to-keep -the-peace-departing-un-troops-leave-a-damaged-nation-in-their-wake-85584.

20. Paisley Dodds, "AP Exclusive: UN Child Sex Ring Left Victims but No Arrests," Associated Press, April 12, 2017, https://apnews.com/article/e6ebc331460345c5ab d4f57d77f535c1.

21. US Embassy Port-au-Prince, "Why We Need Continuing MINUSTAH Presence in Haiti."

22. US Congress, House, Committee on Foreign Relations, *Haiti: From Rescue to Recovery and Reconstruction; Hearing Before the Committee on Foreign Relations,* 111th Cong., 2nd sess., January 28, 2010 (statement of James Dobbins, director of RAND International Security and Defense Policy Center), https://www.govinfo .gov/content/pkg/CHRG-111shrg62792/html/CHRG-111shrg62792.htm.

23. US Embassy in Qatar, "Engaging Al Jazeera on Haiti," January 20, 2010, in Public Library of US Diplomacy, WikiLeaks Cable: 10DOHA24_a, https://wikileaks.org /plusd/cables/10DOHA24_a.html.

24. Ginger Thompson and Damien Cave, "Officials Strain to Distribute Aid to Haiti as Violence Rises," *New York Times,* January 16, 2010, https://www.nytimes.com/2010 /01/17/world/americas/17haiti.html.

25. Associated Press, "Haiti Flight Logs Detail Early Chaos After Quake," NBC News, February 18, 2010, https://www.nbcnews.com/id/wbna35463490.

26. Rory Carroll and Daniel Nasaw, "US Accused of Annexing Airport as Squabbling Hinders Aid Effort in Haiti," *The Guardian,* January 17, 2010, https://www .theguardian.com/world/2010/jan/17/us-accused-aid-effort-haiti.

27. CNN, "Security Concerns Cause Doctors to Leave Hospital, Quake Victims," January 17, 2010, http://www.cnn.com/2010/WORLD/americas/01/16/haiti.abandoned .patients/index.html.

28. Moni Basu, "Buried Alive for Six Days, Earthquake Survivors Reunite for First Time," CNN, December 28, 2010, http://www.cnn.com/2010/WORLD/americas /12/27/haiti.earthquake.survivors.reunion/index.html.

29. Associated Press, "Haiti Flight Logs Detail Early Chaos After Quake."

30. Tom Brown, "Haiti Aid Effort Marred by Slow U.N. Response," Reuters, February 26, 2010, https://www.reuters.com/article/us-quake-haiti-relief/haiti-aid-effort -marred-by-slow-u-n-response-idUSTRE61P03N20100226.

31. Ben Ehrenreich, "Why Did We Focus on Securing Haiti Rather Than Helping Haitians?," *Slate,* January 21, 2010, https://slate.com/news-and-politics/2010/01/why -did-u-s-aid-focus-on-securing-haiti-rather-than-helping-haitians.html.

4. THE OPPORTUNITY

1. Centre for Research on the Epidemiology of Disasters, Emergency Events Database, distributed by the Université Catholique de Louvain, https://public.emdat.be/.

2. The Richter scale is the most commonly used measure of the strength of an earthquake. For the conversion into TNT equivalent, see: Friedemann Freund, "Rocks That Crackle and Sparkle and Glow: Strange Pre-Earthquake Phenomena," *Journal of Scientific Exploration* 17, no. 1 (March 2003).

3. Haitian government figures place the death toll at 220,000 or more. The anthropologist Timothy Schwartz, who did household research as part of a USAID project, places the figure at the low end of roughly 65,000.

4. Government of the Republic of Haiti, *Haiti Earthquake PDNA (Post-Disaster Needs Assessment): Assessment of Damage, Losses, General and Sectoral Needs* (Washington, DC: World Bank Group, March 1, 2010), http://documents.worldbank.org/curated/en/355571468251125062/Haiti-earthquake-PDNA-Post-Disaster-Needs-Assessment-assessment-of-damage-losses-general-and-sectoral-needs.

5. Eduardo A. Cavallo, Andrew Powell, and Oscar Becerra, "Estimating the Direct Economic Damages of the Earthquake in Haiti," Inter-American Development Bank Working Paper Series 163 (February 2010), https://publications.iadb.org/en/publication/estimating-direct-economic-damage-earthquake-haiti.

6. Centre for Research on the Epidemiology of Disasters, Emergency Events Database.

7. Virginie Montet, "Haitian Who Predicted 'Big One' Speaks Up," IOL, January 25, 2010, https://www.iol.co.za/mercury/news/world/haitian-who-predicted-big-one-speaks-up-471418.

8. Data from World Development Indicators (database), World Bank, Washington, DC, https://databank.worldbank.org/source/world-development-indicators.

9. John Burnett, "Haitians Find Lifeline in Local Radio Station," *All Things Considered,* NPR, January 25, 2010, https://www.npr.org/templates/story/story.php?storyId=122948825.

10. Infoasaid, "Haiti Media and Telecoms Landscape Guide," *Internews,* March 22, 2013, preserved in internet archive, May 14, 2021, http://web.archive.org/web/20210514170928/https://internews.org/resource/haiti-media-and-telecoms-landscape-guide/.

11. For a more detailed discussion of the US occupation and the growth of the urban population, see Laurent Dubois, *Haiti: The Aftershocks of History* (New York: Metropolitan Books, 2012).

12. Coordinating Committee of Progressive Organisations, "Haiti: After the Catastrophe, What Are the Perspectives?," translated by Mike Gonzalez, January 27, 2010, reprinted in *Monthly Review,* February 4, 2010, https://mronline.org/2010/02/04/haiti-after-the-catastrophe-what-are-the-perspectives/.

13. L'Agence Haitienne de Presse, February 18, 2010, news, translated (unofficial) as "News-Feb. 18: L'Agence Haitienne de Presse (AHP)—"Coup Under Cover of Humanitarian Aid? Haiti to Become International Protectorate? and More," by *HCVAnalysis* (blog), posted February 24, 2010, https://hcvanalysis.wordpress.com/2010/02/24/news-feb-18-lagence-haitienne-de-presse-ahp-coup-under-cover-of-humanitarian-aid-haiti-to-become-international-protectorate-and-more/.

14. Juan Forero, "Haiti's Elite Sees Business Opportunities Emerging from Reconstruction,"

Washington Post, February 10, 2010, https://www.washingtonpost.com/wp-dyn /content/article/2010/02/14/AR2010021403322.html.

15. As an example, USAID administrator Raj Shah was asked at a January 14, 2010, press briefing if he was "going to be the Paul Bremer of Haiti." See Cheryl Mills and Raj Shah, "Briefing on the Situation in Haiti," US Department of State, January 14, 2010, https://2009-2017.state.gov/r/pa/prs/ps/2010/01/135210.htm.

16. US Congress, House, Committee on Foreign Relations, *Haiti: From Rescue to Recovery and Reconstruction; Hearing Before the Committee on Foreign Relations,* 111th Cong., 2nd sess., January 28, 2010, https://www.govinfo.gov/content/pkg/CHRG -111shrg62792/html/CHRG-111shrg62792.htm.

5. THE PLAN

1. OECD, *Paris Declaration on Aid Effectiveness* (Paris: OECD Publishing, 2005), https://doi.org/10.1787/9789264098084-en.

2. Jonathan M. Katz, *The Big Truck That Went By: How the World Came to Save Haiti and Left Behind a Disaster* (New York: St. Martin's Press, 2013).

3. Bill Clinton, "The Situation Room: Thousands Feared Dead in Haiti; Interview with Former President Bill Clinton," interview by Wolf Blitzer, *The Situation Room,* CNN, January 13, 2010, https://transcripts.cnn.com/show/sitroom/date/2010-01-13 /segment/03.

4. Karen Tumulty, "That Time Bill and Hillary Clinton Went to a Voodoo Ceremony in Haiti," *Washington Post,* March 20, 2015, https://www.washingtonpost.com /news/post-politics/wp/2015/03/20/that-time-bill-and-hillary-clinton-went-to-a -voodoo-ceremony-in-haiti/.

5. Hillary Clinton, "Remarks at the Haiti Donors Conference," US Department of State, April 14, 2009, https://2009-2017.state.gov/secretary/20092013clinton/rm /2009a/04/121674.htm.

6. UN News, "Former US President Clinton Appointed UN Special Envoy for Haiti," May 19, 2009, https://news.un.org/en/story/2009/05/300442.

7. Cheryl Mills, "Haiti Recovery Blueprint Includes Foreign Donors," email to Hillary Clinton, March 20, 2010, in Hillary Clinton Email Archive, WikiLeaks, email-ID 3222, https://wikileaks.org/clinton-emails/emailid/3222.

8. Raymond A. Joseph, *For Whom the Dogs Spy: Haiti: from the Duvalier Dictatorships to the Earthquake, Four Presidents, and Beyond* (New York: Arcade, 2015).

9. Joseph Guyler Delvia, "Haiti Sees Aid Boost from Bill Clinton Appointment," Reuters, May 20, 2009, https://www.reuters.com/article/instant-article/idUSN20530642.

10. Raphael Yves Pierre, *Haitians Talk About Rebuilding the Country After the January 12, 2010 Earthquake* (Oxfam, 2010), https://www.preventionweb.net/files/13645_a pril2010oxfamhaitipublicopinionpol.pdf.

11. Paul Collier, *Haiti: From Natural Catastrophe to Economic Security: A Report for the Secretary-General of the United Nations* (Oxford University Department of Economics, 2009), http://www.securitycouncilreport.org/atf/cf/%7B65BFCF9B-6D27-4E9C -8CD3-CF6E4FF96FF9%7D/Haiti%20Collier%20report.pdf.

12. World Bank, "Indonesia: A Reconstruction Chapter Ends Eight Years After the Tsunami," December 26, 2012, https://www.worldbank.org/en/news/feature/2012/12 /26/indonesia-reconstruction-chapter-ends-eight-years-after-the-tsunami.

13. US Department of State, "Draft of a Convention Between the United States and

the Republic of Haiti with Letter from William Jennings Bryan to Arthur Bailly-Blanchard," July 2, 1914, in *Papers Relating to the Foreign Relations of the United States, with the Address of the President to Congress December 8, 1914,* US Department of State Office of the Historian, document 525 (file no. 838.51/341a), https://history.state.gov/historicaldocuments/frus1914/d525.

14. Cheryl Mills, "From Paul Collier," email to Hillary Clinton, January 24, 2010, in Hillary Clinton Email Archive, WikiLeaks, email-ID 3845, https://wikileaks.org/clinton-emails/emailid/3845.

15. Cheryl Mills, "Haiti Recovery Blueprint," WikiLeaks.

16. Katz, *The Big Truck That Went By.*

17. Jon Bougher, *Mozayik* (Haiti, 2013), film, 32 min.

18. For a further discussion on the camp population and how people were drawn into the camps, see Timothy Schwartz, *The Great Haiti Humanitarian Aid Swindle* (CreateSpace Independent Publishing Platform, 2017).

19. Mona Augustin, interview with author, January 2021, virtual.

20. World Bank and International Finance Corporation, *Country Assistance Strategy for the Republic of Haiti for the Period FY09–FY12,* report no. 48284-HT (World Bank Group, May 4, 2009), http://documents1.worldbank.org/curated/en/230791468037528189/text/482840CAS0P1061C0Disclosed061191091.txt.

6. THE AID-INDUSTRIAL COMPLEX

1. Monsanto, "Monsanto Company Donates Conventional Corn and Vegetable Seeds to Haitian Farmers to Help Address Food Security Needs," PR Newswire, Cision, May 13, 2010, https://www.prnewswire.com/news-releases/monsanto-company-donates-conventional-corn-and-vegetable-seeds-to-haitian-farmers-to-help-address-food-security-needs-93713444.html.

2. Ayiti Kale Je, "Monsanto in Haiti," *Haiti Grassroots Watch,* March 30, 2011, http://haitigrassrootswatch.squarespace.com/6mon1eng.

3. Mark Weisbrot, Jake Johnston, and Rebecca Ray, "Using Food Aid to Support, Not Harm, Haitian Agriculture," Center for Economic and Policy Research, April 2010, https://www.cepr.net/report/using-food-aid-to-support-haiti/.

4. Ayiti Kale Je, "Seeding Reconstruction?," *Haiti Grassroots Watch,* March 30, 2011, http://haitigrassrootswatch.squarespace.com/6sem1eng.

5. American Red Cross, IRS form 990 for 2009 calendar year, filled by Brian J. Rhoa, February 13, 2014, https://www.redcross.org/content/dam/redcross/atg/PDF_s/Publications/Financial_Statements/2010_American_Red_Cross_Tax_Return.pdf.

6. Henrietta Brackman, "Haiti's Hospitality: The Island's Rich Folklore Tradition Is One of Its Many Attractions," *New York Times,* November 4, 1956, https://www.nytimes.com/1956/11/04/archives/haitis-hospitality-the-islands-rich-folklore-tradition-is-one-of.html.

7. Collection of Johnson administration documents regarding foreign relations with Haiti, in "Foreign Relations, 1964–1968, Volume XXXII, Dominican Republic; Cuba; Haiti; Guyana," US Department of State Office of the Historian, documents 325–369, https://2001-2009.state.gov/r/pa/ho/frus/johnsonlb/xxxii/44658.htm.

8. Claire Antoine Payton, "Building Corruption in Haiti," *NACLA Report on the Americas* 51, no. 2 (May 2019): 182–187, https://doi.org/10.1080/10714839.2019.1617488.

9. UN Office of the Special Envoy for Haiti, *Has Aid Changed? Channelling Assistance to Haiti Before and After the Earthquake* (New York: UN, June 2011), https://www.lessonsfromhaiti.org/download/Report_Center/has_aid_changed_en.pdf.

10. "Obituaries," *Washington Post,* April 2, 2005, https://www.washingtonpost.com/archive/local/2005/04/02/obituaries/df510a5b-ef1d-4c50-a076-51cf9465d01d/.

11. Diana B. Henriques and Dean Baquet, "Cozy Links to a U.S. Agency Prove Useful to a Rice Trader," *New York Times,* October 11, 1993, https://www.nytimes.com/1993/10/11/business/cozy-links-to-a-us-agency-prove-useful-to-a-rice-trader.html.

12. United States v. Kay, 359 F.3d 738 (5th Cir. 2004), https://www.justice.gov/criminal-fraud/case/united-states-v-david-kay-et-al-district-court-docket-no-01-cr-914-court-appea-0.

13. *Washington Post,* "Washington in Brief: Helms Suspends Haitian Aid," April 11, 2000, https://www.washingtonpost.com/archive/politics/2000/04/11/washington-in-brief/87bcac4e-f890-4d86-a7ee-dc3b8e6456e0/.

14. Alex Dupuy, "Beyond the Earthquake: A Wake-Up Call for Haiti," *Latin American Perspectives* 37, no. 3 (May 2010): 195–204, https://www.jstor.org/stable/25700524.

15. *Democracy Now!,* "'We Made a Devil's Bargain': Fmr. President Clinton Apologizes for Trade Policies That Destroyed Haitian Rice Farming," April 1, 2010, https://www.democracynow.org/2010/4/1/clinton_rice.

16. Michael Wines, "3 Top Duvalier Aides Living in Splendor in U.S.," *Los Angeles Times,* February 13, 1986, https://www.latimes.com/archives/la-xpm-1986-02-13-mn-23226-story.html.

17. David Rohde, "Visit Afghanistan's 'Little America,' and See the Folly of For-Profit War," *Atlantic,* June 1, 2012, https://www.theatlantic.com/international/archive/2012/06/visit-afghanistans-little-america-and-see-the-folly-of-for-profit-war/257962/.

18. Rachel M. McCleary, "The Virtues of Non-Profit Humanitarian Aid," *Washington Post,* September 2, 2010, preserved in Internet Archive, September 2, 2010, https://web.archive.org/web/20100902181124/http://voices.washingtonpost.com/political-bookworm/2010/09/virtures_of_non-profit_humanit.html.

19. Jake Johnston, "GAO Report Suggests That USAID Remains 'More of a Contracting Agency Than an Operational Agency,'" Center for Economic and Policy Research, November 21, 2011, https://cepr.net/usaid-more-of-a-contracting-agency-than-an-operational-agency/.

20. American Academy for Diplomacy and Stimson Center, *A Foreign Affairs Budget for the Future: Fixing the Crisis in Diplomatic Readiness* (Washington, DC: AAD, October 2008), https://www.academyofdiplomacy.org/wp-content/uploads/2015/12/Long_Final_10_22_08.pdf.

7. THE TRANSITION INITIATIVE

1. Julia F. Irwin, "The Origins of U.S. Foreign Disaster Assistance," *American Historian,* Organization of American Historians, February 2018, https://www.oah.org/tah/issues/2018/february/the-origins-of-u.s-foreign-disaster-assistance/.

2. German Marshall Fund, "The Spirit of the Marshall Plan," accessed January 2023, https://www.gmfus.org/spirit-marshall-plan.

3. US National Archives, "Foreign Aid and Counterinsurgency: The United States

Agency for International Development (USAID), and Other United States Foreign Assistance Agencies in Vietnam, 1950–1967," https://www.archives.gov/research /foreign-policy/assistance/vietnam.

4. John F. Kennedy, "Address Before the General Assembly of the United Nations, September 25, 1961," JFK Presidential Library and Museum, https://www.jfklibrary .org/archives/other-resources/john-f-kennedy-speeches/united-nations-19610925.

5. For a more thorough discussion of this dynamic, and the human toll of the Cold War, see Vincent Bevins, *The Jakarta Method: Washington's Anticommunist Crusade and the Mass Murder Program That Shaped Our World* (New York: PublicAffairs, 2020).

6. Collection of Johnson administration documents regarding foreign relations with Haiti, in "Foreign Relations, 1964–1968, Volume XXXII, Dominican Republic; Cuba; Haiti; Guyana," US Department of State Office of the Historian, documents 325–369, https://2001-2009.state.gov/r/pa/ho/frus/johnsonlb/xxxii/44658.htm.

7. Ibid.

8. Ibid.

9. Ronald Reagan, "Text of Reagan's Address to Parliament Addressing Democracy," remarks at British Parliament transcribed by the Associated Press, *New York Times*, June 9, 1982, https://www.nytimes.com/1982/06/09/world/text-of-reagan-s -address-to-parliament-on-promoting-democracy.html.

10. The National Endowment for Democracy's website describes it as a "private, non-profit foundation," despite the fact that the majority of its budget comes from the US government. The National Democratic Institute and the International Republican Institute describe themselves as "non-governmental organizations." They are, however, expressly *governmental* organizations.

11. David Ignatius, "Innocence Abroad: The New Era of Spyless Coups," *Washington Post*, September 22, 1991, https://www.washingtonpost.com/archive/opinions /1991/09/22/innocence-abroad-the-new-world-of-spyless-coups/92bb989a-de6e 1bb8 99b9-162c76b59a16.

12. Andrew S. Levin, "Civil Society and Democratization in Haiti," *Emory International Law Review* 9, no. 2 (Fall 1995): 389–457.

13. Data from World Development Indicators (database), World Bank, Washington, DC, https://databank.worldbank.org/source/world-development-indicators.

14. Jeffrey D. Sachs, "From His First Day in Office, Bush Was Ousting Aristide," *Los Angeles Times*, March 4, 2004, https://www.latimes.com/archives/la-xpm-2004 -mar-04-oe-sachs4-story.html.

15. Monika Kalra Varma, Margaret L. Satterthwaite, Amanda M. Klasing, Tammy Shoranick, Jude Jean, Donna Barry, Mary C. Smith Fawzi, James McKeever, and Evan Lyon, "Wòch nan Soley: The Denial of the Right to Water in Haiti," *Health and Human Rights* 10, no. 2 (December 2008): 67–89, https://www.jstor.org/stable /20460104.

16. Data from World Development Indicators (database), World Bank, Washington, DC, https://data.worldbank.org/indicator/BX.TRF.PWKR.CD.DT?locations=HT.

17. Walt Bogdanich and Jenny Nordberg, "Mixed U.S. Signals Helped Tilt Haiti Toward Chaos," *New York Times*, January 29, 2006, https://www.nytimes.com/2006/01/29 /world/americas/mixed-us-signals-helped-tilt-haiti-toward-chaos.html.

18. Apaid was born in New York and held a US passport. In 2004, he said he had filled out the paperwork to renounce his US citizenship. Haiti does not allow for dual citizenship. See: Carol J. Williams, "Several Figures Emerge to Fill Power Void in Post-Aristide Haiti," *Los Angeles Times*, March 7, 2004, https://www.latimes.com/archives/la-xpm-2004-may-07-fg-leaders7-story.html.

19. Sasha Kramer, "USAID and Haiti," *Counterpunch*, October 14, 2005, https://www.counterpunch.org/2005/10/14/usaid-and-haiti/.

20. US Agency for International Development, *USAID Field Report Haiti Aug 2005* (USAID, August 31, 2005), https://reliefweb.int/report/haiti/usaid-field-report-haiti-aug-2005.

21. Reed Lindsay, "Massacre Erupts at USAID Soccer Game," *Washington Times*, August 29, 2005, https://www.washingtontimes.com/news/2005/aug/29/20050829-100803-6942r/.

22. International Monetary Fund, World Economic Outlook: Database, multiple years.

23. The term was first introduced by Robert Rotberg, a Harvard University professor, who, in 2005, performed an evaluation of OTI programs for USAID. "OTI can be regarded as the special forces of developmental assistance," he wrote. Robert I. Rotberg, "The First Ten Years: An Assessment of the Office of Transition Initiatives," John F. Kennedy School of Government, Harvard University, 2005, https://corpora.tika.apache.org/base/docs/govdocs1/087/087623.pdf.

24. Jake Johnston, "USAID/OTI's Politicized, Problematic Cash-for-Work Programs," Center for Economic and Policy Research, December 21, 2010, https://www.cepr.net/usaidotis-politicized-problematic-cash-for-work-programs/.

25. Dan Beeton and Alexander Main, "The Latin America WikiLeaks Files," *Jacobin*, September 29, 2015, https://jacobin.com/2015/09/latin-america-wikileaks-hugo-chavez-rafael-correa-obama-venezuela-intervention/.

26. USAID Contract with Chemonics International, obtained via Freedom of Information Act request.

27. US Agency for International Development, *USAID Political Party Assistance Policy* (USAID, September 2003), https://pdf.usaid.gov/pdf_docs/pdaby359.pdf.

28. Jake Johnston, "Revealed: USAID Funded Group Supporting Haitian President in 2011," Al Jazeera, July 15, 2015, http://america.aljazeera.com/articles/2015/7/15/usaid-funded-group-supporting-haitian-president.html.

29. Jake Johnston, "USAID's Largest Post-Quake Program Comes to a Close; More Questions Than Answers," Center for Economic and Policy Research, October 8, 2013, https://cepr.net/usaids-largest-post-quake-program-comes-to-a-close-more-questions-than-answers/.

8. THE DISPENSABLE MAN

1. UN General Assembly, official meeting records, A/65/PV.15 (September 24, 2010), https://digitallibrary.un.org/record/693956?ln=en.

2. See, for example: Vincent Bevins, *The Jakarta Method: Washington's Anticommunist Crusade and the Mass Murder Program That Shaped Our World* (New York: PublicAffairs, 2020).

3. For an excellent discussion of this historical dynamic, see Ha-Joon Chang, *Kicking Away the Ladder: Development Strategy in Historical Perspective* (London: Anthem Press, 2002).

4. Mark Weisbrot and Rebecca Ray, "The Scorecard on Development, 1960–2010: Closing the Gap?," Center for Economic and Policy Research, April 14, 2011, https://cepr.net/report/the-scorecard-on-development-1960-2010-closing-the-gap/.

5. Juan Forero, "Documents Show C.I.A. Knew of a Coup Plot in Venezuela," *New York Times*, December 3, 2004, https://www.nytimes.com/2004/12/03/washington/world/documents-show-cia-knew-of-a-coup-plot-in-venezuela.html.

6. UN General Assembly, official meeting records, A/61/PV.12 (September 20, 2006), https://digitallibrary.un.org/record/583260?ln=en.

7. Just two months after the Summit of the Americas, the president of Honduras was overthrown in a military coup. Though Obama condemned it, the United States worked to keep the ousted president from returning to the country and helped to consolidate the coup. Any goodwill that the new US president had in the region evaporated. For more details on the Honduras coup, see Jake Johnston, "How Pentagon Officials May Have Encouraged a 2009 Coup in Honduras," *The Intercept*, August 29, 2017, https://theintercept.com/2017/08/29/honduras-coup-us-defense-departmetnt-center-hemispheric-defense-studies-chds/.

8. David Smith, "Haiti's Exiled Former President Vows to Return," *Guardian*, January 15, 2010, https://www.theguardian.com/world/2010/jan/15/haiti-exiled-former-president-aristide.

9. US Embassy Port-au-Prince, "Haiti: A/S Shannon's Meeting with MINUSTAH SRSG," August 2, 2006, in Public Library of US Diplomacy, WikiLeaks, cable 06PORTAUPRINCE1407_a, https://wikileaks.org/plusd/cables/06PORTAUPRINCE1407_a.html.

10. Cheryl Mills, "Urgent: New Info on Aristide," email to Hillary Clinton, January 18, 2010, in Hillary Clinton Email Archive, email-ID 25789, WikiLeaks, https://wikileaks.org/clinton-emails/emailid/25789.

11. US Embassy Vatican City, "Vatican on Haiti: Church Losses and Responses," January 20, 2010, in Public Library of US Diplomacy, WikiLeaks, cable 10VATICAN11_a, https://wikileaks.org/plusd/cables/10VATICAN11_a.html.

12. While at *VICE*, investigative journalist and FOIA expert Jason Leopold filed a request for Hillary Clinton's emails. They were released in 2016. WikiLeaks has since archived all of them on its website.

13. Brian Concannon Jr., "Counterin[g] Some of the Votes in Haiti," *Counterpunch*, February 15, 2006, https://www.counterpunch.org/2006/02/15/counterint-some-of-the-votes-in-haiti/.

14. Joseph Guyler Delva, "Charges of Vote-Count Manipulation Hit Haiti Poll," Reuters, February 12, 2006, https://reliefweb.int/report/haiti/charges-vote-count-manipulation-hit-haiti-poll.

15. Dan Coughlin and Kim Ives, "WikiLeaks Haiti: The PetroCaribe Files," *The Nation*, June 1, 2011, https://www.thenation.com/article/archive/wikileaks-haiti-petrocaribe-files/.

16. Peter Hallward, "An Interview with Jean-Bertrand Aristide," *London Review of Books*, February 22, 2007, https://www.lrb.co.uk/the-paper/v29/n04/peter-hallward/an-interview-with-jean-bertrand-aristide.

17. US Embassy Port-au-Prince, "Deconstructing Preval," June 16, 2009, in Public Library of US Diplomacy, WikiLeaks, cable 09PORTAUPRINCE575_a, https://wikileaks.org/plusd/cables/09PORTAUPRINCE575_a.html.

18. US Embassy Port-au-Prince, "Donor Ambassadors Initiative Dialogue on Election Support," December 4, 2009, in Public Library of US Diplomacy, WikiLeaks, cable 09 PORTAUPRINCE961_a, https://wikileaks.org/plusd/cables/09PORTAUPRINCE961 _a.html.

19. Kenneth H. Merten, "Briefing by U.S. Ambassador Merten on Haiti," US Department of State, November 23, 2010, https://reliefweb.int/report/haiti/briefing-us -ambassador-merten-haiti.

20. Alexander Main, "Elections in the Time of Cholera, Part IV," Center for Economic and Policy Research, November 28, 2010, https://www.cepr.net/elections-in-the -time-of-cholera-part-iv/.

9. THE ELECTORAL CARNIVAL

1. Janet Reitman, "Beyond Relief: How the World Failed Haiti," *Rolling Stone,* August 4, 2011, https://www.rollingstone.com/politics/politics-news/beyond-relief-how -the-world-failed-haiti-242928/.

2. Center for Economic and Policy Research, "Election Live-Blog," November 28, 2010, https://cepr.net/election-live-blog/.

3. Seitenfus's experiences on election day are recounted in his book, which was recently translated into English. Ricardo Seitenfus, *Haiti: International Dilemmas and Failures* (São Paulo: Alameda Casa Editorial, 2020).

4. Center for Economic and Policy Research, "Election Live-Blog."

5. Catherine Porter, "Haiti's René Préval Says UN Tried to Remove Him," *Toronto Star,* May 13, 2013, https://www.thestar.com/news/world/2013/05/13/haitis_ren_prval _says_un_tried_to_remove_him.html. The *Toronto Star* article quotes from a documentary on the reconstruction period where the president recounts the election day intervention of the international community. See Raoul Peck, *Fatal Assistance* (Haiti/France/US/Belgium, 2013), 100 min. Préval had made similar remarks in January 2011 to journalist Amy Wilentz: Amy Wilentz, "Haiti: Not for Amateurs," *The Nation,* January 27, 2011, https://www.thenation.com/article/archive/haiti-not -amateurs/.

6. Seitenfus, *Haiti: International Dilemmas and Failures.*

7. Associated Press, "Major Candidates Call for Halt to Haiti Election," NBC News, November 28, 2010, https://www.nbcnews.com/id/wbna40402414. And Ivan Watson, "Haitian Candidates Allege Widespread Fraud in National Election," CNN, November 28, 2010, http://www.cnn.com/2010/WORLD/americas/11/28/haiti.elections /index.html.

8. Emily Troutman (@emilytroutman), "I asked @presidentmicky if he was the mastermind of today's event. He said, 'You always ask the weirdest questions.' lolllllll," Twitter, 2:15 P.M., November 28, 2010, https://twitter.com/emilytroutman/status /8962153356730368.

9. The following account comes from Seitenfus, *Haiti: International Dilemmas and Failures.*

10. Elise Ackerman, "His Music Rules in Haiti," *Miami New Times,* May 29, 1997, https://www.miaminewtimes.com/news/his-music-rules-in-haiti-6360759 ?showFullText=true.

11. For a firsthand account of the day's events, see Jonathan M. Katz, *The Big Truck That*

Went By: How the World Came to Save Haiti and Left Behind a Disaster (New York: St. Martin's Press, 2013).

12. Agence France-Presse, "Haïti : Manigat a de 'bonnes chances,'" *Le Figaro*, November 29, 2010,https://www.lefigaro.fr/flash-actu/2010/11/29/97001–20101129FILWWW00675 -haiti-manigat-a-de-bonnes-chances.php.

13. Seitenfus, *Haiti: International Dilemmas and Failures*.

14. Pascal Fletcher, "Interview—Haiti Elections Process 'Stabilized,' on Track—UN," Reuters, November 30, 2010, https://reliefweb.int/report/haiti/interview-haiti -elections-process-stabilized-track-un.

15. The following account comes from a book written by one of the electoral councilors at the time: Ginette Chérubin, *Le ventre pourri de la bête: Une femme dans les allées du pouvoir et la saga d'une élection fissurée* (Port-au-Prince: Éditions de l'Université d'État d'Haïti, 2013).

16. Anonymous official, message to author, 2015.

10. THE STATISTICAL COUP

1. Center for Economic and Policy Research, "Elections Were Marred Long Before November 28," December 8, 2010, https://cepr.net/elections-were-marred-long -before-november-28/.

2. A source claimed to have been trapped in a hotel that night, unable to leave because of the barricades and violence. While they rested on the couch in the lobby, a group of armed men entered the hotel in a jubilant mood. Asked how they were able to make it to the hotel given the situation outside, one of the men responded that it had been them at the barricades. The source said that one of those individuals was Laurent Lamothe, a close friend of Martelly and the country's future prime minister.

3. The United States experienced this firsthand in the 2020 election and with the January 6, 2021, storming of the US Capitol Building. At the time there was much commentary on how this would affect the US "democracy promotion" activities abroad. For example: Emma Ashford, "America Can't Promote Democracy Abroad. It Can't Even Protect It at Home," *Foreign Policy*, January 7, 2021, https://foreignpolicy.com /2021/01/07/america-cant-promote-protect-democracy-abroad/.

4. Jake Johnston, "Clinton E-Mails Point to US Intervention in 2010 Haiti Elections," Center for Economic and Policy Research, September 7, 2016, https://cepr.net /clinton-e-mails-point-to-us-intervention-in-2010-haiti-elections/.

5. Jake Johnston, "Revealed: USAID Funded Group Supporting Haitian President in 2011."

6. René Préval, interview with author, April 2016, Washington, DC.

7. Mark Weisbrot and Jake Johnston, "Haiti's Fatally Flawed Election," Center for Economic and Policy Research, January 8, 2011, https://cepr.net/report/haitis-fatally -flawed-election/.

8. The point here is not that Célestin should have moved on to the second round; it is simply that there was no basis for the decision the OAS and others made regarding the outcome of the election. It was clear, well ahead of the vote, that the election would not be taking place in a totally free nor fair environment. The problem was trying to move forward with the flawed vote rather than rerunning it.

9. René Préval, interview with author, April 2015, Washington, DC. And anonymous US Embassy employee, message to author, 2015.

10. Fritz Scheuren, discussion with author, 2011, Washington, DC.

11. Jean-Max Bellerive, interview with author, January 2015, Haiti. In 2014, speaking at a symposium on Haiti in Washington, DC, Colin Granderson confirmed the role that international actors had played in the 2010–2011 electoral process. "The international community intervened, working with representatives of the private sector, and managed to get two of the candidates to reverse themselves, to renege on their commitment, and this rescued the electoral process," he said, adding: "But what I think was most unsettling was that following this attempt to have these elections cancelled, was the intervention of certain members of the international community basically calling on President Préval to step down." See Jake Johnston, "Head of OAS Electoral Mission in Haiti: International Community Tried to Remove Préval on Election Day," Center for Economic and Policy Research, June 6, 2014, https://cepr.net/head-of-oas-electoral-mission-in-haiti-international-community-tried-to-remove-preval-on-election-day/.

12. Damian Merlo, interview with author, February 2016, Washington, DC.

13. William Booth, "Duvalier's Return Adds to Turmoil in Haiti," *Washington Post*, January 18, 2011, https://www.washingtonpost.com/national/duvaliers-return-adds-to-turmoil-in-haiti/2011/01/17/ABwtLkD_story.html.

14. Ibid.

15. Center for Economic and Policy Research, "US, UN Increasing Pressure on Haiti to Accept Flawed Election," January 20, 2011, https://cepr.net/us-un-increasing-pressure-on-haiti-to-accept-flawed-election/.

16. Cheryl Mills, "Update on Dr Meeting," email to Hillary Clinton, January 22, 2011, in Hillary Clinton Email Archive, WikiLeaks, email-ID 6830, https://wikileaks.org/clinton-emails/emailid/6830.

17. Cheryl Mills, "Re:," email to Hillary Clinton, January 29, 2011, in Hillary Clinton Email Archive, WikiLeaks, email-ID 28945, https://wikileaks.org/clinton-emails/emailid/28945.

18. Hillary Clinton, "Interview with Wendell Theodore of Radio Metropole," US Department of State, January 30, 2011, https://2009-2017.state.gov/secretary/20092013clinton/rm/2011/01/155611.htm.

19. Jean-Max Bellerive, interview with author, January 2015, Haiti.

20. Center for Economic and Policy Research, "In Haiti, Controversy over Election Continues; In U.S., Media Goes Silent," February 15, 2011, https://cepr.net/in-haiti-controversy-over-election-continues-in-us-media-goes-silent/.

21. Mark Weisbrot, "Aristide Should Be Allowed to Return to Haiti," *HuffPost*, January 21, 2011, https://www.huffpost.com/entry/aristide-should-be-allowe_b_812401.

22. Isabeau Doucet and David Smith, "Jean-Bertrand Aristide Defies US by Heading Back to Haiti," *The Guardian*, March 17, 2011, https://www.theguardian.com/world/2011/mar/17/jean-bertrand-aristide-haiti-return.

23. Associated Press, "Back in Haiti, Aristide Gets Celebrity Welcome," CBS News, March 18, 2011, https://www.cbsnews.com/news/back-in-haiti-aristide-gets-celebrity-welcome/.

24. Cheryl Mills, "1600 Update," email to Hillary Clinton, March 19, 2011, in Hillary

Clinton Email Archive, WikiLeaks, email-ID 6568, https://wikileaks.org/clinton-emails/emailid/6568.

25. Martelly's campaign advisor later told me he wanted to contest the results because their own polling showed they had won 69 percent of the vote. It was Martelly's favorite number.

26. As recounted in Ricardo Seitenfus, *Haiti: International Dilemmas and Failures* (São Paulo: Alameda Casa Editorial, 2020).

27. For a detailed accounting of this, see: Peter Hallward, *Damming the Flood: Haiti and the Politics of Containment* (New York: Verso Books, 2007).

11. THE COMMISSION

1. For more on the commission and the overall failure of the reconstruction period, see Raoul Peck, *Fatal Assistance* (Haiti/France/US/Belgium, 2013), 100 min.

2. Interim Haiti Reconstruction Commission members' letter to Commission co-chairs, *Le Matin* newspaper, December 14, 2010, translated by Isabeau Doucet and reprinted in Norman Girvan, "Protest Letter from Haitian HRC Members to Commission Co-Chairs," *Real News Network,* December 31, 2010, https://therealnews.com/protest-letter-from-haitian-ihrc-members-to-commission-co-chairs.

3. Jake Johnston, "Outsourcing Haiti," *Boston Review,* January 16, 2014, https://www.bostonreview.net/articles/jake-johnston-haiti-earthquake-aid-caracol/.

4. Ibid.

5. Martin Kaste, "After Quake in Haiti, Who's the Boss?," NPR, March 31, 2010, https://www.npr.org/templates/story/story.php?storyId=125328026.

6. Cheryl Mills, "Approval," email to Doug Band, April 14, 2010, in Hillary Clinton Email Archive, WikiLeaks, email-ID 3054, https://wikileaks.org/clinton-emails/emailid/3054.

7. Gabriel Verret, interviews with author, multiple dates, Haiti.

8. René Préval, interview with author, April 2016, Washington, DC.

9. Interim Haiti Recovery Commission, "Minutes of the Board Meeting," June 17, 2010.

10. Former Haitian government official, interview with author, 2013, Haiti.

11. *Democracy Now!,* "Land Ownership at the Crux of Haiti's Stalled Reconstruction," July 14, 2010, https://www.democracynow.org/2010/7/14/land_ownership_at_the_crux_of.

12. Josef Leitman, interview with author, March 2013, Washington, DC.

13. Former commission official, interview with author, January 2013, Haiti.

14. Interim Haiti Recovery Commission, "Minutes of the Board Meeting," August 17, 2010.

15. US Government Accountability Office, *Haiti Reconstruction: U.S. Efforts Have Begun, Expanded Oversight Still to Be Implemented*, Report to Congressional Committees (GAO-11-415, May 19, 2011), https://www.gao.gov/products/gao-11-415.

16. Trenton Daniel, "Haiti PM Softens Stance on Clinton Quake Panel," Associated Press, May 26, 2011, found on *Boston.com,* http://archive.boston.com/business/articles/2011/05/26/haiti_pm_softens_stance_on_clinton_quake_panel/.

17. Hillary Clinton, "New PM Would End Haiti Quake Panel (AP)," email to Cheryl Mills, May 25, 2011, in Hillary Clinton Email Archive, WikiLeaks, email-ID 24198, https://wikileaks.org/clinton-emails/emailid/24198.

18. Jake Johnston, "Haiti Reconstruction Fund: Building Back . . . When?," Center for Economic and Policy Research, April 12, 2012, https://cepr.net/haiti-reconstruction -fund-building-back-when/.

19. Hillary Clinton, "Ambassador Meets with President-Elect Martelly," email to Cheryl Mills, April 6, 2011, in Hillary Clinton Email Archive, WikiLeaks, email-ID 24351, https://wikileaks.org/clinton-emails/emailid/24351.

20. Hillary Clinton, "Remarks with Haitian President-Elect Michel Martelly After Their Meeting," US Department of State, April 21, 2011, https://reliefweb.int/report/haiti /remarks-haitian-president-elect-michel-martelly-after-their-meeting.

21. The following account is based on internal emails obtained through FOIA.

12. THE SLOGAN

1. Associated Press, "Inauguration of Michel Martelly as Haitian President," May 14, 2011, uploaded on July 30, 2015, AP Archive, YouTube video, 0:02:51, https://www .youtube.com/watch?v=1x9UmC0KDKQ.

2. Michel Martelly, "Important Moments of the Speech of Michel Martelly," transcribed in *Haiti Libre,* May 15, 2011, https://www.haitilibre.com/en/news-2957 -haiti-inauguration-important-moments-of-the-speech-of-michel-martelly.html.

3. Laurent Dubois, *Haiti: The Aftershocks of History* (New York: Metropolitan Books, 2012).

4. Clyde H. Farnsworth, "Haiti's Allure for U.S. Business," *New York Times,* June 17, 1984, https://www.nytimes.com/1984/06/17/business/haiti-s-allure-for-us-business .html.

5. Farnsworth, "Haiti's Allure for U.S. Business."

6. The interview is from *Bitter Cane,* released in 1983 by Director Jacques Arcelin. The film was made clandestinely in Haiti during the Duvalier dictatorship. The entire work provides rich background on migration from Haiti and its connection to Haiti's foreign-imposed development model. Jacques Arcelin, *Bitter Cane* (Haiti Films/Crowing Rooster Arts, 1983), documentary film, 75 min, https://vimeo.com /125611719.

7. Ayiti Kale Je, "Haiti—Open for Business," *Haiti Grassroots Watch,* November 29, 2011, http://haitigrassrootswatch.squarespace.com/haiti-grassroots-watch-engli /2011/11/29/haiti-open-for-business.html.

8. AFL-CIO Solidarity Center, *A Post-Earthquake Living Wage Estimate for Apparel Workers in the Sonapi Export Processing Zone* (Port-au-Prince: Solidarity Center, March 3, 2011), https://www.solidaritycenter.org/wp-content/uploads/2014/12 /haiti_livingwagesnapshot030311.pdf.

9. Dan Coughlin and Kim Ives, "WikiLeaks Haiti: Let Them Live on $3 a Day," *The Nation,* June 1, 2011, https://www.thenation.com/article/archive/wikileaks-haiti -let-them-live-3-day/.

10. US Embassy Port-au-Prince, "Minimum Wage Demonstrations Become Violent," June 19, 2009, in Public Library of US Diplomacy, WikiLeaks, cable 09PORTAUPRINCE 592_a, https://search.wikileaks.org/plusd/cables/09PORTAUPRINCE592_a.html.

11. Timothy Schwartz, *The Great Haiti Humanitarian Aid Swindle* (CreateSpace Independent Publishing Platform, 2017).

12. A partial quote from Sassine was used in mid-February in the *Washington Post;*

the full quote only aired in an NPR piece a few weeks later. Juan Forero, "Haiti's Elite Sees Business Opportunities Emerging from Reconstruction," *Washington Post*, February 15, 2010, https://www.washingtonpost.com/wp-dyn/content/article /2010/02/14/AR2010021403322.html. And Juan Forero, "After Quake, Haiti Seeks Better Business Climate," *Morning Edition*, NPR, March 10, 2010, https://www.npr .org/templates/story/story.php?storyId=124077512.

13. Perhaps one of the most well-known books about this dynamic comes from Naomi Klein, whose 2008 book, *The Shock Doctrine*, deeply influenced my own thinking and was a source of inspiration for this project: Naomi Klein, *The Shock Doctrine: The Rise of Disaster Capitalism* (London: Picador, 2008).

14. Hillary Clinton, "Call List," email to Lauren Jiloty and Huma Abedin, June 27, 2010, in Hillary Clinton Email Archive, WikiLeaks, email-ID 25, https://wikileaks.org /clinton-emails/emailid/25.

15. Many of the details relating to the deal between the State Department and Sae-A, the Korean manufacturing giant, were first reported in Deborah Sontag, "Earth-quake Relief Where Haiti Wasn't Broken," *New York Times*, July 5, 2012, https:// www.nytimes.com/2012/07/06/world/americas/earthquake-relief-where-haiti -wasnt-broken.html.

16. Inter-American Development Bank, "Haiti, United States, IDB and Korean Firm Sign Industrial Park Pact," news release, January 11, 2011, https://www.iadb.org/en /news/haiti-united-states-idb-and-korean-firm-sign-industrial-park-pact.

17. Ayiti Kale Je, "Haiti—Open for Business."

18. ActionAid, *Building Back Better? The Caracol Industrial Park and Post-Earthquake Aid to Haiti* (Washington, DC: ActionAid, January 2015), https://www.actionaidusa .org/wp-content/uploads/2016/10/Building-Back-Better.pdf.

19. Associated Press, "Clinton Joins Martelly Advisory Board of 32 to Promote Haiti Investment," *South Florida Times*, September 15, 2011, http://www.sfltimes.com /news/caribbeannews/clinton-joins-martelly-advisory-board-of-32-to-promote -haiti-investment.

20. Larry Luxner, "Two Years After Quake, Haiti Lobbies for Investment," *Washington Diplomat*, January 2, 2012, https://washdiplomat.com/two-years-after-quake-haiti -lobbies-for-investment/.

21. Lois Romano, "Michel Martelly, Haiti's New President, Gets Mixed Reviews," *Daily Beast*, September 21, 2011, https://www.thedailybeast.com/michel-martelly-haitis -new-president-gets-mixed-reviews.

22. Sontag, "Earthquake Relief Where Haiti Wasn't Broken."

23. Ayiti Kale Je, "Haiti—Open for Business."

24. Chemonics' actions in support of the Caracol Industrial Park are detailed in inter-nal reports and emails obtained through FOIA.

25. Cheryl Mills, "Industrial Park Traffic," email to Hillary Clinton, November 28, 2011, in Hillary Clinton Email Archive, WikiLeaks, email-ID 25051, https://wikileaks.org /clinton-emails/emailid/25051.

26. Inter-American Development Bank, "Haiti Investment Forum Draws Hundreds of Businesspeople," news release, November 29, 2011, https://www.iadb.org/en/news /haiti-investment-forum-draws-hundreds-businesspeople.

27. Sontag, "Earthquake Relief Where Haiti Wasn't Broken."

13. THE MUSICIAN AND HIS BAND

1. Many key biographical details concerning Martelly come from Liz Balmaseda, "The Sweet Life of Sweet Micky," *Palm Beach Post,* June 12, 1997.
2. Elise Ackerman, "His Music Rules in Haiti," *Miami New Times,* May 29, 1997, https://www.miaminewtimes.com/news/his-music-rules-in-haiti-6360759 ?showFullText=true.
3. Michael E. Miller, "Michel Martelly Is Haiti's New President. But the Former Palm Beach County Resident Has a Dark Side," *New Times* (Broward/Palm Beach, FL), June 9, 2011, https://www.browardpalmbeach.com/news/michel-martelly-is-haitis-new -president-but-the-former-palm-beach-county-resident-has-a-dark-side-6344960.
4. Balmaseda, "The Sweet Life of Sweet Micky."
5. Ackerman, "His Music Rules in Haiti."
6. Ibid.
7. Ibid.
8. Michael Norton, "Popular Singer Flees Haiti After Being Warned of Plot," Associated Press, September 2, 1996.
9. Ackerman, "His Music Rules in Haiti." Ackerman reported that Martelly paid the bond for Champagne. Florida court records show that the address Champagne listed when he was arrested was Martelly's apartment.
10. Ackerman, "His Music Rules in Haiti."
11. Peter Prengaman, "Haiti Protests Draw Musicians, Artists," Associated Press, December 23, 2003.
12. Balmaseda, "The Sweet Life of Sweet Micky."
13. Ben Patterson, *Sweet Micky for President* (Haiti/Canada/US: Prasperity Productions/Onslot Films/RYOT Films, January 2015), film, 89 min.
14. Damien Merlo, interview with author, 2016, Washington, DC.
15. Merlo interview.
16. Jennifer Wells, "Campaign Fixer Sweetens Prospects for Haiti's Michel Martelly," *Toronto Star,* December 6, 2010, https://www.thestar.com/news/world/2010/12/06 /campaign_fixer_sweetens_prospects_for_haitis_michel_martelly.html.
17. Frances Robles, "Haiti Candidate Martelly Lost Three S. Florida Properties to Foreclosure," *Miami Herald,* March 7, 2011, preserved in *Wehaitians.com,* http://www .wehaitians.com/haiti%20presidential%20candidate%20Martelly%20says%20I%20 stop%20paying%20lost%20three%20properties%20to%20foreclosure.htm.
18. The analysis of shell companies and property holdings is based on public documents available from Florida's Clerks of Court, corporation databases, and property records.
19. Juan Iglesias, phone conversation with author, April 2016.
20. Bill Hardin, phone conversation with author, April 2016. In April 2016, a Global Voice Group spokesperson responded to my questions regarding Lamothe and Martelly's ownership stake in the company, the British Virgin Islands–based shell company Lightfoot Ventures, and their ownership of the property at 560 Gate Lane. The spokesperson denied that Lamothe or Martelly had any ownership stake in Global Voice Group, Lightfoot Ventures, or the home at 560 Gate Lane. Further, he added that any loan taken out in connection with the property had nothing to do with Martelly or his political campaign. He further added that "any interest that

Laurent Lamothe and/or Michel Martelly may have held in these entities was relinquished entirely before getting involved in Haitian politics." This was not true, according to multiple sources who worked with both over the years. In 2021, the International Consortium of Investigative Journalists (ICIJ) obtained a massive trove of leaked documents pertaining to offshore shell companies. Some of the documents concerned Lamothe, Global Voice Group, and Lightfoot Ventures. "In 2010, Lamothe resigned as director of one of those companies, Lightfoot Ventures Ltd., but remained as beneficial owner. Trident Trust email correspondence describes Lightfoot Ventures as 'one of the major telecommunications providers in Haiti . . . with offices in South Africa, the U.S. and a number of other countries,'" ICIJ reported at the time. "The Power Players: Haiti, Former Prime Minister, Laurent Lamothe," International Consortium of Investigative Journalists, 2021, https://projects.icij.org/investigations/pandora-papers/power-players/en/player/laurent-lamothe.

14. THE GHOSTS OF THE PAST

1. Jessica Desvarieux, "Duvalier 2.0? Rebranding Haiti's Former Dictator," *Time*, January 24, 2011, https://content.time.com/time/world/article/0,8599,2044039,00.html.
2. For far more on Chamblain and others involved in Haiti's paramilitary history, see Jeb Sprague, *Paramilitarism and the Assault on Democracy in Haiti* (New York: Monthly Review Press, 2012).
3. Trenton Daniel, "Haiti Gov't Links to Old Regime Prompt Scrutiny," Associated Press, October 13, 2011, found in *San Diego Union-Tribune*, https://www.sandiegouniontribune.com/sdut-haiti-govt-links-to-old-regime-prompt-scrutiny-2011oct13-story.html.
4. William Booth, "In Haiti, Former Dictator 'Baby Doc' Duvalier Is Thriving," *Washington Post,* January 17, 2012, https://www.washingtonpost.com/world/americas/in-haiti-the-former-dictator-duvalier-thrives/2012/01/13/gIQAaYbM6P_story.html.
5. Joseph B. Treaster, "Haitians Report Tracing Transfer of Millions Abroad by Duvalier," *New York Times*, May 12, 1986, https://www.nytimes.com/1986/05/12/world/haitians-report-tracing-transfer-of-millions-abroad-by-duvalier.html.
6. Donald W. Swinton, "Federal Court Awards $500 Million Judgment Against Duvalier," Associated Press, January 20, 1988, https://apnews.com/article/1a6410f510ee2ca5397a9a7a6e6895cc.
7. Dan Coughlin and Kim Ives, "WikiLeaks Haiti: The PetroCaribe Files," *The Nation*, June 1, 2011, https://www.thenation.com/article/archive/wikileaks-haiti-petrocaribe-files/.
8. An additional aspect worth considering is if US officials encouraged the relationship as a way to collect intelligence on Venezuela. Interestingly, in 2015, two nephews of the Venezuelan president were arrested and accused of drug trafficking. The arrest took place in Haiti, where the nephews had been lured by an undercover agent. They were quickly transferred to the US without a formal extradition process.
9. Many of the contracts under question had been awarded to a Dominican firm owned by a prominent politician, Félix Bautista. Years later, a Dominican investigative journalist obtained internal receipts that appeared to indicate that Bautista had given hundreds of thousands of dollars to candidates in Haiti's 2010 election,

including both Manigat and Martelly. Manigat even acknowledged she had taken the money. In 2018, Bautista was sanctioned by the US Treasury Department, which noted: "Bautista has reportedly engaged in bribery in relation to his position as a Senator, and is alleged to have engaged in corruption in Haiti, where he used his connections to win public works contracts to help rebuild Haiti following several natural disasters, including one case where his company was paid over $10 million for work it had not completed." See US Department of the Treasury, "Treasury Sanctions Two Individuals and Five Entities Under Global Magnitsky," press release, June 12, 2018, https://home.treasury.gov/news/press-releases/sm0411.

10. Hillary Clinton, "LG's Messages All Attached," email to Robert Russo, February 27, 2012, in Hillary Clinton Email Archive, WikiLeaks, email-ID 18613, https://wikileaks.org/clinton-emails/emailid/18613.

11. In a 2013 deposition, Lamothe said that the owners of Global Voice Group were himself, Michel Martelly, Patrice Baker, and Franck G. Cine.

12. Hatab Fadera, "Gambia: National Team Gets a New Foreign Coach," *Daily Observer* (Banjul), April 25, 2007, reprinted in *AllAfrica*, https://allafrica.com/stories/200704250699.html.

13. Damien Merlo, interview with author, 2016, Washington, DC.

14. Jean-Max Bellerive, discussion with author, multiple years, Haiti.

15. Global Voice Group, "International Gateway Traffic Verification System Now Fully Operational in Rwanda," PR Newswire, Cision, November 8, 2012, https://www.prnewswire.com/news-releases/international-gateway-traffic-verification-system-now-fully-operational-in-rwanda-177810111.html.

16. Stephanie Strom, "A Billionaire Lends Haiti a Hand," *New York Times*, January 6, 2012, https://www.nytimes.com/2012/01/07/business/digicels-denis-obrien-helps-rebuild-haiti.html.

17. Sara Rafsky, "Was Letter to Haiti Website Just Part of Martelly's Theatrics?," Committee to Protect Journalists, February 24, 2012, https://cpj.org/2012/02/was-letter-to-haiti-website-just-part-of-martellys/.

18. Paul Cullen, "Attracting Trade Now Focus for Haiti's President," *Irish Times*, January 30, 2012, https://www.irishtimes.com/news/attracting-trade-now-focus-for-haiti-s-president-1.454048.

19. Associated Press, "Haiti Names Sean Penn 'Ambassador at Large,'" CBS News, February 1, 2012, https://www.cbsnews.com/news/haiti-names-sean-penn-ambassador-at-large/.

20. *Caribbean Journal*, "Petra Nemcova Joins Sean Penn as Haiti's Newest Goodwill Ambassador," June 6, 2011, https://www.caribjournal.com/2012/06/11/petra-nemcova-joins-sean-penn-as-haitis-newest-goodwill-ambassador/.

21. Sarah Fitzmaurice, "Sean Penn and Petra Nemcova Enjoy Romantic Mini-Break in Mexico," *Daily Mail*, June 1, 2012, https://www.dailymail.co.uk/tvshowbiz/article-2153282/Sean-Penn-Petra-Nemcova-enjoy-romantic-mini-break-Mexico.html.

22. In that same 2013 deposition, Lamothe said he began dating Nemcova in December 2012.

23. Susana Ferreira, "The Clintons in Haiti: Can an Industrial Park Save the Country?," *Time*, October 25, 2012, https://world.time.com/2012/10/25/the-clintons-in-haiti-can-an-industrial-park-save-the-country/.

24. Larry Luxner, "Two Years After Quake, Haiti Lobbies for Investment," *Washington Diplomat,* January 2, 2012, https://washdiplomat.com/two-years-after-quake-haiti -lobbies-for-investment/.

15. THE PROMISED LAND

1. Deborah Sontag, "Rebuilding in Haiti Lags After Billions in Post-Quake Aid," *New York Times,* December 23, 2012, https://www.nytimes.com/2012/12/24/world /americas/in-aiding-quake-battered-haiti-lofty-hopes-and-hard-truths.html.

2. Lauren Moraski, "Golden Globes 2013: Former President Clinton Makes Surprise Appearance," CBS News, January 15, 2013, https://www.cbsnews.com/news/golden -globes-2013-former-president-clinton-makes-surprise-appearance/.

3. Beginning a few months after the earthquake, I started to compile my own database of US contracts and grants for work in Haiti. All the data is from USASpending.gov, though the calculations are my own.

4. Timothy Schwartz, *The Great Haiti Humanitarian Aid Swindle* (CreateSpace Independent Publishing Platform, 2017).

5. For more on Haiti's history, a good introductory text is Laurent Dubois, *Haiti: The Aftershocks of History* (New York: Metropolitan Books, 2012).

6. *Democracy Now!,* "Land Ownership at the Crux of Haiti's Stalled Reconstruction," July 14, 2010, https://www.democracynow.org/2010/7/14/land_ownership_at_the _crux_of.

7. Jonathan Katz, "Fights over Land Stalling Haiti Earthquake Recovery," Associated Press, July 11, 2010, found at CBS News, https://www.cbsnews.com/news/fights -over-land-stall-haiti-quake-recovery/.

8. For much more on the Mozayik community and their struggle for safe housing, see Jon Bougher, *Mozayik* (Haiti, 2013), film, 32 min.

9. Sontag, "Rebuilding in Haiti Lags After Billions in Post-Quake Aid."

10. Jake Johnston, "Haiti's Increasingly Hidden Displacement Disaster," Center for Economic and Policy Research, January 7, 2013, https://cepr.net/haitis-increasingly -hidden-displacement-disaster/.

11. As seen in Bougher, *Mozayik.*

12. Mona Augustin, interview with author, January 2013, Haiti.

13. Johnston, "Haiti's Increasingly Hidden Displacement Disaster."

14. Ayiti Kale Je, "Housing Exposition Exposes Waste, Cynicism," *Haiti Grassroots Watch,* September 24, 2012, http://haitigrassrootswatch.squarespace.com/20eng.

15. Jake Johnston, "Outsourcing Haiti," *Boston Review,* January 16, 2014, https://www .bostonreview.net/articles/jake-johnston-haiti-earthquake-aid-caracol/.

16. Guilaine Victor, interview with author, January 2013, Haiti.

17. For further discussion of this dynamic, see Schwartz, *The Great Haiti Humanitarian Aid Swindle.*

18. Georges E. Fouron, "Haiti's Painful Evolution from Promised Land to Migrant-Sending Nation," Migration Policy Institute, August 19, 2020, https://www.migrationpolicy .org/article/haiti-painful-evolution-promised-land-migrant-sending-nation.

19. Philip Bump, "A Searchable Index of Clinton Foundation Donors," *Washington Post,* February 26, 2015, https://www.washingtonpost.com/news/the-fix/wp/2015 /02/26/a-searchable-index-of-clinton-foundation-donors/.

20. Fulton Armstrong, discussion with author, February 2023, virtual.

21. Chemonics' role in securing land for the Caracol Industrial Park's housing complex is detailed in internal documents obtained through FOIA.

16. THE BATTLE FOR REFORM

1. Bill Vastine, discussion with author, January 2013, Haiti.
2. Martin Patriquin, "'We Are Living in Hell'—Haiti Six Months Later," *Maclean's,* July 22, 2010, https://www.macleans.ca/news/world/we-are-living-in-hell/.
3. Jake Johnston, "GAO Report Suggests That USAID Remains 'More of a Contracting Agency Than an Operational Agency,'" Center for Economic and Policy Research, November 21, 2011, https://cepr.net/usaid-more-of-a-contracting-agency-than-an -operational-agency/.
4. Anonymous USAID official, interview with author, October 2011, Haiti.
5. Vijay Ramachandran and Julie Walz, "US Spending in Haiti: The Need for Greater Transparency and Accountability," Center for Global Development, February 2013, https://www.cgdev.org/sites/default/files/archive/doc/full_text/CGDBriefs/1426965 /US-Spending-in-Haiti-The-Need-for-Greater-Transparency-and-Accountability .html.
6. Jake Johnston, "With Poor Track Records For-Profit Development Companies Team Up to Fight Reform," Center for Economic and Policy Research, December 1, 2011, https://www.cepr.net/with-poor-track-records-for-profit-development-companies -team-up-to-fight-reform/.
7. Martha Mendoza and Trenton Daniel, "US Pledge to Rebuild Haiti Not Being Met," Associated Press, July 21, 2012, preserved in Internet Archive, July 25, 2012, http:// web.archive.org/web/20120725081754/http://news.yahoo.com/us-pledge-rebuild -haiti-not-being-met-170346036.html.
8. Charles Kenny, "It's Time to Reform USAID," *Bloomberg,* March 18, 2013, https:// www.bloomberg.com/news/articles/2013-03-18/its-time-to-reform-usaid.
9. Jake Johnston, "Barriers to Reform: The Big Business of Shipping Food Aid," Center for Economic and Policy Research, November 2, 2011, https://www.cepr.net /barriers-to-reform-the-big-business-of-shipping-food-aid/.
10. Jon Greenberg, "Most People Clueless on U.S. Foreign Aid Spending," *PolitiFact,* November 9, 2016, https://www.politifact.com/factchecks/2016/nov/09/john-kerry /yep-most-people-clueless-us-foreign-aid-spending/.
11. Kenny, "It's Time to Reform USAID."
12. UN Office of the Special Envoy for Haiti, *International Assistance to Haiti: Key Facts as of December 2012,* December 2012, https://www.lessonsfromhaiti.org/download /International_Assistance/1-overall-key-facts.pdf.
13. Mike McIntire, "Haiti and Africa Projects Shed Light on Clinton's Public-Private Web," *New York Times,* October 16, 2016, https://www.nytimes.com/2016/10/17/us /hillary-clinton-cheryl-mills.html.
14. Data from: "Secteur Réel," Banque de Republique d'Haiti, https://www.brh.ht /statistiques/secteur-reel/.
15. Business Wire, "Clinton Bush Haiti Fund Invests to Complete Construction of Haitian-Owned Hotel and Conference Center in Port au Prince," May 9, 2011, https://www.businesswire.com/news/home/20110509007201/en/Clinton-Bush -Haiti-Fund-Invests-to-Complete-Construction-of-Haitian-owned-Hotel-and -Conference-Center-in-Port-au-Prince.

16. CNN, "Clinton Foundation Facilitates $45 Million Haiti Hotel Deal," November 28, 2011, https://www.cnn.com/2011/11/28/world/americas/haiti-hotel-clinton/index .html.

17. World Bank Group, "IFC Invests in Haiti Hotel to Support Essential Business Infrastructure, Job Creation and Tourism," July 3, 2013, https://pressroom.ifc.org/all /pages/PressDetail.aspx?ID=18641.

18. International Finance Corporation, *Poverty and Social Inclusion in Haiti: Social Gains at Timid Pace,* press detail, World Bank, 2014, http://documents1.worldbank .org/curated/en/643771468257721618/pdf/895220BRI00pau00Box385284B00PU BLIC0.pdf.

19. Jake Johnston, "Another Inspector General Audit, Another Failing Grade for USAID in Haiti," Center for Economic and Policy Research, March 5, 2013, https:// www.cepr.net/another-inspector-general-audit-another-failing-grade-for-usaid-in -haiti/.

20. Center for Economic and Policy Research, "'Assessing Progress in Haiti Act' Passed by Congress," June 25, 2014, https://www.cepr.net/assessing-progress-in-haiti-act -passed-by-congress/.

21. Amy Davidson Sorkin, "What the Clinton Foundation Is Costing Hillary," *New Yorker,* February 26, 2015, https://www.newyorker.com/news/amy-davidson/what -the-clinton-foundation-is-costing-hillary.

22. Matthew Mosk, Brian Ross, Brian Epstein, and Cho Park, "In Haiti, a Factory Where Big Money, State Department and the Clintons Meet," ABC News, October 11, 2016, https://abcnews.go.com/Politics/%20aiti-factory-big-money-state -department-clintons-meet/story?id=42729714.

17. THE DIPLOMAT'S JOB

1. Diplomatic cable, obtained by author via Freedom of Information Act request.

2. Former Haitian government official, interview with author, January 2015, Haiti.

3. Associated Press, "Haiti Prime Minister Quits Following Violent Protests," *The Guardian,* December 14, 2014. https://www.theguardian.com/world/2014/dec/14 /haiti-prime-minister-quits-following-violent-protests.

4. Pamela A. White, interview with author, June 2016, Virginia.

5. Larissa Liburd, "An Interview with Pamela A. White, U.S. Ambassador to Haiti," *The Politic,* August 14, 2013, https://thepolitic.org/article/an-interview-with-pamela-a -white-u-s-ambassador-to-haiti.

6. Patrick Saint-Pré, "L'Exécutif signe un nouvel accord avec les partis politiques," *Le Nouvelliste,* January 12, 2015, https://www.lenouvelliste.com/article/140233 /lexecutif-signe-un-nouvel-accord-avec-les-partis-politiques.

7. US Embassy Port-au-Prince, "Statement of the US Embassy in Haiti on the Political Impasse," press release, January 11, 2015, preserved in Internet Archive, September 10, 2015, https://web.archive.org/web/20150910042135/http://haiti.usembassy.gov /press-rel-pol-impasse-usemb-statement.html.

8. Email exchanges involving Cheryl D. Mills, Pamela A. White, and Thomas C. Adams, July 15, 2011, in Hillary Clinton Email Archive, WikiLeaks, email-ID 8838, https://wikileaks.org/clinton-emails/emailid/8838.

9. White interview.

18. THE PARTY

1. International electoral official, interview with author, August 2015, Haiti.
2. Democracy International, *Haiti Democracy, Human Rights, and Governance (DRG) Assessment* (USAID, October 2016), https://pdf.usaid.gov/pdf_docs/PA00MHFX .pdf.
3. Jean-Max Bellerive, interview with author, January 2015, Haiti.
4. Roudy Choute, interview with author, April 2015, Haiti.
5. Danio Darius, "PHTK prêt pour les elections, selon Danielle St-Lot," *Le Nouvelliste*, December 19, 2013, https://www.lenouvelliste.com/article/125480/phtk-pret-pour -les-elections-selon-danielle-st-lot.
6. Haiti Inter Presse, "La Présidente du Parti Haïtien Tet Kale (PHTK), Ann Valérie Timothée Milfort, a reçu samedi 17 Mai 2014, le Représentant Spécial Adjoint pour la Mission des Nations Unies pour la Stabilisation en Haïti (MINUSTAH), Carl Alexandre, a appris Haïti Inter Presse," May 17, 2014, https://haitiinterpresse .com/la-presidente-du-parti-haitien-tet-kale-phtk-ann-valerie-timothee-milfort-a -recu-samedi-17-mai-2014-le-representant-special-adjoint-pour-la-mission-des -nations-unies-pour-la-stabilisation-en-hai/.
7. Femmes en Démocratie, "Vital Voices—Femmes en Démocratie (Haiti)," January 20, 2012, https://fed.org.ht/2012/01/20/vital-voices-femmes-en-democratie -haiti/.
8. Embassy of the Republic of Haiti, "Official Visit of the President of the Republic of Haiti, Michel Joseph Martelly, to Washington, D.C.," https://www.haiti.org /official-visit-of-the-president-of-the-republic-of-haiti-michel-joseph-martelly-to -washington-d-c/.
9. United Nations Development Programme, "Mission de Revue du Projet Élections du PNUD 2010–2011 ou le Retour d'Expérience," October 2011.
10. *Haitinews2000*, "Le Groupe HAITI CHERIE lance ses activités," November 26, 2014, https://haitinews2000.net/14887/le-groupe-haiti-cherie-lance-ses-activites/.
11. Pierre Antoine Louis, message to author, 2015.
12. Jacqueline Charles, "'Legal Bandits' Could Take Charge in Haiti's Parliament," *Miami Herald*, August 7, 2015, http://www.miamiherald.com/news/nation-world/world /americas/haiti/article30459984.html.

19. THE LEGAL BANDITS

1. *Haiti Libre*, "The New Hotel Complex El Rancho NH Under Construction," August 23, 2013, https://www.haitilibre.com/en/news-9285-haiti-tourism-the-new-hotel -complex-el-rancho-nh-under-construction.html.
2. Larry Lebowitz, "Long-Sought Haitian Drug Suspect Arrested, Taken to Miami," *Miami Herald*, June 19, 2003, text preserved in email by Bob Corbett to Haiti mailing list, Webster University, June 19, 2003, http://faculty.webster.edu/corbetre/haiti -archive-new/msg15931.html.
3. John Dinges, *Our Man in Panama: The Shrewd Rise and Brutal Fall of Manuel Noriega* (New York: Crown, 1991).
4. Paul DeRienzo, "Haiti's Nightmare: The Cocaine Coup and the C.I.A. Connection," *High Times*, April 1994, reprinted in *Village Sun*, July 11, 2021, https://thevillagesun .com/haitis-nightmare-the-cocaine-coup-the-c-i-a-connection.

5. *New York Times* News Service, "Spy Unit Formed by CIA in Haiti Tied to Drug Trade; Three of Its Leaders Accused of Helping Keep Aristide Out," *Baltimore Sun*, November 14, 1993, https://www.baltimoresun.com/news/bs-xpm-1993-11-14-1993318005 -story.html.

6. René Préval, discussion with author, April 2016, Washington, DC.

7. Richard Cole, "Files Show Haiti Ignores Top Colombian Trafficker," Associated Press, April 3, 1993, https://apnews.com/article/bfe8fac2abb373d65661d95f68aa8 a46.

8. Juanita Darling, "Once-Feared Haiti Chief Has a Turn Behind Bars," *Los Angeles Times*, April 2, 1997, https://www.latimes.com/archives/la-xpm-1997-04-02-mn -44460-story.html.

9. Kyle Swenson, "The Rise and Fall of Haitian Drug Lord Jacques Ketant," *Miami New Times*, May 27, 2015, https://www.miaminewtimes.com/news/the-rise-and-fall-of -haitian-drug-lord-jacques-ketant-7641123.

10. Steven Dudley, "Drug Allegation Gave US Leverage on Aristide," *Boston Globe*, March 1, 2004, http://archive.boston.com/news/world/articles/2004/03/01/drug _allegation_gave_us_leverage_on_aristide/.

11. Préval interview.

12. Jay Weaver, "Trial Lifts Lid on World of Haiti's Drug-Smuggling Cops," *Miami Herald*, August 3, 2015, https://canada-haiti.ca/content/trial-lifts-lid-world-haiti%E2%80%99s -drug-smuggling-cops.

13. Reuters, "Haitian Businessman Pleads Not Guilty in Miami to U.S. Drug Charges," April 29, 2013, https://www.reuters.com/article/us-usa-haiti-drugs/haitian-businessman -pleads-not-guilty-in-miami-to-u-s-drug-charges-idUSBRE93S10T20130429.

14. The disclosure was made by an attorney in a deposition of Claude Thelemaque, one of the Haitian police officers arrested in the 2012 bust. In 2022, Jaar was arrested in the Dominican Republic for his involvement in the assassination of Haiti's president, and his role as a DEA informant received significant media attention. See, for example, David C. Adams, "One of the Main Suspects in Haitian President's Assassination Captured in Dominican Republic," Univision, January 8, 2022, https://www.univision .com/univision-news/united-states/rodolphe-jaar-suspect-in-assassination-of -haitian-president-jovenel-moise-captured-in-dominican-republic.

15. Frances Robles, "Haitian Leader's Power Grows as Scandals Swirl," *New York Times*, March 16, 2015, https://www.nytimes.com/2015/03/17/world/americas/haitian -president-tightens-grip-as-scandal-engulfs-circle-of-friends.html.

16. Anonymous DEA informant, message to author, August 2021.

17. Keith McNichols, interview with author, November 2018, Haiti.

18. Jacqueline Charles and Jay Weaver, "How the DEA Let One of Haiti's Biggest Drug Busts Slip Through Its Fingers," *Miami Herald*, August 17, 2018, https://www .miamiherald.com/news/nation-world/world/americas/haiti/article215793990 .html.

19. Mitchell A. Seligson and Dominique Zéphyr, *Democratic Values in Haiti, 2006–2008*, LAPOP, Vanderbilt University, May 2008, https://www.vanderbilt.edu/lapop /ab2008/haiti-en.pdf. And François Gélineau, Claire G. Evans, Carole Wilson, María Fernanda Boidi, and Elizabeth J. Zechmeister, *The Political Culture of Democracy in Haiti and in the Americas, 2016/17: A Comparative Study of Democracy and Governance*, LAPOP, Vanderbilt University, December 2019, https://www

.vanderbilt.edu/lapop/haiti/AB2016–17_Haiti_Country_Report_English_V7_W
_05.19.20.pdf.

20. THE ELECTORAL TEST

1. Organization of American States, "OAS Mission in Haiti: Elections Marked a Step Forward," August 10, 2015, https://www.oas.org/en/media_center/press_release .asp?sCodigo=E-218/15.

2. Jake Johnston, "Fraud, Violence, and Protests Cloud Results of Haitian Election," *VICE,* September 6, 2015, https://www.vice.com/en/article/wjan7x/fraud-violence -and-protests-cloud-results-of-haitian-election.

3. Roudy Choute, interview with author, 2015, Haiti.

4. Jessica Leeder, "The King of Jacmel," January 7, 2011, *Globe and Mail,* https://www .theglobeandmail.com/news/world/the-king-of-jacmel/article561131/.

5. Maura R. O'Connor, "Subsidizing Starvation," *Foreign Policy,* January 11, 2013, https://foreignpolicy.com/2013/01/11/subsidizing-starvation/.

6. Steeve Khawly, interview with author, 2015, Haiti.

7. Jake Johnston, "Full Breakdown of Preliminary Legislative Election Results in Haiti," Center for Economic and Policy Research, August 22, 2015, https://cepr.net /full-breakdown-of-preliminary-legislative-election-results-in-haiti/.

21. THE MOST VOTES MONEY CAN BUY

1. Jon Lee Anderson, "Aftershocks," *New Yorker,* January 24, 2016, https://www .newyorker.com/magazine/2016/02/01/aftershocks-letter-from-haiti-jon-lee -anderson.

2. Fritz Longchamp, interview with author, August 2015, Haiti.

3. US Embassy Haiti, "Kenneth H. Merten Is the New Haiti Special Coordinator," August 14, 2015, preserved on Internet Archive, September 6, 2015, https://web .archive.org/web/20150906030902/http://haiti.usembassy.gov/press-rel-new-haiti -special-coordinator-aug-14-2015.html.

4. Foreign diplomat, interview with author, October 2015, Haiti.

5. Jake Johnston, "Presidential Elections in Haiti: The Most Votes Money Can Buy," Center for Economic and Policy Research, November 3, 2015, https://www.cepr.net /presidential-elections-in-haiti-the-most-votes-money-can-buy/.

6. Pierre Antoine Louis, phone conversation with author, October 2015.

7. Rosny Desroches, phone interview with author, October 2015.

8. Jake Johnston, "An Analysis of the October 25 Preliminary Results," Center for Economic and Policy Research, November 16, 2015, https://www.cepr.net/an-analysis -of-the-october-25-preliminary-results/.

9. Jake Johnston, "Haiti Announces Preliminary Election Results, but Race Far from Settled," Center for Economic and Policy Research, November 7, 2015, https://www .cepr.net/haiti-announces-preliminary-election-results-but-race-far-from-settled/.

10. Kenneth Merten, discussion with author, December 2015, Washington, DC.

11. Jake Johnston, "Martelly Forms Commission to Evaluate Haiti Elections, But Can It Break Impasse?," Center for Economic and Policy Research, December 17, 2015, https://cepr.net/martelly-forms-commission-to-evaluate-haiti-elections-but-can-it -break-impasse/.

12. Georgianne Nienaber, "Haiti's Martelly and His Henchman Set the Stage for

Tragedy," *HuffPost,* January 25, 2016, https://www.huffpost.com/entry/haitis
-martelly-and-his-h_b_9068496.

13. Organization of American States, "Haiti: OAS Electoral Observation Mission Expresses Concern over Political Impasse Ahead of Second Round of Elections," January 19, 2016, https://www.oas.org/en/media_center/press_release.asp?sCodigo=E
-002/16.

14. Jake Johnston, "Haiti Election Hangs in the Balance as Political Negotiations Continue," Center for Economic and Policy Research, January 22, 2016, https://www
.cepr.net/haiti-election-hangs-in-the-balance-as-political-negotiations-continue/.

15. France24, "Présidentielle en Haïti: La communauté internationale ou l'"obsession de
la stabilité,'" January 22, 2016, https://www.france24.com/fr/20160122-presidentielle
-haiti-communaute-internationale-obsession-stabilite.

16. Joseph Guyler Delva, "Former Haitian Coup Leader: 'We Are Ready for War,'" Reuters, January 25, 2016, found on *Business Insider,* https://www.businessinsider.com
/former-haitian-coup-leader-we-are-ready-for-war-2016-1.

17. Jake Johnston, "Guy Philippe Threatens 'Civil War' as Haiti Struggles with Political Impasse," Center for Economic and Policy Research, March 21, 2016, https://
www.cepr.net/guy-philippe-threatens-civil-war-as-haiti-struggles-with-political
-impasse/.

22. THE TRANSITION

1. Organization of American States, "OAS Delegation Welcomes Constructive Discussions in Haiti," February 1, 2016, https://www.oas.org/en/media_center/press
_release.asp?sCodigo=E-006/16.

2. Pascale Roussy, interview with author, February 2016, Haiti.

3. Organization of American States, "Haiti: Agreement for Peaceful Transition of Government Accomplished," February 6, 2016, https://www.oas.org/en/media
_center/press_release.asp?sCodigo=E-012/16.

4. Simon Gardner and Joseph Guyler Delva, "Jailed Aristide Aide Denies Haiti Massacre," Reuters, April 8, 2004, text preserved in email by Bob Corbett to Haiti mailing list, Webster University, April 8, 2004, http://faculty.webster.edu/corbetre/haiti
-archive-new/msg21203.html.

5. Subsequent reporting indicated that while many more than five individuals died, there were victims on both sides. See, for example, Anne Fuller, "La Scierie Killings," *Le Nouvelliste,* April 8, 2004, preserved on Internet Archive, January 17, 2006, https://web.archive.org/web/20060117073853/http://irsp.org/cgi-bin/index.cgi?id
=211&display=1.

6. Joseph Guyler Delva, "Haitian Ex-Minister Freed from Jail," Reuters, June 19, 2006, found on Institute for Justice and Democracy in Haiti's website, http://www.ijdh
.org/pdf/RoundupJune3-82006.pdf.

7. Joseph Guyler Delva, "'We're Back'—Aristide Allies Toast Haiti's Interim President at Palace," Reuters, February 14, 2016, https://www.reuters.com/article/us
-haiti-election/were-back-aristide-allies-toast-haitis-interim-president-at-palace
-idUSKCN0VN0OF.

8. André Lafontant Joseph, "Politique: Comment réaliser, sans délai, de bonnes élections en Haïti? (I)," *Alterpresse,* February 5, 2016, https://www.alterpresse.org/spip.php
?article19647#.Vr5fyuYYNCJ. And André Lafontant Joseph, "Politique: Comment

réaliser, sans délai, de bonnes élections en Haïti? (II)," *Alterpresse,* February 5, 2016, https://www.alterpresse.org/spip.php?article19672#.Vr5fkOYYNCJ.

9. Jake Johnston, "Guy Philippe Threatens 'Civil War' as Haiti Struggles with Political Impasse, March 21, 2016, Center for Economic and Policy Research, https://www.cepr.net/guy-philippe-threatens-civil-war-as-haiti-struggles-with-political-impasse/.

10. Jake Johnston, "Haiti President Calls for Electoral Verification Mission Opposed by International Donors," Center for Economic and Policy Research, April 14, 2016, https://cepr.net/haiti-president-calls-for-electoral-verification-mission-opposed-by-international-donors/.

11. Jacqueline Charles, "Haiti Panel Calls for Re-Run of Presidential Elections," *Miami Herald,* May 30, 2016, https://www.miamiherald.com/news/nation-world/world/americas/haiti/article80825277.html.

12. Mark C. Toner, "Daily Press Briefing—June 8, 2016," US Department of State, June 8, 2016, https://2009-2017.state.gov/r/pa/prs/dpb/2016/06/258228.htm.

13. John Kirby, "Daily Press Briefing—May 31, 2016," US Department of State, May 31, 2016, https://2009-2017.state.gov/r/pa/prs/dpb/2016/05/257836.htm.

14. *Haiti Elections: A Resource and News Blog,* "Haiti Elections News Roundup—June 20," June 20, 2016, http://haitielection2015.blogspot.com/2016/06/haiti-elections-news-roundup-june-20.html.

15. Jake Johnston, "US Withdraws Funding for Haiti Elections," Center for Economic and Policy Research, July 8, 2016, https://cepr.net/us-withdraws-funding-for-haiti-elections/.

16. Jake Johnston, "As Haiti Political Crisis Deepens, International Pressure Grows," *AlterNet,* March 25, 2016, found on Center for Economic and Policy Research's website, https://www.cepr.net/as-haiti-politic-crisis-deepens-international-pressure-grows/.

17. Jean Marie Vorbe, discussion with author, January 2020, Haiti. At the time we spoke, his company had been seized by the Moïse government and he was engaged in a protracted legal dispute. For his part, Privert would say he had no control over who would or could run in the election. What is clear, however, is that the transitional government, in the end, did not intervene to hurt Moïse's candidacy. When I met with Privert in the aftermath of Hurricane Matthew, I asked about the upcoming vote and if he had a preference between the two apparent front-runners, Jude Célestin and Jovenel Moïse. "They are both the same," he responded. It didn't sound like a compliment.

23. THE BANANA MAN

1. Reginald Boulos, phone interview with author, January 2021.

2. Maria Abi-Habib, "Haiti's Leader Kept a List of Drug Traffickers. His Assassins Came for It," *New York Times,* December 12, 2021, https://www.nytimes.com/2021/12/12/world/americas/jovenel-moise-haiti-president-drug-traffickers.html.

3. Foreign diplomat, interview with author, October 2016, Haiti.

4. Michael Norton, "Aristide Ends 'Peasant' Stigma on Birth Records," Associated Press, May 16, 1995, found in *Seattle Times,* https://archive.seattletimes.com/archive/?date=19950516&slug=2121384.

5. Jamesky Blaise, interview with author, November 2017, Haiti.

6. Jocelerme Privert, interview with author, October 2016, Haiti.

7. Bette Gebrian, interview with author, October 2016, Haiti.

8. Roudy Choute, interview with author, October 2016, Haiti.

9. Foreign diplomat, interview with author, 2016, Haiti.

10. Sandra Honoré, "Statement of the Special Representative of the Secretary-General for Haiti Sandra Honoré to the Security Council 11 October 2016," United Nations Stabilization Mission in Haiti (MINUSTAH), October 11, 2016, https://minustah .unmissions.org/r%C3%A9union-du-conseil-de-s%C3%A9curit%C3%A9-sur -ha%C3%AFti.

11. The voting-age population at the time was a little more than six million.

12. Haiti Vote Blog (@HaitiVoteBlog), "The meaning of 'banana republic': a country in which foreign corps push the govt around," Twitter, 1:51 P.M., December 23, 2015, https://twitter.com/haitivoteblog/status/679736818049355776.

13. Much of this section is drawn from Jake Johnston, "Amid an Uprising, Can Haitian President Jovenel Moïse Deliver on His Promises?," *The Nation*, July 27, 2018, https://www.thenation.com/article/archive/amid-uprising-can-haitian-president -jovenel-moise-deliver-promises/.

14. Port International official, email to author, February 2018.

15. Erlin Tierjino, interview with author, November 2017, Haiti.

16. Nadia Joseph and others, meeting with author, November 2017, Haiti.

17. Jennifer Vansteenkiste, "Haiti's Peasantry as *poto mitan*: Refocusing the Foundations of Prosperity and Development," *Canadian Journal of Development Studies / Revue canadienne d'études du développement* 38, no. 4 (2017): 523–41, https://doi .org/10.1080/02255189.2017.1304365.

18. Jean Edmond, interview with author, November 2017, Haiti.

19. Blaise interview.

20. World Food Programme, *Post-"Matthew" Emergency Food Security Assessment*, January 2017, https://documents.wfp.org/stellent/groups/public/documents/ena /wfp290561.pdf.

21. United Nations Office for the Coordination of Humanitarian Affairs, Financial Tracking Service, "Haiti Flash Appeal: Hurricane Matthew 2016," https://fts.unocha .org/appeals/527/summary.

24. THE SEARCH FOR LIFE

1. Philomise Pierre, interview with author, November 2017, Haiti.

2. Data from World Development Indicators (database), World Bank, Washington, DC, https://data.worldbank.org/indicator/BX.TRF.PWKR.CD.DT?locations=HT.

3. Richard A. Haggerty, ed., *Haiti: A Country Study* (Washington, DC: GPO for the Library of Congress, 1989), full text at https://countrystudies.us/haiti/.

4. Naeisha Rose, "From Haiti to Tijuana: One Activist's Quest to Ease the Plight of Haitian Migrants in the Americas," *Haitian Times*, July 4, 2019, https://haitiantimes .com/2019/07/04/from-haiti-to-tijuana-one-activists-quest-to-ease-the-plight-of -haitian-migrants-in-the-americas/.

5. Guerline Jozef, phone interview with author, March 2022.

6. Data elaborated from International Migrant Stock 2020 (database), United Nations Department for Economic and Social Affairs, New York, https://www.un.org /development/desa/pd/content/international-migrant-stock.

7. Sandra Dibble and Tatiana Sanchez, "San Diego a Stopping Point for Haitian Migrants," *San Diego Union-Tribune*, June 17, 2016, https://www.sandiegouniontribune.com/news/border-baja-california/sdut-christ-methodist-haitians-shelter-2016jun17-story.html.

8. Kirk Semple, "U.S. to Step Up Deportations of Haitians amid Surge at Border," *New York Times*, September 22, 2016, https://www.nytimes.com/2016/09/23/world/americas/haiti-migrants-earthquake.html.

9. Daniella Silva, "Trapped in Tijuana: Migrants Face a Long, Dangerous Wait to Claim Asylum," NBC News, March 18, 2019, https://www.nbcnews.com/news/latino/trapped-tijuana-migrants-face-long-dangerous-wait-claim-asylum-n981721.

10. Michael D. Shear and Julie Hirschfeld Davis, "Stoking Fears, Trump Defied Bureaucracy to Advance Immigration Agenda," *New York Times*, December 23, 2017, https://www.nytimes.com/2017/12/23/us/politics/trump-immigration.html?_r=0.

11. There has been significant commentary and research on this. See, for example, Phillip W. D. Martin, "Cuba, Haiti: Racism or Hypocrisy? Cubans and Haitians Arrive in the Same Boat but Only One Group Is Detained; U.S. Policy Is Dreadfully Wrong," *Los Angeles Times*, March 17, 1994, https://www.latimes.com/archives/la-xpm-1994-03-17-me-34957-story.html.

12. Carl Lindskoog, "How the Haitian Refugee Crisis Led to the Indefinite Detention of Immigrants," *Washington Post*, April 9, 2018, https://www.washingtonpost.com/news/made-by-history/wp/2018/04/09/how-the-haitian-refugee-crisis-led-to-the-indefinite-detention-of-immigrants/.

13. *New York Times*, "Deportations of Haitians from Miami Center on Rise," June 8, 1981, https://www.nytimes.com/1981/06/08/us/deportation-of-haitians-from-miami-center-on-rise.html.

14. Lindskoog, "How the Haitian Refugee Crisis Led to the Indefinite Detention of Immigrants."

15. Lee Lescaze, "Coast Guard to Intercept Aliens' Ships," *Washington Post*, September 30, 1981, https://www.washingtonpost.com/archive/politics/1981/09/30/coast-guard-to-intercept-aliens-ships/1ee08458-3116-4608-b017-ed683e3c0504/.

16. Of course, there is a much longer history of US immigration laws and detention. See, for example, Freedom for Immigrants, "A Short History of Immigration Detention," https://www.freedomforimmigrants.org/detention-timeline.

17. Associated Press, "Haitians Removed from AIDS Risk List," April 10, 1985, found in *New York Times*, https://www.nytimes.com/1985/04/10/us/haitians-removed-from-aids-risk-list.html.

18. Michael Ratner, "How We Closed the Guantanamo HIV Camp: The Intersection of Politics and Litigation," *Harvard Human Rights Journal* 11 (1998): 187–220.

19. Elaine Sciolino, "Clinton Says U.S. Will Continue Ban on Haitian Exodus," *New York Times*, January 15, 1993, https://www.nytimes.com/1993/01/15/world/clinton-says-us-will-continue-ban-on-haitian-exodus.html.

20. Taylor Branch, *The Clinton Tapes: Wrestling History with the President* (New York: Simon & Schuster, 2009).

21. Josh Dawsey, "Trump Derides Protections for Immigrants from 'Shithole' Countries," *Washington Post*, January 12, 2018, https://www.washingtonpost.com/politics/trump-attacks-protections-for-immigrants-from-shithole-countries-in-oval-office-meeting/2018/01/11/bfc0725c-f711-11e7-91af-31ac729add94_story.html.

22. Jacqueline Charles, "Haitians Gamble on a Better Life in Chile. But the Odds Aren't Always in Their Favor," *Miami Herald,* March 5, 2018, https://www.miamiherald .com/news/nation-world/world/americas/haiti/article202590949.html.

23. See also Deborah Sontag, "Earthquake Relief Where Haiti Wasn't Broken," *New York Times,* July 5, 2012, https://www.nytimes.com/2012/07/06/world/americas /earthquake-relief-where-haiti-wasnt-broken.html.

24. For more on the history of the case, see Accountability Counsel, "Haiti: Caracol Industrial Park," https://www.accountabilitycounsel.org/client-case/haiti-caracol -industrial-park/#overview.

25. Accountability Counsel, AREDE, and ActionAid Haiti, "Haitian Farmers Harmed by Caracol Industrial Park Reach Historic Agreement," *Medium,* December 10, 2018, https://accountcounsel.medium.com/haitian-farmers-harmed-by-caracol -industrial-park-reach-historic-agreement-76f4919edbff.

25. THE $80,000 HOUSE

1. "Martelly à la Banque Mondiale et au FMI," *Le Nouvelliste,* April 19, 2011, preserved on Internet Archive, April 22, 2011, https://web.archive.org/web/20110422225311 /http://lenouvelliste.com/article.php?PubID=1&ArticleID=91570&PubDate =2011-04-19.

2. Harold Charles, "Partnering for Haiti's Future Conference (Part 3)," US Department of State, September 23, 2011, preserved on Internet Archive, April 13, 2013, https://web.archive.org/web/20130413191227/https:/www.state.gov/s/hsc/releases /2011/176298.htm.

3. All contracts award information in this section comes from the USASpending.gov database.

4. Former government official, interview with author, January 2016, Haiti.

5. Greg Higgins, "Architectural Peer Review of Caracol EKAM Housing, Haiti—March 16, 2012 (Rev. April 16, 2012)," preserved on Internet Archive, March 22, 2016, https:// web.archive.org/web/20160306035322/http://www.hrdf.org/research-development -and-innovation-in-construction/architectural-peer-review-caracol-ekam.

6. Hillary Clinton, "Remarks at the Caracol Industrial Park Opening Ceremony," US Department of State, October 22, 2012, https://2009-2017.state.gov/secretary /20092013clinton/rm/2012/10/199451.htm.

7. Bill Vastine, interview with author, January 2013, Haiti.

8. Jerry Erbach, email to author, July 2013.

9. US Government Accountability Office, *USAID Infrastructure Projects Have Had Mixed Results and Face Sustainability Challenges,* Report to Congressional Committee (GAO-13-558, June), 2013, https://www.gao.gov/assets/gao-13-558.pdf.

10. Ed Royce, Eliot Engel, and Ileana Ros-Lehtinen, "Royce, Engel, and Ros-Lehtinen Release GAO Report Documenting Failings in U.S. Assistance for Haiti Reconstruction," US House of Representatives, Foreign Affairs Committee, June 2013, https://democrats-foreignaffairs.house.gov/2013/6/royce-engel-and-ros-lehtinen -release-gao-report-documenting-failings-us.

11. US Congress, House, Committee on Foreign Relations, *Haiti: Is U.S. Aid Effective? Hearing Before the Committee on Foreign Relations,* 113th Cong., 1st sess., October 9, 2013, https://www.govinfo.gov/content/pkg/CHRG-113hhrg85105/pdf/CHRG -113hhrg85105.pdf.

12. Erbach, email message.

13. Yvon St-Martin, phone interview with author, 2014.

14. US Army Corps of Engineers, Jacksonville District, "Post Construction Technical Assessment Report for Caracol-EKAM Housing Development Project Caracol, Haiti," August 14, 2014.

15. Some of this section is drawn from Jake Johnston, "How the US Plan to Build Houses for Displaced Haitians Became an Epic Boondoggle," *VICE*, March 5, 2015, https://www.vice.com/en/article/438jpw/how-the-us-plan-to-build-houses-for -displaced-haitians-became-an-epic-boondoggle.

16. Jake Johnston, "USAID Houses Found to Be of Poor Quality, Will Cost Millions to Repair," Center for Economic and Policy Research, November 20, 2014, https://cepr .net/usaid-houses-found-to-be-of-poor-quality-will-cost-millions-to-repair/.

17. U.S. Congress, House, Tom Lantos Human Rights Commission, *Aid Delivery in Haiti: Development Needs, Capacity Building, and Challenges: Hearing Before the Tom Lantos Human Rights Commission,* 113th Cong, 2nd sess., December 3, 2014, https://humanrightscommission.house.gov/sites/humanrightscommission.house .gov/files/documents/2014_12_03_Haiti_0.pdf.

18. Jake Johnston, "Second USAID Contractor Suspended Following Caracol Housing Debacle," Center for Economic and Policy Research, March 30, 2015, https://cepr .net/second-usaid-contractor-suspended-following-caracol-housing-debacle/.

19. Larry Smith, "America's Top Police Officers," *Parade,* October 4, 2009, https:// parade.com/37630/larrysmith/04-americas-top-police-officers/.

20. Anonymous, phone interview with author, May 2016.

21. Tetra Tech, "Engineering Design & Construction Supervision Program: EKAM Observed Deficiencies Report," USAID, January 14, 2015.

22. CEEPCO, "CEEPCO Statement on Relationship with USAID," preserved on Internet Archive, March 15, 2016, https://web.archive.org/web/20160315152831/http: /ceepco.com/index.php/en/ceepco-statement-on-relationship-with-usaid.

26. THE APOLOGY

1. UN News, "INTERVIEW: Haiti on Path to Stability, Development Thanks to UN Mission, Says Envoy," October 13, 2017, https://news.un.org/en/story/2017/10/568552 -interview-haiti-path-stability-development-thanks-un-mission-says-envoy.

2. The United Nations sought to cover this crime up, claiming that it could not locate the victim. However, a cell phone video of the attack was leaked to the press. Journalists were easily able to locate the victim. Ansel Herz, Matthew Mosk, and Rym Momtaz, "U.N. Peacekeepers Accused of Sexually Assaulting Haitian Teen," ABC News, September 2, 2011, https://abcnews.go.com/Blotter/peacekeepers-accused -sexually-assaulting-haitian-teen/story?id=14437122. In 2017, the Associated Press reported: "The men never faced trial in Haiti; four of the five were convicted in Uruguay of 'private violence,' a lesser charge." See Paisley Dodds, "AP Exclusive: UN Child Sex Ring Left Victims but No Arrests," Associated Press, April 12, 2017, https://apnews.com/article/africa-arrests-united-nations-only-on-ap-e6ebc331460 345c5abd4f57d77f535c1.

3. Mark Snyder, "Sexual Exploitation and Abuse at the Hands of the United Nations' Stabilization Mission in Haiti," Center for Economic and Policy Research, January 2017, https://cepr.net/images/documents/UNSEA_11JAN17_FINAL.pdf.

4. Sabine Lee and Susan Bartels, "'They Put a Few Coins in Your Hands to Drop a Baby in You'—265 Stories of Haitian Children Abandoned by UN Fathers," *The Conversation*, December 17, 2019, https://theconversation.com/they-put-a-few -coins-in-your-hands-to-drop-a-baby-in-you-265-stories-of-haitian-children -abandoned-by-un-fathers-114854.

5. Paul Benkimoun and Béatrice Gurrey, "Haïti: 'Je n'ai jamais vu une épidémie de choléra démarrer avec une telle violence,'" *Le Monde*, March 23, 2019, https://www .lemonde.fr/sciences/article/2019/03/23/haiti-je-n-ai-jamais-vu-une-epidemie-de -cholera-demarrer-avec-une-telle-violence_5440358_1650684.html#.

6. Rick Gladstone, "Cholera Deaths in Haiti Could Far Exceed Official Count," *New York Times*, March 18, 2016, https://www.nytimes.com/2016/03/19/world/americas /cholera-deaths-in-haiti-could-far-exceed-official-count.html.

7. United Nations Security Council, 2017, *Resolution 2350 (2017) Adopted by the Security Council at Its 7924th meeting, on 13 April 2017*, S/RES/2350, available at https://minujusth.unmissions.org/sites/default/files/sc_2350e_0.pdf.

8. Jonathan M. Katz, "U.N. Admits Role in Cholera Epidemic in Haiti," *New York Times*, August 17, 2016, https://www.nytimes.com/2016/08/18/world/americas /united-nations-haiti-cholera.html.

9. Somini Sengupta, "U.N. Apologizes for Role in Haiti's 2010 Cholera Outbreak," *New York Times*, December 1, 2016, https://www.nytimes.com/2016/12/01/world /americas/united-nations-apology-haiti-cholera.html.

10. For more details on the case and its history, see "*Georges v. United Nations*: The Lawsuit Against the UN for Cholera," Bureau du Avocats Internationaux and Institute for Justice and Democracy in Haiti, http://www.ijdh.org/our-work/accountability /cholera-accountability/cholera-litigation/.

11. Jake Johnston, "Haiti Cholera Victims Get First Hearing in Court," Center for Economic and Policy Research, October 23, 2014, https://www.cepr.net/haiti-cholera -victims-get-first-hearing-in-court/.

12. Rick Gladstone, "Lawmakers Urge John Kerry to Press U.N. for Haiti Cholera Response," *New York Times*, June 29, 2016, https://www.nytimes.com/2016/06/30 /world/americas/haiti-cholera-john-kerry-congress.html.

13. Beatrice Lindstrom, interview with author, 2022, virtual.

14. Colum Lynch, "Trump Won't Pay a Penny for U.N. Cholera Relief Fund in Haiti," *Foreign Policy*, June 1, 2017, https://foreignpolicy.com/2017/06/01/trump-wont -pay-a-penny-for-u-n-cholera-relief-fund-in-haiti/.

15. United Nations MPTF Partner Gateway, "Haiti Cholera Response Multi-Partner Trust Fund: Financial Status," as of October 2017, available at https://mptf.undp .org/fund/clh00.

16. *New York Times*, "Haiti 'Ransom' Project," article series, 2022, https://www.nytimes .com/spotlight/haiti.

17. Portions of the following section are drawn from Jake Johnston, "A U.N.-Backed Police Force Carried Out a Massacre in Haiti. The Killings Have Been Almost Entirely Ignored," *The Intercept*, January 10, 2018, https://theintercept.com/2018/01 /10/haiti-raid-united-nations-police-grand-ravine/.

18. Susan D. Page, phone interview with author, March 2021.

19. Jake Johnston, "Haitian Government on the Defensive Following UN Welcoming of Corruption Investigation," Center for Economic and Policy Research, March 7, 2018,

https://cepr.net/haitian-government-on-the-defensive-following-un-welcoming-of
-corruption-investigation/.

20. Catherine Porter and Natalie Kitroeff, "'It's Terror': In Haiti, Gangs Gain Power as
Security Vacuum Grows," *New York Times,* October 21, 2021, https://www.nytimes
.com/2021/10/21/world/americas/haiti-gangs-kidnapping.html.

21. Police Nationale d'Haiti, "Rapport d'Enquete: Incident grave a Grand-Ravine," In-
spection Generale, No 981–17 (2017).

22. Gregory George, phone discussion with author, 2020.

27. THE TWEET

1. Jake Johnston, "Is Haiti Awakening to Change?," *New York Times,* December 26,
2018, https://www.nytimes.com/2018/12/26/opinion/haiti-corruption.html.

2. US Department of State, *2013 Country Reports on Human Rights Practices—Haiti,*
February 27, 2014, https://www.refworld.org/docid/53284ad014.html.

3. Kim Ives, "Accusing President Martelly of Lying and 'Treason,' Senate Report Calls for
His Impeachment," *Haïti Liberté,* August 14, 2013, https://canada-haiti.ca/content
/accusing-president-martelly-lying-and-%E2%80%9Ctreason%E2%80%9D
-senate-report-calls-his-impeachment.

4. Samuel Madistin, interview with author, November 2018, Haiti.

5. Roberson Alphonse, "Petrocaribe: La Banque mondiale critique, le gouvernement
s'enflamme," *Le Nouvelliste,* December 4, 2013, https://www.lenouvelliste.com
/public/article/124778/petrocaribe-la-banque-mondiale-critique-le-gouvernement
-senflamme.

6. Amelie Baron, "World Bank Envoy Criticizes Lack of Transparency in Haiti Oil
Program," Reuters, December 5, 2013, https://www.reuters.com/article/haiti
-oil/world-bank-envoy-criticizes-lack-of-transparency-in-haiti-oil-program
-idINL2N0JJ2AN20131205.

7. Haitian-Caribbean News Network, "Venezuela Blasts World Bank Envoy over Haiti
Handling of PetroCaribe Funds," December 11, 2013, https://www.prnewswire
.com/news-releases/venezuela-blasts-world-bank-envoy-over-haiti-handling-of
-petrocaribe-funds-235473851.html.

8. Mary Barton-Dock, interview with author, 2019, Washington, DC.

9. Anonymous, interview with author, February 2019, Haiti.

10. Damian Merlo, interview with author, February 2016, Washington, DC.

11. Jacqueline Charles, "Haiti Owes Venezuela $2 Billion—and Much of It Was Em-
bezzled, Senate Report Says," November 15, 2017, https://www.miamiherald.com
/news/nation-world/world/americas/haiti/article184740783.html.

12. Sandra Lemaire, Matiado Vilme, and Renan Toussaint, "Haiti's President Launches
PetroCaribe Investigation," *Voice of America,* October 19, 2018, https://www.voanews
.com/a/haiti-s-president-launches-petrocaribe-investigation-/4620196.html.

13. For a detailed account of the events, see Réseau National de Défense des Droits
Humains, "The Events in La Saline: From Power Struggle Between Armed Gangs
to State-Sanctioned Massacre," December 2018, https://web.rnddh.org/the-events
-in-la-saline-from-power-struggle-between-armed-gangs-to-state-sanctioned
-massacre-eng/?lang=en.

14. Harvard Law School International Human Rights Clinic and Observatoire Haïtien
des crimes contre l'humanité, *Killing with Impunity: State-Sanctioned Massacres in*

Haiti, April 2021, http://hrp.law.harvard.edu/wp-content/uploads/2021/04/Killing_With_Impunity-1.pdf.

15. Jacqueline Charles, "Dozens Brutally Killed, Raped in Haiti Massacre, Police Say. 'Even Young Children Were Not Spared,'" *Miami Herald,* May 15, 2019, https://www.miamiherald.com/news/nation-world/world/americas/haiti/article230380739.html.

16. Jake Johnston, "The Overpass to Nowhere," Center for Economic and Policy Research, June 6, 2019, https://cepr.net/the-overpass-to-nowhere/.

17. Samuel Madistin, interview with author, February 2018, Haiti.

18. Foreign diplomat, interview with author, February 2018, Haiti.

19. Bernardo Álvarez, interview, 2015, Washington, DC.

20. Melius Hyppolite, phone interview with author, 2018.

21. Roberson Alphonse, "TPTC, Agri-Trans épinglés par la BID, " *Le Nouvelliste,* May 27, 2016, preserved on Internet Archive, July 2, 2016, https://web.archive.org/web/20160702044240/https://www.lenouvelliste.com/lenouvelliste/article/159328/TPTC-Agri-Trans-epingles-par-la-BID.

22. Jacqueline Charles, "Before Haiti's President-Elect Even Takes Office, He's Battling Money-Laundering Suspicions," *Miami Herald,* January 24, 2017, https://www.miamiherald.com/news/nation-world/world/americas/haiti/article128501399.html.

23. Jake Johnston, "Did Trump Take a Page out of Haiti's Presidential Playbook?," Center for Economic and Policy Research, May 17, 2017, https://cepr.net/did-trump-take-a-page-out-of-haiti-s-presidential-playbook/.

24. Jean-Baptiste Bien-Aime, interview with author, 2019.

25. Jacqueline Charles, "Haiti President Accused of Embezzlement Scheme in Government Audit of Venezuela Aid Money," *Miami Herald,* June 4, 2019, https://www.miamiherald.com/news/nation-world/world/americas/haiti/article231122978.html.

26. There was a noticeable difference in the political space this time around, however. In March 2017, René Préval had passed away peacefully in his Port-au-Prince home due to heart disease. The man who had quietly kept the Aid State on its tracks for more than a decade, to whom the international community had always turned in their attempts to cobble together short-term political deals, was no longer there to lean on. Préval's political coalition fractured into dozens of, at times, competing factions. It came as little surprise that the two-time president hadn't left behind a robust political party to carry on his project. "After thirty years of building democracy, parties have failed," Préval had told me in May 2016 in a wide-ranging discussion. "I'm an anarchist," the former president explained. "I believe each must act on their own initiative and the sum of that is a democracy. Many think anarchy is no order, but that's not true. It's a philosophy, it's a way to learn." Rather than building a traditional party, Préval spent his last years trying to support civil society. "Today, the sectors that are strong are not the parties, they are civil society. . . . We are trying to put them together." I thought about his comments often over the following years. During the Moïse administration, civil society did emerge as virtually the only countervailing force in Haitian politics, a dynamic that has continued to the present day and is embodied in efforts such as the Commission for a Haitian Solution to the Crisis.

27. Johnson administration documents regarding foreign relations with Haiti, col-
    lection, Documents 325–369 in "Foreign Relations, 1964–1968, Volume XXXII,
    Dominican Republic; Cuba; Haiti; Guyana," US Department of State Office of the
    Historian, https://2001-2009.state.gov/r/pa/ho/frus/johnsonlb/xxxii/44658.htm.

28. Mark Weisbrot, "The United States Shows Its Contempt for Venezuelan Democ-
    racy," *The Guardian,* April 22, 2013, https://www.theguardian.com/commentisfree
    /2013/apr/22/united-states-contempt-venezuelan-democracy.

29. Andrés Oppenheimer, "Obama's Plan to Counter Venezuela's Oil Clout," *Miami Her-
    ald,* September 6, 2014, https://www.miamiherald.com/news/local/news-columns
    -blogs/andres-oppenheimer/article1990026.html.

30. Mark Weisbrot, "Obama Absurdly Declares Venezuela a Security Threat," Al Jazeera,
    March 10, 2015, http://america.aljazeera.com/opinions/2015/3/obama-absurdly
    -declares-venezuela-a-national-security-threat.html.

31. Edward Wong and Nicholas Casey, "U.S. Targets Venezuela with Tough Oil Sanc-
    tions During Crisis of Power," *New York Times,* January 28, 2019, https://www
    .nytimes.com/2019/01/28/us/politics/venezuela-sanctions-trump-oil.html.

32. Joshua Goodman, "Trump Pressed Aides on Venezuela Invasion, US Official Says," As-
    sociated Press, July 4, 2018, https://apnews.com/article/north-america-donald-trump
    -caribbean-ap-top-news-rex-tillerson-a3309c4990ac4581834d4a654f7746ef.
    And Brian Ellsworth, "Trump Says U.S. Military Intervention in Venezuela 'an Op-
    tion,' Russia Objects," Reuters, February 3, 2019, https://www.reuters.com/article
    /us-venezuela-politics/trump-says-u-s-military-intervention-in-venezuela-an
    -option-russia-objects-idUSKCN1PS0DK.

33. Christopher Woody, "The US Is Putting a Full-Court Press on Venezuela, but It
    May Not Get to Call All the Shots," *Business Insider,* June 7, 2018, https://www
    .businessinsider.com/us-latin-american-diplomacy-to-isolate-venezuela-mixed
    -success-at-oas-2018-6.

34. US Mission to the Organization of American States, "Permanent Council Approves
    Resolution to Not Recognize the Legitimacy of the Maduro Regime," January 10,
    2019, https://usoas.usmission.gov/permanent-council-approves-resolution-to-not
    -recognize-the-legitimacy-of-the-maduro-regime/.

35. US Mission to the Organization of American States, "OAS Member States Issue
    Joint Statement on Venezuela," January 24, 2019, https://usoas.usmission.gov/oas
    -member-states-issue-joint-statement-on-venezuela/.

36. Jacqueline Charles, "As Crisis in Venezuela Escalates, Caribbean Nations Take
    Sides, Haiti Joins U.S.," *Miami Herald,* January 25, 2019, https://www.miamiherald
    .com/news/nation-world/world/americas/haiti/article225070430.html.

37. Roberta Rampton, "Trump Dangles Investment to Caribbean Leaders Who Back
    Venezuela's Guaido," Reuters, March 22, 2019, https://www.reuters.com/article
    /cnews-us-venezuela-politics-caribbean-idCAKCN1R313H-OCATP.

38. Information on lobbyists is available from FARA.gov.

28. THE MERCENARIES

1. This section draws from a long investigative report, available here: Jake Johnston,
   "Our Boss Will Call Your Boss," Center for Economic and Policy Research, March
   12, 2019, https://cepr.net/our-boss-will-call-your-boss/.

2. Augusto Lewkowicz, phone interview with author, February 2019.

3. Miguel Marquez, Devon M. Sayers, and Caitlin Hu, "Haiti PM Says Detained Americans Are 'Terrorists' Targeting Government," CNN, February 20, 2019, https://www.cnn.com/2019/02/20/americas/haiti-detainees-prime-minister-allegation-intl/index.html.

4. Matthew Cole and Kim Ives, "U.S. Mercenaries Arrested in Haiti Were Part of a Half-Baked Scheme to Move $80 Million for Embattled President," *The Intercept*, March 20, 2019, https://theintercept.com/2019/03/20/haiti-president-mercenary-operation/.

5. Chris Osman, interview by Mike Ritland, *The Mike Drop*, podcast audio, April 19, 2019, https://www.youtube.com/watch?v=r8Sd_UfcYDY.

6. Mario Andresol, interview with author, February 2019, Haiti.

7. *Loop News*, "PNH: Un arrêté présidentiel réduit les pouvoirs du DG Gédéon," May 30, 2018, https://haiti.loopnews.com/content/pnh-un-arrete-presidentiel-reduit-les-pouvoirs-du-dg-gedeon.

8. Jake Johnston, "Meet the New Haitian Military? It's Starting to Look a Lot Like the Old One," Center for Economic and Policy Research, March 16, 2018, https://cepr.net/meet-the-new-haitian-military-it-s-starting-to-look-a-lot-like-the-old-one/.

9. Andres Martinez Casares and Joseph Guyler Delva, "Haitian Army Set to Make Controversial Return After Two Decades," Reuters, November 18, 2017, https://www.reuters.com/article/us-haiti-military/haitian-army-set-to-make-controversial-return-after-two-decades-idUSKBN1DJ01M.

10. *Haiti Libre*, "The National Palace Deploys Its Special Unit Equipped with Weapons of War," November 21, 2018, https://www.haitilibre.com/en/news-26176-haiti-flash-the-national-palace-deploys-its-special-unit-equipped-with-weapons-of-war.html.

11. Jake Johnston, "State Department Awarded Contract to Politically Connected Security Firm," August 31, 2017, https://cepr.net/state-department-awarded-contract-to-politically-connected-security-firm/.

12. Kim Ives, "Haiti's Police Chief Replaced," *Haïti Liberté*, August 28, 2019, https://haitiliberte.com/haitis-police-chief-replaced/.

13. U.S. Congress, House, Committee on Foreign Relations, *Haiti on the Brink: Assessing U.S. Policy Toward a Country in Crisis: Hearing Before the Subcommittee on the Western Hemisphere, Civilian Security, and Trade of the Committee on Foreign Affairs*, 116th Cong., 1st sess., December 10, 2019 (Statement of Testimony of Pierre Esperance, Executive Director of the Haitian National Human Rights Defense Network).

14. Amnesty International, "Haiti: Amnesty International Verifies Evidence of Excessive Use of Force Against Protesters," October 31, 2019, https://www.amnesty.org/en/latest/news/2019/10/haiti-amnesty-verifies-evidence-excessive-force-against-protesters/.

15. Sandra Lemaire, "Haiti Policemen Protest Demanding Better Work Conditions, Union," *Voice of America*, October 28, 2019, https://www.voanews.com/a/americas_haiti-policemen-protest-demanding-better-work-conditions-union/6178348.html.

16. *Haitian Times*, "Haitian Authorities Declares Fantôme 509 Gang a Terrorist Group," May 18, 2020, https://haitiantimes.com/2020/05/18/haitian-authorities-declares-fantome-509-gang-a-terrorist-group/.

17. Stuart Schrader, *Badges Without Borders: How Global Counterinsurgency Transformed American Policing* (Oakland: University of California Press, 2019).

18. Jake Johnston, "Despite Track Record, U.S. Hires Contractor to Provide Troops to U.N. Haiti Mission," Center for Economic and Policy Research, April 11, 2013, https://www.cepr.net/despite-track-record-us-hires-contractor-to-provide -troops-to-un-haiti-mission/. And Tetra Tech, "Haitian National Police Capacity Building," https://www.tetratech.com/en/projects/haitian-national-police-capacity -building.

19. For a more detailed discussion on the history of paramilitarism in Haiti, see Jeb Sprague, *Paramilitarism and the Assault on Democracy in Haiti* (New York: Monthly Review Press, 2012).

20. A pejorative Haitian term often directly translated as "ghost," but which was used to refer largely to Aristide loyalists allegedly involved in gang activity.

21. Chelsea Kivland, "The Semantics of the Gang in Haiti Today," Society for Cultural Anthropology, May 3, 2022, https://culanth.org/fieldsights/semantics-of-the-gang. This was also something I heard frequently while speaking to friends in Haiti around the time.

22. Harvard Law School International Human Rights Clinic and Observatoire Haïtien des crimes contre l'humanité, *Killing with Impunity: State-Sanctioned Massacres in Haiti,* April 2021, http://hrp.law.harvard.edu/wp-content/uploads/2021/04/Killing _With_Impunity-1.pdf.

23. Johnston, "State Department Awarded Contract to Politically Connected Security Firm."

29. THE ONGOING REVOLUTION

1. Anonymous, interview with author, January 2020, Haiti.

2. Mona Augustin, interview with author, January 2021, virtual.

3. Jovenel Moïse (@moisejovenel), "Ce lundi 13 janvier 2020, ramène la fin de la 50ème législature. Nous constatons la caducité du Parlement et nous prenons acte de ce vide institutionnel occasionné par le départ de la chambre . . . ," Twitter, 12:02 A.M., January 13, 2020, https://twitter.com/moisejovenel/status/1216586192164204544.

4. Jake Johnston, "The OAS Picks Sides in Haiti . . . Again," Center for Economic and Policy Research, June 4, 2020, https://cepr.net/the-oas-picks-sides-in-haiti-again/.

5. Jake Johnston and David Rosnick, "Observing the Observers: The OAS in the 2019 Bolivian Elections," Center for Economic and Policy Research, March 10, 2020, https://cepr.net/report/observing-the-observers-the-oas-in-the-2019-bolivian -elections/.

6. Sarah Marsh, "Exclusive: Haiti's Moise Plans to Use New Powers to Overhaul Constitution," Reuters, January 16, 2020, https://www.reuters.com/article/us-haiti -politics-exclusive/exclusive-haitis-moise-plans-to-use-new-powers-to-overhaul -constitution-idUSKBN1ZG0A5.

7. Associated Press, "President Replaces Controversial Minister," September 11, 1985, https://apnews.com/article/c894a630801cf15232d2bc347df1f2ff.

8. While this was certainly the atmosphere in Port-au-Prince, outside the capital the story was a little different. Though his lofty rhetoric had not exactly translated into policy successes, Moïse did retain a significant level of support in more rural areas. When I spoke with individuals who had been kicked off the land for his banana plantation, for example, many said they would still vote for Moïse. At least, they said, he was from their community and understood rural Haiti.

9. Jean Casimir, *The Haitians: A Decolonial History,* translated by Laurent Dubois (Chapel Hill: University of North Carolina Press, 2020).

10. Richard Morse, interview with author, January 2020, Haiti.

11. Greg Chamberlin, "Aubelin Jolicoeur," obituary, *The Guardian,* February 18, 2005, https://www.theguardian.com/media/2005/feb/18/guardianobituaries.pressandpublishing.

12. Don A. Schanche, "An Appropriate Setting in Land of Voodoo: Quirky Old Hotel in Haiti Returns from Dead, with Couple's Help," *Los Angeles Times,* June 11, 1988, https://www.latimes.com/archives/la-xpm-1988-06-11-mn-4320-story.html.

EPILOGUE

1. Jacqueline Charles, "Made in Miami: How a South Florida Plot to Oust Haiti's Jovenel Moïse Led to His Murder," *Miami Herald,* December 6, 2022, https://www.miamiherald.com/news/nation-world/world/americas/haiti/article264470076.html.

2. References in this chapter to phone calls are based on phone records that investigators pulled in the weeks after the assassination and which I later obtained.

3. Jacqueline Charles, "'My Life Is in Danger. Come Save My Life.' Haitian President's Desperate Final Pleas," *Miami Herald,* July 19, 2021, https://www.miamiherald.com/news/nation-world/world/americas/haiti/article252866418.html.

4. Police Nationale d'Haïti, Direction Centrale de la Police Judiciare Bureau des Affaires Criminelles, DGPNH/DCPJ/BAC-D-21, Haiti, 2021.

5. Parts of this chapter are drawn from a longer investigative report: Jake Johnston, "'They Fooled Us,'" Center for Economic and Policy Research, February 7, 2022, https://cepr.net/report/they-fooled-us/.

6. Jake Johnston, "The OAS Picks Sides in Haiti . . . Again," Center for Economic and Policy Research, June 4, 2020, https://cepr.net/the-oas-picks-sides-in-haiti-again/.

7. Gregory W. Meeks, Albio Sires, and Andy Levin, "Meeks, Sires & Levin Issue Joint Statement on Haiti," Office of Representative Gregory Meeks, December 22, 2020, https://meeks.house.gov/media/press-releases/meeks-sires-levin-issue-joint-statement-haiti.

8. Ned Price, "Department Press Briefing—February 5, 2021," US Department of State, February 5, 2021, https://www.state.gov/briefings/department-press-briefing-february-5-2021/.

9. More details on the February 7, 2021, "coup" plot are available here: Johnston, "'They Fooled Us.'"

10. Christian Emmanuel Sanon, phone interview with author, September 2019.

11. Daniel Whitman, interview with author, February 2021, Washington, DC.

12. Jean Sénat Fleury, phone interview with author, March 2021.

13. More details are available in Johnston, "'They Fooled Us.'"

14. Police Nationale d'Haïti, Direction Centrale de la Police Judiciare Bureau des Affaires Criminelles.

15. Video of the speech is available here: Jovenel Moïse, "Prezidan Jovenel Moïse di li koke nan gòj nèg yo," Radio Tele Ginen, February 5, 2021, https://www.youtube.com/watch?v=YS7SGEizfoM.

16. Multiple sources close to the president.

17. iciHaiti.com, "Diplomacy: New Russian Ambassador Accredited to Haiti," June 2, 2021, https://www.icihaiti.com/en/news-33881-icihaiti-diplomacy-new-russian-ambassador-accredited-to-haiti.html.

18. *Haiti News Hub,* "Alix Thybulle and the Jake Johnston Affaire: Corruption and Arms," September 22, 2020, https://haitinewshub.com/top-stories/f/alix-thybulle -and-the-jake-johnston-affaire-corruption-and-arms.

19. Jake Johnston, "EXCLUSIVE: Head of Haiti's Palace Guard Subject of US Law Enforcement Investigation into Arms Trafficking," Center for Economic and Policy Research, July 9, 2021, https://cepr.net/exclusive-head-of-haitis-palace-guard -subject-of-us-law-enforcement-investigation-into-arms-trafficking/.

20. Anonymous official, interview with author, June 2021, Haiti.

21. Keith McNichols, phone interview with author, February 2023.

22. Maria Abi-Habib, "Haiti's Leader Kept a List of Drug Traffickers. His Assassins Came for It," *New York Times,* December 12, 2021, https://www.nytimes.com/2021 /12/12/world/americas/jovenel-moise-haiti-president-drug-traffickers.html.

23. Emily Horne, "Statement by NSC Spokesperson Emily Horne on U.S. Government Delegation to Haiti," White House, July 12, 2021, https://www.whitehouse.gov /briefing-room/statements-releases/2021/07/12/statement-by-nsc-spokesperson -emily-horne-on-u-s-government-delegation-to-haiti/.

24. Jake Johnston, "Haitians Don't Need Another President Chosen Behind Closed Doors," *American Prospect,* July 19, 2021, https://prospect.org/world/haitians-dont -need-another-president-chosen-behind-closed-doors/.

25. United Nations Integrated Office in Haiti (BINUH), "Communiqué du Core Group," July 17, 2021, https://binuh.unmissions.org/fr/communiqué-du-core-group-4.

26. The following analysis is made based on the phone records I obtained.

27. Anatoly Kurmanaev, "Haitian Prime Minister Had Close Links with Murder Suspect," *New York Times,* January 10, 2022, https://www.nytimes.com/2022/01/10 /world/americas/haitian-prime-minister-assassination-suspect.html.

28. Caitlin Hu and Etant Dupain, "Haiti Prime Minister Orders Firing of Top Prosecutor in Presidential Assassination Case," CNN, September 14, 2021, https://www .cnn.com/2021/09/14/americas/haiti-prime-minister-ariel-henry-jovenel-moise -assassination-intl/index.html.

29. Matt Rivers, Etant Dupain, and Natalie Gallón, "Haitian Prime Minister Involved in Planning the President's Assassination, Says Judge Who Oversaw Case," CNN, February 8, 2022, https://www.cnn.com/2022/02/08/americas/haiti-assassination -investigation-prime-minister-intl-cmd-latam/index.html.

30. Charles, "Made in Miami: How a South Florida Plot to Oust Haiti's Jovenel Moïse Led to His Murder."

31. David C. Adams, "Is There a U.S. Intelligence Agency Link to the Assassination of Haiti's President?," Univision, April 26, 2022, https://www.univision.com/univision -news/latin-america/cia-link-assassination-president-moise-haiti.

INDEX